DISCARD

IRWIN T. SANDERS, Ph.D., Cornell University, is Professor of Sociology and Co-Director of the Community Sociology Training Program, Boston University. Dr. Sanders was formerly Associate Director of the International Training and Research Program of the Ford Foundation and Research Director, Associates for International Research, Inc. He has taught at the University of Kentucky (where he founded the Bureau of Community Service) and has held many advisory government posts both here and abroad.

THE
COMMUNITY

IRWIN T. SANDERS *Boston University*

THIRD EDITION

THE RONALD PRESS COMPANY • NEW YORK

Library of Congress Catalog Card Number: 75–14949
PRINTED IN THE UNITED STATES OF AMERICA

To My Wife

Preface

This book describes community life in its many and varied forms, large and small, industrial and rural, at home and abroad. It reflects the significant changes in the field of sociology and the study of the community that have taken place during the last decade. From a predominant concern with the social system approach of community analysis—an approach that still retains value—the study of the community has moved to greater problem-orientation as reflected in present chapters on conflict and social action. More people are now aware that any program designed to benefit large numbers of people will eventually have to be carried out in local communities, the so-called "grass-roots."

This edition, although based on the very well received previous ones, reflects the changes in sociology as a discipline. One of these is the increased interest in social inequalities and conflict. Another change is the growing impatience of some sociologists with analysis that does not lead to application of the findings to serve the community. This can be described as a shift to applied sociology about which many leading sociologists are talking today and toward which they are slowly moving. The text recognizes the challenge to the comfortable assumptions of "value neutrality" of an earlier decade. It is difficult for a sociologist to claim today that his job is only to describe the facts and leave up to others the task of applying his findings to real life situations.

Within American society during the past few years a number of changes have occurred that affect the local community; they are fully recognized in this volume. The master social processes of urbanization, industrialization, bureaucratization, and commercialization show how these seeming impersonal processes influence the lives of individuals in very personal ways. There have also been consciously planned policy changes designed to shift some decision-making from the centers of power in the national and state capitals back to the local communities.

This survey of the community in its many forms, then, employs the paradigms of the social system, conflict theory, and the social field to describe and understand the continuity and persistence of community life along with its imbalances and modifications. The term "community" is a complex concept. It is hoped that its variety, vitality, and significance are adequately presented in this volume.

Appreciation should first be expressed to the numerous students with whom interaction in the field and in the classroom helped clarify my ideas; second, to my professional colleagues whose critical reactions often led me to reshape my thinking; third, to the many authors who let me quote from their articles and books in order to illustrate basic topics; finally, to Johnnie Scott, Susan Van Horne, and Laura Willard for assistance in manuscript preparation and to Marian Hughes for dealing with the copyright permissions. A special note, too, is due to the many community-minded men and women who agreed to long interviews in various community studies and thereby helped me gain insight into current problems and how local groups are trying to cope with them.

IRWIN T. SANDERS

Boston, Massachusetts
July, 1975

Contents

PART IV THE COMMUNITY IN PROCESS: INEQUALITY AND CONFLICT

PART V THE COMMUNITY AS SOCIAL ACTION

PART VI CONCLUSION

1

PERSPECTIVES

Each person experiences community to a greater or lesser degree. For some, it is limited to a small group of people or a restricted geographical area; to others, community has a spacious meaning and includes many people and an ever-expanding physical base. Some think of community in psychological terms, preferring to deal with a "sense of community" rather than with a given locality. The chapter which follows addresses itself to this question and argues that a basic requirement for a sense of community in our modern era is a recognition of interdependence among people, groups, and institutional arrangements.

Others look at the community in social science terms, where community is seen in relation to the larger society or may even be viewed itself as a local society. Chapter 2 indicates approaches some of the social sciences take in their treatment of the community. This same chapter points out options available within the socio-logical perspective and explains how these provide the themes around which this book is organized.

1

The Search for Community in a Complex Society

Many people today are seeking a sense of community. They want to be thought of as whole persons and not simply as customers, passengers, clients, or social security numbers to be processed through computers. On the other hand, many residents of larger cities seem to enjoy the anonymity that such a milieu affords and work out a style of life with interesting diversions but with few social contacts involving any real friendship.

What is there about American society, or about any postindustrial society for that matter, which affects people in such ways? Why do those who feel deracinated try to get their roots down into friendlier social soil? Many traits of our society could be mentioned as shedding some light on this situation. These need to be placed in a context such as that which Robert A. Nisbet (1962) provides in his book *The Quest for Community* (retitled *Community and Power*). He believes:

> . . . that the ominous preoccupation with community revealed by modern thought and mass behavior is a manifestation of certain profound dislocations in the primary associative areas of society, dislocations that have been created to a great extent by the structure of the Western political State . . . (p. 47).

3

He sees the problem as social and political:

> . . . social in that it pertains to the statuses and social memberships which men hold, or seek to hold. But the problem is also political—political in that it is a reflection of the present location and distribution of power in society. (p. 47).

SELECTED TRAITS OF MODERN AMERICAN SOCIETY

In dealing with the "sense of community" we are looking at those factors which affect psychological states: how people feel and how they evaluate their feelings, which influence the interaction of us all. The feeling most frequently expressed today is one of confusion, due to differences among us in perceptions of events, and disagreements as to the direction our American society is taking and should take. Of course, individual interpretations of each situation may differ and each experience may affect some members divisively, others cohesively. The four societal traits discussed below influence a person's social orientation and, therefore, that person's interpretation of the experience. They relate to one's sense of community.

Range of Options

In contrast to earlier societies, where tradition dictated within limits what people did or did not do, our society confronts an individual with almost unlimited possibilities, at least, held out as options even though realistically the individual might qualify for relatively few. At any rate the whole range needs to be taken into account in any rational consideration of choice.

Put another way, our society is highly differentiated. Compare the types of jobs open to young people today with those available thirty or forty years ago. When a young person tells his or her parents that he or she is going to be a computer programmer, the parents probably do not even know what a computer looks like and what such a computer program is. The careers of doctor, lawyer, or engineer would seem familiar to the parents, despite the fact that these three professional fields have been going through radical internal change.

Another wide range of options is connected with recreation and the use of leisure time. The pages of any metropolitan newspaper illustrate the choices confronting the individual with ability to pay. For those who do not prefer or cannot afford the highly advertised leisure time activities there are various options on television, in loafing or visiting groups, or in outdoor activities. Some of these activities give a temporary sense of community. Most of the time, one is merely a ticket-holder or spectator who is being diverted for a while.

Another option often cited as an advantage of our society is the chance to choose from among many life styles. This can vary from the relatively homogenized pattern in the affluent suburbs to the preferred anonymity of urban apartment living or to a hippie existence in certain areas of larger cities. With young people in particular the influence of the peer group conflicts with that of the parents. Along with this presumed range of options is the assumption that people can find the economic means to move ahead into more and more desirable situations. But the fact of the matter is that wide options are open to only a certain segment of the population, whereas limitations based on income, race, sex, and job opportunities hold back many people. In such cases, the sense of community does not arise from sharing the benefits of the system but out of mutual opposition to certain features of the system.

Rapid Tempo of Change

Many social critics have pointed out that changes come along faster than individuals or the social structures which they tend to undermine can adjust to them. The widely read book *Future Shock* by Alvin Toffler (1971) develops the theme of the rapidity of change and points out its many social effects. He notes:

> . . . We are simultaneously experiencing a youth revolution, a sexual revolution, a racial revolution, a colonial revolution, an economic revolution, and the most rapid and deepgoing technological revolution in history . . . (p. 186).
> . . . The powerful bonds that integrated industrial society—bonds of law, common values, centralized and standardized education and cultural production—are breaking down. (p. 301).

Along with this increased tempo of change there is a diversification of values, leading to a crack-up of consensus:

> . . . Most previous societies have operated with a broad central core of commonly shared values. This core is now contracting, and there is

little reason to anticipate the formation of a new broad consensus within the decades ahead. The pressures are outward toward diversity, not inward toward unity. (p. 301).

Few Americans realize that, in contrast to most other societies, the United States has built innovation into the basic American social structure. In the technological field, every major corporation has a research division that is constantly seeking to improve or modify the product it offers to the public; the whole research arm of the defense establishment is also involved in subsidizing research into all areas of science that might lead to more sophisticated weaponry. The National Aeronautics and Space Administration (NASA) supports extensive research in several scientific fields. In the area of physical planning, experts are constantly trying to devise new ways of utilizing urban space, providing the transportation and public services (utilities; waste disposal) required of densely-packed populations. Developers of real estate properties seek to erect on the land available to them structures which bring in more revenue than those now standing. In education, the effort is being made in hit-or-miss fashion to prepare young people today for a different kind of world which will exist in the year 2000. Courses on The Sociology of the Future try to project forty or fifty years ahead the trends which even now can be discerned and predicted. Those familiar with large scale organizations, such as government bureaus, hospitals, correctional systems cannot help but be impressed with the numerous reorganizations which such bureaucracies experience in an effort to introduce what seem at the time to be desirable innovations. Conscious, planned, purposeful change is thus a basic feature of American society.

Accompanying this is the popular belief that what is *new* is *good* or, at least, *better*. This explains much faddism that sweeps across the country and partially accounts for the fact that college generations just a few years apart dress differently, behave differently in some ways, and even seem to have different thought patterns. Having the latest model of any product: automobile, television, kitchen stove, lawn mower, apparel is a desired end in itself. But when one is not able to keep up with the endless procession of newly available products, when the children who watch television begin to ask for advertised toys which the family cannot afford, then one begins to get a feeling of falling behind in the procession. This can alienate, cause a partial loss of whatever sense of community one might have had.

This is closely related to the phenomenon of rising expectations, where the relatively deprived begin to hope that they too can share in some of the desirable goals or good things. And even if there is some modest improvement in their situation, such improvement is so little and comes so slowly, that those who had hopes begin to despair and fall back again into the psychology of "the have nots." Periodically, when government programs are set up to accomplish certain goals for categories such as "the urban poor," "the senior citizens," "disadvantaged ethnic minorities," these categories may let their expectations go beyond the possible benefits which such programs can provide. Disillusionment results.

The tempo of change, however, is most noticeable in its relationship to sense of community in the realm of customs, conventions, values. People who have been taught to support a strictly segregated society find it very difficult to readjust their thinking and their behavior to one that is non-segregated; men (and many women) who have accepted the supremacy of the male as a fact in every walk of life find it hard to adjust to situations in which women begin to play non-traditional roles; older professors and those in other professional fields, who have painstakingly climbed the ladder of prestige over a long period of time, find it unfair and even bewildering to accept at the top rung very young professionals who want immediate participation in decision-making and recognition as persons; parents who grew up in a social setting where parents had the last word wonder why they should try to relate democratically to their children and their children's friends.

As differences arise among groups over the rightness or wrongness, appropriateness or inappropriateness of types of social change, communication tends to break down and with it whatever sense of community that may have existed. The answer, of course, is that such changes make possible the creation of a different type of understanding where the sense of community may again reappear. But this is always a time-consuming process.

Confusion as to Direction of American Society

Those familiar with earlier periods of American history are often tempted to wish for the public certainty and self-assurance which these periods exhibited. In America's past one is reminded of the period of expansion, at home and abroad, around the turn of this century. In that period each individual was supposedly working out his own social and economic salvation. At one extreme the so-called "robber barons" were amassing gigantic fortunes and at the other extreme even the poorest immigrants felt some progress in giving their children a better life than they had enjoyed. Each nation, too, was working out its own salvation under what has now come to be called imperialism. At this historical period, most Americans were self-confident. They knew where they stood and they had a sense of direction. Whether the concept of "manifest destiny" was mere jingoism or hard social reality is not the point at issue. What is important is the sense of community that existed, the shared feeling that America was on the move all together.

In World War I America was united in its effort "to save the world for democracy." World War II provided a more recent "sense of community" in the desperate fight against totalitarian dictatorships. And, for many Americans, the cause of "rebuilding the war torn world," was a serious one which gave pride in being an American.

With the turn inward upon domestic problems, particularly the cause of civil rights, attention was called to inequalities and social injustices in American life. Here were situations that ran counter to the American value system of equal opportunity, individual rights, and democratic participation. Sharp divisions appeared in the body politic, which became even more accentuated as the Indo-China embroilment became deeper and deeper. This led some to look beyond remedial programs for our society to the questioning of the basis of society itself. Each generation, of course, defines what its problems are. The problems selected in this generation are those which go to the very heart of not only individual values but the American value system itself. This questioning has occurred simultaneously with a shift from an emphasis upon production (building a bigger, more productive America) to a postindustrial emphasis upon consumption, where the stress is upon distribution of production.

The Watergate episode and its aftermath have shown the directions which the technocratic, power-seeking approach would take America. Apparently it is being rejected in favor of a more humane approach where individual rights take precedence over a few officials' perception of national interest. But the reestablishment of the moral order, the reformulation of goals for the society, and the decision as to whose goals are to predominate will profoundly affect the extent to which American citizens will feel again a sense of community.

Rapid Communication of the Tragic

Another characteristic of modern society is the rapidity with which tragedy in one part of the world is communicated. Communications satellites beam TV programs from one continent to another instantaneously. And the news tends to permeate daily life: in written, oral, aural fashion. An essential feature of many tragic occurrences is the breakdown in the sense of community highlighted by the incident being reported.

Natural catastrophe is news: an earthquake in Peru, a typhoon in Japan, a drought in Sub-Saharan Africa, a crop failure on a vast scale in Southeast Asia. Such reporting confronts us with suffering humanity with whom we may or may not feel a degree of empathy. It does make us aware, however, that in parts of the world these catastrophes are tearing down resources and social structures on which the people had depended and concerning which they may have had a sense of community; now a new start has to be made; the road ahead will be long and difficult despite the sudden rush of community feeling in dealing with the emergency by those who forget themselves in an effort to help others.

Social upheaval is news. Here the focus is on discontent and some effort to register it. It too signals the breakdown of community. As we hear and see about strikes and revolution against the government in Chile, the expulsion of Asians from Uganda, the attempted coup d'etat in one country after another, the mass protests of striking workers, striking students, striking housewives or farmers, we begin to wonder whether there is a sense of community anywhere in the world. Up to a point the number of tragic occurrences may not be much greater than in the past, but the communication of these events—compacted into a thirty minute TV news program—certainly acquaints people around the globe with what seems to be wrong everywhere.

The individual misconduct or act of violence is news. The alienated individual who tries to assassinate a political figure, destroy

his own family, hijack an airliner or take his own life in a futile
gesture of protest is announcing to the world that he has no sense
of community, except with a very small group of like-minded individuals. Again, the news media can become saturated with the
acts of a relatively few people and thereby give the impression that
a sense of community is no longer commonplace.

Many other facets of American or other modern societies could
be mentioned but these four at least illustrate some of the factors
which negate a sense of community in some ways characteristic of
the past, while they also point to some new directions that a sense
of community may have in the future. But before looking too far
ahead a backward look may be useful.

CHANGING SOCIAL BASIS OF THE COMMUNITY

The pendulum of history has many curious swings; it does not
always beat an ordered movement back and forth between two
extremes. If we examine the basis for the sense of community in
the past, we find at least four emphases which, though not mutually
exclusive, do seem to characterize the range of possibilities. These
four are tradition, individualism, communality, and interdependence.

Tradition and the Community

Where people act in keeping with traditions, where they farm,
marry and otherwise conduct their lives in keeping with time-
honored custom, they can claim a very basic sense of community.
Their traditions are what they have in common and their community consists of those ancestors who have gone before and those
descendants who are to follow. Many descriptions have been
written of these traditional communities, most of which are agricultural and therefore tied in with the cycle of the seasons and
changing moods of nature. A traditional community does not question the rightness or wrongness of the past. When asked why they
do a certain thing in a given way its members reply quite simply:
"That is the custom." They are in the pre-scientific era; a supernatural explanation of an event is just as plausible as a scientific one.
Furthermore, they live in a relatively small society. Their village
and perhaps the nearest market town tend to constitute their social

universe and they can comprehend fairly well what they observe within the universe. Their society is relatively undifferentiated in that most farmers have learned to do many kinds of tasks for which an urbanite would call a repairman or specialist.

Their sense of community is built on a familistic society, with the principle of patriarchy guiding various relationships. Individuals gain their security from submitting to the authority of the head of their family and their individual status is tied in with the respect (or lack of it) that others in the community have for one's own kinship group. People following a traditional pattern are usually conservative as judged by city people, but this is not because they resist change for its own sake but because they are so close to the margin of subsistence that they do not have enough resources to spare for experimentation. If you are head of a family of four and someone asks you to try a new type of rice or to cultivate it in a way with which you are not familiar you will think twice before you jeopardize your family's very existence by experimenting with a new idea which may or may not work.

Unquestionably people who live in such rural communities, whether in the open country communities of the United States or the villages of other parts of the world, are aware of being a part of community. They may tend to associate primarily with their own relatives; they may even avoid association with certain families in the community but they all know that they share a common fate and that the clue to whether a person is to be respected or not is the extent to which he observes the expected traditional behavior associated with someone of his status. To say that people in such localities have a sense of community is not to deny the fact that a number of them may find the controls implied in such a system restrictive and unpleasant. They welcome a chance to move away and strike out on their own; yet they always carry with them the conditioning that they experienced while growing up in the tradition-bound community.

Individualism and the Community

With the swing away from tradition to the more rational, scientific approach to farming and to other economic sectors, people had to find a substitute for tradition if they were to experience any sense of community. In the days of "rugged individualism" at the turn of the century, to which allusion has already been made, the community existed to help people get ahead. Its institutions were to be used for that purpose and everybody understood the rules of the game. The policy of laissez-faire or "live and let live" seems a strange principle on which to develop a sense of community, but this seems to have happened in one period of American society. This is not to idealize the Gay Nineties and the decades which followed for a number of historians have shown just how difficult these times were for large numbers of people.

When the main goal of life was to get ahead (in some cases hold what you have), then a sense of community could spring up among those who had the same goal. Outright competitors of course felt no urge to assist each other, but one could lend a helping hand to those who were not competitors on the theory that bread cast upon the waters would return with manifold blessings. This meant that one really had no *social* concerns except those that promoted *individual* concerns; those who were at the top of the system through their acceptance of *noblesse oblige* did render some assistance to the unfortunate, such charity being a part of one's Christian duty.

Where the market place became the controlling factor, with everyone accepting its operations as central, then there could be a sense of community about that. The market could either become the villain to be castigated or it could bring favorable advantages to perspicacious individuals.

To look back upon those days through the lenses of contemporary insight can lead to a misunderstanding of what people actually felt and thought at that time. One's present condition, even if unfortunate, was not the main concern but rather the hope and even conviction that if one worked hard enough and had a stroke of luck now and then life would get much easier. There was a new continent to be conquered, a disintegrating Spanish empire whose vassals should be freed (the Spanish-American war) and taught English, mineral deposits around the world to be developed—many of them right here at home, and new industries to provide for a rapidly expanding population.

Though it seems paradoxical, it is clear that in the days of individualism there was a sense of community in localities throughout the United States. This was due perhaps to the lingering common cultural traditions but was also due to the heady intoxication of rapidly expanding economic power from which an individual might benefit. The Protestant Ethic so fully described by the German sociologist Max Weber was at work; it was the same America described earlier by the Frenchman Alexis de Tocqueville where organizations and associations of many kinds were devised to serve the needs of individual members. Through such group efforts more and more services, both material and nonmaterial, became available. The standard of living rose for much of the population and one could evaluate one's own worth by what one was able to acquire and hopefully enjoy. Even though with the booms there came the busts and hard times, the sense of community was still strong enough to weather the strains.

To conclude, the age of individualism was the kind of community one develops in playing a game where the rules are known, where some were destined to be losers and others winners, and where very few referees or umpires were around to be sure that the rules were kept. But the fact that the game—namely the Great American Dream—was the common basis upon which those born here and the millions attracted here framed their lives provided a sense of community both locally and nationally.

Many social critics have pointed out the limitations of individualism as a central culture theme. Philip Slater (1970) in *The Pursuit of Loneliness* portrays, almost to the point of caricature, where such emphasis has led. He states:

> The belief that everyone should pursue autonomously his own destiny has forced us to maintain an emotional detachment (for which no amount of superficial gregariousness can compensate) from our social and physical environment, and aroused a vague guilt about our competitiveness and indifference to others; for, after all, our earliest training in childhood does not stress competitiveness, but cooperation, sharing, and thoughtfulness—it is only later that we learn to reverse these priorities. Radical changes to our society, then, always rap a confused responsive chord within us that is far more disturbing than anything going on outside. They threaten to reconnect us with each other, with nature, and with ourselves, a possibility that is thrilling but terrifying—as if we had grown a shell-like epidermis and someone was threatening to rip it off.
>
> Individualism finds its roots in the attempt to deny the reality and importance of human interdependence. One of the major goals of technology in America is to "free" us from the necessity of relating to, submitting to, depending upon, or controlling other people. Unfortunately, the more we have succeeded in doing this the more we have felt disconnected, bored, lonely, unprotected, unnecessary, and unsafe. (pp. 25–26).

Communality and the Community

Throughout history there have been many utopian schemes to set up communities in which all members would have a satisfactory life and where many of the abuses so evident in society at large could be eliminated. The stories of Brook Farm and the transcendentalists, of the Oneida Community, the Shakers and a number of others illustrate the intensity with which groups have sought a true sense of community. In the past such groups foundered on the dilemma of utopianism: how to find and maintain communalism in a noncommunal world. They were always limited in size for their communalism was a vision not capable of being made—under existing conditions—a large-scale social reality.

Today there are also many intentional communities reacting against present social evils. The *kibbutzim* of Israel are some of the best known, but the communes in the U. S. of the 1970's also fill important social needs for those who participate.

The characteristic of such efforts is the shared experience. Ordinarily, the various tasks are cooperatively carried out with as little distinction of sex and economic roles as possible. There is a common ideology binding the members together, a common locus for their activities, and a shared daily routine. Communes vary as to their requirement that the members bring in to the group the income from their jobs. One of the most largescale set of communes was set up under Father Divine in New York City many years ago. He was a charismatic personality who inspired devotion chiefly but not exclusively among black supporters. He set up living centers known as heavens and required that each member turn over all his earnings to the furtherance of his religious mission. While the more recently established communes, according to Rosabeth Kantor (1972) stress personal fulfillment (how good are the 'vibes') rather than group continuity, they do represent an effort to gain a sense of community by sharing with others.

Roszak (1969) notes that these communes reflect the existence of a counterculture which seeks to offer to their members alternate ways of coping with what to them are grim social problems. One of the characteristics of the counterculture, if one can take *The Greening of America* by Charles Reich (1970) as one of its apocalyptic visions, is liberation:

The meaning of liberation is that the individual is free to build his own philosophy and values, his own life-style and his own culture from a new beginning. . . . In place of the world seen as a jungle, with every man for himself . . . or the world seen as a meritocracy leading to a corporate hierarchy of rigidly drawn relations and manoeuvers for position . . . the world is a community. In personal relations the keynote is honesty, and the absence of socially imposed duty. (pp. 241; 243–4)

Such an approach would lead to communalizing of social relations, which would prove to be the basis of a new approach to a sense of community. Interpersonal relations would be honest in that there would be true sharing of feelings, thoughts, and intentions. This is carrying communalism to its ultimate extreme.

Interdependence and the Community

As we move farther away from the global and national perspective to the local community (where each of us lives), we can see that a sense of community can develop out of a realization of mutual interdependence.

One might take the university community as an illustration. For centuries it was assumed that intellectual pursuits were the central concerns of the university collective. Students were embryonic scholars who were to be processed through a guild system into full-fledged masters and doctors; everybody was motivated by the pursuit of knowledge and some in the community were senior, others junior. With the changing role of the university in society, it is no longer a luxury institution where detached scholars can contemplate the problems of humanity; it has become in part, at least, a certification mechanism providing a piece of paper to an individual who needs it to get the kind of job that he wants. This means that the interest of the student and the teacher are no longer the same. In the words of an Oxford don, the purpose of the faculty is to stay around the institution as long as possible and that of the student is to get out as fast as possible. If one thinks commonality necessary for community, then obviously there is little in common between student and faculty. If one adds to this the third power bloc in the university—the administration—then there is even greater discrepancy as to commonality. The goals of the administration are to keep the institution fiscally viable, to bring about greater efficiencies so that salaries can be met, and to stress those activities which will set well with possible donors, whether these be private individuals, organized philanthropies, or state legislatures. What we are driven to, therefore, is the realization that each of the three major sub-systems of the university—faculty, student, and administration—has different functions to perform if the institution is to survive in our kind of society. Simultaneously we see that one party cannot exist without the assistance of the other parties. Therefore, there must develop by the very exigencies of the situation an interdependence which far transcends any stress on commonality. The realization of this interdependence, this mutual reinforcement, is the first step toward developing a sense of community (Sanders, 1973).

Much the same applies to a national society or a local community where interdependence exists on an infinitely larger, more complex scale than on a university campus. This is first shown in the meshing of the local institutional order, to be described in Chapter 8. It is also indicated in the various allocative mechanisms whereby goods and services, jobs, prestige, and power become distributed throughout the community, differentially to be sure. Every organization finds itself in a field of action with other organizations and the so-called power structure consists of much more than a few easily recognized members of the top elite. There is a whole power grid that is involved in decision-making, with interdependence one of its major characteristics.

This theme of interdependence is not of recent origin. Classic sociological theory has for a long time been stressing what happens as societies move from the more simple types to the more complex. The French sociologist Emile Durkheim, in particular, showed how the division of labor in complex societies brought about an organic interdependence that led to a collective conscience or collective "representations" which differed from those in the traditional or mechanical society. Where the interdependence breaks down, the sense of community suffers.

Therefore, as one looks to the future it is most likely that tradition will not be the binding force for a sense of community; likewise extreme individualism seems to have run its course; nor does the answer lie in the emphasis upon communalism if it is assumed that everybody is to be stripped to the same common denominator. If we are to maintain some of the obvious benefits of a complex society, we will have to find our sense of community in two ways: first, we may seek commonality of interests with a relatively few people where intimacy can prevail; second, we may develop some kind of appreciation for and accommodation with the larger community, seeing our connection with it in terms of an acknowledged interdependence.

INTERDEPENDENCE

Since this book endeavors to help provide an understanding of the local community, one might well ask how a sense of community, based on interdependence is tied up with locality. Four dimensions of interdependence can be observed in any home town.

Symbolic Interdependence

When papers are not delivered, when garbage is not collected on schedule, when buses or subway trains fail to run, or when the snow is not plowed one is suddenly made aware that there are many operations being carried out behind the scenes. One does not usually have face-to-face contact with those who are contributing to one's personal welfare; relations remain impersonal, but they are built on a type of interdependence.

Economic Interdependence

Not only is there a connection between supplier, retailer and customer, but there are differences in services offered in localities of various sizes. Thus communities from smaller to larger form a hierarchy with respect to services available in them.

The Local Institutional Order

Within a given spatial domain the institutional complexes have worked out an accommodation to each other, and continue to do so. They represent the normative order, or the expected standards of the community (Wilson, 1968). The home, the school, the church, and various other associations are usually mutually supportive in this regard. With rapid social change, such as the kind we are experiencing today, challenges to this normative order weaken the sense of community as traditionally defined and call for a re-definition. These local institutional complexes, however, go beyond merely representing the normative order; they actually perform many functions which keep the community a viable social unit.

Allocation of Prestige and Power

Finally, the local interdependence is also revealed in the way prestige and power, income and services are allocated among the different social groupings. There is an interdependence among these allocating mechanisms. Local groups who work on problems of social inequality know very well how strong is the tendency for existing mechanisms to favor those already enjoying a privileged position. But through the political process the allocation procedures are being modified in many communities. This is what the War on Poverty was all about in the minds of its more ardent partisans.

One of the interesting current trends is that, whereas formerly only the more advantaged groups took time or felt it worth their while to become involved, now people at every economic level, in all sections of a city or town are making their concerns known, frequently in strident ways. Protest or action groups do more than try to deal with a particular issue; they try to provide for their members a channel of participation which will increase a sense of community. Since the interests of various segments of the community are not identical, this broader base of participation makes the local community a much livelier place than in the past and introduces factors to take into account by those who had formerly been making decisions in behalf of the community.

Gerald D. Suttles (1972) has studied urban slums as well as other parts of metropolitan areas. In addressing the problem of communion and community, he comes to this conclusion:

> Although this (quest for a community of sentiment—one where everyone can be his true moral self) is a growing symbolic representation of the local community, I suspect that it is poorly realized in most actual communities. To a large extent Americans still live where they have to and, in any case, have to move so often that the community of limited liability is the most prevalent form. The coerciveness of the work place and other institutions not only creates a yearning for community but makes it difficult to realize in the residential community. Thus people seek for alternatives in other institutions: the student community, the political community, the business community, and so on. The extent to which these other institutions can offer either communion or community is limited by their institutional dependencies. They cannot be fully liberated and continue to function. *The focus of the desire for community, then, will probably continue to return to the local residential community, and if people seem shallow and inauthentic elsewhere, the*

pressure for a community of sentiment may increase. [italics mine]
(p. 266)

We thus face one of the many interesting paradoxes of our time: as we move toward a mass society in vast metropolises, the need to maintain the strength and even to revitalize the smaller local community (within the metropolis as well as outside) assumes much greater importance. We need to understand local communities better in order to develop social policies which make them more satisfactory to their residents. The search for a sense of community will go on, and when found it will reduce confusion and alienation by linking the individual in a meaningful way to the larger society.

2

Theoretical Approaches to Community Analysis

One can study the community in varying degrees of thoroughness. The simplest level is *personal observation and individual interpretation.* Everyone "experiences" the community in which he lives because many of his daily activities are connected with the use of local services, with the organizations made up of other community members, and with his reactions to what is occurring around him. This personal description is thus available to everyone and affords a good starting-point for developing skills in community analysis. But there are three cautions to be kept in mind. First, most people have a partial or "keyhole" view of their community. They see it from their own particular vantage point; they know their own part of town and may be uninterested or poorly informed about other areas. They may be so engrossed in one particular line of work—managing a business, going to school, running a household, driving a bus—that they see the community in terms of their own occupational segment.

A second caution is the need for objectivity. This means putting oneself in the place of other people instead of looking at every matter merely from the personal vantage point. This leads one to ask:

What are the reasons for the behavior of certain groups? Why do some people like and some dislike certain cliques or groups to which the individual observer might belong? Objectivity requires that one seek to understand "the definition of the situation" held by varying kinds of groups and not assume that one's own assessment is the only appropriate one. A third caution is the exercise of greater care in describing what one sees. When a new driver is being trained, his instructor first insists that he learn a specialized vocabulary that includes such words as "hand brake," "accelerator," "gear shift," "starter," and "carburetor." If one wishes to analyze a community, one needs a special vocabulary to describe the kind of social phenomena one observes. Sociology seeks to provide such a vocabulary.

Another level of community study—beyond that of personal observation and interpretation—is the self-survey. (Kimball and Pearsall, 1954) (Warren, 1955) In the self-survey, a group of local citizens, often with the assistance of an outside consultant, examines various aspects of the community, frequently concentrating on problem areas in the search for solutions. Such studies go beyond the observations of a single individual and rely upon the data from many sources.

A third level, the most thorough of all, is social science research. In this case professionally trained personnel employ tested scientific methods to collect and analyze data about the underlying social structure and basic processes of a community. They know what statistical sources to tap (Munson, 1968), how to select a representative sample of informants, how to make up questionnaires and conduct interviews, how to analyze newspapers and other available documents, and particularly how to tabulate and classify the data in order to arrive at and present findings about the community. This approach may be a careful reconnaissance (Sanders, 1960) or a social survey (Devine and Falk, 1972), or it may be "research in depth" in which no effort is spared to do as complete a job as possible. The costs may run into thousands of dollars, but the findings may result in savings to community agencies of much more than the original research expenditures. Or, even if the local community does not expect immediate, specific benefits, the research may add important knowledge to the related social science fields.

Social scientists, however, do not all use the same kind of research approach, as is pointed out by Bell and Newby (1972) in their brief summaries of American and European community studies. This is because they have different intellectual interests and are trying to answer different questions about the community (Simpson, 1965). Some are more interested in reform than analysis; others in thoroughly understanding one particular facet in contrast to those who view the community as a total functioning system; some want to participate in the community and experience for themselves what the community is like while others prefer to make use of the mass of statistical data already available in data banks about American metropolitan areas and political subdivisions. We can characterize at least four significant social science approaches: the qualitative approach (the community as a place to live); the ecological approach (the community as a spatial unit); the ethnographic approach (the community as a way of life); and the sociological approach (the community as an arena of social interaction).

THE COMMUNITY AS A PLACE TO LIVE (QUALITATIVE APPROACH)

There is obviously no perfect community, no matter what criteria one may use. But there are relative advantages that one community may have over others.[1] In a comparison of Durham and Greensboro, North Carolina, an attempt was made to define livability as the sum total of the qualities of the urban environment that tend to induce in a citizen a state of well-being and satisfaction. People of these two cities were interviewed to find out what kind of physical city they wanted. The interview techniques, because of their originality, deserve special mention (Wilson, 1962):

> The interview itself contained several distinct parts. The first, a series of oral questions, dealt with the amount of experience living in other cities and/or on farms, along with reasons for moving to the current location. General satisfaction, likes, and dislikes about the city as a whole were next. City size preferences and questions about the relative importance of certain social and physical characteristics of cities in general followed. A number of questions dealt with the relative importance to the respondent of his neighborhood, compared with the city as a whole,

[1] For pioneering efforts in this approach see E. L. Thorndike: *Your City* (1939) where he presents a factual index for 117 cities based on 23 items; Bradley Buell and his colleagues (1940) who sought to establish a rate of social breakdown for several cities, and Robert C. Angell's work on "moral integration" of 43 cities (1951).

and with his view of the desirable and undesirable features of that neighborhood.

Direct questions were varied by a second part of the interview, called a "game" because of its mechanical similarity to familiar parlor games. A series of alternative choices among various types of residential utilities and services (described on the board) was "bought" with a limited amount of "money" supplied in the context of the game. (Briefly, the respondent had won a free house. The decisions in the game were those necessary to determine the kind of neighborhood in which to build the house.)

A second part of the game was similar, but dealt with neighborhood facilities such as schools and churches, and distance relationships desired between those facilities and the respondent's home. During the course of the game, the interviewer rated the house and neighborhood environment for certain qualitative aspects.

A third major element of the interview utilized a series of photos of miscellaneous neighborhoods. The respondent was asked to indicate by a rating scale the extent to which each of the photos contained certain specified qualities, such as "privacy," "beauty," etc., and to rank the photos in order of preference.

The interview ended with a series of personal questions: attempts to get information about the basic personality of the respondent, social and economic data, occupation, etc. (pp. 364–65)

As the following table shows, the people of Greensboro were more satisfied with their community than the people of Durham:

TABLE 2–1

**Relative Satisfaction of Residents with Their City,
Greensboro and Durham, N. C.**

	Greensboro	Durham
Very much satisfied	43%	23%
Satisfied	39	58
Neutral	14	16
Dissatisfied	2	3
Very much dissatisfied	2	0
	100%	100%

Source: F. Stuart Chapin and Shirley F. Weiss, *Urban Growth Dynamics in a Regional Cluster of States,* New York: John Wiley & Sons, Inc., 1962, p. 371.

In a different study an effort was made to see whether professional people in rural areas varied in their feeling of community satisfaction. A series of interviews was conducted with teachers, clergymen (social-helping professionals), lawyers, doctors, dentists (technical-helping professionals) (Jesser, 1967). The social-helping professionals were found to have lower community satisfaction scores than the technical-helping professions. These lawyers, doctors and dentists who were most satisfied participated in the community's formal organizations and those teachers and clergymen who were most satisfied were those who had made the largest number of moves in their career.

In another study (Johnson and Knop, 1970) rural and urban people were compared with respect to community satisfaction. Urban residents were more satisfied with shopping and medical facilities, teacher ability, employment opportunities and entertainment-recreation potentials. Rural residents, on the other hand, appear more satisfied with local democratic processes and their general geographical milieu.

These studies of residents' qualitative perceptions of a community's livability represent one kind of social science analysis of the community.[2] In each case the researchers used statistical techniques to arrive at their findings about the way people evaluated aspects of community life (Zehner and Chapin, 1974).

Closely related to the qualitative approach to community study is what has been called the social indicators movement. Just as economists use economic indicators to describe the state of the economy at any given time, so sociologists are trying to devise and utilize indicators of certain social conditions. Social indicators have been defined as *quantitative data that serve as measures of socially important conditions of society.* These indicators may measure both "objective" conditions of society and persons (e.g., health, education, crime, mobility, etc.) and "subjective" perceptions of life experiences (e.g., satisfactions, aspirations, alienation, etc.) (Henriot, 1972; *The Annals,* 1967).

A New York *Times* article by Robert Reinhold (1973) has described this movement as "trying to get desire on a graph." He writes:

> . . . the refinement of opinion sampling methods and the adaptation of statistical analysis to the study of social problems have given the profession some powerful new tools to monitor social programs . . .

[2] For an effort to look at habitat qualities from the standpoint of ecological psychology, see Roger G. Barker and Phil Schoggen, *Qualities of Community Life: Methods of Measuring Environment and Behavior Applied to an American and an English Town.* San Francisco: Jossey-Bass, Inc. 1973.

Decency and dignity may be elusive goals, but many contend that they cannot be achieved by using standard economic indicators, such as gross national product, and conventional social statistics as a guide. Raymond Bauer, the social psychologist at the Harvard Business School who coined the term social indicators in 1966, put some of the questions that need answering to a 1971 Senate subcommittee on social planning: "While we would reduce hunger, we do not know just who is hungry. While we would reduce crime, our knowledge of even how many crimes of what type are committed is highly imperfect. While we would improve the 'quality of life' we do not know what our citizens value in our lives." . . .

Once valid indicators are determined, how should they be used? Some believe they should gauge the relative costs and benefits of achieving specific goals, such as higher employment and less crime . . .

But some advocates of social indicators urge caution in their application. "Far too many promises and claims have been made for social indicators, and not enough delivered," writes Eleanor Bernert Sheldon, president of the Social Science Research Council. "The risks are too great that a continual oversell could indeed transform the indicators movement into a passing fad." (p. 8; © 1973 by the New York Times Company)

Obviously, those primarily interested in the quality of community life will follow the results of the increased use of social indicators at the community level, where they can be particularly helpful in the study of social change (Clark, 1973a).

THE COMMUNITY AS A SPATIAL UNIT
(ECOLOGICAL APPROACH)

Although Chapter 3 will deal with this general topic, the ecological approach can be briefly illustrated here by reference to a series of three studies by Frank L. Sweetser (1961–63) on the social ecology of Metropolitan Boston. Sweetser has prepared maps showing how forty statistical measures of social or economic characteristics are distributed among 471 "social areas" of Metropolitan Boston. A few of the measures are: foreign or mixed parentage, sex ratio of the single population, young families with working mothers, residential migration into the metropolitan area, median family income, commutation to work, male clerical and service workers, and social rank. There is nothing very dramatic about these measures in and of themselves, but when one sees them marching, as it were, across the series of maps of the big metropolitan area, shifting some between 1950 and 1960, one senses changes in the life of the communities comprising Greater Boston. Professor Sweetser expects the same main trends to be borne out in the 1970 census figures.

Notice in the following findings, selected from many others of equal interest reported by Sweetser, that the element of *space* or physical location is always present.

> In Metropolitan Boston between 1950 and 1960 those tracts [3] which were gaining population faster than the average tract tended also to be rising faster than the average tract in socioeconomic status.
>
> Tracts showing gains in population also tended to have higher relative increases in proportions of elementary school children than have tracts tending to lose population.
>
> Relative increase in population for specific areas is associated with relative decrease in proportions of foreign born, and vice versa.
>
> Although the non-white (or Negro) population remains largely concentrated in the urban core of the metropolis, there is a definite centrifugal movement toward the outer urban zone, and away from the inner urban tracts.
>
> Housing quality in the inner zones has probably changed but little (it may, in fact, have deteriorated) in Metropolitan Boston between 1950 and 1960. On the other hand, there can be no doubt about the marked improvement in average housing quality in the three outer zones.
>
> Between 1950 and 1960 the Western and Northwest sectors of Metropolitan Boston gained professionals and managers and lost blue collar workers, while the South Central sector gained blue collar workers and lost professionals and managers. Occupational segregation among these residential sectors has thus increased.

Even though one has no familiarity with the Greater Boston area, the above findings show that attention to spatial distribution of social and economic traits provides some meaningful insights into community forces and local problems.

Alvin Boskoff (1962), who is conducting studies of Metropolitan Atlanta, views the ecological approach as one of the essential preparatory tools used by the urban sociologist. It focuses, he reminds us, upon three related aspects: (1) the spatial distribution of groups and activities; (2) the conditions or factors in adjustment to subareas; and (3) the nature of the interrelations between and among

---

[3] As defined in the 1970 Census, "Census tracts are small, relatively permanent areas into which large cities and adjacent areas are divided for the purpose of providing comparable small-area statistics. Tract boundaries are determined by a local committee and approved by the Census Bureau; they conform to county lines. Tracts are originally designed to be relatively homogeneous with respect to population characteristics, economic status, and living conditions . . ." U. S. Department of Commerce, Bureau of the Census: *1970 Census Users' Guide*, Part I, p. 86. October, 1970.

subareas in an overall sociogeographic division of labor. Interdependence is thus an accepted fact.

Occasionally, the demographic approach is cited as one of the ways of viewing the community. The value of looking at a community in terms of its population is taken up later (in Chapter 4), but will not be treated here as a separate approach. The ecological approach makes full use of population statistics as linked with census tracts, thus providing more revealing information than the population statistics taken alone.

Some sociologists (Murdock and Sutton, 1974) have called attention to what they term the "new ecology," which has gone far beyond the work of Park (1952; see Chapter 3). It is based most notably on the studies of Hawley, Duncan, and Schnore. The last two writers (1959) view ecological processes as composed of four elements: population, organization, environment and technology. Murdock and Sutton point out that ecology viewed in such terms can usefully join with other approaches to the community (e.g., social systems) to formulate much sounder theory and more penetrating insights.

THE COMMUNITY AS A WAY OF LIFE
(ETHNOGRAPHIC APPROACH)

There are literally hundreds of community studies carried out in an effort to describe the total way of life of the local residents. Each investigator decides for himself just what methods he will use, what relative emphasis he will give to various aspects of the culture, and how much he will rely upon his own personal impressions and observations. It is common in this approach for the social scientist (often an anthropologist) to learn the language used in the community if it is foreign to him, to stay in residence for a year or more, and to participate as fully as he can in all the local activities so that he can watch the people under many different conditions as they engage in all kinds of activities.

The characteristic of this method which supposedly gives it special merit is the all-around, comprehensive view presented. Not just the spatial and demographic considerations, but insight into the total culture is the goal. The table of contents of a recent study shows how the author sought to cover as wide a slice of life as possible. Irene Winner (1971) described life in a Slovenian village, in the northwestern part of Yugoslavia. Her chapter headings, while following the ethnographic tradition, tend to stress the social more than the material aspects of culture: The Village and Its Setting; The Village in History; The Early Society; The Stem Family and Traditional Elites; The Village Socioeconomic Structure and the Outside World; The Village Economy; Local Government and the State; Social Aspects of Village Life; Religion; The Life Cycle; The Question of Modernization; and The Peasant World View.

This approach, however, is supposed to do more than give a complete community picture; it often is said to represent in minuscule the whole society of which the community is but a part. Conrad Arensberg (1965), in a very valuable article, examines the extent to which a single village can be a sample of the larger society. In his view, there are the problems of representativeness, completeness, inclusivensss, and cohesiveness. A village is representative of the society when its population reflects the kind of demographic and other groupings found in the latter: two sexes, several ages, several classes, several sects, major and minor ethnic groupings, several professional or full-time technical and economic specializations.

As for completeness, the basic question is one of boundaries. When does the settlement grade off and articulate with a neighboring or overlapping community? One way of determining completeness as a sample for the larger society is to be sure that the village contains some instances of every kind of individual in which the species manifests itself: baby, child, adolescent, adult, and oldster, of each sex. Arrangements must also be made to fill these statuses in a regular way. Furthermore, people may assemble as a community, then disperse, only to reassemble later on, conscious of their common identification.

Inclusiveness may be adequate to permit the village to serve as a mirror of the society if there is some penetration of the community by the national culture but not to the point that the community has become so highly specialized (for instance, formed around an atomic laboratory research station) that it is atypical. "As long as specialties do not dominate community experience and community culture, and as long as citizens are aware of and prepare their children to recognize, again at least minimally, the outer reaches of such specialization stretching away from their own lores and skills, the community will serve 'as a sample.' " (p. 259)

How integrated must the community be and how much should it reflect the fissions of society if it is to serve as a representation of the society? Arensberg assumes that the people will alternate between strife and accommodation, solidarity and antagonism. But there must be limits to strife if the community is to continue. "A sample community must reflect both the unities and the fissions of the parts it samples in its table of organization of the whole society it mirrors. But it need do that again only within the outer limits of its own continuance." (p. 260)

In the ethnographic tradition a community description is as much a creative as a scientific act. Robert Redfield (1955), whose book on *The Little Community* is a masterful summing up of this approach, writes:

> An account of a little community is not something that is given one as out of a vending machine by putting in the appropriate coins of method and technique. There is no one ultimate and utterly objective account of a human whole. Each account, if it preserves the human quality at all, is a created product in which the human qualities of the creator—the outside viewer and describer—are one ingredient. (p. 136)

Within the past few years anthropologists, who have had most experience with the ethnographic approach and its stress upon interdependence of cultural traits, are turning from the study of small communities to urban settings. They believe that the methods they have developed for studying rural communities in other cultures can contribute to a deeper understanding of complex urban life (Weaver and White, 1972; Plotnicov, 1973–74).

THE COMMUNITY AS AN ARENA OF SOCIAL INTERACTION (THE SOCIOLOGICAL APPROACH)

Instead of describing the total culture in all of its many details, as in the ethnographic approach, the sociologist concentrates upon the social interaction characterizing the community. In order to trace the various emphases in the social interaction approach it is first essential to understand the nature of such interaction and to distinguish it from communication, function and dynamics, which are terms to be used in much of the analysis which follows.

The Nature of Interaction

The view of the community as an arena of interaction may seem an oblique approach to the daily activities one observes in a home town. "Everybody knows" that the county school board does not get along well with the city school board; that the Lions and Kiwanis clubs will always cooperate when there is some worthy community project under way; that there is apt to be trouble at the small steel mill every three years or so when the national labor union representing the workers negotiates a new contract with the management of the big steel companies; that the Country Club excludes certain ethnic elements of the population and consequently this minority group has organized a country club of its own; that certain businessmen are looked down upon by other businessmen for what the latter consider "shady practices" in selling cars or real estate. Also, the community has been disturbed over juvenile delinquency since a gang of boys from a good residential area was caught stealing crates of candy bars from a railroad car. Item after item could be listed to illustrate the kinds of interpersonal relationships found in a community. In order to deal analytically with these one can use the concept of interaction—the observable and meaningful behavior of groups and individuals with each other.

Interaction and Communication. These two words are really interchangeable if communication is defined as the contact of mind with mind, the interchange of meaningful symbols between two or more people. Anyone who watches the spy stories on television or at the movies realizes that the major problem in intelligence work is that of communicating, of interacting with some other agent, without being caught. The reason for this difficulty is the readiness with which a third party can observe the various levels of communication, whether a nod of the head, sign language, an exchange of messages, or clandestine or open conversations.

But communication is far more complex than one at first assumes. A subfield of sociology known as "symbolic interaction" deals with these complexities. In his analysis of interpersonal behavior Murray Melbin (1972) notes:

> Just as speech is "a structured scheme of oral communication, behavior repertoires are structured systems of gestural communication, verbal and other, used by persons in social relationships . . . (p. 10)

Looking beyond the individual one finds that many group and community differences arise because of the failure of those involved to communicate effectively. Proposals are often presented in such vague, ambiguous language that one person will make one interpretation while a second and third person will reach very different interpretations. Some people in the community may be considered "haughty" or "uncooperative" because this is the impression they communicate to others, whereas they may really not think of themselves in those terms and would do much to change the impression if they understood the nature of what they were communicating. If meaningful symbols lie at the bottom of true communication (and therefore smooth interaction), then it is necessary for any person or group to be sure that others understand the meanings they attach to these symbols. This means that others must not only be able to repeat the words used by the first party, but they must also know the connotation given to those words. For example, groups that come together in the interest of more efficient government may find eventually that they *mean* different things when they speak of "efficient government." The League of Women Voters may stress orderly election procedures, a system of civil service, and a full debate of campaign issues by rival candidates in a public meeting. A businessman's group may think of efficient government as the one that costs the least, whereas a group of social workers may point out that in order to save money (in terms of the costs of human problems) governmental agencies may have to spend money (in terms of preventive programs) and that the test of good government is how the money is used in the public interest once it is collected. Political scientists may think of good government in some of the terms mentioned above but may also be interested in the exercise of constitutional powers by the different agencies of government. Therefore, the term "efficient government," unless it is spelled out in greater detail, is not an effective symbol of communication. It is apparently meaningful to most people, but the meanings attached to it will vary.

Interaction and Function.   At first glance, it might seem that interaction and function are much the same thing. It is common to say that a thing functions when it "works" and certainly interaction, as used here, would describe the "working together" of individuals and groups within a community. For purposes of clarity, however, function has been given a different meaning in scientific writing from that of simply "working." It more and more has come to mean the contribution that a unit, such as a social group, makes to the total environment, such as a community, of which it is a part. This means that in describing the community function of a particular group such as the Chamber of Commerce one does not ask merely what are the purposes of the Chamber as drawn up in its charter and as believed in by its members; instead, one assumes that the Chamber has connections with many other groups and groupings of the community and that one can best describe the actual functioning of the Chamber, from the community viewpoint at least, by tracing these social relationships between it and other groups. If, for example, the City Council will not decide on a problem of physical planning and zoning until it knows how the members of the Chamber of Commerce feel, then the connection between the Council and the Chamber has functional significance; if local labor leaders consider the activities of the Chamber somewhat antagonistic to their interests and tend to oppose any course of action proposed by the Chamber, than again the Chamber has functional significance in that it serves as a focus of cooperation among labor leaders and as a target for them in supporting what they consider the self-interest of their union membership. To continue the description, one would ask about the interaction between the Chamber of Commerce and the United Way, the Farm Bureau, the Woman's Garden Club, the Board of Education, to mention but a few possibilities. When one has traced all of the significant ramifications of the Chamber of Commerce's interaction with all other possible groups, then one has described the function of that particular organization.

Thus function is more than interaction in a general sense; it is rather an analysis of interaction between some part of the community structure and other parts. This is why it is almost impossible to talk clearly of function without thinking of structure, or the social organization through which functions are traced. "Social structure" consists of all the social relationships in a community viewed from the status standpoint. Those occupying at a given time the statuses of husband and father, wife and mother, daughter and sister, son and brother, are bound together structurally in a family unit; this unit becomes associated with other family units, and quite unconsciously on the part of the various members of the different families, these family units become the family aspect of the total structure. Just as in the case of the Chamber of Commerce, one can trace the function of the family as an important subsystem by showing how the family units interact with economic, political, religious, educational, or recreational units.

Robert K. Merton (1957) has correctly pointed out that many functions are *manifest* or evident. People know that the exclusive Nineteenth Century Club for many years has promoted the baby milk fund and considers this one of its most important community contributions during the year. This would be a manifest function to which members and nonmembers would readily agree. But the same group may serve a *latent* or hidden function which a few perceptive individuals may discern but which they are not apt to talk about or, at any rate, get much agreement about. Membership in the Nineteenth Century Club may serve the latent function of showing a small upper class that a woman has "arrived" socially and can therefore be invited to exclusive functions by the "best families" and that her daughter can be included among the list of debutantes. The members of this group when pressed to name the function of their club would stress the baby milk fund and the importance to them personally of the informative club meetings. Very few, if any, would list as a chief function this social selectivity, which is decidedly "functional" for those who are trying to climb from the upper middle class to the upper class.

Through this and the other illustrations given, it should be clear that function can only be interpreted by watching the social interaction, but it goes a step beyond merely listing what happened in terms of activity or communication of symbols. The functional description must include the relevancy of this activity and communication to the community (or social unit) as a whole, taking account of both the manifest and latent aspects.

Interaction and Dynamics.   When one speaks of a dynamic person, one usually thinks of someone who gets things done, who radiates vitality, and who is definitely action-oriented. "Social dynamics," like many terms in the social sciences, has a connection with this popular meaning but requires a more precise definition. Pitirim A. Sorokin (1937–41), who has done the most exhaustive study of sociocultural dynamics, would view the dynamics of a community or a society as dealing with that which is moving, changing. He also seeks to show that throughout this flux there are certain uniformities of change that can be discerned and analyzed.

The concept of dynamics thus adds the element of *change* to interaction, which itself usually has a neutral tone. It is obvious that no two people and no two groups that interact are ever the same after the interaction; they are either on friendlier or unfriendlier terms as a result. Furthermore, without interaction change could not occur. Thus social dynamics would look at the community as a changing system and try to work out the laws governing the change within it. The concept of dynamics needs to be added to that of structure-function to give a complete account of a social system. Underlying it all is the basic fact of continuing interaction among the units of the community.

By comparing and even equating interaction with communication and by contrasting it with function and dynamics one gets a clearer picture of the nature of interaction.

Types of Interaction Within the Community

Sociologists have worked out terms to describe some of the chief types of interaction: cooperation, amalgamation, competition, assimilation, conflict, accommodation. These are useful when characterizing a *single situation,* such as the interaction between the Woman's Christian Temperance Union and the local bartenders' union, which in this case would probably illustrate conflict. The same six terms can be employed to describe a *series of occurrences* or the flowing of interaction through time, in which case one would call them social processes. They would still be types of interaction but would designate many single situations in sequence. A social relationship between two groups may move from competition into conflict, then into accommodation, and perhaps finally into cooperation. The description of what happened from one point of time to another is a description of the social process.

These terms, to be explained presently, are also useful when drawing up the social characteristics of a community. A community will tend to highlight one process more than others, with the result that the traditions of conflict or cooperation have much to do with the way interacting individuals and groups define the situation and either belligerently or peaceably try to work their way out of a problem.

Although discussion here is limited to these types of interaction, there are many other social processes that are useful in describing what occurs in community life. For instance, ecological processes are mentioned in Chapter 3 in the treatment of the community as a place; in Chapter 9 socialization and social control will be viewed as important motivational processes; whereas in Chapter 11 attention is paid to industrialization and urbanization and their connection with social change. All of these processes consist of human interaction, and each deals with some particular aspect of this interaction sequentially. The six processes being discussed here treat interaction from the standpoint of goals of the participating units and the degree to which these units either help or hinder the other in reaching these goals.

Many different sociologists have written on these six processes, and each tends to follow some individualistic treatment. The most complete analysis of the social processes in the community setting has been done by Jessie Bernard (1962), who treats organization, conflict, and competition as the basic concepts. She then works out on a continuum the stages through which conflict passes from elimination to assimilation and through which competition passes from the cutthroat stage to monopoly. She pays little attention to cooperation as a process.

On the other hand, Kimball Young (1949) thinks of opposition and cooperation as the two basic processes: Opposition "may be defined as a struggle *against* another or others for a good, goal, or value; cooperation is joint striving with another or others for a good, goal, or value." He then divides opposition into competition and conflict, defining competition as a less violent form of opposition "in which two or more persons or groups struggle for some end or goal but in the course of which attention is focused chiefly on reward rather than on the competitor." (p. 64) In conflict the person or group thwarts, injures, or destroys the opponent in order to secure the wanted goal or reward. Young looks upon the three processes—accommodation, assimilation, and amalgamation—as being derived from the others previously mentioned.

Accommodation as a process, according to Young (1949), has to do "with the conscious efforts of men to develop such working arrangements among themselves as will temporarily suspend conflict and to make their relations more tolerable and less wasteful of energy." Assimilation means "the common blending and sharing of folkways, mores, laws, and ways of life generally of two or more groups or societies or peoples that formerly had distinctive patterns." (p. 75) He treats amalgamation, particularly the biological type, as the only way to complete assimilation. However, other writers frequently think of amalgamation in the nonbiological sense of a business merger, for instance, where each of the interacting firms loses its original identity and becomes a part of a new firm that carries on independently. Churches, college organizations, and welfare agencies, for example, can amalgamate if some new group comes into being to take the place of two or more that formerly existed as separate units.

With this introduction to the types of interaction, each type will now be illustrated with reference to a community setting.

Cooperation. Conflict and acute competition are spectacular; they catch the headlines. Cooperation is much more common and certainly more basic to the operation of life in many small communities (Mead, 1937). Yet, cooperation is difficult to treat concretely, since there are so many ways in which there can be "joint striving with another or others for a good, goal, or value."

For example, there can be an impersonal cooperation, or symbiosis. It grows out of the division of labor and specialization of tasks that increase as society grows more complex. Certainly the men who collect the garbage in the early morning before the householder is up are engaged in a cooperative activity, since they render a service for which the householder has paid. Also, the householder has cooperated to the extent of wrapping the garbage in paper, putting it in proper containers, and locating these containers at some spot acceptable to the collectors. To try to describe all such types of cooperation in a community would be almost an endless task; what does become quickly evident is the breakdown in some chain of cooperation because some partner to the interaction does not play the role expected of him.

Another type of cooperation occurs in what might be called mutual aid groups. In early frontier days in America and even today in some rural areas people would come together to help a neighbor rebuild a barn that has burned or to assist a bedridden farmer get his crop in. In many cultures these mutual aid groups are important features of community life (Sanders, 1956). In Brazil the word *mutirao* is used to designate a group of workers called upon in an emergency by a neighbor to aid without remuneration in completing rapidly a particular piece of work (Marcondes, 1948).

> When a farmer needs to make a road, clear brush, plant, cultivate, or harvest speedily but lacks sufficient help to carry out his tasks, he calls on the *mutirao* to come to his assistance. He agrees to reciprocate and pay back this service by himself being ready to work for the others when they call upon him. The day almost always ends in a fiesta which strengthens a moral obligation between the one who sought the cooperation and those who participated (p. 374).

Usually the day chosen for the *mutirao* is a Saturday or the day before a holiday, which gives everyone a chance to rest on the following day.

It is but a step from these traditional, informal mutual aid groups to the purposive formation of what are called cooperatives, or associations to further the mutual interests of those joining together. In one sense, the cooperative is primarily an economic union, but in many ways it goes beyond that and becomes a social outlet, a way of class expression for those who have become convinced of the need to stick together.

Amalgamation. Amalgamation deserves but brief treatment, since it is less frequently found. Groups decide to merge, or amalgamate, and lose their former identity in becoming a part of a new group. This happens over and over again in business and is best illustrated in the union of two banks, with the merger preserving in its name parts of the titles of the original banks. The Citizen's Bank merges with the Union Trust Company and becomes the Citizen's Union Trust Company.

Minor political parties find competition with the two major parties difficult and may regroup their forces under a new name. The case of the coming together of three branches of Methodism in 1939 resulted in amalgamation known as The Methodist Church. Illustrations could be multiplied to show this type of interaction viewed from the standpoint of shifting goals of groups involved in the interaction.

Competition. Perhaps the process most consciously stressed in American communities is that of competition. It runs through the warp and woof of American life, receiving encouragement in school with the competition for grades, for membership in honorary societies, and for places on athletic teams. Not only is there rivalry within the school, but competition between schools is highly accentuated, chiefly in athletics. Such competition builds up an in-group loyalty, but when very intense can affect other educational practices such as scholastic performance, hiring and firing of school officials because of interest expressed or not expressed in successful competition, and even the use of school funds for areas of competition in place of strengthening libraries, laboratories, and other facilities not involved in interschool comparisons.

Competition, furthermore, is looked upon as the process that keeps the free enterprise system operating successfully, although with increasing frequency the government has had to step in as an umpire, to organize agencies to watch over the stock exchanges, the trends toward monopoly, and public utilities. Churches compete for members and even organize their Sunday schools so that pupils compete with each other. Much use is made of competition in youth groups, civic clubs, and women's organizations, both locally and nationally. Many of the rewards held out to those involved in community development are couched in competitive terms, with one community competing against another.

Political competition, especially with a two-party system, is deeply ingrained in the American way of life. Once a man enters politics he must think about re-election and continuing in a position of influence. This means that he must learn "the political game" and understand the nature of political competition. Communities vary in their willingness to support candidates who conduct what are frequently called "vigorous" campaigns by some and "dirty" campaigns by others; they demand different standards of performance from those who have been elected to office. Some communities show great indifference or apathy to political matters until conditions get so bad that the "general public" feels its interests are not properly protected or its sense of fairness has been violated. Then the people of the community rise up "to throw the rascals out," after which they sink into another period of unconcern and indifference.[4]

Within communities there are frequently borderline cases between conflict and competition. Two rival unions may be trying

---

[4] Many professionals in charge of various agencies have been trained to deprecate politics, but in assuming a managerial post, they find themselves deeply immersed in politics. This is especially true in public health. See "The Political Ingredient in Public Health Services: A Neglected Area of Research," *Milbank Memorial Fund Quarterly* 44 (October, 1966), pp. 13–34.

to organize the same nonunionized plant, each claiming the right of representing the workers with the management. As was pointed out earlier, the types of interaction being described here relate to the goals of the interacting parties. If the struggle between the two unions is merely that of getting the support of the workers of this plant, if both are after the same reward, then the interaction can be termed competition. If, however, this is a case in which the main goal is to try to eliminate as an organization the rival union and the support of workers is merely secondary to that primary aim, then the situation can be defined as conflict. In such a case the National Labor Relations Board will most probably be invited in to conduct an election among the workers to determine their preferences in the matter. This is the method of accommodation.

Assimilation. When the people of an Alabama community were asked what they did with newcomers whom they did not like, one of the men replied, "Oh, we simply freeze them out." Further study of that community showed that that was really what happened. Even some residents who had married into the old, established families still were reminded that they were newcomers—though acceptable newcomers—after twenty years of residence. This behavior is not typical of all Alabama communities but does express the situation one finds when the most influential people are self-satisfied and opposed to change.

The study of a Kentucky community showed that its people, quite unconsciously on their part, had arrived at a way of assisting in the assimilation process. When any new professional man or the manager of one of the local businesses moved to town, he would be asked to join one of the civic clubs within the first year and would be given an important committee assignment. Shortly thereafter he was made an officer if he measured up and was thus given a chance to demonstrate to the community what capabilities he had. When this demonstration was added to the other qualities he and his family displayed, the people of the community had a good idea of how that newcomer fitted in.

In many communities church groups are among the most active agents of assimilation, since rival denominational groups go to call on Protestants in an effort to gain them as members. Similarly, Catholics find a ready welcome in their own church-related organizations, as do minorities with other religious orientations.

Assimilation into a community, however, is different in some ways from assimilation into a group. A group is usually able to exercise some choice in the selection of its new members; it has carefully defined rules of attendance, paying dues, and other duties; and it has a self-identity that distinguishes it from other associations in the community. A community, however, has little direct control over those who settle there and cannot bring direct means to bear in the name of the community to teach the new people the values and role expectations of the older residents. Pressure must be indirect. Through various groups where such pressure is recognized and heeded, assimilation occurs; where it is ignored, the new elements remain indigestible lumps in the body politic.

Conflict. Conflict in American communities today can take a variety of forms and can arise over a number of issues. Also, what will disturb one community will have almost no repercussions in another community thirty miles away. Some of the broad conflict areas deserve consideration even though none of these may be a particular problem at a given time in one's home town. These include such areas as industrial conflict, race conflict, oldtimer-newcomer conflict, religious tensions and schisms and between "liberals," "conservatives" and "radicals" over political ideologies. Later chapters will deal with some of these kinds of conflict in greater detail.

Accommodation. Accommodation is the process used for easing conflict so that people who have been spending their energies fighting each other can begin doing something else. It is rational in that men consciously begin to seek a way out of an impasse; it usually means that each party to the conflict has to yield some ground in order to develop working arrangements again. When some conflict besets a community, the first step to be taken by those interested in ending that conflict is to move it into accommodative channels.

THREE INTERACTIONIST EMPHASES:
SOCIAL SYSTEM, SOCIAL CONFLICT, SOCIAL FIELD

The discussion above of interaction and related terms has prepared the way for a brief presentation of three emphases in viewing the community as an arena of interaction: the social system, conflict, and social field.[5] The first to be considered, namely, the *social system* views the community as a relatively enduring system of interaction centered around some locality. (See Chapter 7) It analyzes the system in terms of structure and function (components and operations). The idea of a system is commonplace. An automobile is a mechanical system, made up of parts that must perform satisfactorily if the automobile is to operate smoothly. The human body is a system, a biological organism whose parts must carry out specific functions if the bodily processes are to be uninterrupted. But to understand a social system we do not need to turn to mechanics or biology for helpful analogies; we can see how a family works as a system. It, too, has its parts (or members), each of which has definite roles to perform to keep the family a viable unit; there is production and distribution of goods (e.g., food and clothing) and services; and there is concentration of authority and the exercise of social control; and there is an interdependence accompanied by a sense of belonging to one's own particular family group and not to some other family. Although efforts are made to keep family life on a fairly even keel or in some kind of equilibrium, the mere passage of time and pressures from outside introduce changes calling for adaptation and reintegration of the family as a system. But one need not push even this social analogy too far. It is cited to show that human groups do behave as though they were systems. Of course, there are many differences between a family and a community, even with respect to the way that they behave as systems.

A second way of viewing the community from an interactionist perspective is in terms of *social conflict*. (See Chapter 12) Sociologists using this emphasis see the community primarily as a stratification pattern in which there is unequal distribution of resources, wealth, power, and prestige. They try to account in their analysis, often employing the dialectical method, for the existence of social inequalities; they study trends as to a decrease or an increase in these differences; and they note how antagonisms present in the community find overt expression in patterns of social interaction. This is admittedly a partial approach but its advocates

---

[5] Not discussed specifically in this connection are the two approaches of symbolic interaction and exchange. For an exposition of these see Peter Singleman, "Exchange as Symbolic Interaction: Convergences Between Two Theoretical Perspectives," *American Sociological Review* 37 (1972), pp. 414–424. See also Denisoff, Callahan, and Levine, 1974.

claim that it deals with the sociologically most significant aspects of the community.

A third way to view the community as a *field of interaction*, which can best be understood by concentrating upon actions (e.g., building a community hospital). (See Chapter 17) Each action must be analyzed in terms of (1) the persons involved (actors or participants; (2) associations or groups through which the action takes place; (3) the stages and phases of the action through time. (Kaufman, 1959) Such an emphasis helps show how a community mobilizes to meet some generally felt need.

Before taking up these three interactionist approaches each of which stresses forms of interdependence, we will first look at some setting factors which influence community life. These must be taken into account by the community sociologist whatever his approach might be: social system, conflict, or social field.

THE SETTING

The community as a system of interaction is part of and acted upon by complex environmental factors, which together can be called its *setting*. The following presents the setting factors.

Settings and Components

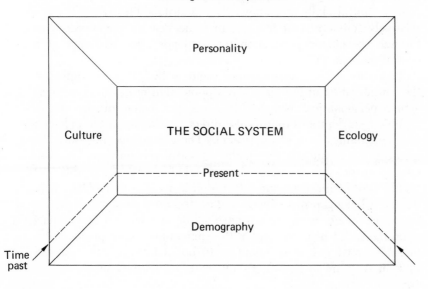

ECOLOGY

A community is a territorially organized system coextensive with a settlement pattern in which (1) an effective communication network operates, (2) people share common facilities and services distributed within this settlement pattern, and (3) people develop a psychological identification with the "locality symbol" (the name).

A major factor in the setting of a community is ecology, which traces some of the adjustments man has made to the natural environment and is described at some length in Chapter 3. Any system of social relationships, whether viewed as a group, a community, or a whole society, must bear some connection to the *place* in which its members must carry on their activities. Community life in the Sahara Desert is much different from that in the lush tropical growths farther south in the African continent, and a New Hampshire village has a different tone from a settlement in Southern California. For any community one wishes to study it is necessary to learn about the adjustment of the people to their natural resources, climate, and the surface features.

DEMOGRAPHY

A community consists of a population in all stages of the life cycle, so that new members are recruited through the biological process of birth. Furthermore, the population must possess sufficient technical skills and knowledge to sustain life, whether on a relatively self-subsistent level as in some peasant communities or through specialized production that depends upon exchange at a central market.

Therefore, a second background factor is that of demography, or the consideration of the people as a population rather than as interacting personalities. Chapter 4 points out many of the demographic considerations that have a direct bearing upon the behavior of a community as a social system. These influence not only the quantity but frequently the quality of social relationships. A community made up of many diverse ethnic groups has different problems of assimilation and integration from one in which the population is homogeneous. Increasing or declining numbers, changing sex ratios or age composition, have subtle but no less real impact upon the social behavior within the community. City planners, for instance, must pay close attention to population growth and mobility if they are to be able to anticipate community needs well in advance.

CULTURE

A third factor of the setting is culture, or the social heritage, which is dealt with in Chapter 5. The cultural aspects are so much a part of our every act that one can separate them out only for purposes of analysis. If we were to place culture in the central position of Figure 1, shifting the social system to the side as one of the background factors, then instead of stressing social relationships we would be paying close attention to values, traditions, norms, belief systems, and the general themes that run like golden threads with all their variations and contradictions through the life of a given community. The knowledge of such matters is essential if one is to interpret correctly the interaction among the component parts of the social system; but in this present analysis, the cultural factor, rich as it is, is background and not central.

PERSONALITY

Few community studies, because they try to describe a different level of the social universe, delve into the problem of personality development and personality types within a given community. When such topics can be incorporated, the picture of community life assumes a new dimension. In our analysis this fourth factor of the setting indicates whether or not there are any special personality types developing within or attracted to a given community. It throws light on the prevalent attitudes and their formation (relating these to the belief systems), and it gets at the problem of motivation of the community members to conform to or deviate from the established patterns of conduct. In view of the complexity of these psychological problems and of the different methodological procedures involved in their study, most sociologists accept as granted the fact that the community is made up of persons who have been "socialized" into the ways of that community and who are sufficiently motivated to act as reasonable, relatively predictable participants in group and community life. Although personality is here placed as a setting factor, this does not mean that it is irrelevant or unimportant but rather that it is being studied in this connection in terms of how it influences the social relations, the main focus at this time. More will be said about personality in this connection with culture in Chapter 5.

TIME

The past definitely lives on in the present; without a knowledge of this past, contemporary events cannot be fully understood. The temporal factor should involve more than just tracing a sequence of events; it should also include some effort to reconstruct the interrelationships that existed at a given time in the past among important social units of the community and the relevance of such interrelationships to present behavior in the community. The study of the past also helps one find out why communities that are reasonably close together and quite similar from the standpoint of the physical environment and population characteristics differ so much in their approach to many problems of the day.

Time, however, can be contemporary as well. Community events frequently have a periodic rhythm that can be anticipated with pleasure (a festival) or dreaded (a perennial spring flood). Wilbert E. Moore (1963) has written a provocative book showing the importance of time in daily intercourse. He observes:

Time presents itself in human experience as a boundary condition, but also as a sequence. The hands of the clock move, calendar pages are torn off, birthdays are celebrated with growing regret, officers retire, and eras come to an end.

Short of major and sudden geophysical events, space principally acquires any dynamic qualities it may have by virtue of changes in social values, interests, and techniques. In other words, space is generally a passive condition of behavior, variable only as human behavior makes it so. Time, on the other hand, is intrinsically dynamic, and indeed the idea of dynamic (or static) is impossible without reference to conceptions of time.

Much of social behavior depends for its orderly qualities on common definitions, assumptions, and actions with regard to the location of events in time. Certain activities, for example, require simultaneous actions by a number of persons, or at least their presence at a particular time—the starting of a work shift at a factory, the departure of a fishing boat from a wharf or beach, or the calling of an association meeting to order. Thus one element of temporal ordering is synchronization. Other activities require that actions follow one another in a prescribed order; thus sequence is a part of the temporal order. For still other activities the frequency of events during a period of time is critical; thus rate also is one of the ways that time impinges on social behavior. For all of these elements of social coordination the term timing is useful, since it denotes precisely the critical importance of some temporal order, while leaving open the kind of requirement or the rigidity with which the activity in question is to be related to time as an inexorable variable. Although any of the dimensions of temporal ordering may be subject to some latitude, some tolerable degree of looseness or approximation, timing is an intrinsic quality of personal and collective behavior. If activities have no temporal order, they have no order at all. (pp. 8–9).

THE LARGER SOCIETY

A crucial setting factor for any community is the larger society of which it is a part. A community is not a closed system but is influenced by a wide variety of pressures which originate in the economic, political, educational centers far beyond its boundaries (Martindale and Hanson, 1969). According to a logical outline, one should devote a special chapter to this factor as is done in the case of place, people, and culture and personality. To do so, however, would anticipate so much material that will be taken up in later chapters that undue repetition would occur. Part of the task of the analysis which will follow throughout the book is to show the interdependence between local and national systems. Though the focus is on the patterns of local interaction, these cannot be understood without some reference to the national scene where social change is occurring on an accelerated scale.

3

The Community as a Place

Inexorably, a Copper Mine is Eating Away Butte, Montana. This is a headline for the following newspaper story (Franklin, 1973):

> Butte, Mont. About noon most days here the Anaconda Company blasts loose another chunk of Butte, bringing the rim of the largest open-pit copper mine in the country closer to the center of what was once Montana's largest city. Pieces of Butte are literally going down the hole. Anaconda's enormous Berkeley pit—the yawning, spirally terraced excavation into "the world's richest hill" is a mile and a quarter long, a mile wide and 1,000 feet deep—has already swallowed up the saloons and sporting houses of the Meaderville section of Butte and half of McQueen next to it.
>
> "Uptown" Butte—really the downtown business district, but so named because it is up the Hill—is next. The blasting that precedes excavation is coming nearer. . . .
>
> What is happening in Butte is, in some sense, a dramatic—if not bizarre—example of a conflict that is taking place across the country between America's demand for minerals and energy and a growing unease among ordinary citizens over the penalties of industrial progress. (p. 78; © 1973 by the New York Times Company)

The article then describes a plan to move Butte to flatlands away from the pit but also tells of the difficulties in carrying out this plan when businessmen do not feel that they will be adequately compensated for giving up the buildings they now own. This illus-

49

tration of the effect upon one city of environmental (as well as economic and political) factors highlights the importance of seeing the community as a *place*, as a settlement pattern.

THE COMMUNITY AS A SETTLEMENT PATTERN

The settlement pattern, represents an adjustment to the physical environment, usually called the *habitat*, which consists of location, shape, and size as well as surface features, climate, and natural resources. Part of this adjustment is also cultural. In contrast to habitat which is natural, *culture* is man-made. It is the accumulation of things, ideas, and social arrangements that a given people has invented or borrowed from other people. All of these different culture traits are woven together into a way of life that is passed on as a social heritage to each succeeding generation. Thus, the lay of the land around any community is natural; what man does to this physical setting becomes a part of his culture, since he uses his tools and draws upon his ideas of technology or even his sense of what is beautiful or utilitarian.

This is why the community as a settlement pattern is an important illustration of man's adjustment to his physical surroundings, or habitat, through the use of his culture, or social heritage. Although most of this book is devoted to a discussion of those topics that might be called *sociocultural*, at this point brief attention will be paid to some of the physical aspects of the community as they are reflected in social life.

Location

It is interesting to speculate about the reason for the location of any particular community. The reasons advanced by residents of the community may correspond to the facts or they may be very fanciful indeed. Some Greek villagers, in explaining why their village was located where it was, told the story of a conflict that had broken out among the people of their former village many years before at a village dance. There had been an argument and violence had ensued. The spirits of those killed were soon thought to haunt the village, so the elders decided to change its location. They took three large pieces of meat, placed each piece at what appeared to be a favorable location, and selected the spot where the meat stayed fresh the longest in the belief that it would prove the most

healthful place to live. Again, in a Bulgarian mountain village people believed that their community had been located on its present
site three or four hundred years previously because one day a
peasant widow living on the plain below missed her sow who was
about to bear young. Finally, after a long, tiresome search, Baba
Draganna, the widow, found the sow and her litter far up on the
mountainside. According to the story, she was unable to carry all
the animals back to her home below and decided to build a hut up
there. Because she liked the water as well as the protection from
passing armies that this location afforded, she persuaded others to
join her. And today in this village the people say that the church
stands on the exact spot where Baba Draganna found her sow, and
they call the village Dragalevtsy, in honor of this enterprising
woman. (Sanders, 1949).

For most American communities we do not have to look for leg-
ends to account for the location, nor do we, for that matter, have to
rely upon them in the case of the Balkan villages. For this particular Bulgarian village of Baba Draganna represents what the geog-
raphers would consider an excellent adjustment: an adequate water
supply (both a spring and a small river that turns the water wheels
of the mills), proximity to the forest and upland pastures above,
and easy access to the cultivated land below.

Some communities come into being and develop because of location on some important waterway or seacoast harbor. Others grow
up because there are important mineral resources to be exploited;
others because a rich farming area needs a set of services that only
some expanding settlement can provide. Resort communities owe
much to their scenic surroundings or to the development of some
mineral springs, a sandy beach, or mountain paths.

Thus to understand a particular community, it is important to
know why people located it where they did and whether or not the
same factors still afford it advantages today.

Shape

The shape of a community is directly influenced by its physical
surroundings. Anyone who has flown over Charleston, West Virginia, is at once aware of the limitations set by its topography and
understands why a whole mountain top had to be leveled off in
order to create a place for an airport. True enough, today man
does move his residential areas up and down the slopes of the hills,

but the main part of most towns in rugged terrain tends to be in whatever level land can be found along a river bottom. And the community tends to stretch along this bottom as far as it can before it spreads out to the hills. These variations in shape can best be understood through the various diagrams shown in Figure 3–1.

Size

Perhaps the first question we ask about any community is "How big is it?" Usually we expect an answer in terms of the number of

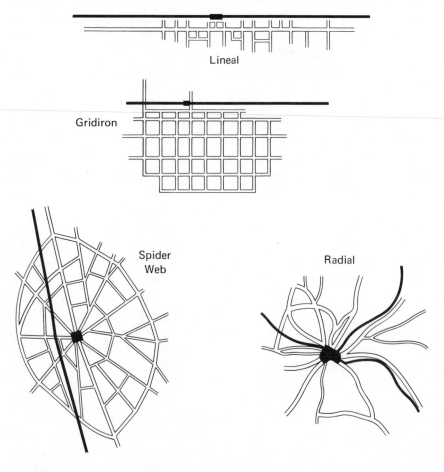

Figure 3–1. Examples of town patterns. *Source:* PEP (Political and Economic Planning), *Report on the Location of Industry* (London: PEP, 1939), p. 157.

people rather than in terms of square miles. The communities considered in this book vary in size from the small, self-subsistent, relatively isolated settlements to the subdivisions of the great metropolitan areas of our country.

The size of a community has much to do with the kind of interaction people have (Terrien and Mills, 1955). The larger the community, the smaller the proportion of people known to the individual member and the greater the tendency toward anonymity and impersonal relations. Also, the individual's contacts tend to center around professional, occupational, or other social groupings rather than upon the immediate neighborhood in which one lives. The larger the community, the greater the likelihood of availability of a wide variety of services, the richer the so-called "cultural offerings," and the higher the degree of educational and economic specialization. These rather obvious facts are what might be called a function of size, which explains why people so often ask "How large is your community?"

Since we do not ordinarily think of the size of a settlement in terms of area but rather in terms of people, the matter of population density becomes important. Communities with a large population per square mile differ in some social respects from those with relatively few people per square mile. For example, in the latter case, part-time farming may be important because a man can hold down a job in a factory or in a business and at the same time, with the help of members of his family, run a small farm to supplement his weekly wages. On the other hand, in a very densely populated area, even vegetable gardens are out of the question. Thus where density is high, the man-made environment (culture) is very influential and even at times overpowering; where density is low there is more opportunity for interaction with the natural environment (habitat).

Communication and Transportation Routes

In the discussion of location above, mention has already been made of the importance of riverways and highways. A sketch of a settlement pattern is incomplete without some discussion of its means or routes of communication with other centers. If the only way out of a community is by way of a rickety bridge, then outside contacts are discouraged much more than in the case of a community at the crossroads of several highways leading in different directions and serving as arteries for the inflow of goods, ideas, and guests. What such roads mean can be illustrated by the case of India, where a great many villages cannot be reached by modern transportation. They are not accessible to trucks, and hence everything has to be carried in on the backs of animals or human beings. If a community's level of living is limited to material that can be carried on a donkey, the chances of rapid technological change are not very great.[1] But donkeys are a rarity even in the most isolated American communities, most of which are increasingly being linked through highways with larger centers. The description of such connections is an important part of the treatment of the community as a settlement pattern.

COMPETITION FOR SPACE WITHIN A COMMUNITY

In most communities a premium is placed upon good location by those living in that community. Where the community is small, the population sparse, and plenty of land available, this competition for space is not pronounced. But as business centers develop here and there, as some areas are known as good residential areas and others as poor residential areas, then location becomes an important factor in community life. After observing this process long enough, one will notice that there are at least two types of competition: that existing among various possible uses of the land for industrial, commercial, institutional, and residential purposes and that existing among individuals looking for desirable sites on which to locate their homes.

Competition with Respect to Land Use

In a growing community this competition is at work every day. Consider, for instance, the area set aside for industry. Usually,

---

[1] A few years ago, a prominent American consulting engineer suggested to an Asian government that it ought to give up the idea of building at prohibitive cost a road network over the whole land. He pointed out how unpredictable the rivers were and how difficult and expensive it would be to construct bridges so strong that they would not be washed away by the periodic floods. His solution was quite modern—too modern for his audience. He suggested that the national government build small airports all over the country and serve the transportation needs of the people through the use of small planes and helicopters. The government officials thought this an impractical suggestion and asked him to delete it from his report. They wanted to follow the conventional approach of having autobuses before airbuses.

people do not want to build homes in the neighborhood of a factory. In the past, a factory has meant smoke, noise, and often ugly piles of materials, railroad sidings, and shifting property values. However, an industrialist who is building a factory wants it near enough to transportation and to utilities to make its operation efficient. It must also be accessible to its workers; before the day of the automobile this meant the factory had to be within walking distance of the workers. Furthermore, the industrialist also wants his plant located near other factories whose products are linked to his own output and he is often prepared to go to great lengths to get his firm situated to best advantage. At the same time, however, he finds himself in competition with those who, for example, oppose his location near a river (where he can empty industrial waste hopefully in non-polluting form) because they think that area might better be used as a park or a residential area.

Although such competition exists, most communities feel that factories are a great asset, or they would not try so hard to persuade companies to locate in their midst. Nevertheless, the arrival of industry means greater competition for space within any community.

Commerce, too, has its preferred points at which businessmen like to be located. It is a maxim of retail business that one does best at a location where the greatest possible number of people pass by daily. As there are only a few places in a city where the maximum is reached, competition for these spots is intense. As business grows, it spreads out from the main center, involving side streets in its expansion, and even moves out to set up suburban centers. This spread brings it into conflict with residents in the areas being invaded.

The use of land for institutional purposes introduces a further competitive element. A university, a state mental hospital, church plants, and a municipal park are all illustrations of institutions taking up part of the area of a community. Some of the institutions may occupy sites desperately wanted by industry or business and yet they remain adamant when requested to move or to give up some of their grounds. These institutions themselves may even be expanding, as in the case of most urban universities which feel forced to enlarge at the expense of residential areas and also at times to buy out business and industrial firms in order to get more land contiguous to the central campus. The larger the amount of nontaxable institutional land in the central area, the lower the tax return from that area. Thus institutional competition often involves not only a competition for mere space but also a competition for sites on which others would pay taxes but on which public institutions do not.

Competition between residential areas themselves is likewise keen in a growing community. Some of those living in what might be called downtown residential areas may protect their values by walling off outside invasion and may preserve many of the advantages of a central location with a rather high residential tone. Others desiring good location give up the struggle, sell out, perhaps at a loss, and move to the suburbs, where they hope to set up legal safeguards through zoning to guarantee them the type of exclusiveness they think in keeping with their social status in the community.

Those at a lower economic position take the poorer accommodations available, frequently having to overcrowd to pay for the higher charges being made. Even so, eventually they are told that they must move, for their dwelling is to be razed for a filling station, a new bank building, a supermarket or a highway extension. Conflict situations often arise under these conditions and the proposal to build the new structure may be either modified or abandoned.

Thus we can see that as far as land use is concerned the community is very active. Here in a physical sense one can observe at work the competition that is part and parcel of the community as a place.

Competition for Residential Sites

Frequently the location of one's home has much to do—in the minds of many people, at least—with the degree to which one is accepted in certain circles. Thus we can say that there is a social selection at work in this competition for residential space. As people rise economically, they often want to rise socially; they say that they want to give greater advantages to their children, so they try to move to a better address.

A further factor, perhaps the basic one, is that of cost. One can afford only so much in the way of rent or of payments on a mortgage. The better areas tend to be purposely priced high in order to give them a greater prestige value; one pays for the location or address as well as for the accommodations. But the reverse does not hold true at the other end of the economic scale. The poorest people, competing as they do for shelter itself, frequently have to pay proportionately higher for their meager accommodations than those better off financially. Thus poverty begets poverty.

This becomes especially evident where there is segregation, whether it be racial, as in the case of the blacks, or cultural, as in the case of immigrants with differing language and social patterns. They are hemmed in, as it were, and are not allowed to expand into areas where their presence may be thought by the dominant group to lower the property values. As their numbers grow, the living space does not grow proportionately, and the competition becomes even more severe. This gives rise to many social problems and brings into existence both private and public welfare agencies, among which the public housing program is one of the clearest examples.

We find, therefore, that not only is there competition within a community as to the various uses to which the available space will be put (industrial, commercial, institutional, and residential), but also there is serious competition within the residential areas themselves, where economic, racial, and social factors all play a considerable part.

THE STUDY OF HUMAN ECOLOGY

This impersonal competition for space discussed in the preceding pages is really part of the subject matter of ecology. There are numerous textbooks and special studies that give comprehensive treatment to this subject, for it has become an important area of research in its own right (Duncan and Schnore, 1959; Schmid, 1950; Quinn, 1950; Hawley, 1971). For example, electric and telephone companies in metropolitan areas have large staffs of social scientists who study population and residential trends so that they can decide today whether to put in large or small cables to take care of the anticipated business ten years from today. They need to estimate the outcome of this competition for space that is currently taking place.

The ecologists have set forth certain patterns that they think a city might be expected to follow in its development (Duncan, Sabagh and Van Arsdol, 1962). The sociologists at the University of Chicago, the first to give serious, sustained attention to these spatial patterns, have listed several ecological processes that explain much of the competitive behavior described above. These processes are five in number:

1. *Concentration*—the tendency toward marked population density in certain geographic areas.
2. *Centralization*—while concentration deals with density of populations and social institutions in a given area, centralization denotes the tendency of basic types of institutional services to locate at focal points of transportation and communication (centers of activity).
3. *Segregation*—the tendency of like units to form a cluster is called segregation. This can be applied to business and industry; most often it is used with reference to clustering of well-defined population types.
4. *Invasion*—the process by which new types of institutions or population groups gradually penetrate an area already occupied and displace its institutions or population groups.
5. *Succession*—if invasion results in complete displacement, succession has occurred, for succession means a complete change in population type or use of the land.

R. M. Hurd in 1911 and E. W. Burgess (1925) later on set forth the theory of concentric zones as shown in Figure 3–2.

Because of geographic and other factors, no city expands in such perfect circles but, according to the theory of Hurd and Burgess, some cities do tend to approximate this general scheme.

Another theory seeking to account for the ecological structure of the city is called the sector theory (see B in Figure 3–2). Homer Hoyt (1939) is one of its chief advocates. He held that the city moves out along main transportation routes or at points where its spread meets no resistance. Thus the expansion is not in general waves as the concentric zone theory would indicate but in radii moving out from the center.

For cities having more than one nucleus, or center, the multi-nuclear theory is proposed (C in Figure 3–2). Two formerly separate towns may merge by growth into one built-up area, while the center of each maintains much importance. Or different nuclei related to specialized commercial or industrial activities may develop, and each may become a center for expansion of its type of land use.

Some of these theories supposedly explain suburbanization, a remarkable process of our time. Some view it as a decentralizing or centrifugal tendency in the general pattern of urban growth linked

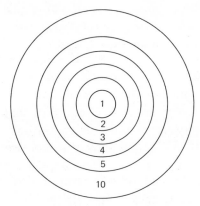

Concentric Zone Theory

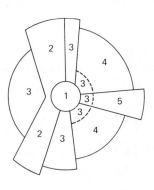

Sector Theory

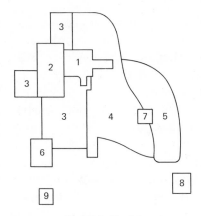

Multiple Nuclei

Three generalizations of the internal structure of cities

DISTRICT

1. Central business district
2. Wholesale light manufacturing
3. Low-class residential
4. Medium-class residential
5. High-class residential
6. Heavy manufacturing
7. Outlying business district
8. Residential suburb
9. Industrial suburb
10. Commuters' zone

Figure 3–2. Three theories about the growth of cities. *Source:* Chauncy D. Harris and Edward L. Ullman, "The Nature of Cities," *Annals of the American Academy of Political and Social Science* 242 (November, 1945), p. 12.

to the deterioration of housing in the central parts of the area. These parts, which are built up first and become obsolescent for residential purposes, are occupied by lower status and in-migrant groups. This movement may also be linked to type and place of work as well as to transportation routes since top white-collar groups, unlike other occupational groups, may choose low-density suburban communities even if these communities are not readily accessible to their work (Farley, 1964). Some research shows this to be much truer of larger, older cities, where deterioration of the downtown areas is more pronounced than of newer cities whose people may actually rank higher in income, education, and occupation than their suburbs (Schnore, 1963).

Of course, if cities are to grow, the population must increase. When this happens, the present area may become more congested or people may settle at a greater average distance from the city center, or both. Hal H. Winsborough (1963) has shown in the case of Chicago that the latter (deconcentration) has been happening since 1860, while congestion increased from 1860 to 1900 or 1910. Since that time it has decreased. He argues that both of these aspects of urban population must be analyzed if we are to understand suburbanization from an ecological point of view.

We may also view suburbs, as well as other types of communities, in terms of the demographic characteristics of the people living there. This is taken up in the next chapter. Or, we may study suburbia as a way of life as shown in participation in various kinds of organizations, cultural values, status-seeking and political attitudes, which move us away from customary ecological analysis (Fava, 1956). The suburb, being a place, is by its very nature closely related to other spatial features of the metropolitan area of which it is a part (Sternlieb, 1971, 1972).

Human ecology, as a field of inquiry, has been moving beyond the mere description of impersonal processes related to the distribution of different kinds of land-use and population types. Ecologists such as Amos Hawley (1968) show an increasing concern with the form and development of territorially based social systems. They deal with the general problem of social organization which they presume arises out of the interaction of the population with its environment. On the contrary, there are some sociologists (Firey, 1945) who hold that sentiment and symbolism tend to operate to keep the land-use pattern from developing as some of the ecological theories would have expected and that cultural factors intervene between the population and environment to influence a community's social organization. Nevertheless, the ecological approach, has provided fruitful insights to the study of the community as a settlement pattern and may in the future shed light on the organizational aspects of community life.

COMMUNITY DELINEATION

One of the most troublesome questions facing community sociologists is setting the territorial limits of a community. No matter how the geographical limits may be drawn the social interaction of people living within these boundaries spills over them. Thus trying to contain a system of social interaction within a specified geographic area is like trying to contain water in a circle pencilled on a table top. This difficulty has led some sociologists to make use of the *statutory* community, whose boundaries are legally fixed: an incorporated village, town, city, or county. In such a case one does not have to be concerned with delineation of the boundaries as one would in the case of the *natural community* being discussed here. There are, of course, other sociologists who discount the utility of the community as a sociological concept and urge that analysis of human behavior be carried out in terms of the large-scale formal and bureaucratic organizations that constitute so much of American society. The individual would thus be related to the mass society, rather than to a place on the map.[2]

Such a procedure would obviously get sociologists out of one difficulty but would plunge them into another. If they study the real world, as they claim to do, they find that most people see themselves as belonging to some local community despite what social theorists might claim for them. Federal programs bog down or move ahead as they are able to deal with local community groups, including the officials in city hall as well as the neighborhood groups supposedly benefiting from the programs. Also, in most towns one finds groups dedicated to the improvement of their community. To tell them that there is no such thing as a community would mystify them and even anger them. It certainly would discredit in their eyes the persons who made such a statement.

This, then, is a definitional problem. Our lives are not confined, in a dynamic society, to the local community where we reside. We may work elsewhere, we may socialize outside, and we may obtain many economic and professional services elsewhere. Certainly, what occurs in our community is very much influenced by

[2] For a good discussion of territoriality, particularly as demonstrated in various types of urban neighborhoods or subcommunities see Gerald D. Suttles (1972).

decisions taken in Washington, D. C., the state capital, and in the headquarters of business corporations and national organizations. The closed community certainly does not exist today, and in a strict sense probably never existed. So the first problem we face is the recognition that a local community is not a total community in that it supplies all of our material and social needs and is not a place where all decisions affecting our welfare are made.

The other side of the dilemma is equally obvious. Most of their activities do occur within the radius of what people call their community. There is a geographical focus to their lives. There is also some interrelationship between the local institutions which meet their needs and even, at times, some organization among the consumers of these needs, such as a Parent-Teachers group. People identify with a place and compare its quality of life with that in another place. In each case they have in mind the geographical area covered by a given community.

Determining this is referred to as community delineation, which is to be understood by reference to four major points: the center, the services, the boundaries, and interpenetration with other communities. Each will be discussed in turn.

The Center

A community as a system of interaction is located geographically around a center where there are available business, professional, and institutional services. Local social interaction is organized around these. As a starting point we need to be aware of variations in these centers according to sufficiency and type.

1. *The isolated, relatively self-sufficient rural community.* The first condition a community must meet is that it have a relative degree of self-sufficiency. That is, it must provide people with many of their basic needs. By this criterion, an isolated rural village where people grow all of their own food, spin their own cloth, make their own shoes, build their houses themselves, and provide for religion and education is a community in that people have a set of services to share in common. By the same measure, in mountainous areas of the United States an isolated settlement that two generations ago had little dealings with the outside world would be considered a community even though it numbered not more than ten or fifteen households.

2. *The town-country community.* With the coming of roads and the opening up of means of communication, rural communities no longer remain isolated. The people there become more involved in the ways of the town where they bank, see a movie, get a part for the tractor, attend a function at the consolidated school, pay taxes, and get United States Department of Agriculture checks. When this happens, their community expands to include the town. Their immediate settlement takes on more of the characteristics of a neighborhood, with its insufficient services, and becomes part of the outreaching community of the town. (Brunn, 1968; Haga and Folse, 1971) Thus most rural people in the United States today, even though they may or may not live in recognizable neighborhood units, are a part of the larger community of some town upon whose services they have become dependent. This means that people who live in these towns can correctly think of their community as extending far beyond the city limits to the rural people who identify themselves with this town as a chief shopping or recreation center. This can be called the town-country community in contrast to the isolated, self-subsistent rural community.

3. *The urban community.*[3] Moving up the scale of size one finds cities, medium-sized and large, which attract into their orbit the surrounding town-country communities. The size of these constellations, including the center and the hinterland, is particularly impressive in the case of the biggest cities. These may be considered communities for planning purposes but usually are more correctly referred to as trade areas. Nevertheless, persons living at some distance from this urban center may identify themselves not only with the town in which they live but also with this urban center and really feel a sense of identification with both places. For example, many residents of small county-seat towns in the vicinity of a center of fifty thousand people, while not denying their affiliation with their home town, would think of themselves as members of the larger community to which they go for the concert and lecture series, for the athletic contests, or for visits with close relatives settled there, for a luncheon party at the best city hotel for some young

---

[3] The U. S. Bureau of the Census classifies as urban those places of 2,500 inhabitants and above incorporated as cities, boroughs, towns, and villages. Obviously, towns with populations close to this figure are really part of the town-country community. See also page 82 for a fuller definition of urban.

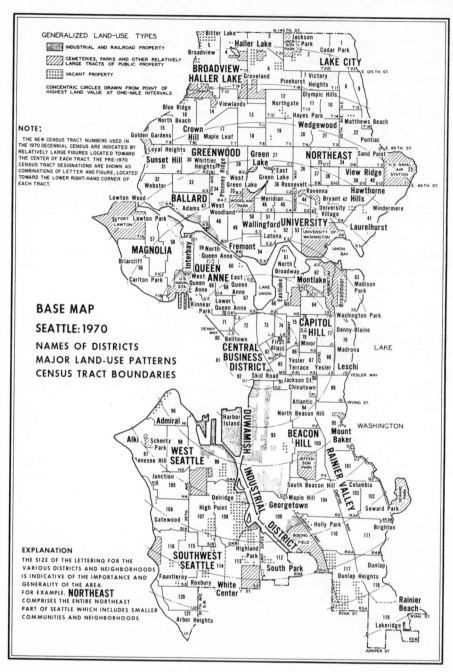

Figure 3–3. Names of districts, major land-use patterns, and census tract boundaries: Seattle. *Source:* Calvin F. Schmid, and Stanton E. Schmid, *Crime in the State of Washington,* Law and Justice Planning Office, Planning and Community Affairs Agency, Office of the Governor, Olympia, 1972, p. 94.

bride-to-be, and often for jobs. There is a general tendency for one's primary loyalty to belong to the smallest, most immediate grouping, but there is no reason why one cannot also belong to expanding concentric circles of association.

4. *The metropolitan subcommunity.* In the case of metropolitan aggregations, however, there is occasionally a very interesting development. In contrast to this movement of identification from the small to the large unit many newcomers to a metropolitan area, while developing an identification with the overall symbol, such as Chicago, also put down their roots in the immediate locality in which they live (Hunter, 1974). The result is that some of them become very much attached to and feel a part of what is really a subcommunity of the big metropolitan areas. Figure 3–3 shows the neighborhoods and communities of Seattle, Washington. These are sufficiently well defined to be mapped; each has its own name which people throughout the area recognize, and many of them have their own local groups through which to act in achieving common purposes. One of the questions now being explored more intensively is this problem of attachment to smaller subareas of the city. Much research done quite a few years ago seemed to indicate that city people, because they tended to associate with acquaintances from all over the city, had little loyalty to the immediate locality in which they lived. Some more recent studies indicate that even in the metropolitan area the locality grouping may still have considerable significance.

H. Laurence Ross (1962) demonstrated in his study of a census tract in Boston, Massachusetts, that residents perceive a city as containing named areas, bounded by such barriers to travel as parks, rivers, and large streets. People knew the names of areas other than the ones where they resided and these names had class and ethnic connotations in harmony with indexes derived from the census.

As indicated, there is usually a hierarchical arrangement among these centers of different size, with the larger centers more and more tending to dominate the smaller ones.

Notice that in the area shown in Figure 3–4 there are three centers of over one hundred thousand within eighty to one hundred miles of each other. These are identified by the Roman numerals I, II, III. In addition there are twenty towns ranging from three thousand to twenty-five thousand in population scattered at varying intervals from the large centers and from each other. These towns are shown by the letters *A* through *T*. Around each of these towns

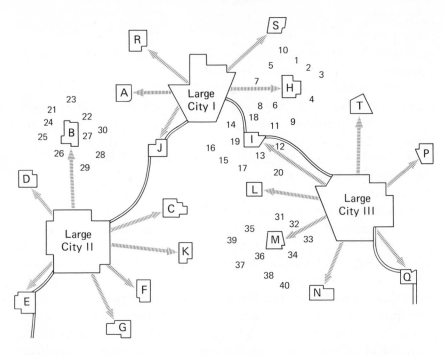

Figure 3–4. Map showing metropolitan dominance over towns (in letters), which in turn dominate smaller localities (in numbers).

are several hamlets or rural neighborhoods, each with its own identity and name, but each so insufficient in services that the people visit some nearby town to fulfill many of their economic and social needs. For four of the towns these neighborhoods have been drawn in, numbered from 1 up to 40.

There is no question but that the three large centers (I–III) exert great significance over the area because of the metropolitan newspapers published there, the radio and TV broadcasts, and certain kinds of facilities that they alone can afford to those demanding them (Bogue, 1949; De Fleur and Crosby, 1956; Pappenfort, 1959). Some examples of these are "cultural" (drama companies with Broadway casts, concerts by prominent artists or musical organizations) or medical (some world-renowned specialist is located there). Also, women wishing the latest styles in dresses or fur shops may visit the large center. Businessmen and industrialists may look to these centers for scarce items or machine parts that they need in a hurry. This illustrates how such large centers really exercise metropolitan dominance over the area although they touch people living at some distance only through one or two interests (Butler and Fuguitt, 1970; Stoeckel and Beegle, 1969).

One effort to analyze how places of different size are connected with each other is *central place* theory which holds that population centers may be placed hierarchically and that different levels of the hierarchy may be related to size of place and types of services offered in that place. (Christaller, 1960; Berry and Garrison, 1958)

The central-place model contains three basic ideas (Mark and Schwirian, 1967):

(1) cities are involved in symbiotic economic relationships with the immediately surrounding agricultural population and are centrally located in their trade area,

(2) within a region manifesting a central-place locational pattern a hierarchy of central places emerges as a result of ecological position and functional differentiation, and

(3) the distance between cities of the same size exhibits regularities which are a function of the mode of transportation at the time of location. (p. 30).

A study of the incorporated urban places in Iowa showed that the central-place theory was not in itself a sufficient explanation for population growth, which resulted from expansions of the local economic base (Mark and Schwirian, 1967). Despite this qualification, central-place theory continues to deserve study despite the disruption of regional ecological patterns on which it was based.[4]

One set of predictions, based on an analysis of Canadian data (Saskatchewan, Eastern Ontario, and Prince Edward Island), is as follows (Hodge, 1966):

1. The number of farm trade centers will continue to decline as increases occur in farm size and farm mechanization, thereby lowering the man-land ratio and the market potential for trade center establishments.

2. Hamlets will satisfy most daily shopping needs, and convenience centers will be bypassed by rural people seeking centers with a wider range of specialized goods and services. Convenience centers will decline to hamlet status in most instances and many present hamlets will disappear.

3. Except for a limited amount of "suburbanization" around large cities, small trade centers will likely disappear within a radius of ten miles of large trade centers and will show substantial decline in areas

---

[4] Frank and Ruth Young (1973) compare their approach (structural, based on social differentiation) with central place theory.

up to fifteen miles away. Only beyond this distance is the trade area integrity of small centers likely to remain secure.

4. As the thinning out of small centers continues, rural people will have to travel as much as one-third farther to reach a center offering even day-to-day necessities. Higher-order centers will tend to emerge in a more regularly spaced pattern to serve the demands created by expanded farm incomes and the ability to exercise choice because of increased mobility. (p. 195).

Using some of the same variables employed in the earlier study of trade centers, Irving L. Allen (1968) studied the extent of cultural activity in 52 Iowa communities over 5,000 population. He constructed a cultural facilities index based on the presence of such items as art galleries, community "little" theaters, community-civic concert series, well-stocked bookstores, larger than median-sized public library, art film series, community symphony orchestra, and professional theater engagements. He found all of the above fairly prevalent among the 52 communities, that the foundation base required to support each of the facilities is smaller than is often presumed, and that such activities formerly associated with larger communities have become prevalent in smaller communities, with many being established in the 1950's and early 1960's. Population size explained 36 per cent of the variance found in the variety of facilities.

Allen used a cultural interests index score as well. This was constructed from paid mail subscriptions by individuals for nine nationally circulated periodicals either devoted to the fine arts or having considerable arts content. The Cultural Interests Index Scores are the cumulated subscription (and membership) rates per 1,000 persons for each of the 52 communities. He tested with this index the hypothesis that the population size of communities is not related to the prevalence of cultural interests in the population, as indexed by the relative proportion of persons in the community with those interests. He found that the larger and smaller communities are similar in the relative density or prevalence of persons with cultural interests. He cites three possible variables that might explain part of the variance not covered by demographic variables: propinquity to larger dominant communities; the social organization of the community by way of providing organized sponsorship and audience patronage of facilities; and the presence of a college or university in the community. His rather optimistic conclusion that the small town in America is not destitute of all of the cultural amenities of larger cities is most interesting and his study is certainly deserving of wider replication.

The theory of metropolitan dominance and central place theory reaffirm what Figure 3–4 illustrates: namely, that centers are of different size and importance and the selection of a center as a starting point for community delineation is the first step. It is correct to select the small center as well as the large center for certain purposes, but in each case the characteristics of the social relations will vary in important ways.

Services

After designating a particular place as the center for delineation purposes, the next task is to decide what services and activities, and their accompanying patterns of social interaction will be the subject of the inquiry. Any local community will be deficient in some services or its members may prefer those offered elsewhere. (Johansen and Fuguitt, 1973) But one must decide what must be present before an area can be mapped; some services require a very small area and others a larger area and a greater population. Table 3–1 indicates some of the choices available. The headings are self-explanatory: a difference is made between institutional services (school, church, local governmental functions) and economic (stores, etc.) and professional (doctors, dentists, etc.) services. Sociation in the last column refers to social life outside the work or economic context.

TABLE 3–1

Possible Combinations of Services and Activities Carried Out by Majority of Members Primarily in Community of Residence.
(X Means Present; O Means Absent)

Community Type	Services and activities as focus of interaction				
	Residence	Job	Economic, Professional Services	Inst. Services	Sociation
A	X	X	X	X	X
B	X	X	O	X	X
C	X	X	O	O	X
D	X	O	X	X	X
E	X	O	X	X	O
F	X	O	O	O	O

In comparing Types A and F, the extreme cases, one finds that in the first case all of the activities are carried out in the community of residence, but in the second case none of them are. In all probability, one trying to delineate communities would not include F as a community if research showed this pattern prevailing for most of the people residing there. It might be given some special name as a "residential" community, but would not be the more composite community being considered here. The question then arises as to where one would draw the line in delineation: Type B would indicate that most people prefer to shop outside their community (perhaps some popular shopping plaza) but in all other respects their social interaction is within the community of residence; in Community Type C they also go for professional services outside the community, but in other respects focus their activities in the place where they live. Type D shows that most people are employed outside the community of residence but that in other respects they are members of the residence community. Type E would indicate that the majority of people, who work outside the community, also tend to lead a social life that takes them outside as well. This is because many of them may "socialize" with people they know at the place of employment or acquaintances met before moving into the present community. Instead of making residence the constant as was done in Table 3–1 one could hold some other activity, such as *job* constant.

This oversimplified typology indicates that one must know what one is mapping. Some delineation may be done to show the correspondence between place of residence and use of economic and professional services; other delineations may relate sociation to residence. Or, one could select Type A as the basic composite community and in delineation note in what respects a given community departs from the full range of activities listed there.

Since the early 1920's sociologists have been mapping communities and have developed a number of techniques which would provide the information on which one could state in what place most residents procured the services or engaged in the activities listed. The problem then is not so much one of research technique but one of definition. The fewer the activities included the more restricted is the community as a system of social interaction and the less able it is to maintain a distinctive identity.

Boundaries

The two chief methods employed for determining boundaries are the objective and subjective methods. In the objective method one gathers data about the location of selected activities and utilization of designated services by asking people themselves or by getting the information from those providing the services. There are also some individuals who have a sufficient overview of the community to make useful observations for more careful testing. A relatively simple way is to ask school children, say in junior high, to tell where their families go for various kinds of services and then relate these to the child's place of residence.

The subjective approach is that of social identification, since it tries to get at the perception of what people themselves consider to be their community or communities. When an individual's place of work and place of residence are in two different localities, he might very properly consider himself a member of both communities. Perhaps a fruitful approach to delineation is not to try to devise a complex typology of communities but rather develop a typology of community memberships, and study these rather than the geographical area.

A study of two counties in Illinois shows a close correspondence between community of residence and community of identity, with 96 per cent of respondents naming where they lived as the community with which they identified. On the other hand, there was weak association between economic interaction (obtaining retail items) and community of identification (Clement, Rojek, and Beck, 1974).

Interpenetration

Where it is obvious that the majority of people residing in a community work or shop outside, then the boundaries should indicate this interpenetration. In the analysis of the system of social interaction the subsystem (e.g., commerce) which is involved would have to be related to the interaction which takes place outside the community. It has spread over the boundaries, so to speak, and in this connection boundaries are meaningless. The sociological analysis needs to follow the interaction. But if a local community really does exist, then one could argue that most of the social interaction occurs within the community boundaries, with some interpenetration to be expected. The assumption can also be made that, just as members of one community may be seeking certain services elsewhere, by the same token people from another community may be crossing boundaries to take advantage of some special services offered in the first community. The concept of *interpenetration* makes it possible to use boundaries when they seem firm, but to open them up when certain patterns of interaction demand. Two or more communities may combine to carry out collective action which affect members of both or all communities. A good case in point would be the establishment of a regional high school where two or more political jurisdictions are involved as well as two or more composite neighborhoods in the sense used above. This social spill-over and resultant interpenetration is becoming increasingly common in American life today.

In our enthusiasm to trace this interpenetration we must not lose sight of the locality reference of much of the social structure. Merely to mention the terms used for the locality-referent indicates that we cannot move too far away geographically or conceptually (i.e., in abstractions), without losing sight of social reality. The existence of locality relevant functions for the community as a social system is shown in the specifically designated areas for the groups and subsystems within the community.

Group or subsystem	Locality-referent
Family	House-yard, apartment, neighborhood
School	School district
Church or religious body	Parish, membership area
Government	Political: precinct, ward, town or city limits county lines
	Service: police, fire districts (often follows political units). sanitary district welfare district
Commercial establishment	Trade area
Professional service	Client-area
Industrial plant	Employment area

Some of these, such as a sanitary district or the employment area of an industrial plant may transcend the boundaries of a local community, but they do have locality reference and are not blurred into a mass society.

PLACE AS A SETTING FACTOR

The community as a set of social relations does not itself adjust to the physical environment but its relations "are mediated through the behavioral organism [of its members]. The perceptual processes of the organism are the source of information about the physical environment, which gains cultural organization from its conceptual and theoretical components." (Parsons, 1968 p. 466). Technology is developed to overcome some of the organismic problems (cold and heat; too much or too little water; food and mineral resources), but this technology is conducted within social structures where people are interacting with each other.

In summary, five points may be made about place as a setting factor:

1. A settlement pattern with definite foci where people can gather to work, shop, play, or worship leads to social relationships more frequent or more highly structured than the settlement pattern lacking such foci.

2. The greater the size of the settlement, the smaller the proportion of the population known to the ordinary resident, not just because of more people but also because of the greater problem of movement throughout the whole community.

3. The social networks that make up the community are influenced by the extent to which population segments are segregated by race, religion, or occupation. This influence shows up in lessened communication among the different segments, greater difficulty in reaching consensus on important issues, and a greater likelihood of manipulating the segregated units as political blocs in the local struggle for power.

4. Ecological analysis can show changes in land use, residential types, and other statistically verifiable modifications involving space. However, other types of studies directly concerned with social interaction must be made to determine whether or not the presumed effects of ecological processes really work out as predicted. For

instance, ecological studies may show that the spread of business establishments into a residential area affects economic values and other objectively measured indexes. But to determine how this spread changes interpersonal relationships, one must study them directly since the bonds among people may be tightened as people rally together to face the new invasion in some cases, or weakened in other cases as people quickly try to get rid of their homes in an effort to buy more desirable dwellings elsewhere. Ecological studies help us infer psychosocial changes; they do not describe them. Since social relations are basically psychosocial, the attributes of place suggest, perhaps limit, but do not describe the major interactional characteristics of the community.

5. The quality of the environment has become a social problem. (See Chapter 18) Pollution has organismic effects; its control calls for new technology, a revised value system (relative importance of pure air or profits), new laws and ordinances, and new social structures to "fight" for a better environment or manage effectively the procedures developed to improve the living space.

4

The People

Some interesting facts about a community come to light when people are viewed as a population rather than as personalities. The study of population is called *demography* and deals with the birth and death rates, the movement and distribution of the people, and other variables such as age, sex, occupation, religion, educational attainment, and the like. In other words, just as one can measure and map the physical layout of the city so one can measure and characterize the various population categories found in the community. To one untrained in statistics and cautious of figures, such study may at first seem puzzling, but these statistics come alive when interpreted in terms of their significance to the community.

GROWTH AND DECLINE IN COMMUNITY POPULATION

Community Size

Few of those who live in metropolitan areas realize that almost half (71.5 million) of the U. S. population (144.8 million) lived in 1970 in communities of less than 50,000 people. In fact, there are 396 places with a population over 50,000 but 20,372 places with less than 50,000. This raises the question as to what size of place would be most representative of U. S. communities?

the six places with a population over 1 million each, whose total population is 18.8 million, or

the 1,143 places, ranging from 10–20,000, but totalling over 16 million, or

the 520 cities, varying from 25–50,000, with a total of 17.8 million, or

the 240 cities, varying from 50–100,000, with a total of 16.7 million, or

the 16,628 communities of less than 5000, whose population totals 19.3 million, a sum more than the largest six places.

This list does not include all of the size categories shown in Table 4–1 but it does indicate that the study of one community, whether it be a metropolitan city or a small country town, provides a poor basis for generalizing about community life in the United States.

TABLE 4–1

Size of Place by Number and Population, 1970

Size	Number	Total Population
1 million and more	6	18,770,773
500,000–1 million	20	12,989,017
250,000–500,000	30	10,466,400
100,000–250,000	100	14,292,614
50,000–100,000	240	16,740,130
25,000– 50,000	520	17,848,705
20,000– 25,000	242	5,404,850
10,000– 20,000	1,143	16,026,535
5,000– 10,000	1,839	12,930,372
2,500– 5,000	2,295	8,041,728
2,000– 2,500	987	2,200,587
1,500– 2,000	1,361	2,353,858
1,000– 1,500	2,182	2,678,402
500– 1,000	3,294	2,371,707
200– 500	3,990	1,332,486
Less than 200	2,519	299,597

Source: Adapted from Table 6. Population of Incorporated and Unincorporated Places, 1973. Bureau of Census, U. S. Department of Commerce, U. S. Summary PC (1) A1, December 1971.

Total Numbers over a Period of Time

Even in a period when our national population is steadily increasing each year, there are many American communities that lose more people than they gain over a five- or ten-year span. What does it feel like to live in a community where numbers are declining? What prospects lie in store for the businessman, the professional person, or the property owner? (Harden, 1960; Keyes, 1958.) The least one can say is that the people in such a community must adjust to this changing situation, thereby altering in part, at least, their customary manner of approaching their problems.

A minimal approach to the study of the people of a community is that of determining their shift in numbers through the years (Tarver, 1972; Fuguitt, 1971). The figures of United States census, taken every ten years, tell the story. For cities of over 50,000 population, special census tracts are drawn up to assist in comparing the numbers in one part of the city with those elsewhere. In using the figures for a given city one must determine whether reference is merely to the incorporated area called the "central city," which does not include all of the surrounding built-up area, or whether the figures include the metropolitan area lying around the central city.

For the United States as a whole, between 1960 and 1970, the population of central cities increased by 6.4 per cent in contrast to 11.6 per cent for the previous decade. The suburban ring grew by nearly 27 per cent during 1960–70, a smaller figure than the 46 per cent recorded during 1950–60. Table 4–2 shows the rates of growth for selected central cities over three decades. Usually, how-

TABLE 4–2

Rates of Population Growth for Selected Central Cities, 1940–50, 1950–60, 1960–70

City	Rate of Growth, % 1940–50	1950–60	1960–70	City	Rate of Growth, % 1940–50	1950–60	1960–70
Atlanta	9.6	47.1	2.0	Los Angeles	31.0	25.8	23.3
Baltimore	10.5	−1.0	−3.6	Minneapolis	6.0	−7.5	−10.0
Boston	4.0	−13.1	−8.1	New Orleans	15.3	10.0	−5.8
Buffalo	0.7	−8.1	−13.1	Philadelphia	7.3	−3.3	−2.7
Chicago	6.6	−1.9	−5.2	Pittsburgh	0.8	−10.7	−13.9
Cincinnati	10.6	− .3	−10.0	Portland	22.3	− .2	2.7
Cleveland	4.2	−4.2	−14.3	San Francisco	22.2	−4.2	−3.3
Columbus	22.8	25.4	14.5	Seattle	27.0	19.1	−4.7
Dayton	15.7	7.5	−7.2	St. Louis	5.3	−12.4	−17.0
Denver	29.0	11.1	4.2	Washington	21.0	−4.7	−1.0
Hartford	6.7	−8.5	−2.6				

ever, people, are interested in knowing about the increase in the whole metropolitan area, which includes the suburbs as well as the central city.

Bases for the Increase or Decrease

The population numbers for a particular community depend upon three factors: natural increase or decrease, migration, and annexation. Each of these will be examined in turn.

Natural increase or decrease. In order to be able to compare the same community at different periods or to compare two communities, birth and death *rates* must be used rather than statistics of the actual number of births and deaths. A birth rate shows the number of live births per thousand people for a particular year. These are called "crude" rates, since they take into account everyone in the community, whether children or octogenarians.

When the death rate is subtracted from the birth rate, we get the rate of natural increase.

Community leaders in any state can see to what degree their community compares with the state average and with the nearby communities. When one town differs significantly from such averages, the search for an explanation may lead to some important findings about the community. County or state public health officials are often in a position to provide these statistics and can advise as to how they should and should not be interpreted. For example, infants born in a city hosiptal to women who come from an area outside the city should not be counted as a part of the natural increase of that city any more than should the deaths of nonresidents brought to the hospitals from outside the city. This is why some well-informed person needs to interpret what population statistics do and do not show, particularly when these are based on a single city or small community.

Migration. In America today there is considerable movement from one community to another as well as within a community. Indeed, nearly 25 million Americans, or 17.1 per cent of those one year of age and over, lived in a different house on April 1, 1950, from on April 1, 1949. From March 1960 to March 1961, 35.5 million, or 20 per cent of the U. S. population one year old or over, had moved at least once. Of this 20 per cent, 13.7 per cent had moved within the same county; 3.1 per cent had moved within counties of the same state; and 3.2 per cent had moved between states. Another fact of importance is the failure of large cities in the past to reproduce themselves; that is, the birth rate of those living there has not been high enough to offset the death rate, although there is recent evidence of a trend now toward a full replacement ratio. Nevertheless, if a city is to grow, newcomers must be attracted. In 1960 the population in standard metropolitan statistical areas (SMSAs-cities of 50,000 or more and the suburban areas surrounding them) accounted for 66.7 per cent of the U. S. population and in 1970 for 68.6 per cent. But there had been a reduction of the proportion inside central cities (33.4 in 1960; 31.4 in 1970), while the ring around the central city (within the SMSA) grew from 33.3 to 37.2 per cent of the U. S. population. Outside these metropolitan areas the proportion decreased from 33.3 per cent in 1960 to 31.4 per cent in 1970. Migration is a partial explanation.

Three questions about migrants are of special interest: (1) Where do these migrants come from? (2) What are their characteristics? (3) Why do they move? Warren S. Thompson (1953) provides some historical background:

1. *Whence the urban migrant?* Before 1900 two main internal movements were of importance. The first was the east-to-west migration. People were rapidly settling west of the Appalachians, and they have been continuing this trend toward the Pacific even in our own day. The second shift was from the country to the city. By 1880 the urban population outnumbered the rural.

Since 1900 four main movements can be described. The first of these is from the South to the North, involving both white and Negro workers. Since the South had a higher birth rate and fewer economic opportunities, migration began during World War I, declined during 1930–40 and was resumed during World War II. The second covers regional shifts, such as that between large cities in different parts of the country. Frequently people move between communities of the same general character. The third movement is a continuation of the shift from rural communities to urban centers. In 1962 only one person out of thirteen lived on a farm. The fourth trend is the suburban one, which is a centrifugal movement in metropolitan areas from the central city to the area surrounding it, but with some reverse flow (Taeuber and Taeuber, 1964; Kirschenbaum, 1971).

2. *What are the characteristics of the migrants?* As far as heredi-tary qualities go, the migrants are a fairly good cross-section of the community from which they come. Also, men move more than women. For example, within a state 101 men move to every 100 females; between contiguous states 103 men; between noncon-tiguous states 110 men. The farther the move, the greater is the proportion of males involved.

Migrants are most commonly found in the 15-to-34 age group. In general, migrants are better educated than the nonmigrants among whom they settle, a fact contradictory to the general impres-sion. Of course, this does not refer to migratory farm workers, since they do not settle down; but it does refer to the newcomers (the migrants) who seek to become definite members of the com-munity.

This characteristic of education ties in with the fact that those occupations requiring most training are more mobile. White-collar workers move more than hand workers, and the higher the social status of the white-collar workers, the more mobile they are (Ladin-sky, 1967); Zuiches, 1970).

3. *Why do people move?* The "push-and-pull" theory of mi-gration attempts to answer this question (Fuguitt, 1959). Mere dissatisfaction with one's situation is not in itself a cause for migra-tion as a rule; it usually is accompanied by some presumed alterna-tive. The migrant may have heard that there is a good job waiting or may have received letters from a friend telling of the great oppor-tunities in a new place. In any case, there must be a desire to change or to improve one's present situation. At times the "pull," as one begins to contrast it with one's opportunities in the home community, becomes the irritant that leads to dissatisfaction, which in turn, forms the "push." In other words, the migrant may have been quite satisfied until he learned of these possibilities elsewhere.

Some recent studies have revealed additional facts about mi-gration. For example, in three isolated mountain communities in Eastern Kentucky it was found that a migrant's social class origin influenced not only when he left the mountains, where he moved, and with whom, but also his subsequent level of living in the urban area (Schwarzweller & Brown, 1967). But a study of former high school students in a rural area of Michigan showed that selectivity in the migration process had less to do with family background and family resources than it did with the situation of the subjects themselves. They did have greater measured ability, higher grades, and higher educational and occupational aspirations, (which could of course reflect early upbringing in the home) (Rieger, 1972). One study of interregional migration indicates that Southern Negroes migrating to the Northern cities had a lower proportion of poverty than did Negroes native to the urban North, which indicates that poverty in Northern ghettoes cannot be blamed upon the influx of Negroes from the South. As the study says, "Poor transplanted rural Southerners may be highly visible in the urban North, but they constitute a minority of the poor living there." They also are less poor than the Negro Southerners left behind. Whites migrating from the South to the urban North were better off than those left behind but with higher incidence of poverty than the populations joined. (Bacon, 1971).

Long (1974) found that black migrants to six of the nation's largest cities were less likely to be poor and on welfare in 1970 than blacks born and reared in these cities.

The migration of the poor is a much-discussed public policy concern, particularly in urban states.[1] If they move in search of a job and find one, then their migration becomes an economic asset; if they move because welfare payments are higher elsewhere than the place they leave, they may bring about misallocation of resources. This is a strong argument in favor of establishing uniform national standards for welfare payments, thereby eliminating welfare as an incentive for migration by the poor.

As earlier comments indicate, noneconomic factors also influence migration. One of these is the availability of information because people in lower economic groups rely heavily on what friends and relatives say about opportunities in other areas (Lansing and Mueller, 1967). Almost half of the migrants with a college education obtained information by a special trip to the destination, but only 24 per cent of migrants with a high school education or less did so.

. . . Recognizing the important role of friends and relatives in the migratory decisions of the poor, several authors have described a pattern of "chain migration." In that process an initial group of migrants leaves

[1] This paragraph and the one that follows is based on Frederic B. Glantz, "Migration and Economic Opportunity: The Case of the Poor," *New England Economic Review*, March/April 1973. 14–19. See also Ritchey, 1974, Rieger and Beegle, 1974.

a given area in search of better opportunities and after a suitable location is found, information is passed back to the "home" area and succeeding groups of migrants follow.[2]

Another factor sometimes mentioned is the size (total population) of an area because (1) people more readily gain information about a large center from the mass media; (2) a large area is more likely to offer attractive social and recreational activities. But the study reported here did not find the size of city as significant statistically as the proportion of the area's population with income below the poverty level. That is, though people may be poor they accept and try to support their relatives from outside.

The effects of migration upon a community will depend therefore upon the type of migrant who arrives and the opportunities he finds.

Annexation.   Cities also increase the number of their inhabitants by annexing the territory lying adjacent to the city. Between 1960 and 1970 the central cities gained 3.9 million people by annexation, or 6.4 per cent of their total population. It is interesting to note in this connection that the number of urban places in the United States in 1930 was 3165; in 1940, 3464; but in 1950, 4054 according to the previous definition of urban and 4741 according to the new definition, which included urbanized areas under 2500 people.[3] By 1960 the figure had grown from 4741 to 6041, and by 1970 it reached

---

[2] Ibid., p. 16.

[3] "In addition to its central city or cities, an urbanized area contains the following types of contiguous areas, which together constitute its urban fringe:
1. Incorporated places with 2,500 inhabitants or more.
2. Incorporated places with less than 2,500 inhabitants provided each has a closely settled area of 100 housing units or more.
3. Towns in the New England states, townships in New Jersey and Pennsylvania, and counties elsewhere which are classified as urban.
4. Enumeration districts in unincorporated territory with a population density of 1,000 inhabitants or more per square mile.
5. Other enumeration districts in unincorporated territory with lower population density provided that they served the following purposes:
   a. To eliminate enclaves.
   b. To close indentations in the urbanized areas of one mile or less across the open end.
   c. To link outlying enumeration districts of qualifying density that were no more than 1½ miles from the main body of the urbanized area."
(Bureau of the Census, 1960 Census of Population, Volume 1, Part A, XIX.)

7062 using the current definition. The shift since 1940 is therefore quite startling.

Certainly anyone using the population figures for a given area such as a community must be sure that the figures all relate to the same geographic base and that what seems to be growth is not merely the accretion of new territories together with their residents (Schnore, 1962).

Annexation, however, should not be confused with consolidation of various types of governmental services. It is quite common for a city department of health to combine with a county department of health to form a more effective unit. Likewise, city and county planning boards may consolidate, or boards of education, or recreation departments. The units of government remain as formerly—quite distinct, but these particular functions have been consolidated and operate jointly.

To summarize, population size whether resulting from ups and downs in natural increase, migration, or annexation does have real community ramifications. Kasarda and Janowitz (1974) used survey data to study community attachment. They found:

> First, location in communities of increased size and density does not weaken bonds of kinship and friendship. Instead, length of residence is a central and crucial factor in the development of these social bonds. Second, location in communities of increased size and density does not result in a substitution of secondary for primary and informal contacts. Rather, the results suggest that formal ties foster more extensive primary contacts in the local community. Third, increased population size and density does not significantly weaken local community sentiments. But community sentiments are compatible with desire to avoid the negative features of local community life. (p. 338).

Such findings may seem to run against popular beliefs about the differences between small and large communities, but this is why sociologists need to continue to test popular ideas and sentiments about various facets of community life.

POPULATION COMPOSITION OF THE COMMUNITY

Only when the total numbers of a community are broken down into special groupings does the true importance of population analysis become evident. There are many possible ways of making these divisions, and some may prove more useful than others.

Sex Ratio

One important fact to know about a community is the sex ratio, the number of men to each 100 women. Washington, D. C., and many other cities in the East where large numbers of secretaries and office workers are needed contain more women than men and thus represent a poor place for a young woman to go in search of a husband. Wars tend to lower the sex ratio, as does the migration from a community by men in search of work. On the other hand, in areas being newly settled, where single men initially comprise the bulk of the population, the sex ratio is very high and a "man's society" tends to develop. Women outnumber the men in the urban population in every age group beginning with the fifteen- to nine-teen-year-old category. But men outnumber the women in almost every age group of the rural-farm population. In Egypt the reverse seems to be true because of differences in selective migration, which in turn are related to the contrasting types of employment opportunities available in the cities of the United States and Egypt.

At the time of birth, there is a sex ratio of about 105 males to 100 females in the white population but an equilibrium is reached in the early adult years, only to be soon turned into a female surplus "by nervous wear and tear, occupational diseases, accidents, homicide, and suicide" (von Hentig, 1952). In 1850 the sex ratio for the United States was 104.3 but by 1950 it had become 98.7, and in 1970, 94.8, indicating a surplus of females.

The influence of an unbalanced sex ratio, whether it be many more males or many more women, is subtle. The mores or customs regarding sexual behavior, ways of spending leisure time begin to change; out-migration of the overrepresented sex is speeded up; and the effects are also seen in the organizational life of the community with respect to kinds of associations or clubs which come into existence, the programs they adopt, and relative participation by males or females.

Age Composition [4]

Age composition is determined by dividing up the population into age groupings based on five-year intervals. For example, to

[4] For a thorough treatment of the age structure of the community and its social effects see Starr (1971).

know how many youngsters there are under five, how many between five and nine years, how many ten to fourteen, and so forth, helps in predicting the structure of the population five or ten years hence. By comparing the oldest age groups with the youngest, for example, the businessman knows whether to deal in wheel chairs or baby buggies, the community whether to open a rest home or a children's nursery, or whether to put a croquet court in the park for the old people or add more slides for the young. Also, planning for the educational needs of the children can only be done in terms of the age distribution.

Communities differ markedly in the proportion of people of working age. There is a tendency for the rural communities, which have many children and old people, to lose those inhabitants in the productive age group to other areas. This means that rural communities must educate the young and care for the old without the benefit of the relatively larger working force found in the cities. Such demographic facts are obviously of great importance. For example, such facts might be used by advocates of an equalization educational fund within a given state providing for an allocation of school money on the basis of need and not merely on the basis of where the taxes are collected, since cities tend to benefit from the work of those who have been educated elsewhere before their migration to the cities.

Many communities have suddenly grown conscious of the larger proportion of elderly people in their midst. This has led to the construction of special homes for the elderly by municipalities or church and fraternal groups. It has also caused some organizations, such as the Young Women's Christian Association, to set up special programs for those in the upper age brackets in recognition of the fact that the aged have special demographic and social characteristics (Kiser, 1962, Talmon, 1961). The elderly are increasing at a faster rate than the total population. Between 1960 and 1970, those over 75 increased 37 per cent, those between 70–74 by 15 per cent, those from 65–69 by almost 12 per cent, and those between 60–64 by almost 21 per cent.

Figure 4–1 is a useful reminder that different generations (cohorts, or those people born at the same time) as a group go through life experiences different from those who preceded or who follow them. Cohort A on the figure will have vivid memories of the economic depression of the 1930's, whereas Cohort C will have no con-

Stages in life course

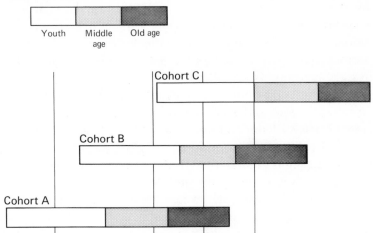

Figure 4–1. Processes of cohort flow and aging showing selected cohorts over time. *Source:* Table 1.3 from Chapter 1, "Elements in a Model of Age Stratification," from *Aging and Society: Vol. 3: "A Sociology of Age Stratification"* by Matida White Riley, Marilyn Johnson, and Anne Foner (New York: © 1972 by Russell Sage Foundation).

ception of what Cohort A experienced. This has been carefully explained by Matilda White Riley (1973) in her comments on the accompanying figure:

> . . . This figure represents schematically the lifespan of three selected cohorts. . . . The people within each cohort *age*. That is, over time they pass through a sequence of roles from birth to death (such as dependent child, student, worker, spouse, retiree), learning to play new roles and relinquish old ones, accumulating knowledge and attitudes and social experiences, and undergoing biological and psychological development and change. As particular individuals are aging and dying, a second crucial process is taking place concomitantly: *new cohorts* of people are continually being born.
>
> Meanwhile, changes in the social structure—designated as "history" at the bottom of the Figure—are constantly occurring (as society undergoes wars, famines, periods of prosperity and depression, changes in the state of science and the arts, revolutions in tastes and beliefs, etc.). As society changes, each new cohort encounters a unique sequence of social and environmental events. Hence the life-course patterns of people in one cohort will differ in some respects from the life-course patterns

of other cohorts. In this sense, different cohorts age in different ways. (p. 36).

It is clear, therefore, that part of the setting for understanding a community as a system of social interaction is the age composition, including the analysis of cohorts and the situations individuals are likely to encounter as they move through different statuses from birth to death.

Race Composition [5]

People in a local community are often unaware of the real distribution of the people by race. On one occasion the leading residents of a community, assuming that the facts corresponded with their prejudices, complained about the high crime rate among a racial minority living in their midst. A careful check of the record of arrests and of the racial composition showed that actually those in the minority grouping were responsible for a smaller proportion of arrests than their share of the population. Generalizations about any minority group are all too commonly based on prejudice rather than fact and need to be checked against the statistical record to assess the true situation.

When large numbers of two or more races live side by side each race tends to develop its own subcommunity, each with its own institutions and social outlets. But despite these discernible differences all inhabitants of a particular area defined as a community, no matter of what race, can be considered as members of that general community and are apt to feel that they should be taken into account when any community-wide program is being formulated. Failure on the part of any race to recognize its dependence on the other results in various manifestations of social disorganization. Thus knowledge of the percentage of each race in the total population of the community is basic to any discussion of full community participation by each race.

One changing aspect of American community life is the redistribution of the black population (Rubin, 1960). In 1960, 60 per cent of all blacks lived in the South, but by 1970 only 50 per cent lived there. In 1960, 34 per cent lived in the North but this had grown to 40 per cent by 1970. Likewise, in the West there was an increase

[5] See Chapter 13 for discussion of interaction between races at the community level.

from 6 per cent to 8 per cent between 1960 and 1970. Furthermore, the blacks are essentially an urban population. By 1970 three out of five lived in the central city of a major metropolitan area. They made up more than half of the central city population of four large cities in 1970: Washington, D. C., Newark, N. J., Gary, Indiana, and Atlanta, Ga. During the past decade the black population in metropolitan areas increased by four million. When one takes into account the 1.5 million blacks lost to the South by net out-migration, it is clear that natural increase is responsible for most of this metropolitan increase, even making allowances for the fact that the four million increase include Southern as well as Northern cities.

While the white population was increasing about 12 per cent between 1960 and 1970 the black population increased by about 20 per cent, accounting for 11 per cent of the total U. S. population. The other nonwhite groups made up 1.4 per cent in 1970. Anyone making a community study can compare local figures with these national figures.

The three aspects of composition discussed thus far—sex, age, and race—are based on biological characteristics which cannot be changed. Cultural definitions surrounding them or their distribution within a community may change, but people cannot change their sex, age, or race. Women, who at one stage of a country's history were looked upon as chattel subservient to men, may attain a position in society where they control far more than half of the wealth of the nation, as they do today in the United States. Young people, who should be seen and not heard according to earlier traditions, may now be given an important place in the scheme of things. Furthermore, life expectancy has increased to the point that many people will live throughout more of the human life span, although the life span itself has not basically changed. Likewise, attitudes toward race that developed in an earlier day undergo marked modification with the passing of time. Thus, clearly the cultural aspects of population composition are subject to change. Some of these aspects are treated briefly in the paragraphs that follow.

Marital Status

A greater proportion of American people are married than ever before. Demographic factors such as a more nearly equal sex ratio and an increased life expectancy may account for much of this change but not for all of it. Furthermore, the young people in many American communities marry at an earlier age than formerly. This has a direct effect upon the interest the young people take in the welfare of the community in which they have settled. A study of the changes in marital status through the years can reveal community characteristics that might not otherwise be apparent—a case in point would be the effect of such trends on the fertility pattern.

Nationality and Language

Because of the assimilative character of American society, most of those who enter the United States as immigrants acquire American citizenship and try to outdo others in becoming "good Americans." The older people find it hard, however, to master English and may feel more comfortable when using their mother-tongue. They may also want to maintain some reminders of their former life; hence they patronize delicatessen stores where they can buy the type of food to which they are accustomed. They may even want to provide elementary schools where their children can be taught their parents' native language as well as English.

Unquestionably, these ethnic divisions, as will be pointed out in Chapter 13, play a great part in community life, particularly where minority groups entertain traditional prejudices toward those of other nationalities who have also emigrated to the same American community. Furthermore, factions tend to arise within these ethnic groups as the immigrants try to adjust to political and economic changes occurring in the "home country." It is not simply that an Armenian-American may be suspicious of the Swedish-American ethnic group in his community; he may be even more at odds with another Armenian-American group.

If a person is to understand the importance of such groups, he must first determine their size. When he has learned from the census or other figures the kinds of nationality and language groups in his community, as well as their relative size, he can then see the total population of his community in a clearer light. He can also try to answer the question as to why some ethnic groups, in the opinion of the local community, "fit in" well and others do not.

Religious Groupings

In some communities religious divisions assume great significance. Knowing the relative size of each major religious grouping aids in understanding the type of problems that may periodically recur. It is important to know, for example, how representative the Ministerial Association is of the whole community or to what degree the Federated Church Women speak for all the churches of the town. To what extent do the Knights of Columbus speak for Catholic men? What organizations represent the divisions of the Jewish people, divided as they frequently are into Orthodox, Conservative, and Reformed congregations?

Communities vary in the extent of church affiliation. In some, church-going is customary and even a matter of social pressure; in other communities, there is much less emphasis upon formalized religious activity. Some churches serve as social centers as well as places of worship, a fact that may show up in higher affiliation statistics. In using the figures from a religious census it is important to remember that some religious bodies count as adherents the entire family when the head of the family is a communicant; other bodies count only those individuals who after reaching maturity voluntarily choose to join as official members of the body.

Educational Attainment

For many purposes it is useful to have a general idea of the number of college graduates or high school graduates in the community. Such data provide still another way of viewing the population. In certain communities where college graduates are proportionately high, it is very likely that there will be considerable support for such organizations as the American Association of University Women, the League of Women Voters, or discussion groups among the men, such as the Torch Club. Such figures help one understand the point of view certain segments of the population take toward the type of school program that will be most enthusiastically supported by the community. Likewise, industrialists seeking a location for a plant are apt to give preference to a community where their highly trained technical staff members will find congenial associates of a comparable educational level.

Rural-Urban Distribution

When the community boundaries have been drawn up as described in the previous chapter, it may well be that both rural and urban people will be included. But rural people are not a homogeneous group. In fact, the United States Bureau of the Census has set up a threefold division of rural residents: *the nonfarm*, who, like the person just beyond the city limits, does no farming; *the part-time farmer*, who derives a certain proportion of his income from farming and the rest from some other economic activity; and *the full-time farmer*, for whom farming is a full-time undertaking.

The term "the urban fringe" has been widely used to describe the nonfarm person and even the part-time farmer who have settled near the cities in what was ten or twenty years ago open countryside. It has been called a new social frontier and is described as follows by Solon T. Kimball (1949):

> The tide is an irresistible one. It sweeps in and through old communities. It engulfs farm after farm, breaking up rural neighborhoods that have had decades of stability. It turns quiet little villages, which have preserved their numbers and institutions for many decades, into places having problems that those who have spent their lives there find they are unable to understand or cope with. (p. 5).

Kimball then goes on to describe one of these fringe communities in southeastern Michigan. He found that farm land was being withdrawn from productive purposes to provide space for people to live and that the number of farmers was diminishing both relatively and absolutely as they retired or died and were not replaced.

He also noted that the village community showed much greater resistance to the invasion of outsiders. Those who supplied professional or retail services actually improved their economic lot because of the larger number to which they catered. The old religious, fraternal, and social groups continued their activities with relatively little disturbance. Only the school system with its overflow of children from the newcomer families found itself inadequate to meet the new problems.

In this fringe community the population was relatively young and heterogeneous. These newcomers plus the grown children of the "old-timers" succeeded through two community-wide organizations (The Mothers' Club and the Civic Club) to help the community face its problems.

This account of what has happened in Lambertville, as this community is called, is reminiscent of many accounts of the frontier. A study by Andrews and Eshleman (1963) of those living in the rural fringe surrounding Columbus, Ohio, describes the differences between the migrants and the old residents there. These investigators conclude that the old residents are being forced to modify their behavior and re-evaluate their established mode of living, while the newcomers welcome the change. Such studies show the usefulness of looking at the people of the community in terms of urban, nonfarm rural, part-time farm, and full-time farm categories. Each of these groupings may have certain unique problems worthy of special study.

Occupational Distribution

A listing of the occupational distribution of the members of the community is indicative of many local characteristics. Together with racial, religious, educational, and similar aspects of population composition, it is useful in presenting an overall demographic picture. With these figures it is possible to trace changes in community patterns—to see, for instance, to what extent the occupational distribution has changed through the years.

Because a community has certain demographic characteristics, it tends to attract those to whom such traits are appealing. Young parents are attracted to communities where there are many other young parents concerned about similar problems; those of a given ethnic background may be drawn to areas where others with comparable backgrounds reside. And so it goes. Statistics help reveal the groupings, and knowledge of the groupings, in turn, affords insight into the patterns of living in a particular community.

HOW HEALTHY ARE THE PEOPLE?

The people of a community are more than an aggregation as measured by numbers and viewed in terms of composition. They are human beings who have to carry on their daily duties as best they can. In other words, students of population are interested in selected *qualitative* as well as quantitative characteristics of the people of any community. Since poor health is one of the greatest drains upon the community's human resources, it should be viewed in community as well as in individual terms, in terms of the extent to which illness disrupts social relationships at home, at work, and in other organizational activities. A sick person in the home sets up a chain reaction that not only affects his relationships with members of his immediate family but also frequently changes the contacts between these family members and other people. The economic burdens of illness are well known: They mean loss of earning power as well as the out-of-pocket expenses for medical services and drugs.

The *morbidity rate*, or incidence of illness, may or may not be available for the local community, depending upon the kind of statistical service that the local health authorities have set up. The task is complicated by the fact that such statistics must be gathered from physicians who may be too busy to fill out complicated reports. Often, however, the information for the more serious types of illness can be obtained from hospital sources. Perhaps the only really satisfactory way of getting relatively accurate information on such matters is to conduct a special investigation within the community itself. A careful sample of the population may be questioned about symptoms of ailments they now have or the illness suffered within the home during a given period. Results obtained can first be checked with local medical authorities for interpretation and then issued as a picture of the health conditions of the community. These findings would provide valuable data on community health patterns.

To summarize, a community is lived in by people who can be counted, studied in terms of the various groupings to which they belong, and understood in the light of the problems that demographic trends reveal. Demographic trends represent only one aspect of the community, but, when added to the knowledge of the community as a place or the community as the provider of jobs and services, they provide a necessary background against which to view the intense social activity of which community life consists.

POPULATION AS A SETTING FACTOR

Population analysis, like ecological study, does not deal with personal or group interaction. It does reveal statistical relationships between certain categories of people as well as numerical trends involving people.[6] As has been pointed out in the previous discussion, these obviously affect the way people live together in a community,

[6] An excellent twenty-page booklet entitled *Census Data for Community Action* describes the kind of information available from the 1970 census. Bureau of Census, U. S. Department of Commerce. November 1972. Available from Superintendent of Documents, Washington, D. C. for fifty cents.

but just what their consequences for social relations are must be learned through a study of social interaction itself.

Kingsley Davis (1959) indicates at least four areas of study in which demographic and sociological skills can be combined to advantage: (1) fertility in connection with attitudes and social institutions; (2) population change in relation to social and economic change; (3) the labor force with respect to population structure and social organization; and (4) the family with regard to demographic behavior. These areas, he points out, involve a two-way relationship between population and social structure and they allow for "the study of motives and attitudes and yet permit the application of demographic techniques as an essential part of the analysis." (p. 314) In this kind of fruitful interplay, the study of the people of a community can provide a rich background of understanding, thus serving as a setting factor.

5

Culture and
Personality

In western New Mexico, two communities, composed of people
with a similar cultural background and living in the same general
ecological setting, reveal striking social differences that can only be
explained satisfactorily by the fact that each group brought different
traditions to its new settlement. The communities, each numbering
about 250 people, are 40 miles apart, and both villages have subsistence patterns based upon combinations of farming and livestock
raising.

"Rimrock," one of these communities, was settled by Mormon
missionaries in the 1870's as an outpost for the conversion of the
Indians; these early settlers were "called" by the church and sent
by the church authorities. Today the church is the central core of
the village. "Homestead," the other community, was settled by
migrants from the South Plains area of western Texas and Oklahoma
in the early 1930's; it was a part of the Okie movement described in
Steinbeck's *Grapes of Wrath*. Each farm unit is operated by a nuclear family, consisting of father, mother, and unmarried children,
and the many different denominations show religious factionalism.

Evon Z. Vogt and Thomas F. O'Dea (1953) in comparing the
differences in value orientations found in Rimrock and Homestead
(both fictitious names for the real communities studied), took four
examples of possible community action and showed how each com-

95

munity responded differently. When land became scarce, the people of Rimrock borrowed money from a church welfare plan agency, bought some land, and instead of breaking the plot up into individually owned units, kept the parcel as a block and put it under the control of a cooperative called Rimrock Land and Cattle Company. On the other hand, in 1934 the people of Homestead had the opportunity of acquiring additional land through the Federal Security Administration. This land would have been managed cooperatively by a board of directors selected by the community. The scheme collapsed because it soon became clear that each family expected to acquire its own private holdings on the range and that a cooperative would not work in that community.

A second illustration was the graveling of the village streets. As late as 1950 the streets of both communities were in bad repair. In that summer a construction company brought much large equipment into the area to build and gravel a section of the state highway. In Rimrock, the villagers, acting through their church organization, decided to take advantage of the presence of these machines, had meetings of representatives from almost every family, and voted that each family would donate $20 to a fund to get the job done. In Homestead the construction company offered to gravel the streets of the center if the residents would contribute enough funds for the purpose. This community plan was rejected by the local people, and an alternative plan was followed. Each of the operators of several of the service institutions independently hired the construction company truck drivers to haul a few loads of gravel to be placed in front of his own place of business, thus leaving the rest of the village streets a sea of mud in rainy weather.

The construction of a high school gymnasium was the third instance. Residents of both communities were told that the funds for materials and for certain skilled labor would be provided from state school appropriations provided the local residents would contribute the labor for construction. In spite of some difficulties the people of Rimrock completed their project by arranging that each able-bodied man contribute at least fifty hours of labor or $50, the latter to be used to hire outside laborers. The homesteaders of the second community were willing to work on the gymnasium only if they were paid a dollar an hour. At this rate, the funds were soon exhausted and construction stopped. A partially completed gymnasium and stacks of some ten thousand adobe bricks disintegrating slowly with the rains, stood as monuments to the individualism of the homesteaders.

The two communities show differences, too, in their dances. The Mormons have always considered dancing to be an important form of recreation, and almost every Friday evening they hold a dance in the village church house. These dances are family affairs and are opened and closed with prayer. On the whole, these Rimrock dances are peaceful, although at the dances held in the local school there has been some evidence of drinking (quite contrary to Mormon rules), and at times fighting has resulted from the presence of nonvillagers. The village dances in Homestead are also important focal points for community activity. These affairs take place several times a year in the school house and are always well attended. They often end in fist fights because of tensions between rival families.

These illustrations show definitely that the people of Rimrock, the Mormon village, respond to group problems as a group and that cooperation has become second nature to them. It has become a part of the institutionalized structure of expectations, reinforced by religious conviction and social control. On the other hand, in Homestead, the researchers found that the strong commitment to an individualistic value orientation has resulted in a social system in which interpersonal relations are strongly colored by a kind of factionalism and in which persons and groups become related to one another in a competitive, feuding relationship.

UNDERSTANDING THE VALUE ORIENTATIONS
OF A COMMUNITY

Values and Value Orientations

Obviously, no individual, no group, no community can possess all that it might want to possess nor achieve all that it might want to achieve. Therefore, possible goals have to be ranked in some order of importance, and available energy and resources spent in pursuing those goals considered most important. *Values* are those things or achievements that the community members consider good, and therefore to be sought, thereby implying that the opposites of these are bad, and consequently to be rejected (Becker, 1956; Warren, 1972; Williams, 1969). From the study of Rimrock it was clear that cooperation was a value, whereas in Homestead individualism was a value ranked higher than cooperation. But these things and achievements do not exist as separate entities. They are part of what has been called value orientations. As defined by Clyde Kluckhohn, (1951) *value orientations* are those views of the world, often implicitly held, which define the meaning of human life or the "life situation of man" and thereby provide the context in which day-to-day problems are solved). Just as customs are what the people do and traditions are the explanations people have for doing specific things, so value orientations are the ways people look at life in general. For instance, American agricultural technologists who are trying to help Asian people increase their farm production are frequently nonplussed at the reluctance of the peasants to follow suggestions based on scientific research. They keep telling the peasants, "If you would treat your ground this way and use this kind of seed, you could increase your crop by a third." This appeal may fall on deaf ears, since the peasant is not always interested in increasing his crop; his concern is not with how much he can grow on a given piece of land but rather with how little he needs to grow to take care of his family and to sell in order to get money for taxes. His value orientation is toward minimum rather than maximum production, and he has a different set of assumptions from the American technician whose whole professional career has been spent in helping people maximize their efforts.

Types of Value Orientations

Without clear-cut categories for the analysis of value orientations the whole concept remains vague and difficult to describe for any particular community. Figure 5–1, prepared by Florence R. Kluckhohn, gives an excellent way of sorting out and classifying what can be learned about the value orientations for any locality. She considers five problems crucial to all human groups. The first category takes up the question of the character of innate human nature (human nature orientation). As the three columns show, it can be viewed as essentially *evil*, as *neutral* (a mixture of good and evil), or as *good*. Likewise in each case it may be considered mutable, that is, subject to change, or immutable. The Puritans stressed the point that human nature was basically evil but perfectible, and many American communities seem to hold to this as a dominant

Innate human nature	Evil (mutable-immutable)	Neutral { mixture of good and evil (mutable-immutable)	Good (mutable-immutable)
Man's relation to nature and supernature	Subjugation to nature	Harmony with nature	Mastery over nature
Time focus	Past	Present	Future
Modality of human activity	Being	Being-in-becoming	Doing
Modality of man's relationship to other men	Lineal	Collateral	Individualistic

Figure 5-1. Ranges of variability in value orientations. *Source:* Florence R. Kluckhohn and Fred L. Strodtbeck, *Variations in Value Orientations* (Evanston, Ill.: Harper & Row, 1961), p. 12. *(Note:* Since each of the orientations is considered to be independently variable, the arrangement in columns of sets of orientations is only the accidental result of this particular diagram. All combinations are considered to be possible. For example, a doing activity orientation may be combined with a mastery-over-nature position and individualism, as it is in dominant American culture, or, as one finds in Navaho Indian culture, it may be in combination with a first order harmony-with-nature position and collaterality.)

value. In other communities where the Puritan tradition is weak or has never been present, the orientation is toward the belief that human nature is a mixture of good and evil. In daily life, this human nature orientation lies behind any community's approach to such matters as juvenile delinquency or reformation of the adult offender. If human nature is thought to be essentially evil, it follows that "bad people" must be constrained and confined, and the emphasis is one of "protecting society" rather than of rehabilitating the criminal. If human nature is considered essentially good, as would be the case in certain communities with strong Quaker or Friends' Society traditions, the problem is chiefly one of finding what influences led the individual astray and of seeking to correct those influences so that the good in the person can really shine forth.

The second orientation is that between man-nature (including the supernatural). The Spanish-American communities of the Southwest illustrate the *subjugation-to-nature* orientation. Many people there believe that there is little that man can do to help himself against the wrath of storms or the scourge of illness. A person says fatalistically, "If it is the Lord's will that I die, I shall die," and may even refuse the services of a doctor because of this attitude. The *harmony-with-nature* approach sees no real separation between man, nature, and supernature and is illustrated by the Navaho Indians or by the traditional orientation of the Chinese peasant. Most American communities, however, stress the *mastery-over-nature* orientation and, as Florence Kluckhohn points out, believe that "the Lord helps those who help themselves." People put up flood walls to control a stream, span the river with bridges, tunnel through mountains, air-condition homes, and conduct surveys to be sure that they are fully utilizing local natural resources.

The *time* orientation represents a third range of variations. All communities have some concern with the *past*, the *present*, and the *future*, but they differ in the importance accorded to each. Where most of the people of a community stress the past, they tend to be complacent and take pride in what their ancestors have done more than in what they have done themselves. They tend to resist change, and stress conformity almost as an end in itself. Most American communities, however, are future-oriented. Civic clubs, women's groups, and many church organizations work untiringly to make the community "bigger and better." People think in terms of their children's future and plan accordingly; they have hopes of improving not only their material status but their social status as well. Change is viewed as inevitable and desirable.

A fourth dimension of value orientation is *activity*. As explained by Florence Kluckhohn, in the *being* orientation the preference is for the kind of activity that is a spontaneous expression of what is conceived to be "given" in the human personality. Mexican society illustrates the *being* orientation in its widely ramified patterning of fiesta activities, which though spontaneous, are nevertheless restrained by definite codes of conduct. The *being-in-becoming* orientation emphasizes the kind of activity that has as its goal the development of all aspects of the self as an integrated whole. This is illustrated in the writings of those such as Erich Fromm who try to get people to accept the total personality and eliminate the split between "reason" and "nature." The *doing* orientation, so common to American life, has as a distinguishing feature the demand for the kind of activity that results in accomplishments that are measurable by standards conceived to be external to the acting individual.

"Getting things done" and "let's *do* something about it" are stock American phrases (Goldstein and Eichhorn, 1961).

The *relational* orientation, the last to be considered here, has three subdivisions: the lineal, the collateral, and the individualistic. These three are present in some form in all systems of human relations but receive different emphases from community to community. When the *lineal* principle predominates, there is stress upon age and generational differences and upon cultural continuity. Social patterns in the community are set by traditions, groups such as the family are more important than the individual, and young people tend to follow the occupations of their fathers. Many of the more isolated rural communities that are strongly family-centered are of this type. *Collateral* relationships are those based not on lineage (father-son) but on laterally extended relationships such as sibling (brother-brother, brother-sister, sister-sister) ties. The stress here is upon the goals and welfare of this laterally extended group, which is always moderately independent of other similar groups. When applied to communities, this principle would result in strong influence of peer groups upon individuals growing up and the desire for the approval of one's contemporaries more than the approval of one's elders. In an *individualistic* orientation a man need not remain in a fixed position and need not so often bow his head in acceptance of a dominating authority. As Florence Kluckhohn points out, he is much more free to be like everyone else. When the individualistic principle is dominant, individual goals have primacy over the goals of specific collateral or lineal groups. At the same time, each individual's responsibility to the total society and his place in it are in terms of goals (and roles) that are defined and structured as *autonomous* ones in the sense of being independent of particular lineal or collateral groupings.

VARIANT VALUE ORIENTATIONS

Student clashes with police as well as racial clashes in the 1960's have demonstrated the existence of groups whose members hold to a value system sometimes at variance with the dominant values.

One of the major contributions made by Florence Kluckhohn (1961) and those working with her has been the clarification of the importance of variant value orientations. Values that at one time may have been simply variant may later on become dominant. The key to understanding these variations lies not only in deciding which of the divisions (such as *being* or *doing*) under any orientation (such as *activity*) apply to a given community but also in finding out the order of importance given by the people of a local community to the possible orientations. While some major groupings in the community will rate some orientations at the top, other groupings may place a different orientation there. Such variant value orientations must be taken into account. Florence Kluckhohn sets forth the following hypothesis *"The rate and degree of assimilation of any ethnic group to dominant American culture will depend in large part upon the degree of goodness of fit of the group's own rank ordering of value orientations with that of the dominant culture."* (p. 26). Such assimilation continues to occur as newcomers shift from any variant values they might have held to the acceptance of the primary emphases of the majority of people with whom they come in contact outside their immediate family or social group.

Assimilation, however, is not the only reaction. There are those who stress confrontation instead; they seek to substitute for the dominant values another set which they champion. One example—the youth counter culture of the late 1960's—pointed up this confrontation.

Youth Counterculture

This has been primarily a student-centered movement ranging from the beat-hip bohemian to the New Left of the Students for a Democratic Society. Various writers have sought to describe the common thread running through the protest, whether it be a retreatism to drugs and withdrawal from contact with conventional society or an activist program to bring about immediate changes in the established order. One interpretation is that the counterculture stresses the nonintellective powers and values; it "strikes beyond ideology to the level of consciousness, seeking to transform our deepest sense of the self, the other, the environment." (Roszak, 1969) This stands in contrast to the scientific world view which supposedly has alienated people by deadening man's sensitivity to man.

An effort to inject such values into the bureaucratic decision-making of a university calls for a readiness to change and a creativity in organizational restructuring for which most professors and administrators have not been prepared. And in any confrontation many other considerations such as power become so involved that the variant values themselves are lost sight of. Suffice it to say that college communities both in the United States and abroad have gone through a conditioning process that alerts them to the fact that there is a set of variant values which some young people, definitely a minority, hold—at least for the time being—as central to their lives, and to which they can attract other young people for periods of time or when a particular circumstance arouses support for their cause. As a summary, we might cite the following observation by Richard Flacks (1971):

> . . . At a minimum, the ambition of the counterculture is to create a new way of life that will serve as a viable alternative to those options that have become established in American culture: most counter-culturalists, however, hope that in time, their values will *prevail* and *supplant* conventional values. At a minimum, the ambition of student revolutionists is to disrupt and frustrate American imperialism and militarism; most new leftists, however, hope to participate in a thoroughgoing transformation of the American economic and political order. (pp. 104-5).

The variant values of the black power militants is familiar to anyone who follows major community issues. They are impatient with the slow process of integration as practiced in the past and seek, through stressing black racial identity and social action, to bring about major changes in American life. They attack racism and white supremacy as dominant values. The same is true of another group—the women's liberation movement—which strikes at a dominant value—male supremacy. These examples show that along with the analysis of dominant values one needs to be familiar with variant values which are claiming public attention.

CULTURE AS A SETTING FACTOR

To study a community one must take its social heritage, or its culture, into full account. This means a familiarity with its historical traditions, the crises through which it has passed, the customary behavior of its people, and the explanations people give for doing what they do—such as going to church or not going to church on a Sunday morning. An analysis of dominant and variant values is also necessary. Ward Goodenough (1963), in explaining the sense in which a community may have a culture, also points out how it operates to influence individual and group behavior within the community.

In the first place, he recognizes that any generalized culture of a community is always a part of someone's private culture and thus is never the same for any two persons. In this sense there are as many working models of a community's generalized culture as there are individuals in the community.

But, in the second place, there is a community culture that is separate from the members' conception of it:

> Regardless of the differences between their own private standards for themselves and those they attribute to their fellows, people are usually at some pains not to reveal these differences in their overt behavior. Insofar as a person tries to conduct himself according to the standards he attributes to others, others are likely to attribute to him a private culture that is in reality a reflection of his generalized culture for them. And it is their generalized cultures for others that people usually use as their operating cultures when their behavior is subject to others' scrutiny. As people who have regular dealings with one another try to conform to the generalized cultures they individually attribute to their mutual fellowship and as they modify their individual conceptions of these cultures in order to increase their predictive value, these conceptions will increasingly converge. Thus a high degree of consensus can develop both regarding the content of the generalized cultures they individually attribute to each other and consequently regarding the content of the operating cultures which they individually use to guide their interactions with one another. To the extent that there is close agreement of this sort among its members, a group may be said to have a *public culture*, a culture that its members share and that belongs to all of them as a group. The public culture of a community, together with the public cultures of its several subgroups, is what many anthropologists seem to have in mind when they speak of a community's culture. . . .
>
> A community's public culture consists of the perceptual and conceptual features embedded in the meanings of the vocabulary of its language and other public symbols, a public body of knowledge and beliefs, a public value system, and a set of public conventions, rules, and recipes with regard to behavior and operational procedure. (pp. 263–64).

PERSONS AS COMMUNITY MEMBERS

If a community system is to operate to the satisfaction of its members, the members must know how to behave acceptably as part of that system. This is what child-rearing is all about. It is designed not only to help the child learn how to gratify his material needs and to mature emotionally, but it is supposed to enable him to become a genuine participant in his community and the larger society to which he belongs. He must learn to play many different roles in many kinds of social situations, in keeping with the public community culture mentioned in the last section.

The Status-Role Bundle

Mr. Ezra Smith, devoted husband and father of five young children, has risen according to schedule, shaved, dressed, breakfasted, and gone over the day's details with his wife. He then backs his car out of the garage of his modest home and is soon lost in the line of traffic of others headed for work. He parks his car behind the shoe store where he is a salesman and goes in for a brief staff session with the manager before the doors are opened to customers. Here he becomes the employee from the standpoint of the manager and a salesman in the eyes of the customers.

At lunchtime he goes to the Lions Club, where he is an officer and where he visits informally with many of his friends. On the way back to his store he stops at a car dealer's showroom to look over a low-priced car that he is thinking of buying. The rest of the afternoon he spends at the store. Occasionally this routine is interrupted when he arranges with the manager to be away for jury duty, to serve on the board of a crippled children's home, to go to the dentist, or to take care of some business affairs of the veteran's organization of which he is a member.

After work he finds life varied enough. Some nights he goes to "pack meetings" with a son who is a cub scout; occasionally he accompanies his wife to a PTA meeting or to a church supper. On other evenings he gathers with some of his friends at the veterans' club for card games or takes others in his family to the drive-in theater or watches television with neighbors, or goes to a night baseball game in a large city sixty miles away, or attends an evening course in salesmanship sponsored by the extension division of the local college.

During his vacation period he introduces further variety into his life, taking a trip by car to visit his relatives in another state or going to a state forest with his family for a camping trip or simply staying at home and doing some much-needed repair work around the house.

Even this brief inquiry into the private life of Mr. Smith is sufficient to indicate several interesting things. First, during his waking hours Mr. Smith moves from one status to another. He is husband, father, motorist, salesman, customer, club member, scout leader, student and vacationist as well as a man an adult, and a member of the middle class. Secondly, each status he assumes carries with it certain roles or behavior patterns that he considers normal and that others around him expect him to perform. As a shoe salesman he is not supposed to play "This little pig went to market, this little pig stayed home . . ." on the toes of his customers, although as a father he does this at the insistence of the baby; as a motorist he is supposed to obey the traffic signals; as an adult he is supposed to "put away childish things" and "act his age." Many of these roles have little to do with the unique traits of Mr. Smith as an individual but have been passed down to him and to others in his community as customs and mores. They constitute learned behavior, but the community has had a hand in deciding what is and what is not to be learned.

A third consideration is the fact that Mr. Smith performs most of these roles in the presence of other people; he communicates and interacts with them. What he does and how he does it are closely tied in with his idea of his status and his understanding of what is an appropriate series of roles for that status; he is guided by the response of other people in deciding whether he has initiated the expected role or not, and, if what he is dong seems to be displeasing, he can change his behavior accordingly.[1] His own idea of what a father should do may differ from his wife's idea of what a father should do in a given situation; as he starts to discipline a child, perhaps as his own father disciplined him, his wife may say, with a glance: "You are not treating this child right. Don't you remember what Dr. Spock said?" and thus cause him to alter his role. Even though his own status as father gets confused from time to time with

---

[1] One study found that in towns between 5,000 and 15,000 businessmen were more conservative than in towns which were both larger and smaller, raising the question as to whether some aspects of personality are related to community size. (Photiadis, 1967).

that of the dutiful husband, he still remains a father; it is the roles and the role expectations that change and not that particular status.

This combination of status and accompanying roles has been called "the status-role bundle" by Talcott Parsons. From one standpoint, a community may be looked at as a gigantic collection of statuses—"rich man, poor man, beggar man, thief . . ."—and each new generation inherits these statuses and adds some new ones. The fact that these statuses and roles persist in time apart from the personality of any one individual or collection of individuals gives a community a predictability; one can anticipate in general how a policeman directing traffic will act no matter which officer is on duty a particular day at a particular spot. Obviously, each individual has some leeway in playing these roles; what we call his personality may seem better adapted for some kinds of role-playing than others, and he is urged or guided into those positions where he can best perform.

The term *social relationship* is useful in describing the bond between two interacting persons. Each has a status vis-à-vis the other, and each supposedly acts in keeping with the role expectations that accompany that status. This means that a social relationship has both static and dynamic (role-playing) aspects. *Social values* assist in ranking statuses as higher or lower, more or less important; *norms*, on the other hand, set the limits within which roles must be played. A school teacher can discipline a child, but community norms tell what he may or may not do in carrying out the discipline. He will probably not be allowed to whip the child with a birch rod, but he may send the child home with the request that the parents seriously consider such a step. The norms are a great deal like the rules covering the game of football in that they tell what a player may and may not do.

But how does Mr. Smith arrive at the point where he can play so many different roles, can enter into social relationships with others, and avoid giving offense by observing the norms which limit his role-playing? He can do so because he, like everyone else in his community, has gone through a long, slow process of personality development. As an ego, as a self-conscious person he has learned that some responses afford him more satisfaction than others; he is also aware, to be sure, that he often faces conflicts in choosing what to do. Viewed from the standpoint of society, this whole process is called *socialization*, or the motivational process which describes the internalization, or the automatic acceptance, of the appropriate roles, values and norms. (Stoll, 1974). This will be described in Chapter 9.

A THEORY OF ROLE STRAIN

No matter how much Mr. Smith or any other community member may have internalized the roles he is supposed to play, he will invariably face role strain in his daily interaction. This is an important background fact that must be borne in mind in understanding the social life of a community.

William J. Goode (1960) has analyzed this role strain, or the felt difficulty in fulfilling role obligations. He views role relations as a sequence of "role bargains," and as a continuing process of selection among alternative role behaviors, in which each individual seeks to reduce his role strain. He recognizes four types of role strain:

> First, even when role demands are not onerous, difficult, or displeasing, they are required at particular times and places. Consequently, virtually no role demand is such a spontaneous pleasure that conformity with it is always automatic.
>
> Second, all individuals take part in many *different* role relationships, for each of which there will be somewhat different obligations. . . . These are conflicts of allocation (civic as against home obligations).
>
> Third, each role relationship typically demands *several* activities or responses. Again, there may be inconsistencies (what the husband does to balance his family budget may impair his emotional relations with members of his household). There may be different but not quite contradictory norms which may be applied to the various behavioral demands of the same role (the clergyman as the emotionally neutral counselor, but as a praising or condemnatory spiritual guide) . . .
>
> Finally, many role relationships are "role sets," that is, the individual engages, by virtue of *one* of his positions, in several role relationships with different individuals. (p. 485. Footnotes in quotation omitted).

No wonder then, as Goode says, that the individual is likely to face a "wide, distracting, and sometimes conflicting array of role obligations." Failure to recognize this is at the bottom of many unsuccessful efforts at community improvement, for the sponsors of such programs frequently fail to recognize the role obligations of those whose help they seek. Participants in such undertakings need help in redefining their role commitments so that they have a rationale for including the community-focused activity in the array of competing role relations. As Goode reminds us, "In general, *the individual's total role obligations are overdemanding.*"

There are, however, socially acceptable ways of reducing the role strain. For example, the individual himself can manipulate his role structure in several ways:

1. *Compartmentalization:* This may be defined on the psychological level as the ability to ignore the problem of consistency. Socially, role relations tend toward compartmentalization because the individual makes his demands on another and feels them to be legitimate, in specific situations where he can avoid taking much account of the claims on that person. . . .

2. *Delegation:* This may be seen, at least in part, as one way of achieving compartmentalization. . . . A wife may delegate housekeeping, and some of the socialization and nursing of the child. Note, however, that the societal hierarchy of values is indicated by what may *not* be delegated: for example, the professor may not hire a ghost writer to produce his monographs, and the student may not delegate examinations.

3. *Elimination of role relationships:* Curtailment may be difficult, since many of our role obligations flow from our status positions, such as those in the job or family, which are not easily eliminated. Of course, we can stop associating with a kinsman because of the demands he makes on us, and if our work-group sets norms which are too high for us to meet, we can seek another job . . .

4. *Extension:* The individual may expand his role relations in order to plead these commitments as an excuse for not fulfilling certain obligations . . . In addition, the individual may expand his role system so as to *facilitate* other role demands, for instance joining an exclusive club so as to meet people to whom he can sell stocks and bonds.

5. *Obstacles against the indefinite expansion of ego's role system:* Although the individual may reduce his felt strain by expanding his role system and thereby diminishing the level of required performance for any one of his obligations, this process is also limited . . . The rewards cannot increase at the same rate as the expansion even if at first he increases his skill in role manipulation, because eventually he must begin to fail in some of his obligations, as he adds more relationships; consequently, his alters (those with whom he is interacting) will not carry out the counterperformances which are expected for that role relationship.

6. *Barriers against intrusion:* The individual may use several techniques for preventing others from initiating, or even continuing, role relationships—the executive hires a secretary through whom appointments must be made, the professor goes on a sabbatical leave. The administrator uses such devices consciously, and one of the most common complaints of high level professional men and women and executives is that they have no time. This feeling is closely connected with the fact

that they *do* have time, that is, they may dispose of their time as they see fit. Precisely because such men and women can accept a wider array of role opportunities, demands, and even temptations than do others, they must make more choices and feel greater role strain. (pp. 486–87); also see his *Explorations in Social Theory.* New York: Oxford University Press, 1973, pp. 97–120.

The six points listed above explain what an individual may do to reduce role strain. Or, if we view a role relationship as a transaction or "bargain," the individual may further reduce strain by "obtaining as gratifying or value-productive a bargain as he can with each alter in his total role pattern."

Yet an individual is not a free agent with respect to the other partners to the role relationships in which he is engaged; nor are the partners. There are structural limits set by the community to the individual's ability to bargain freely. As we note these structural limits, we see in closer detail the pressures upon a person as a member of a community. Again, Goode specifies six structural elements. The first is the hierarchy of evaluations (or value system as described in the preceding chapter) that the community or society tends to accept. An individual's evaluation of what he can and cannot do cannot be very far out of line with the guidance given by the loose, society-wide hierarchy of evaluations. Second, third parties may intrude into the bargaining process going on between two people if they become concerned with the way an individual is manipulating his role structure. For example, parents are criticized by kinsmen, neighbors, and friends if they do not press their children in the direction of assuming a wider range of roles as they grow older. Third, norms of adequacy define what is an acceptable role performance in keeping with the age, rank, and esteem of the individual. Such norms also apply to the total system of roles assumed by the individual because if he has too narrow a system, his performance is thought to be inadequate. (The wife complains, "We never go out and meet people.")

A fourth limit is the linkage between roles in different major community systems, or institutional orders. Thus, to carry out the obligation of the father requires the fulfillment of job obligations. In this case having to link roles in two systems limits the individual's freedom to manipulate his role system. In the fifth place, there is little room for bargaining in the ascriptive statuses (mother, female, "native American") that we occupy. Finally, since two people are involved in a role relationship and are mutually dependent upon the performance of the other, mutual deviation will only rarely reduce their role strain. It is usually less wearing to carry out the expected role performance.

PERSONALITY AS A SETTING FACTOR

This discussion shows at once the difficulty of separating even for analytical purposes, personality, culture, and the social system. They are all intimately intertwined. But one does need to concentrate on one of them at a time if there is to be any clarity of focus. Since this is a book about the community, the central place is held by the patterned social interaction and the setting factors will have to be taken as given.[2] For example, this chapter recognizes that a community is made of people. Sociologically speaking, they *are* the community if they are thought of as persons involved in a network of social relationships. This means that they can respond to social overtures, gestures, social situations in ways that are mutually meaningful to other community members. Their personality traits may vary widely, but they share enough in common to make daily life possible. The deviant, to be discussed briefly in Chapter 9, has so organized his personality that in some ways at least he cannot or does not behave as other community members expect him to behave. He may conform to the pressures of his own little in-group, which is itself deviant with respect to community values and norms. Fundamental to community life, therefore, is the requirement that most members behave as integrated personalities, not only possessing a wholeness as far as the individual's identity is concerned, but also an integration that has incorporated and reacts positively to expectations of other community members.

As we noted in Chapter 3, some communities highly publicized for certain purposes—such as Las Vegas—tend to attract certain personality types; other communities hold out the welcome sign to perhaps a different sort. Communities vary too in the demand that they make upon their members to participate or not participate in certain forms of social life, which again is a selective factor in screening out those types of persons that do not find the community congenial.

---

[2] Talcott Parsons (1968) observes: "Although they interpenetrate crucially with social systems, the personalities of individuals are not core constituents of social system (nor vice versa) but precisely environments of them." *International Encyclopedia of the Social Sciences*, vol. 15, p. 469.

Once the choice has been made to settle or once a person has been born into a community and remains there, the process of socialization with all of its subtle pressures is set in motion by relatives, neighbors, tradesmen, parents of one's own children's playmates, various organizational representatives, and fellow-workers. Paradoxically, personality that is a *sine qua non* for the operation of the system, and is therefore a setting factor, is also produced or largely shaped by the system for which it is the basis.

6

Dilemmas Within
Community Sociology

The discussion of the Setting Factors, covered in the preceding chapters, has confronted us with some of the problems faced in trying to formulate a neat, systematic approach to the community. As we shall note in the chapters which follow, the field of community sociology is becoming structured according to different perspectives. Thus, it is no longer useful to seek some all-embracing definition, or even a set of properties which most community sociologists would accept. Instead it seems more productive to describe some of the choices which have to be made and then to recognize that each choice leads in a particular direction.

This, then, is a proper juncture to take a backward look at some of the dilemmas related to describing the community as a place, or in terms of other setting factors. Likewise, a forward look alerts us to the need to decide for a particular analysis whether to use the social system, conflict, or social field perspective.

Before turning to the presentation of five dilemmas, some justification should be given for calling them dilemmas and not merely options or choices. A dilemma has been defined as "a necessary choice between equally undesirable alternatives; a perplexing predicament." The alternatives are "undesirable" in the sense that the choice of one rules out the choice of the other, whereas many community sociologists (present author included) have preferred in the past not to make choices but to keep all possibilities under the umbrella term "community." Not only does choosing one horn of a dilemma eliminate the other but it affects the selection of available alternatives in other dilemmas encountered. Of course, from the standpoint of forcing greater precision in community studies, these dilemmas may prove highly "desirable" in the long run.

The five dilemmas to be taken up in turn are: local versus non local; statutory versus natural community; comprehensive versus selective scope of social relations; explicit versus unstated theoretical framework; descriptive versus interactive nature of setting factors.

DILEMMA 1: LOCAL VERSUS NON-LOCAL

As shown in Table 6–1 below, a community sociologist must decide whether to view a community as a locality (that is, spatially limited to a particular settlement) or to think of it in non-local terms. This is the first dilemma.[1]

TABLE 6–1

Local vs. Non-local Dilemma

Spatial Orientation	Types	Characteristics
LOCAL	1. Statutory Community	Political Unit: incorporated village, town, city and county.
	2. Natural Community	Settlement covering part of or more than one political unit; Growth uncontrolled
	3. Specialized Community	Prison, army camp, university
NON-LOCAL	1. Spatial	Broader than locality (e.g., world community)
	2. Non-Spatial	Based on social networks and common interests

Locality

If one considers the locality aspect of community an integral part of the definition, then certain options are open. Three of these should be mentioned.

---

[1] The dilemmas discussed here are not necessarily encountered in the sequence presented.

The political unit. Some community sociologists, primarily those interested in comparative analysis, take as their community the political unit: the incorporated village, the town or township, the city or the county. These are all locally based jurisdictions, which can be drawn precisely on a map. They are statutory creations assigned the responsibility of making certain kinds of decisions and carrying out stated functions in behalf of those who live within the specified geographical limits. Within this area, however, people carry out a wide range of activities which are preponderantly non-governmental, or non-political, but which can be analyzed and compared.

Whenever the investigator chooses the political unit as his spatial area he or she should indicate that the study deals with the *statutory community*. We then know at once the kind of locality under discussion and we are also quickly aware of many characteristics of this kind of community unit.

The settlement. There are times when a community sociologist chooses to study a settlement, or a constellation of houses, services, buildings, parks, institutions which occupy an identifiable geographical area. The settlement may be of two types: first, it may stretch out beyond the actual city limits (the statutory community). At some point, by the use of numerous available methods, one can decide that the fringes of the community have been reached and that the territory of another settlement has been encountered. The edges are at best only approximations for it is taken for granted that between any two adjoining settlements there will be an interstitial zone where the boundary is confused.

A second type of settlement may be a neighborhood or some identifiable local area within a large local political unit. Sociologists in their study of large cities have identified a number of these subcommunities which seem to have many community characteristics although they are not legal entities in their own right.

Such settlements are not the result of legislative acts but the accretion of private acts by hundreds of private individuals in acquiring land, using it for their own purposes, but in proximity to other people. Economic rather than political processes may have been the guiding ones, so much so that one political unit may govern only part of the settlement. For this reason, such a community—which includes a total settlement—can be termed a *natural community*.

The specialized community. Place can also be identified for various specialized communities: a prison, an army camp, a university, a mental institution. These have often been referred to as communities and they do have a *locus;* they exist in space. The extent to which the *locus* is important in the analysis will depend upon the kind of research being undertaken.

Non-local

Spatial. There is widespread precedent for considering the community, in a sociological sense, as a spatial but non-local entity. Robert M. MacIver (1970) makes much use of the concept of community in his writings, contrasting it with an association (an organization of social beings for the pursuit of some common interest or interests). Illustrations of association are marriage, church and state. For him, community is any area of common life, such as a village, town, district, or country, or even wider area. He would thus include localities but would move on to much broader spatial coverage. In this sense one could properly speak of a "world community." What is important in MacIver's characterization of the community is that it is a focus of social life; it is integral and includes much more than one or more common interests (which comprise associations).

In the future we may expect greater use of the term community for non-local spatial units. "The Atlantic Community" may take on sociological characteristics beyond those it now possesses as might "The European Community." Certainly, community sociologists have the conceptual framework and methodological tools for studying the extent to which such collectivities with the increase in social relations are becoming real communities.

Non-spatial. There is a well-established perspective in which the community has no locality referent or, if so, only for convenience of identification. Some would refer to a large-scale body such as the Roman Catholic Church as a community (in contrast to MacIver who calls it an association). Though it has a central headquarters its adherents do not live in any one locale, any one country or continent. The community cannot be identified in spatial terms.

Although he makes reference to the local community from time to time, Robert Nisbet (1962) in his *The Quest for Community* uses the term in a much broader sense (e.g., The Medieval Community or the Political Community), His interest is primarily in social factors which give people a sense of community.

The most recent development derives from the study of social networks, in which spatiality may not be considered an essential characteristic for the definition of community. Works which might be cited in this connection are those by Elizabeth Bott (1957), Jacqueline Scherer (1972), and Barry Wellman and Paul Craven (1973a, b). They implicitly take some territoriality as a given, but do not try to map the communities of which they speak.

To conclude, the dilemma lies in the fact that one either thinks a community has locality features or it does not. Those who use locality may differ widely in the importance they attach to it, but it remains one of the elements in their treatment of community; on the other hand, those who dismiss locality as they study the growing complexity of highly mobile urban life provide us with a different conception of community. The locality approach which some of the urban specialists tend to reject is very useful in the numerous non-urbanized areas of the United States and elsewhere, and need not be discounted because of the current interest in the social network emphasis. At the same time, those who deal with the cities and towns as settlements can profit much from some of the dimensions introduced by those who stress "who is interacting with whom?" However, one cannot use the local and non-local definitions of community simultaneously.

DILEMMA 2: STATUTORY VERSUS NATURAL COMMUNITY

If we assume for purposes of discussion the decision to include *locality* in the definition of a community, we then face the dilemma of deciding what kind of locality to study. Although the preceding section brought out some of the major differences between the statutory and natural communities, Table 6–2 listed below calls attention to additional factors to be considered in a resolution of the dilemma.

Some of the advantages and disadvantages of each type may be noted.

Boundaries

The boundaries of the statutory community are already determined; those of the natural community must be delineated.

TABLE 6–2

Statutory Versus Natural Community Dilemma

Issues	Statutory Community (local politcal unit)	Natural Community (local settlement)
1. Boundaries	Already determined	To be delineated
2. Decision-making	Through local government	Coping through coalitions
3. Subunits	Political districts (wards) and/or neighborhoods	Neighborhoods
4. Utility or application	Large-scale statistical comparisons (Much data available) plus problem-solving in terms of political unit	Problem-solving for a particular community; use of several cases for deriving and testing propositions

Obviously, in studying the natural community the researcher has to be concerned with the outer reaches of the unit. There are various ways; interviewing a sample of people who live beyond the built-up area to find out what they consider their community to be; having local merchants, bankers, service people indicate the distance from which people come to use their stores and services; checking the membership lists of organizations and churches, or subscriptions to the local newspaper to get some index of the extent of the natural community. Suffice it to say, that there is a long tradition of determining the boundaries of a natural community, though this becomes more difficult with the increased mobility of local residents. Just as we think of the statutory community as a political unit, while recognizing that it is much more than that, so we think of the natural community as basically an economic and service-centered unit, while recognizing that local government—even on a partial scale—has to be taken into account.

Decision-making

A major consideration in selection of a statutory community is its ability to act; through local government it can make decisions about a wide variety of local concerns. This is why the statutory community has been the subject of so many studies of decision-making and why political scientists as well as sociologists use the statutory community in what they term "community studies."

In a natural community no *official* decisions affecting the whole settlement may be taken, but often decisions are made which—though not official—are generally accepted. Such decisions may go through specific community-wide organizations, or representatives of organizations. When problems arise, a coalition of interested persons and groups come together and they cope with the problems. It may not be the same kind of decision as that made by a city council or a county board of commissioners, but it does deal for the time being with the situation. Frequently, some controversy in a natural community, since there is no overall governmental body to resolve the matter, goes to the proper court for adjudication as a lawsuit.

The natural community is thus not based on residence within a political unit (the statutory community) but may include people who are parts of two statutory communities (the city and the county, for example). A city may be part of the territory of a county, for instance, but it has jurisdiction over its specified area to the exclusion of county interference, while the county government serves all those not within the city limits.

Yet, study after study has confirmed that those who live in the city and those who live outside the city all consider themselves the members of the community represented by the settlement. In fact, many of the leading personalities of the institutions and groups operating within the city may actually reside outside the city but contribute their time and money to projects affecting the whole natural community. It is often true that local residents do not know where the city limits are.

Subunits

Both the statutory and natural communities may have subunits which can prove useful both in terms of analysis and in terms of local action. First, there are the political subunits whose voting records and other behavior can be studied. Political parties may be organized around these official subunits (wards, districts, etc.) Second, both kinds of communities also are likely to have neighborhoods which do not follow lines of the political subunits, although there is at times some correspondence. These are natural neighborhoods which change perceptibly over time as types of residents change and as major developments take place in the settlement as a whole.

Since these two types of subunits (political and natural neighborhoods) are found in each community (statutory and natural) they do not constitute a very useful criterion in making a choice between the two. The political subunits taken together add up to form the statutory community, which makes the analysis neater and perhaps more conclusive in the discussion of political issues. On the other hand, units of social action—which increasingly come into play in large-scale efforts to deal with local problems—do not usually follow precinct or ward lines. They embrace localities which have a tradition of sorts and which are recognized by residents and others as a distinct sub-locality; they may include formal associations designed to promote the interests of those in the neighborhood (Suttles, 1972). Such neighborhood initiative has meaning for the sociologist whether he uses the statutory or natural community specification.

Utility or Application

One attractive feature of the political unit (statutory community) is the rich accumulation of data collected by the U. S. Census Bureau as well as by other agencies. This holds true both for cities and counties. If the natural community has sufficient population size it may be part of a Standard Metropolitan Statistical Area. Once its boundaries have been determined by whatever means are chosen, the area enclosed can then be described in terms of census tracts. Unfortunately, many of the smaller natural communities cannot be served in this way.

Mention has already been made of the utility of a particular community type for local problem-solving. Some problems can be dealt with simply at the city or county level, but many go beyond these to the whole settlement where cooperation across political boundaries is required. The United Way recognizes this social fact in that it transcends political units.

Neither the statutory nor the natural community is necessarily the *right* way to define a community. The same researcher may use one in one study and the second type in another study, all depending upon the purpose. To illustrate, if a single community is intent upon doing something about a range of problems and if the local government boundaries do not coincide with the area of action, then the natural community concept might be best. In such a case, resources can be mobilized from throughout the whole settlement, not just from the city limits. But this is a matter to be decided in each individual case.

DILEMMA 3: COMPREHENSIVE VERSUS SELECTIVE SCOPE OF SOCIAL RELATIONS

An assumption reaffirmed at the beginning of this chapter is that every community of whatever type, in the sociological sense, consists of social relations. Others might question this assumption, but accepting it does involve one in a further dilemma: namely, what is the scope of the social relations. Are they to be contained within the geographical limits set or do they spill beyond the bound-

TABLE 6–3

Comprehensive Versus Selective (Limited) Scope of Social Relations

Types of Social Relations	Actors	Locale
COMPREHENSIVE		
All social behavior (A local society)	A. Residents and non-residents	Within community
	or	
	B. Residents and non-residents plus residents	Within community
SELECTIVE (limited)		
1. Public behavior only (as opposed to private behavior)	A. Residents and non-residents	Within community
	or	
	B. Residents and non-residents plus residents	Within community Without community
2. Intergroup behavior (including formal organizations, temporary coalitions, social action groups)	C. Local and external groups Local groups	Within community Without community

aries of the statutory or natural community? Table 6–3 illustrates some of the possibilities.

It is possible to maintain that all social relations within the community should be considered and, on the contrary, it is also possible to argue in behalf of a selective scope.

Comprehensive Scope

If one considers the local community as a local society, then one could insist that all social behavior which occurs in the community is relevant to the description of community life. For instance, the training that parents give children within the private domain of the home is important to the community in that "good" training produces "desirable" members of the community. Deciding upon this comprehensive scope does not answer all the questions, for one must then decide what actors are to be included and in what situations. A tenable position would be that the scope of social relations in the comprehensive sense would include all social behavior of both residents and non-residents within the defined limits of the community. Others might counter with the suggestion that this is not comprehensive enough, but that in addition to what happens locally the behavior of residents without the community should also be included with the local social relations. The question not posed at this level on the chart is whether the relations among individuals only or that among groups is to constitute the general body of social relations.

Selective Scope

Some of the same kinds of problems arise even though one chooses to be more selective in defining local social relations. If not *all* social behavior is to be included, how is a selection to be made? Is it possible, for instance, to draw up categories of private behavior and public behavior by saying that the behavior connected with certain statuses (father) is non-communal and that connected with other statuses (president of a PTA—though the same father as above) is communal? Is the behavior of an official to be noted while that of the member of the Elks Club in his clubhouse is considered private? And if one can define public behavior, does it refer to what is carried out only within the confines of the local community or does it also refer to such behavior by local residents outside of the community?

One tempting decision is to limit community social relations only to intergroup behavior on the thesis that an individual at the community level acts through groups; therefore, studying these groups is the most effective way of dealing with local social relations. Here, again, to what extent should the activities of local residents outside the community be counted as local social relations?

A further possible basis for selectivity might be described as communal social actions: a campaign for the building of a local hospital, the formulation and operation of a school bussing program; the substitution of modern low-cost governmental housing for the elderly in the place of substandard housing provided by a slum landlord. The illustrations could proliferate.

Here, as elsewhere, the decision as to scope of social relations will depend upon the problem which the community sociologist is investigating. At some point, however, the investigator must face up to the dilemma of the scope to be covered, both as regards the kinds of social relations and the locale in which they are supposed to be carried out.

DILEMMA 4: EXPLICIT VERSUS UNSTATED THEORETICAL FRAMEWORK

This dilemma is not unique with the community sociologist. It holds true for other fields of sociology as well. Should the theoretical framework he made explicit, or be left unstated? Table 6–4 suggests some of the possibilities.

TABLE 6–4

Explicit Versus Unstated Theoretical Framework

	Paradigm Options (Social Relations)
Explicit Framework	1. Social System (Structural-Functions) 2. Conflict-Inequality (Dialectical) 3. Field Theory (Social Action) 4. Others (Exchange, Symbolic Interaction)
Unstated Framework	1. Descriptive, Avowedly non-theoretical. 2. Eclectic. Theory selected according to community phenomena being analyzed.

Recent literature in community sociology highlights the close connection between theoretical orientation and the results of a given community investigation.

Explicit Framework

It is a truism that social relations appear in a different light if viewed from a different theoretical scheme. For example, if one looks at a community *as if* it were a social system (though recognizing that it is really *not* a unitary actor) one will be impressed by the persistence or continuity of the system, will describe its parts or components, and will notice how these relate to each other to maintain the system through functions or operations. The changes observed will be largely adaptive to both internal and external conditions.

If one takes the dialectic paradigm, where the stress is on conflict, inequality, and shortcomings of the community as measured against some ideal, a different set of observations will be stressed. Different data will be collected, social relations will reveal another patterning, and findings about community behavior may contradict those of an investigator looking at the same community from the social system paradigm.

Other theoretical orientations likewise lead to other ways of analyzing the community. A field theory which stresses social actions or illustrations of community problem-solving, may or may not relate to an exchange theory paradigm.

Unstated Framework

Suppose, however, the investigator claims that no particular framework is espoused but that "the facts will speak for themselves." This approach ignores the possibility that some implicit paradigm guides the selection of the facts collected. What may be meant is that the investigator is primarily interested in describing the community in terms of ordinary sociological concepts, hoping to provide a case of usefully organized data so that any community sociologist can use the case in working out whatever theoretical propositions are being tested against actual community studies.

A community study may also be done from an eclectic stance. Without a commitment to a major theoretical position, the researcher may choose to use theories of the middle (or lower) range, selecting them from any sociological perspective to the extent they have explanatory value for the particular community phenomena he is investigating.

Finally, should one select and specify a theoretical scheme, one needs to decide whether this scheme is simply to help select and classify data collected about the community or whether it is to be used to provide definite propositions which are to be proven, dis-̇ proven, or remain unproven. Accepting the first use does not necessarily imply the second.

This dilemma comes increasingly to the fore with the impatience of some community sociologists with the structural-functional (social systems) approach; they claim that it gives few guidelines for changing the status quo in the interest of a disadvantaged group in the community. At the same time, others accuse various community sociologists of trying to initiate change in the community without ever developing a clear idea of *what* it is they seek to change. The debate continues; the dilemma remains.

This dilemma should make us try to understand why community theory is relatively underdeveloped in comparison with theories in other areas such as the family. (Hillery, 1972). There is much new interest in the community but our knowledge of how communities work is still not adequate to the demand being placed upon it. Four reasons have been cited for this lack of cumulative knowledge.[2] First, the tendency to confuse studies of community-related phenomena with analysis of the community. Any study which deals with a single problem of the community such as crime or housing needs usually does not focus on the community itself as the object of study. Its incidental information about the community is therefore not used to test hypotheses about the nature of community life. Second, the perpetuation of competing and noncomplementary approaches to the study of community—such as have just been described above—means that what is learned in one approach, with its different interests and assumptions, cannot be fitted easily into the findings of a different approach. A case in point is the lack of success to date in relating findings from the ecological approach to those obtained in the study of social interaction itself. Third, the emphasis upon viewing each community as a spatially and temporarily unique phenomenon does not lead to the testing of generalizations necessary for the development of useful theory. This is a criticism often leveled at the ethnographic approach. Fourth, the

---

[2] These four points, to which I have added my own explanations, are taken from Gene F. Summers, John P. Clark, and Lauren H. Seller, "The Renewal of Community Sociology," *Rural Sociology*, 35, (June 1970) p. 219.

schism between rural and urban (or nonrural) sociologists persists even though they are both studying communities, admittedly of different size.

It is, of course, not possible nor even desirable that social scientists select a single approach and abandon all others. Those using different approaches, however, may agree to test in their various ways some of the disputed findings about community life and thus lead to a more coherent theory upon which everyone can build more confidently.

DILEMMA 5: SETTING FACTORS AS DESCRIPTIVE VERSUS INTERACTIVE

Somewhere along the line a community sociologist must decide what community-related variables affect the social relation to be described. The theoretical scheme may direct the researcher to some more than to others, but nevertheless a decision has to be made whether the setting factors are to be used simply for description or background or whether they are to be translated into variables which interact with the social relations. Examples, as shown in Table 6–5, would include:

TABLE 6–5

Setting Factors as Descriptive Versus Interactive

Setting Factors	Descriptive	Interactive
Ecosystem	Ecological and economic background	Social relations as influenced by ecosystem variables
Demography	Population numbers, composition and other characteristics	Social relations as influenced by demographic variables
Historic-cultural heritage	Historical events, value systems, belief systems, etc.	Social relations as influenced by cultural variables

Ecosystem

Obviously the patterning of social relations does not occur in a vacuum; it occurs within a given economic arrangement as well as in a habitat which may be hospitable toward human life or full of natural obstacles to be overcome. The given community may be satellite to a larger economic center; factories may be opening up or shutting down; unemployment may be high or low. Should all such facts be described so that the user of the community study can draw his own conclusions, or should an effort be made to demonstrate the effect such properties of the ecosystem have upon social relations?

Demography

Every community consists of a population. Is it sufficient to give the descriptive aspects of the population: numbers and growth, composition, and other characteristics or should demographic variables be related to social relations as one means of explaining community life? Some hold for instance that the greater the population density the less the neighboring which occurs in a given place. What use in a community study is there for such demographic considerations?

Historico-Cultural Heritage

The same kind of dilemma confronts one in the use of the historico-cultural heritage. Is the history of the community simply a conventional introduction which one leaves after Part One, or are there aspects of it (value system, etc.) which need to be applied analytically to the sociology of the community? To what extent, one might ask, do different communities have their own individuality and, if so, how much of this uniqueness is a function of a specific historical series of events as well as of the basic value system of those who originally settled the place and left their imprint?

Other setting factors could be mentioned as well, but these suffice to illustrate the dilemma: once the significant factors have been chosen (probably in keeping with some theoretical framework) how are they to be used? Simply as descriptive, background material from which others can draw their own conclusions or as variables to enrich the understanding of the social interaction occurring in the community? The answer, of course, lies in the kind of community study being done, which in turn is a function of the kind of community sociologist the researcher happens to be.

✻   ✻   ✻

These dilemmas have been presented in the hope of demonstrating the growing divergencies in and increasing richness of the field of community sociology. They also highlight the difficulty of finding any over-arching definition or theory which encompasses all that is being done in the name of the field. The preferential treatment given to some of the alternatives posed in this discussion, has been for the purpose of carrying the analysis along rather than to argue for their superiority. Nor have all of the possible dilemmas been explored here. Enough have been mentioned to alert one to the kinds of issues to be encountered in later chapters.

This discussion should also indicate to anyone interested in understanding the local social scene that there is no simple cookbook-like recipe. Instead, what is needed is a series of informed insights which can then be related to each other to form some glimpse of the whole. At the same time, it is important to realize what is left out of the picture as one opts for a given emphasis. It also reminds us that when our neighbor is speaking of the community he may not be talking about the same area or the same concepts that we prefer to use.

III

THE COMMUNITY AS A PERSISTING SOCIAL SYSTEM

Part III emphasizes ways in which a community persists through time, with one generation succeeding another and maintaining the social institutions and organizations begun by preceding genera-tions. The stress is on continuity, on how consensus is developed and maintained. The selected topics covered in the next five chap-ters deal only partially with the community as a social system. Suffi-cient details will be provided, however, to give one an introduction to the social system perspective.

Some of the essential features of the social system approach to community study can be briefly mentioned here. First, the focus—as clearly indicated above—is on social relationships, interaction, the associational networks through which daily activities are carried out. Since these are the central considerations, other matters such as the ecological, demographic, cultural, personality, and temporal become setting factors, or part of the total environment in which the community as a social system operates.

Second, this approach to community study assumes an interdependence of the social units. Not every unit is linked directly to every other unit, and this relative autonomy of parts has been called "structural free-wheeling." (Hillery, 1968). Yet but there are discernible chains of action and reaction much more extensive than most people would ordinarily assume. Indeed, one of the purposes of this approach is to identify those units which are not functionally part of community life, as well as to trace the interdependencies that do exist. Insight into ways in which the units or *components* are fitted together in the performance of their activities gives us a picture of *community structure*.

In the third place, a system, if it is to exist as a going concern, must fulfill certain conditions that will differ in the case of automobiles, biological organisms, and communities. Certain requirements must be met, and their absence leads to inexorable consequences. Those sets of activities prerequisite to the existence and persistence of a community as a system can be called *operations* and related to the numerous social processes that are found in every community.

Since the subject being analyzed is the local community, the social system approach tries, in the fourth place, to define the boundaries of the community and also relate, to the extent possible, the components and operations of the system to the locality thus identified. In other words, not all behavior in a community (e.g., a family having a cookout in the backyard) is *communal.* Some is *private* and personal, rather than communal, whereas some is also *societal*, rather than communal, such as enlistment of volunteers for the United States Armed Forces, since units of the larger society reach into the community to accomplish their purposes.

A fifth characteristic of the social systems approach is its study of ways in which the community adapts to internal and external forces that modify both the components of the system as well as its operations. Continuity as a system requires continuous adjustments, acceptance of innovations, as well as shifts in structure and in individual attitudes on which community consensus is based. This does not, of course, deny the fact of continuing and, at times, rapid social change, but it does mean that modifications in some sectors of the community do influence other sectors which are related.

7

The Social System
Paradigm

In order to understand a community as a social system a person does not have to bear in mind simultaneously all of the thousands of facts about that community. Rather, he needs a conceptual scheme into which these facts can be fitted. This is somewhat like having a "social map" to consult. While concentrating on the northeastern section of an ordinary map, the investigator is aware that there is a southwest and that there are some intermediate points. Thus on a "social map" of the community anyone examining the area dealing with family-church relationships will at the same time know that this particular topic is also related to education and the economy, as well as to local government. The social map affords this awareness of the existence of the other parts not under immediate examination, but when the scope of the inquiry is broadened, these other areas become involved in an orderly way.

THE COMPONENTS OF THE COMMUNITY

Any system, even one that is moving very fast, has parts. In the case of a social system these parts may really be patterns of interaction (for that is what a group is). In other words, the dynamic aspect may be frozen at one point in time so that an analysis can be

131

made of its structure, or of the relationship of the parts to each other. The comparison is often made with a motion picture film that tells the story only as it moves from one frame to the next. But it is possible to halt the projector and show one particular frame on the screen as long as desired so that some special detail can be studied. Social scientists have to catch "society on the run," since people never stop interacting, but they can trace the patterns of behavior and separate out a particular cluster of these behavior patterns for further study. It is in this sense that one can talk of components of a social system.

Since these components are analytical concepts, or a part of the social world set aside for study, it is possible to select those that deal with a relatively few people or those that deal with many, depending upon the kind of problems one wishes to study. The accompanying Figure 7–1 shows their range in size, moving from the single person through successively larger units to the total community. One could, of course, relate the community to a region and a whole society by continuing this figure into more comprehensive components. The figure should be carefully studied before moving on to the discussion of each of the components. Note that the basic unit of analysis for the study of a community is the subsystem (combined into major systems) and that the behavior of a community as a total system is greatly dependent upon the interaction among these subsystems. These subsystems are in turn made up of widespread networks of groups, which give expression to the kinds of activities associated with each subsystem; the groups are for their part made up of social relationships. The component called a "grouping" is introduced because it refers to certain categories of people, or publics, found in any community. Although these are not related to each other by bonds of interaction, they nevertheless constitute a component of importance for the community as a whole, as later discussion will show. A few more words about each component may further clarify Figure 7–1.

THE PERSON

The person, or the socialized individual, as pointed out in Chapter 5, is a social product. He also becomes a partner in teaching what he has learned to those about him, particularly the younger

Community System (Reference is made to communal properties of these major systems)

Economy ⟷ Religion
Government
Family ⟷ Education

Major System (Institutionalized unit meeting basic human needs)	Family	Economy	Government	Religion	Education and Public Information
Subsystem (Widespread social network)		Transportation, Banking, Industry, Commerce, Agriculture, Medicine, Organized labor	Political Party Officialdom	Various religious bodies	School Press Radio and TV
Social Grouping (Categories of people with common characteristics)	Parents with preschool children	Cotton-growing farmers, Homeowners	Aliens	Churchgoers	University graduates
Social Group (3 or more people in social contact)	The household	A hospital staff, A construction crew, Members of a law firm	Local League of Women Voters	Ministerial association	Members of adult education course
Social Relationships (2 people or units in social contact)	Parent-child	Merchant-consumer	Official-citizen	Clergyman-member	Teacher-pupil
The Person (as a type)	Parent	Consumer	Citizen	Member or adherent	Teacher

Figure 7–1. Components of a community system, with examples. (Major community systems of health, welfare, and recreation do not appear above, although some are discussed extensively in separate chapters.)

people whom he may be trying to influence in definite directions that he considers proper. Whether his psychological mechanism is more similar to a gyroscope (as in the case of the inner-directed person) or a radar (as with the other-directed person), he is nevertheless able and ready to interact with other people in ways he considers expected and appropriate (Riesman, Glazer, and Denney, 1953). As Figure 7–1 shows, the person occupies many different statuses (parent, consumer, citizen, church member, teacher, etc.) within a community.

THE SOCIAL RELATIONSHIP

The generalized social relationship, such as that between any parent and child, merchant and consumer, official and citizen, clergyman and church member, or teacher and pupil, frequently provides a convenient way of looking at some of the crucial characteristics of groups or even subsystems. It is a fair question to ask, "In this community, what is the relationship between the worker and management?" The person will understand the meaning of the question and may try to generalize in one of several ways. If labor is unorganized in the community and each worker seeks to establish a personal connection between himself and his employer, then this worker-manager relationship will be described in such terms; if labor is highly organized, militant, and powerful, then this particular relationship will be described in different terms. Or, if the picture is spotty, with some firms unionized and others not, then a third variation appears. This illustrates in quite simple terms how the analysis of any one relationship might give considerable insight into some of the important areas of social life.

The class (or caste) relationships between race or ethnic groups; the generalized relationships between husbands and wives; among Catholics, Protestants, and Jews; between college people and townspeople—all reveal much about a community even though the analysis of each of these is in terms of those occupying two particular statuses. At times the situation varies so much from person to person that generalization about some relationships should be avoided; but even this fact itself has social significance, for it shows the existence of at least deviant behavior patterns and the possibility of variant values.

Although the examples in Figure 7–1 do not indicate this, social relationships can exist among groups or subsystems in as real a sense as they exist among persons. This should be borne in mind as these more inclusive units are fitted into the general scheme of the community system.

THE SOCIAL GROUP

Social groups are also components. Their types are many and their number, even in a medium-sized city, is difficult to calculate, particularly as one thinks of the informal cliques as well as the recognizable formal organizations. Through them things get done or proposals get blocked; in groups people spend their leisure, carry on their jobs, worship, acquire schooling, and become acquainted with those whom later they will marry.

Beyond any question someone who could trace the behavior of all the groups of a community would have an omniscient view of that community, but such a comprehensive view is impossible even with the most ambitious research designs. What is possible, however, is the study of the behavior of various types of groups, with enough samples of each type to enable one to generalize about that type.   For instance, men's service or luncheon clubs or mental health associations fall into general patterns about which a great deal can be said without knowing the specific details of every such group in the community.   One can also determine through a preliminary survey what specific groups in the community have a bearing upon the special research problems under investigation and then study these groups in great detail.

Whatever the approach, if one is intent upon a community study, the groups that are studied must be seen not as entities within themselves but as components of a larger social system. This means that one will stop and ask such questions as, "What would this community lack or what changes would be effected if this particular group (or others like it) were to disappear?" If definite answers can be made to that question, then one is describing "the function" of that group in the community. If family groups were to be abolished, certain consequences would follow; the same would hold true for particular kinds of economic, governmental, religious, and recreational groups upon whom the community members seem to have developed a dependence even though not all of them are participants. Relatively few people serve on the City Council, but without the proper functioning of this Council many community services would suffer and almost everyone in the community would be affected. It thus follows as a matter of definition as well as of fact that if a community is a system (with interrelated parts), the failure of any one significant part to perform as expected impairs the functioning of other parts closely tied in with it and eventually cripples the whole system.

The problem of analysis then turns to the meaning of the term *significant part*, for in a community as in the bodily organism there are parts such as the appendix that have little to do with the operation of the system. They may be fleeting and evanescent or may be so old that they have outlived their usefulness. Albert J. Reiss, Jr. (1954) would consider *as communal* only those forms of interaction that arise within the values that have been locally defined and implemented (put into practice). Therefore, he uses criteria internal to the system, since something is communal only if local people consider it so. Before taking up the subsystem, the next interactional component which follows logically as a step beyond the group in inclusiveness, it would be well to consider a different kind of component—the social grouping.

THE SOCIAL GROUPING

For anyone interested in the study of public opinion in the community or in the planning of political appeals, the *grouping* provides an important component. If the word *group* is reserved for those who are in direct social contact, then some other word such as *grouping* must be found for those who, because they possess certain characteristics in common, fall into the same categories, but who do not interact with each other on a face-to-face basis.

These groupings, many of which are included in the decennial U. S. Census, can be studied through statistical methods. Demographers concern themselves mainly with the groupings based on biological, economic, and some of the social criteria; the economists study some of these as well. Other social scientists, such as sociologists and social psychologists, have an interest not only in these but also in those involving personal achievement and common interests. Where the categories can be studied statistically it is possible to show the association between two or more of these groupings. For example, when the proportion of youth in the population rises, certain statistical correlations appear among such variables as family status, educational attainment, social views, and interests in sports. In other words, these relationships can be "qualified." Such findings have a bearing upon the study of the community as a social system when it can be shown that the behavior of the subsystems and their constituent groups are affected, a matter not too difficult to do when the statistical analysis has been carefully done and the theoretical model used is empirically sound.

THE SUBSYSTEM

Groups, as has been pointed out, for the most part do not exist in isolation any more than does an individual. Most of them come into existence and survive in response to deep-seated human needs to which society has worked out numerous adjustments in the past. New groups arise as the life of the community becomes more specialized, and additional groups develop for the purpose of tying together into some sort of coordinated fashion the new groups of a highly specialized sort. For example, where occupation becomes so specialized that people learn only one narrow pursuit, classes in "do-it-yourself" spring up to impart to shopkeepers, housewives, busdrivers, insurance salesmen, and lawyers the ordinary technical skills that most people had in an earlier era. Coordinating councils of many kinds also become a necessity. These illustrate the fact that groups do become tied together in widespread interrelated social networks that in turn are a part of the age-old institutions that have been satisfying in various ways the familial, economic, religious, educational, and political needs of man. It does not matter that many of these felt needs are acquired (and therefore social) rather than biological; the fact that they exist is sufficient explanation for the presence of these institutionalized networks that we can call a subsystem.

But what are these networks and how does one know what groups are interconnected? As already indicated, the answer must be sought in the needs of the community system, for it is in response to these needs, felt and mediated by community members, of course, that the networks come into existence.

The size of a community has much to do with the number of such networks. For example, in a large city there may be many Baptist churches that for that community constitute a subsystem, or a network of interacting groups. But in a small town there will probably be only one Baptist church and no "Baptist subsystem," although this single church is representative of the subsystem existing in the larger society. Yet, in the small town there will be a family subsystem, a commercial subsystem, an agricultural subsystem, as well as others representing a joining of forces to meet community needs as highlighted by the value orientation of the community members. It is useful, however, to identify these subsystems as they exist in the larger society and then ask if their local counterparts are found within the community, remembering all the while that this analysis of the community as a social system is in terms of a theoretical scheme that will not apply 100 per cent to any given community. But having such a scheme helps one know what components to seek and how to interrelate those that are found.

MAJOR SYSTEMS

The major systems listed on Figure 7–1 are convenient analytical constructs for grouping together the subsystem into functional contexts. For example, it is only common sense to tie together the subsystems of agriculture, the professions, commerce, industry, transportation, banking, etc., into one major system called "the economy." When a person is describing the economy he is talking about the behavior of these subsystems toward each other and toward subsystems outside of the economy. The totality of the interaction of these subsystems, within limits at least, characterizes what might be termed the "economic segment" of the community. But the economy interacts with government, which in turn is made up of its constituent subsystems, and out of such interaction community welfare is influenced. A pointed illustration is the continuing debate as to whether there should be more taxes to provide more public services or lower taxes and decreased services to the citizenry. The tendency of government is to expand its activities, and the tendency of those in charge of economic matters is to resist its expansion and control.

Not all activities that occur within any one of these major systems are communal. Much that goes on within the home, the business office, or on the playing field is serving the private interests of those engaged in the activities there. The community, however, becomes directly involved when, for example, parents neglect their children, or when a husband and a wife seek a divorce. This is another way of saying that the term *communal* must be understood with reference to the value orientation of a given community, since in one place what is considered a public matter is elsewhere considered a private matter.[1]

This brief catalogue of the components of a community system should provide the basis for classifying and describing most of the social units in the community. Such an approach does indicate that in the study of a particular type of unit (such as an industrial plant) it is helpful to see that it too consists of components and is at the same time a part of a larger unit. It is important to remember that some of the components described are *concrete* and can actually be seen: a person, two people in a social relationship, a social group. The rest of these components are *inferred* from the behavior of people and their groups. One cannot at any one place or point of time see an economy, a family system, a religion, but one can see human behavior that demonstrates what we have come to associate with these major systems. This dealing with *analytic* as opposed to *concrete structures* (terms given special meaning by Marion J. Levy (1952)) is common in any scientific research. We cannot see weight but we can see evidences of what weight does and so use it as a concept in everyday life as well as in the most intricate laboratory experiments. Therefore these complex patterns of relationships (subsystems and systems), so intertwined with other patterns that they cannot be separated even theoretically, assist one in finding out what is behind the observable group behavior and make possible not only the analysis of a community but the description of a total society as well (Williams, 1969).

[1] See especially suggestions for measuring "communityness" made by Willis A. Sutton, Jr., and Jiri Kolaja (May, 1960).

THE COMMUNITY IN OPERATION

In addition to asking, "What are the parts?" the student of the community also wants to know how these parts fit together to make the whole system work. One of the best ways to begin to think in dynamic rather than static terms is to list some of the processes that need to be considered in community study. For present purposes the ecological processes and demographic processes can be omitted, but attention should be directed to the following:

Processes descriptive of types of goals in interaction (Chapter 2)

Conflict	Competition
Accommodation	Cooperation
Assimilation	Amalgamation

Processes descriptive of social control (Chapter 9)

Socialization	Persuasion
Suggestion	Coercion

Processes descriptive of social change (Chapter 11)

Regimentation	Industrialization
Mechanization	Commercialization
Urbanization	Secularization

The *processes* listed above are really descriptive terms for a series of observable acts occurring between components of the system. They sum up and classify streams of interaction looked at from various standpoints (goals, change, control) to which one can attach labels. *Operations*, on the other hand, have to do with the behavior of the whole system and describe the behavior within the system that keeps it going as a system. Urbanization, for example, is a process of change that may occur within a large social system, but it is not to be considered a fundamental operation necessary to the survival of such a system. Rather, it is a method of adaptation that goes on within the system when certain conditions are present. *Processes* are useful in various kinds of analyses, but in the working out of an overall conceptual scheme they need to be supplemented by certain fundamental systemic *operations*. Such operations are listed and briefly characterized in Figure 7–2.

Recruitment of New Members

For any system to survive, new components are necessary as replacements for old ones that wear or die out. In a biological

Operations of the Community System	Characteristics of the Operation
Recruitment of new members	Through birth and immigration
Socialization	Preparation of new members for full-scale participation in society
Communication	Face-to-face contact through transportation; flow of ideas on which individual decisions are made and public opinion formed
Differentiation and status allocation	Division of labor and specialization of status-role bundles serving the community; assignment of community members to these statuses
Allocation of goods and services	Production, exchange from outside, distribution, and consumption of necessary material items and nonmaterial services; special systems worked out for distribution of scarce items
Social control	Mechanisms for maintaining regularity and order and for control of deviant behavior on the part of those insufficiently "socialized" or "improperly" motivated
Allocation of prestige	Ranking of community members prestige-wise on the basis of degree to which they embody the major values of the community; differentiation on the basis of social class (horizontally) rather than on occupational, ethnic, and other vertical divisions, though the two are usually interconnected as is this type of allocation with allocation of status, goods and services, and power
Allocation of power	Filling of important leadership positions crucial to the functioning of the community and its subsystems
Social mobility	Movement up or down the social scale from one class position to another. Usually intraclass rather than interclass shift. Important motivational factor in an "open" society which provides opportunity for mobility
Integration through adjustment	The establishment and maintenance of "running equilibrium" between the components, leading to social cohesion and solidarity. Done through internal accommodation and through adjustment to forces inside and outside the system

Figure 7–2. The operations of a community system.

organism, such as the human body, new cells are constantly being formed; or again, anyone owning an automobile two or three years old knows about the need for replacement of parts. These analogies should not be carried too far in their application to a social system such as the community but do at least serve as reminders that a community keeps going only through the recruitment of new members, the most obvious way being through the birth of children.

A second means of recruitment is in-migration of people from other places. Where these newcomers arrive in family groups, there is a replacement of people at all age levels. In general, however, the young adults tend to move to cities in search of work opportunities, which means that an above-average concentration of minor children and elderly people is left in rural communities.

With this replenishment of *persons* there are sufficient members available for the groups that local people consider essential, and these in turn keep the subsystems going.

It is not surprising that community leaders become alarmed when they note a total population decline for their community or watch a heavy out-migration of young people. Although they have never thought about it in social system terms, the community leaders nevertheless recognize the fact that this recruitment of new members and replacement of those leaving or dying are fundamental operations in the survival of the community.

A further problem develops when people who are physically located in a community do not participate in the statuses and roles that are a definite part of that community system. In every community, as Hiller (1941) has pointed out, there are guests, or transients; those in transitional status who are temporary residents but not guests; provisional members who are under the test of acceptance or rejection by fellow residents; and permanent members with recognized statuses and roles in the community. How one moves from one of these stages of acceptance to the next is tied in with the recruitment characteristics of the community. The problem of transforming strangers, once they are recruited, into neighbors and loyal residents is obviously related to the communication patterns and the methods of socialization existing in the total community.

Communication

Again, if we were to use an organic analogy, solely for illustrative purposes, we could say that communication is to the social system what circulation is to the biological organism. In the case of the community, not only do people need to move about physically, but ideas and information need to circulate. These ideas and this information must and do go beyond ordinary news events to include ideas about what is desirable and undesirable for the community.

It is only through such interchange that people can arrive at a consensus or agreement about common action or recognize serious conflicts.

Communication has even more meaning in that a social system survives only as each significant component performs its particular specialty for the total system. In the social world this is not done by a unit isolating itself and following its own interests but by participating as expected in a network of relationships. This implies that the failure of any component to perform as expected disturbs other parts of the network. Studies show that, where such failures in performance occur, the underlying problem often proves to be one of communication or the inability to "read the signals" of interaction correctly. Whenever some committee chairman or some professional leader of a subsystem says, "Oh, but I didn't know we were supposed to do that" (or help out in this way), he is indicating a breakdown in communication.

Community problems therefore arise when various groups keep to themselves without developing a community-wide perspective or fail to realize that much of what they do has a bearing upon what others do. Where there is misunderstanding, it is a rule-of-thumb procedure, long recognized by successful community workers, to get the parties in dispute talking to each other. The mere establishment of communication often tends to clarify issues and lead to better understanding.

Differentiation and Status Allocation

A complex community in today's world needs to do many things that are no longer within the ability or resources of any one or even any small group of individuals. If it is to maintain itself as a properly functioning system, some mechanism must operate in the community to determine what specialties are needed and deserving of reward and then to assign or allocate sufficient members (or groups) to the carrying out of those specialties. In a planned community, such as one run by the leaders of a planned totalitarian society, all of these details are supposedly anticipated in a specific way with formal plans for officials to read and try to follow. In American communities this operation of perpetuating and adding to the wide variety of statuses occurs much more spontaneously, with the result that very few people are aware that such an operation is actually occurring in the community.

There is present in every community, of course, the differentiation of statuses related to differences in age, sex, marital condition (married, unmarried, etc.), kinship, and some occupational specialization. As society grows more complex, the communities, reflecting the larger social changes, become more highly differentiated. Not only is each person called upon to hold a larger number of statuses in his daily routine, but some of these statuses are held by a relatively few people. The result is that any individual member differs from his neighbor according to the varying repertory of statuses-roles held by each. Obviously, this differentiation heightens the difficulty of the communication.

But even though a community in a theoretical sense may boast of having many specialties, its members may feel deprived if some of the more important specialties are not filled. The part of the operation that accompanies differentiation is status allocation, or the assignment of persons (or groups) to the statuses needing to be filled.

One community had no doctor, a status it considered necessary to its remaining a "good community." Its members got together sufficient funds for a health building, provided living quarters for the doctor in this building, and guaranteed a certain amount of practice with the result that it induced a well-trained doctor to come into that community. Here was one example of allocation. Another example is that of elections, when the allocation of people to public posts is carried out in a formal way. Though less spectacular, the informal ways of persuading people to enter different types of work are very important. Intangibles such as prestige, fringe benefits, and the direction of change in the community enter into the decision by individuals—the fundamental mechanism through which this allocation is achieved—to assume a particular position.

Groups develop specialties too. Where there are recognized community needs, available groups are sorted both formally and informally into the part they are to play. This is revealed by the tendency on the part of a community member to think of a particular group whenever he thinks of the Plug Horse Derby, or again to think of the League of Women Voters, for example, when he thinks of good government, or to think of the Shriners and the hospitals they sponsor when he thinks of crippled children. The picture is of course much more complex than this but does involve groups as well as individuals.

Allocation of Goods and Services

Not only do people have to be allocated to the whole array of statuses within a community, but the existing goods and services have to be allocated to the people in terms of the statuses they hold. Since the acquisition of goods and services in American communities is through the medium of the market place (they are paid for in dollars and cents), those who hold the highest paying positions are in the most advantageous location. There are certain minimum essentials that any community member should receive (food, clothing, shelter, education, medical care), although the quality of these essentials will vary with the economic standing of their users.

Aristotle pointed out long ago that the least stable communities were those consisting of very rich and very poor people. If the allocation of material goods in such communities is too one-sided, there are consequent disruptive social effects.

Socialization

Not only must new members be recruited but they must be trained (Becker and Strauss, 1956). In this sense, socialization— can also be termed a basic operation of the system. Needless to say, in times of drastic change the community leaders find it much more difficult both to select the best methods of training and to agree upon goals so that the young people can be made ready for their adult responsibilities. Socialization, as used here, not only includes the inculcation of values and the recognition of what roles are to be played in keeping with given social statuses in specified situations; it also involves a technical efficiency in the carrying out of these roles. A major status each adult is supposed to hold in the community is that of bread-winner (if a man) or housewife (if a married woman), although in modern times many modifications occur. To perform the roles tied in with such traditional statuses the adult male must know some occupation, the housewife must know the mechanics of managing a home. Learning how to do these is a part of the operation of socialization, and a community that fails to teach these economic skills along with a value orientation, etiquette, and the rest is functioning poorly as a system. The situation becomes confused, however, as the woman's liberation movement tries to bring about an overdue redefinition of male and female roles in U. S. society.

Social Control and Allocation of Power

Every individual exercises some control in the social space that he occupies. But the ultimate legitimate control of force is in the hands of those acting in behalf of the governmental institution. In addition, there is often another power structure, largely socioeconomic, which in the case of some communities allocates power to a relatively few individuals who are involved in the most important decisions affecting the community. There is no need to review here the basic points about social control as long as one recognizes that it describes how and to whom power is distributed and the manner in which the power is exercised, particularly with reference to deviant behavior and the introduction of new enterprises or divergent points of view into the community.

Allocation of Prestige

Although this is most commonly tied in with the other kinds of allocation, such need not be the case. For this reason it deserves treatment as a special operation. The status allocation, mentioned as a third operation of the system, refers to all of the numerous statuses in the community, whether they carry any prestige or not. It is based on the fact that many different kinds of things have to be done, and there are certain types of positions whose occupants are supposed to do these things. From the standpoint of community welfare the status of the bus driver is highly significant (as would be readily apparent if he or others did not perform his duties for two or three weeks), but this status has little prestige. Status allocation, therefore, is an operation by which essential positions up and down the line are filled. It is also possible in many communities for a man or woman to be able to buy much more than his or her share of scarce goods and services and yet be lacking in prestige, since in those communities the possession of wealth has only a coordinate position with family background, certain personality traits, and service to the community. On the other hand, in some communities "money talks the loudest," and prestige accrues to those who have the most wealth. In the case of another kind of allocation, the possession of power is not in itself an assurance of prestige, for the community members make a distinction between the kinds of power (economic, political, social, etc.) and ascribe prestige to a considerable extent on the way power is exercised.

The social layers, or class system, of a community are correlated with allocation of prestige (Simpson, 1956). This system is based on a number of interconnected factors that vary in importance from community to community. Nevertheless, the sorting out of people into social ranks is an operation that continues quietly but effectively.

Having prestige carries with it certain responsibility toward the community. In a community with an aristocratic tradition, the elite may develop a sense of *noblesse oblige* and think it their duty as upper class people to render service to the less fortunate, although such an approach to the problem in a democratic society is apt to be misunderstood. But the leader who enjoys the esteem of others in the community usually realizes that he does exert influence and therefore must be responsible; he also knows that to continue to hold this esteem he must play the roles expected of one in his position. This is why he goes through a round of activities that serve the community, even though as an individual he might prefer to spend time in quite different ways.

Social Mobility

Another community operation describes the movement of people from one stratum to another. Since it involves changes related to social class, it is frequently a combination of the various types of allocation mentioned. For example, the leaders of the community know that they will not hold their positions indefinitely; thus many of them try to select protégés who can carry on when the original leaders have retired. This movement within the community class system means that qualified persons from lower rungs can by demonstration of ability and interest rise to higher rungs. At the same time, some people in favored positions may fail to measure up and therefore suffer a mobility downward, since members of the community do not rank them as highly as formerly. Just as a community needs a circulation of ideas (referred to as communication), so it needs a circulation of ability, which is often reflected in the rise of those who are qualified for higher position.

Communities vary in the avenues through which people can rise, but such channels must exist if the community is to survive for long as a social system. This is why sociologists frequently study the origins of the present leaders of any community; they want to trace the extent of social mobility and learn how upward mobility is achieved.

Integration

What holds a community together as a system? There is no simple answer that can be described in mechanical or mathematical terms. People, because they live in proximity and share a common past, share the accumulation of that past—their culture. To the extent that they agree about the importance of certain traits in this culture—values, norms, etc.—they have a consensus or agreement that makes community members tend to define the same social situations similarly and behave accordingly; they discourage those who would do things differently unless it becomes evident that the innovation has certain demonstrated superiority over traditional ways. But community members also live in a common geographical setting, which means that they must organize, even if in rudimentary fashion, to overcome space, to use whatever local resources they know how to use, and to develop a division of labor that enables individuals to specialize along lines that they can do best or in which they are most interested. The more individuals specialize, the more interdependent they become and the greater the need for functional integration, as a strike of transportation workers, for example, quickly demonstrates. This means that in addition to a common heritage (culture) there are common needs to be met in the present. But the culture and the personal experience of living members indicate ways in which these needs may or may not be met. To the extent that community members feel involved in the conduct of what is considered essential to the community—to that extent they develop a feeling of social solidarity, of being integrated into the community. There is thus a tendency to stick together, to act corporately and not as hundreds of isolated, disorganized individuals. Some term this "social cohesion," which is only another way of speaking about integration.

In summary, when we speak of integration as an operation of the system, we are using it as a label to describe all of those tendencies within the system to give a common orientation (communication and socialization), a sense of participation and identification, and a smoothing out of obstacles to the performance by each interdependent component of the contributions (functions) that it is expected to make to the system.

There is no way to summarize the various operations that have been mentioned, for they do not move progressively from small to more inclusive concepts. Rather, they are ways of describing the kind of behavior that must occur if the community is to continue to exist as a system. All operations are obviously related to each other; recruitment of new members is related to socialization; communication, to integration; one type of allocation to the other types; and social mobility to allocation of prestige, to mention only some of the connections.

The components, whether persons, groups, or subsystems, are the units that are involved in these operations. Some operations refer more specifically to some units than others. To illustrate, socialization is carried out through the family, play group, school, and church; allocation of scarce goods and services through the economy, with the family and the class system also being involved. In other words, to begin to delineate all of the possible interrelationships would prove a tremendous task; yet, one by one, each of these must be individually investigated if scientific knowledge about the community as a system is to be accumulated. The purpose of this chapter, however, has been to show the kind of conceptual scheme in terms of which such testing can be carried out.

THE COMMUNITY AS A CHANGING SYSTEM

Somehow or other the community must manage to maintain, at least in all crucial areas, some balance between too little and too much change. There will never be any constant equilibrium, but for fairly long periods there may be what is called "a running equilibrium," connoting that there are many shifts of position, as among runners in a mile relay, but they all stay on the track. Disequilibrium would be present if some of the runners tried to take a short cut to the finish line without following the set course, or if some started running the wrong way. Some conflict theorists take exception to any model of the community which relies upon an equilibrium concept. Their ideas will be covered in Chapter 11 along with the implications of such views for the social system model of community analysis.

Since a community is by definition and by fact a part of the larger society, it is invariably influenced by what happens outside its boundaries. Even if its leaders wished, they could not shut out the outside world. For a while they might condition their members not to pay very much attention to these influences, but minorities of this sort fight a losing battle through time. Any thoroughgoing study of the community should include therefore an analysis of the impacts of the larger society upon the community, the points of receptivity in the system, and the means by which the influences from outside are communicated and translated into changed behavior.

It is often assumed that to think of a community as a social system is to put it into a static, unchanging theoretical straitjacket, which does not allow for a satisfactory description of change. True enough, an effort is frequently made to describe the system at a given point in time and to connect the important components with each other so as to clarify the function that each performs; but the term "system" also implies operation or movement. Some mechanical systems may be considered "closed" in that their parts do not adjust or change, but even in them wear and tear produces some accommodation. In the case of biological organisms, however, adjustment or change is an accepted fact of life. So it is with social systems.

Thus, integration is not an effort to bring back into unison what was joined together before some event occurred but rather an operation through which components of the system accommodate to each other as new circumstances arise and as pressures from outside (via the setting) impinge upon the working of the system. To put it in other terms, social change occurs when social units face problems and have to do something about these problems. From the standpoint of the system, integration occurs when these units make decisions having a favorable rather than an unfavorable effect upon the capability of other components to react to the problems that they face. There exists, therefore, this constant internal accommodation or adjustment, which is the essence of social change and is also the key feature of integration as a systemic operation.

THE VILL

An important contribution to our understanding of the community as a social system is that of George A. Hillery, Jr. (1968). He starts out with the assumption that a folk village is a community and would so qualify under almost any definition that might be used. He noted the characteristics of such village life by analyzing descriptions of ten villages in various parts of the world. He then did the same for five cities. He then used a term—the vill—to refer to a more general model than either the folk village or the city. To this neutral term he could ascribe the common elements found in varying degrees in these two extreme types of recognizably different settlements.

What, then, are the foci around which the vill as a system is integrated? They are space, cooperation, and family. In fact, he defines the vill as a localized system integrated by means of families and cooperation. He uses the term "system" advisedly to denote some integration in the vill, in which members interact more with each other than with outsiders. The vill is located in only one place; if moved it would lose its identity. Furthermore, most people are attached to the vill in part because they are members of a family. The family emphasis may be greater in the folk village than in the city where contractual relations are more frequent, but even in the city the family is a major component. This means that cooperation in the vill can take two forms: one is mutual aid, more commonly found in folk villages where families exchange labor, and the contractual arrangements just mentioned above.

In his sophisticated treatment Hillery indicates the interrelationships among the locality, familial, and cooperative foci. He also points out that a social system such as the vill is held together by interaction which is based on symbolic behavior and slightly differing interpretations of the actors. It is this lack of completely uniform interpretation of symbols that keeps a community from being mechanistic and automatically repetitive, allowing for creativity and some "slippage," which he calls "structural free-wheeling."

THE LOCAL COMMUNITY AND THE LARGER SOCIETY

A local community (such as Butte, Montana) and American society can both be viewed as social systems. More than that, most of the concepts used in analyzing and describing the community will be useful in describing the national society, which also has a setting, components, and operations. Although it is easy *in fact* to distinguish between a community and the larger society, it is not so easy to show their differences in social system terms. Looked at from an individual standpoint, when is one acting as an American and when as a member of one's hometown community? And when is one acting as neither?

There are two ways of attempting to resolve this problem: One is to maintain that the differences between a community and a society as social systems are differences of degree; the other approach argues that there are significant differences in kind, or attributes found in one system but not in the other. The ethnographic approach, described in Chapter 2, views the community as the smallest locality unit in which the characteristics of the total society are found. So the application of this approach to a particular community revolves around the degree to which this locality actually manifests the salient traits of the larger society.

This emphasis upon difference in degree can be very useful and productive in research findings. By taking any relevant characteristics, one can not only demonstrate the extent to which they are more closely identified with the community than with the larger society, but also just as importantly show how communities vary with respect to a specific characteristic. For instance, the local community value system may coincide with or depart in certain respects from the national value system—a matter of degree; and communities themselves may differ to the extent that they incorporate the national values. Explaining such differences may lead to useful community typologies. Albert J. Reiss, Jr., (1959) has shown that stratification, which certainly exists in the larger society as well as in the local community, can be given specific community properties that can serve as the bases for intercommunity comparisons. Thus, one may correctly conclude that many, if not most, of the characteristics of social systems will be relevant both for the community and the society. Each characteristic may be placed upon a continuum, at one end of which is its manifestation in the simplest social unit and at the other end is located its manifestation for the most complex social unit—namely, the society. Just where the community as a social unit will fall upon the continuum of this characteristic is a matter for empirical research and description.[2]

But are there system properties or characteristics that apply only to the community and not to the society? One can cite at least three that relate uniquely to the community as defined in this book. They are (1) locality; (2) institutional concreteness; (3) and mediating social mechanism between individual and society. Obviously, each of these requires fuller explanation.

Locality

We must grant from the start that all social systems have what Charles P. Loomis calls *territoriality*. He observes: "Territoriality determines within limits, how much space each person or group may have, the frequency and intensity of interaction within the group and the probabilities of systemic linkages between groups." [3]

This territoriality that Loomis mentions differs according to the social system under study. A group has a locale in terms of which it operates; a society has a territory, although a member of a society may still be a member even though he goes to live for twenty years in some place distant from that territory. But a community possesses locality, which means much more than territoriality in the ordinary sense. Locality means pinpointing some individual's residence, some activity, some institution in a specific geographic spot that can be comprehended as an area. Furthermore, locality has centrality in the community social system, whereas territoriality is less central in a society, though it can assume importance in time of enemy invasion. Lawrence W. Drabick and Roy C. Buck (1959) have this locality dimension in mind when they write:

> Each individual is inexorably tied to some of the basic institutions of the community in much the same way as each other individual inhabitant. He pays taxes to the governmental unit, is influenced by its decisions, and regulated by its policing structure. He supports the educa-

---

[2] For one of the most detailed examples of this in terms of the Gemeinschaft (Community)-Gesellschaft (Society) Continuum, see Charles P. Loomis, *Social Systems: Essays on Their Persistence and Change.* "The Division of Labor, the Community, and Society," Essay 2 (Princeton, N.J.: D. Van Nostrand Co., Inc., 1960).
[3] *Ibid.*, p. 37.

tional structure and is influenced by its actions and decisions. He is, at least, aware of the religious structure and is probably a part of it. Few individuals will be identically affected by all institutional ties, but each will participate in them to a greater or lesser extent. (p. 110)

This geographical focus, this sense of sharing a common area with its own name and identity, and this permeation of social life by the centrality of locality have been so much discussed by others and are treated so fully in later chapters that they need not be further explained here.

Institutional Concreteness

Anyone well drilled in English grammar remembers the distinction between an abstract and a concrete noun. Religion is an abstract noun, whereas a church (in the sense of a building) is concrete. Therein lies a major difference between the community and the society. The latter must be understood primarily in terms of abstract concepts, whereas in the community people confront the visible manifestations of society's major institutional complexes. A society does not have stores, police stations, water works, picnic grounds, but a community does. State and national authorities may concern themselves with such matters through providing financial support, supervision of activities, such as banks, and even in the construction of highways that go between communities. But most of the facilities that these larger social units provide are located in some community and often become a part of the local institutional arrangements though keeping a strong tie outside the community.

Even when the society does provide services in some tangible form, they are usually provided to municipalities, agencies, or groups and not primarily to individuals. It is in his community that the member of a national society—as an individual—finds expression of the overarching institutions mixed in with those that are local in origin. Nor does the individual have any way to participate in the deliberations of Congress should he happen to be in Washington, D. C. Instead, he helps elect people from his locality (or its vicinity) to go to the House of Representatives and from his state to go to the Senate. In essence then, the community gives visible, physical, concrete, local expression to its members of the abstract institutional systems that make up the larger society.

Mediating Social Mechanism Between the Individual and Society

The third unique feature of the community as a social system is the function it performs, through the use of institutional services provided locally, *to relate the individual to the larger society, helping to satisfy the needs of each.* Thus to think of the community as a service center simply in terms of providing needed supplies—medical and welfare assistance, etc.—to local residents is to tell but half of the story; in addition, the community is simultaneously servicing the larger society in its systemic needs. The nurturant function of preparing the youngster for his proper adult roles makes community life run more smoothly, but it is also indispensable for the continuation of a society.

This articulation between the individual and societal needs is thus preeminently a community responsibility. To satisfy requirements of both parties thus related, the community must more and more fit itself for the task by becoming sufficiently specialized. School systems that were adequate for all social needs thirty years ago now have to be changed to service both the individual and society. So it runs through all aspects of life. Furthermore, a geographical area (such as a village) that was adequate to serve as the mediating mechanism in days when families were relatively self-sufficient in food and clothing is now not large enough. So the community may have to expand to include the market town, especially if the people are growing accustomed to traveling there frequently for the satisfaction of their daily requirements. Frank W. and Ruth C. Young (1962) have studied the problems that Mexican villages have had in their articulation with the larger Mexican society and note three emphases associated with simultaneous internal and external elaboration of social organization: local autonomy, representative external contacts, and interpenetration of the community and national systems. As new balances between individual and societal needs are struck, then the geographical base may also expand. Frequently, the expansion may not demand greater expenditure of time since improved transportation and communication may help the individual resident overcome distance fairly easily.

Roland Warren (1972) defines the community as *"that combination of social units and systems which perform the major social functions having locality relevance.* This is another way of saying that by 'community' we mean the organization of social activities to afford people daily local access to those broad areas of activity which are necessary in day-to-day living." The five social functions that he lists can be considered as those that mediate, at the community level, between individual and societal needs. His five are (1) *production-distribution-consumption,* which deals with the local participation in the process of producing, distributing, and consuming those goods and services that are a part of daily living and access to which is desirable in the immediate locality; (2) *socialization,* a process by which society or one of its constituent units transmits prevailing knowledge, social values, and behavior patterns to its individual members; (3) *social control,* or the process through which a group influences the behavior of its members toward conformity with its norms; (4) providing local access to *social participation* through religious organizations and other formal and informal associations; (5) providing *mutual support* in time of need. Warren then organizes his presentation of the American community around these five locally based functions, thus documenting in many ways how the community serves in what the present writer would call a mediating social mechanism between individual and societal needs.

This preview of the community as a social system is designed, as was pointed out earlier, to give a quick summary of one perspective for which community social interaction can be viewed. There are many unanswered questions in the application of social systems theory to a community which this treatment will not presume to resolve, nor are there many studies of communities where this approach has been thoroughly tested. Without question, however, it does help a person organize what he knows about a single community or many communities so as to bring out interrelationships, thus going beyond the mere collection of facts and their simple tabulation. This approach helps give meaning to those facts because of the context against which they are viewed.

8

The Local Institutional Order

The continuity or persistence of the community as a social system occurs because many of the local activities are institutionalized and because many of the social units of the community are interconnected. The major systems mentioned in the previous chapter and shown in Figure 7–1 are sometimes referred to as social institutions, or time-honored, sociocultural configurations centering around a basic human need. (Etzioni, 1968). We shall first look at the characteristics of these major systems which comprise the local institutional order using the family, religion, and government as examples, and then discuss the linkage of various major systems to each other in the community.

CHARACTERISTICS OF A MAJOR COMMUNITY SYSTEM

Each of the major community systems has at least six important characteristics, the analysis of which gives us an insight into the nature of that system. These can be taken up in turn.

1. *A structure, or network of agencies, organizations, or establishments, which frequently can be viewed as subsystems.* Most groups can be connected with a single major system—the Woman's Missionary Society with the religious system, the Family Service Society with the welfare system, and the Saturday Afternoon Bridge

Club with the recreation system. But there are groups that belong to two or more systems, acting as bridges oftentimes between the two. Examples would be the Parent-Teacher's Association, linking the family and education; the Taxpayers' Association, hopefully linking government and the economy.

But these groups do not exist in isolation; they tend to be clustered around the activities which characterize the system. As we look at the major community systems, we find variations in the extent to which we can view their constituent groups as subsystems. The family, for instance, has the simplest structure in that it consists of individual households which, in most American communities, are not connected into large kinship or tribal units. The situation would be different in many developing countries where definite sections of the town or city might be occupied by people from the same clan or from the same tribe, thus forming identifiable subsystems. Nor is there in American communities any overarching organization trying to coordinate family life, although many church, educational and welfare groups do have family interests very much in the forefront. Thus the family as a major community system in United States communities may be thought of as relatively amorphous in structure, although there is nothing amorphous about the patterns of relationships within any single family or between it and other family units to which it may be related. At the other extreme we find local government relatively cohesive, though it sometimes seems amorphous when scattered actions (or inactions) are considered. Its structure hangs together, partly because it is designed to serve the whole community and so has to have some kind of overall approach to problems; partly because many of its constituent groups are created by legislative acts and have an authority within specified spheres. Much attention is given in the community, as well as by legislators and judges, to the proper jurisdictional boundaries of these governmental subsystems.

In between the amorphous community system (such as the family) and the cohesive community system (such as the government) are the other systems, whose components may not be related in formal, legal ways but whose behavior is affected by that of the other components (the subsystems of the public school and of the parochial school; of public recreation and of private recreation; of private medical practice and of group practice).

In many communities each of these major systems has certain dominant figures who very often are able to keep the relationships among the various subsystems moving fairly smoothly, enabling the structure of the major system to hang together. If the subsystems of a major community system are in deep conflict in a given community, then that system may be losing its systemic character in that it can no longer carry out the operations expected of it and therefore fulfill the community needs that it formerly provided. An example would be a prolonged labor dispute between the subsystems of industry and organized labor, which in turn would affect the whole economy of the community. This leads into the second characteristic of a major community system.

2. *A set of functions, manifest and latent.* If the members of the community are to derive the expected satisfactions from living in that community, then different components of the community must perform in such a way as to provide these satisfactions. One might list the functions of each component; or one might ask a more penetrating question: What other components in the community would be affected if a particular component (the police subsystem, the hospital subsystem) failed to carry out its duties? The answer to this question, if fully provided, would show all of the existing relationships between that component and the rest, which is the approach to the study of function used in the analysis of social systems.

Some of the functions are obvious, easily visible, commonly accepted, and repeated over and over again. These are the *manifest* functions of a system. There are other functions, however, that a component does for the whole system which are not readily seen and may be entirely unnoticed by the individuals most fully involved in the work of that social unit. These are *latent* functions (Merton, 1957). Although personnel in the health system are primarily concerned with the prevention and curing of illness, one of their main latent functions may be that of providing opportunities for people to talk to others, often for a fee, as a reaction against what to them has proved an anonymous social existence in which the community seems disinterested and impersonal.

But identification and description of these functions are not always easy. Part of the problem lies in the many connotations that the term *function* has and part in the shifting importance of various systems in our society.

3. *Ideology or rationale.* This provides justification for the continuation of the system or subsystem. Part of the training of the functionary lies in the rationale of religion, public education, the free enterprise system, and public health. Why does this set of organized activities exist? Why should some major system be tax-supported or allowed to make public appeals to the community? How does it fit into the American way of life? In many communities of the United States today there is a debate, sometimes smouldering, sometimes bursting into flame, among citizens who differ as to the desirability or lack of desirability of certain kinds of subsystems in the community. The labels used, conservative or liberal, American or un-American, and many more, mislead more than they describe. But behind the labels is a very real difference in points of view.

There are critical areas where these differences come into the open. The institutionalized setting for this is the political process: local elections to this or that. But it is not in the race for city councilman, town supervisor, or town selectman, that the divergent philosophies are most in evidence—it is in the bitter struggle for places on the library board or the school board. Those participating in this struggle recognize that this is a contest for men's minds, as it is often put. Some argue that the younger generation needs to be taught what is "right"; others say that it should be given the "right" to explore for itself any inquiries it chooses; some claim that the books provided must reflect a particular point of view; others insist that they should reflect several possible shades of opinion; some believe that a teacher must instruct along lines prescribed by non-educational vigilante groups in the community, while others feel that he must be allowed to teach what he considers proper for the course he is conducting.

Ideologies respond in other ways to the needs of the times. In most communities the justification for education in the past has been limited to the traditional functions of an intellectual sort with an occasional recognition that the high school served a useful purpose in helping youngsters from many ethnic and nationality backgrounds fit into the overall community system. More recently, however, from presidents of the United States to local leaders there have been expressions to the effect that the school system itself must contribute to the realization of fuller civil rights by all members of the community. This newer development—some would say long overdue—

does call for a reformulation of the rationale within education and by community leaders who have not been intimately connected with education.

4. *Norms and standardized procedures.* Not only do the major systems of a society and their counterparts in a community develop an ideology, they also formulate standards of right and wrong for those connected with them. These norms may apply differently to the varied statuses within the leadership hierarchy, but some may apply to everyone. We often think of the rules governing behavior by members of religious bodies, but there are just as rigid rules governing behavior in educational institutions, although they do not deal so precisely with moral questions as would the norms connected with religion. They do indicate what is appropriate and inappropriate and often legal or illegal.

But these complex systems also become bureaucratized in the sense that procedures become standardized. Ritual is a classic example of this, but there are other kinds of procedures that are required of those connected with different units of the major system. There are set ways to get a wedding license, a hunting license, a driver's license, or official permission to add an extra room to one's house. There are standardized ways for conducting athletic events, tournaments, paying the performers through expense allowances or salaries, making reservations at the national parks. Some of these are determined locally, others not. But the local expression of the major system generally subscribes to both the norms and the procedures.

5. *Functionaries.* These are people charged with the responsibility for watching out for the interests of the major system. Many functionary statuses are readily recognized: the clergyman, the school superintendent, the mayor or city manager, the city recreation director, or the secretary of the county medical society. Since the family is structurally amorphous, as was pointed out earlier, it has no functionary to speak in its interests. But outraged, irate housewives, deeply disturbed by some condition affecting their homes or their children, can make their views known in very vivid ways. But they combine their efforts only long enough to work for the correction of a particular situation in one part of the community; they are not spokesmen for the overall family needs of the community.

Many functionaries receive special training for their tasks. Part of the training at a theological seminary is designed to help clergymen represent the interests of organized religion not only before their own congregations but before the community as a whole.[1] The United Way Executives may go through a two-year course in a school of social work with a program designed just for their kind of duties; school superintendents may have advanced degrees in educational administration: Chamber of Commerce executives may attend one of the regional workshops held every summer to help them better understand ways of analyzing the communities in which they work and to carry out effective programs in behalf of the businessmen they represent. Not all of these functionaries view themselves as watchdogs or champions of the major systems that pay their salaries. But if they compromise their position too far by yielding functions of their own system to another, then their constituency will be apt to demand a replacement. Thus, the functionary is in a circumscribed role; he has to act in accord with the role expectations of those who appointed him and whom he is supposed to serve. Some of the most difficult tasks any public-spirited functionary faces are those of (1) recognizing at what points the interest of his system and the interest of the community coincide; (2) knowing how far the interest of his own group can be promoted at the expense of other groups before the damage to other groups becomes disorganizing to the community system; and (3) deciding on what occasions to stand and fight for his own system or subsystem to protect its integrity so that it can continue to perform its functions for the community. For example, how far should clergymen be parties to the extremes of conspicuous consumption, as revealed in expensive burials which some funeral directors now advocate? Very often the competition and conflict one notices between segments of community life are interpreted as rivalry between individuals who are reacting personally to each other; the more subtle and correct view might be that each functionary is the champion of his own segment, each doing what he is paid and trained to do, and each thoroughly convinced that his set of activities is basic to the survival of the community.

6. *Paraphernalia.* These are material resources and artifacts re-

---

[1] Clergymen who hold formal authority from their denomination are most apt to move out ahead of their parishioners in social questions such as civil rights (Wood, 1970). For basic differences between liberal and conservative religious leaders see Johnson (1967).

quired for the operation of the major system. This topic looms large in the cost of equipping hospitals for the demands made by medical man and patient alike; it is raised when the school board has to decide between a new gymnasium or an enlarged school library, or the town council has to decide where to locate an incinerator so as not to antagonize too many of the local residents. The kinds of factory buildings that are constructed, the way the transportation routes move the goods through the town, the kinds of church buildings the community groups finance, and the whole playground system with its costly equipment illustrate how important a characteristic the paraphernalia can be in the operation of a major system.

Some of the problems arise out of the speed of technological advance, which means that some equipment deemed by many as satisfactory are viewed by the specialists as already out-of-date. For example, local institutions (such as local health bodies) that were content with handsorting the data they needed for their programs now say that they cannot get along without access to computers. Some problems arise out of the allocation of funds, always seemingly in scarce supply, among the many demands for physical resources and equipment by community groups, public and private.

There is a tendency in some communities to confuse the pleasing, attractive appearance of the expensive school buildings with the program that goes on inside. Heavy expenses for outside appearance may really be budgetarily starving the inside programs, since there are not enough local funds to support both. But no matter what major community system one has in mind, it must depend in many ways upon the physical plants, whether homes or churches, and the furnishings and equipment inside for carrying out its expected functions.

THE FAMILY SYSTEM

Differences in Family Types

John Sirjamaki (1947) characterizes the American family system as follows:

> *Family:* monogamous marriage; conjugal family with limited kin reckoning; considerable divorce and remarriage; family reduced in size and functions; increased individuation of family members, with approach-

ing husband-wife equality and particular emphasis on children; marriage as a sacrament, but with considerable secularism. (p. 255).

Although such a description accurately describes the overall family system in the United States, marked regional variations still remain. The Spanish-American family in New Mexico differs from the middle-class suburban family of Lake Forest, Illinois, in the authority accorded the father. The rural family of the Appalachian mountains has traits that seem most unusual to long-time residents of Flint, Michigan (Brown, Schwarzweller, and Mangalam, 1963). In a few communities and among some social groupings the home is a place to eat and sleep, but most activities are carried on elsewhere; in most communities though, even where the patriarchal tradition no longer prevails, the home is much more than a boarding-house.

Furthermore, there seem to be differences among the social classes in many family behavior patterns. Two studies, one made in Boston and the other in Chicago, agreed that:

> The lower class is more severe in punishment in toilet training.
> The middle class has higher educational expectations of their children.
> Middle class children are allowed more freedom of movement away from home during the day.[2]

On the other hand, the studies showed that there was no class difference in amount of care given the children by the father and no class difference in display of aggression by children in the home, excluding aggression toward siblings. But there are sufficient indications of family differences within any community to make it extremely dangerous for one to assume that one's own family or that of a close friend can be used as a basis for generalization about the community as a whole. Racial, religious, and occupational factors all play their part, as do such traumatic experiences as divorce, desertion, or death, which lead to "broken homes."

[2] Robert J. Havighurst and Allison Davis, "A Comparison of the Chicago and Harvard Studies of Social Class Differences in Child Rearing," *American Sociological Review* 20 (August, 1955), 441. Also see Melvin L. Kohn, "Social Class and Parent-Child Relationships: An Interpretation," *American Journal of Sociology* 68 (January, 1963), 471–80, for an analysis in terms of parental values rather than child-rearing practices. Also see Howard S. Erlanger "Social Class and Corporal Punishment in Childrearing: A Reassessment," *American Sociological Review* 39 (February 1974), 68–85, who questions the idea that the use of physical punishment by parents is correlated with social class.

Nevertheless, it is fair to say that a visitor to America from some peasant society such as India would be more impressed by the similarities he observed in all American families than by the differences, because he would be comparing what he saw with the family-centered, traditionalistic society in which he had been reared.

Functions of the Family

One writer, Blaine E. Mercer (1956), takes strong issue with those who claim that the American family is *losing* many of its functions. He states:

> Affectionally, it (the family) is more significant than ever in an increasingly industrial society in which an individual can be "lost in a crowd." Economically, family, while not so important as formerly as a production unit, is the basic earning and spending unit. Protectively, it is in the family that concern for individual welfare is still most effectively expressed. Recreationally, we have recently experienced a revitalization of family activities. . . . Educationally, the family is expressing concern for child training through growing membership in P.T.A. and other home-school organizations, through emphasis on the study of child psychology, care in selection of books and recordings; even the recent outcries against unfunny comic books and horror films have come largely from parents and family life organizations. (p. 198).

The functions of the family, as discussed thus far, are stated chiefly in terms of the individual. That is, what does the family do for him? It is necessary also to see how the family participates in the operation of the community as a total social system. One of the most important contributions of the family in this regard is so obvious that it hardly needs to be stated: namely, the biological replacement of the population. But even this function is subject to various pressures. A case in point is Hamtramck, Michigan, an immigrant Polish Catholic community, which had four of the characteristics ordinarily associated with high fertility of its residents: rural origin, foreign birth, low socioeconomic status, and Roman Catholicism. In 1920 its birth rate was much above the average in the United States; by 1950 the two were very similar. What had happened, in spite of the characteristics mentioned, to make the rates there more like the rest of the country? Albert J. Mayer and Sue Marx (1957), who tried to account for the change, suggest that the Poles had as their reference group Americans with a higher standard of living, particularly for the children. They desired to avoid group ridicule, to enjoy this higher standard of living. And they found it increasingly difficult to support a large family at even a subsistence level. Also, they had a decided prejudice against accepting welfare funds. These pressures and incentives were strong enough to make the people prefer small families and resort to birth control. Furthermore, Hamtramck was such a cohesive and close-knit community that once the values related to lower birth rates began to be accepted, the knowledge of birth-control methods could rapidly spread through the community.

Another very important contribution made by the family to the operation of the community as a system is the socialization of the young, which also aids in the socialization of parents, involving them much more in community affairs than would otherwise be the case. Certainly, participation in community affairs seems definitely linked with the presence of children in the home, and particularly younger children, according to evidence from a study of Prince Georges County, Maryland (Rohrer and Schmidt, 1954). The parents themselves go through a socialization process, which gives them a more active community concern, although when the children grow up and move away, interest in organized community effort may hold much less attraction unless such participation is "good for business" or unless prestige-involvement provides sufficient motivation.

In a study of Banbury, England, Margaret Stacey (1960) views the family as being particularly important in two respects: in teaching certain fundamental social and moral attitudes and in its influence upon social status. Yet, she points out that social change is possible only if older assumptions and attitudes are rejected—that is, if family teaching is rejected. The net effect is that of widening the always existing gap between the generations. Frank Furstenberg (1971) questions some of the underlying assumptions about transmission of parental attitudes to children, particularly mobility orientation.

Thus a study of any community would have to take into account not only what the family system is like but also those changes within the systems, such as lowering birth rates, which may affect the future of the community. The family as a major system lacks the several subsystems that the economy possesses, for it lacks the differentiation of statuses found in the economy. As far as family life is concerned, people are distributed into small disconnected but roughly similar units. Such units can be typed by size and composition, but those conforming to a given type, such as three-member families, do not comprise an extended network of social interactions. The only major intermediary network in America between the individual family groups and the total family system (as an institutionalized set of statuses, roles, values, and norms) is the kinship group, which again binds only a relatively few people together and does not cut across most communities in the way that subsystems previously described would do. In a study of an upper-middle-class suburb of a North Central State, Winch and his colleagues (1967) found that Protestants were less familistic than either the Jewish or Catholic groups. In a familistic, peasant society the kinship group would step in to exercise social control when this was necessary, but in most American communities each individual family unit operates independently. When these family units fail to perform their functions effectively, the community becomes acutely aware of juvenile delinquency, truancy, desertion, and a breakdown in consensus about dominant values. It is only as these "problems" become evident that the average citizen realizes that the family system, though working in small units, is actually in its totality a major system in the community.

THE RELIGIOUS SYSTEM

The Church and the Sect

In order to speak with clarity and accuracy about religion and society, sociologists find it necessary to make distinctions among the different kinds of religious bodies. For example, there are such tremendous differences between Jehovah's Witnesses and the Eastern Orthodox Church that each will have a different relationship to its social environment, although as religious organizations they will have some points in common. Each writer in this field is apt to formulate his own system for distinguishing between religious bodies, but the most widely used classification centers around the use of the terms *church* and *sect*. Harold W. Pfautz has found it desirable in his discussion of the development of Christian Science to use a fivefold classification of religious bodies based on degree of secularization, as shown in Figure 8–1.

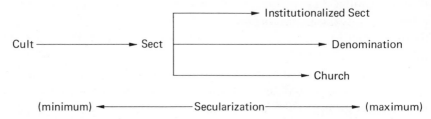

Figure 8–1. Development relationship among types of religious "groups." *Source:* Harold W. Pfautz, "The Sociology of Secularization: Religious Groups," *American Journal of Sociology* 61 (September, 1955), p. 121.

According to Pfautz[3] five distinct frames of reference can be employed in the construction of types: the demographic, ecological, associational (oriented to group organization), structural (social differentiation within the group and type of leadership), and social-psychological. Once a sect has developed, it can become either an institutionalized sect, a church, or a denomination. Figure 8–2 summarizes Pfautz's main points. This figure should prove particularly useful in indicating the main points stressed by sociologists in their study of religion as a social system.

Many studes have shown that new sects are closely connected with socioeconomic status, which has some bearing upon the choice that an individual makes. Benton Johnson (1963) sees the sect as a powerful agent in socializing lower-class groups in the values and usages of our predominantly middle-class society. In his study of Columbus, Ohio, Russell R. Dynes (1955) verified the hypothesis that Churchness (represented by Episcopalians and Presbyterians) is associated with high socioeconomic status and, conversely, that Sectness (Holiness, Pentecostal, Church of God, Church of the Nazarene, and Baptist) is associated with low socioeconomic status.

Religious Subsystems

Each denominational subsystem is replete with its own professional leaders, or functionaries, who differ in their ideas about the extent to which they or their parishioners should become involved in community affairs. Their job as functionaries is not to represent

[3] See his article for reference to those (Troeltsch, Pope, Niebuhr, Yinger) who have been most responsible for the development of this terminology and on whose work he bases his classification.

the community but rather their own denomination and in many cases their own local congregation. The long training that most of them have had in theological seminaries plus the special roles, which in some ways set them apart, makes most of them content to leave community problems to others.

But the subsystem, in addition to the functionaries, has its own set of beliefs—perhaps formulated in creed and worked out as theology—which gives it a distinctiveness from many other though not all religious bodies. Particularly in the case of the newer sects, as well as periodically with the more established ones, a feeling of being different heightens the *esprit de corps*. This difference may be that of a minority group conscious that only as all members stick together will any of them gain; or the sense of difference may be one that grows out of the feeling of being "better" or "more pious" than nonmembers. These beliefs, in addition to embracing creed, also indicate conduct and practice, thereby giving guidance for daily life. To be told that one should not consume pork products, as is the case of some of the small sects in the Protestant tradition, sets the members apart from those people who do eat pork. This is a part of the belief system one embraces in joining that particular group.

The religious subsystem, like other subsystems, is composed of social groups or organizations. In some churches [4] this phase receives such stress that much time is put into many activities that to the outside observer have little connection with traditional religious behavior. But those in charge of such programs visualize the church as a social as well as a spiritual center, pointing out oftentimes that there is little difference between the two. Other church groups try to set up a rigid distinction between the human and social on the one hand and the divine and spiritual on the other. All of these differences have a marked influence on participation in community affairs. If a church satisfies most of their social needs, its members are much less interested in becoming involved in community matters; if a compartmentalization takes place between religion and everyday life, the individual brings to community activity a different orientation (Liu, 1961).

[4] The typology in Figure 8–2 refers to national bodies, where it is possible to distinguish usefully between church and denomination. In the discussion of religion in the local community, the word "church" will be used in the everyday sense and will refer to the local groups of all religious types.

Sociological Perspective

Type of Religious Body	Demographic	Ecological	Associational	Structural	Social-Psychological
Cult (many "store-front churches")	So small that every member is acquainted with others personally Heterogeneous in racial and ethnic composition	Confined to local community and technically segregated because of smallness	Lacks internal differentiation Members interact with one another totally Typically isolated outside the mores Interaction chiefly non-symbolic (Note 1) Recruitment voluntary	Little status differentiation present Leadership is personal, residing more in personal qualities of leader than in social response and definition Rules few but contain a total way of life	A fellowship; affectual motives are primary, solidarity based on psychic dividends
Sect (Dunkers and Amana Society)	Increases in size to point where secondary relationships are necessarily reached Remains heterogeneous	"On the move" Because of its conflict ideology, as well as smallness, it remains ecologically segregated; if it disperses, does not do so at random	Increasing internal associational differentiation Symbolic elements increase because goals (ideology) become clarified In conflict with larger society Recruitment primarily voluntary	Status differentiation has increased Functionaries identified Leadership has become charismatic (Note 2) Norms more specific but continue to cover entire range of social life Prestige low	A following in which affectual and value-rational motives are combined

Institutionalized Sect (Quakers, Mormons, Christian Scientists)	Too large for all members to know each other even impersonally Grows more homogeneous, since recruiting is more selective Rate of growth decreasing	National and even international in distribution Highly segregated	Much internal differentiation; numerous formal groups develop; balance between symbolic and nonsymbolic elements Conflict with larger society institutionalized Has structured forms; legal, ceremonial Traditional membership becomes significant	Formal status more common Leadership is official but not professionalized Directives for conduct highly specific Power has grown with respect to other groups in larger society; "respectable"	Approximates a "community" with a balanced motivational texture among the emotional, the self-interest, the traditional, and value-rational orientations
Church (Roman Catholics)	Large but heterogeneous Grows as larger society grows	Members scattered and not segregated	Highly differentiated; assimilated into larger society Recruitment traditional rather than voluntary	Social structure complex and formal Leadership offical and professionalized Normative system explicit, specific, comprehensive	An institutional locus of control in the larger society Membership conveys prestige

Type of Religious Body	Demographic	Ecological	Associational	Structural	Social-Psychological
Denomination (more important Protestant bodies)	Large but homogeneous — Growth slow, may be static	Segregated	Highly differentiated symbolic elements outweigh nonsymbolic — Relationship to larger society is accommodative — Members belong because parents belonged	More power than institutionalized sect but less than the church, with such power employed for reform — "Respectable" — Behavior as institution relatively rational	Associations rather than communities

Figure 8–2. Types of religious bodies within American Christianity. *Source:* Adapted from Harold W. Pfautz, "The Sociology of Secularization: Religious Groups," *American Journal of Sociology* 61 (September, 1955).

Note 1: "Throughout religion symbolism plays an important part. Symbols are substitutes or representations of some object or situation. They may be verbal or tangible. A commonly recognized religious symbol assists the person to identify himself with his fellows. It promotes a sense of solidarity. . . . For the religious worshiper, the object and its symbol are combined into an indivisible emotional experience that asserts itself whenever the situation calls for contact with the supernatural powers." Kimball Young, *Sociology: A Study of Society and Culture,* 2d ed. (New York: American Book Co., 1949), p. 372.

Note 2: Charismatic Authority: resting on devotion to the specific and exceptional sanctity, heroism or exemplary character of an individual person, and of the normative patterns or order revealed or ordained by him. A. M. Henderson and Talcott Parsons (trans.), Max Weber: *The Theory of Social and Economic Organization* (New York: Oxford University Press, 1947), p. 328.

Along with creeds and ethics go important symbols, which signify to the fully initiated member much that words fail to convey. Symbols, too, can be divisive in the community sense, as in the case of Jewish minorities to whom the Star of David is as meaningful as the Cross is to Christians. At a certain level of communal activity, however, it is possible to work out an accommodation—at high school commencement exercises, for example—where a Catholic priest, a Protestant clergyman, and a Jewish rabbi can all participate without conflict of symbols or at least with a toleration of their use by the rest.

Usually, too, there is some kind of established hierarchy within a given religious subsystem. Great honor is paid to the hierarchy, which consists of those persons most closely associated with the more sacred aspects of the religious body. Quite often, in the case of laymen, the hierarchy does not correspond to social position in the community, since individuals who have been blocked in mobility drives in other ways find genuine satisfaction in devoting most of their energies to working in church groups. This is a common phenomenon in community life that applies to masonic orders, civic and woman's clubs, as well as to religious bodies.

However, these various religious subsystems from time to time find themselves in severe competition and occasionally in conflict. Religion, for example, may be the precipitating cause of some unfortunate incidents in the community when actually other causes may have been more basic. As a matter of fact, most church bodies may be characterized under one of three types. There is the *circumscribed* church whose leaders and most of whose members keep to themselves and have little to do with community problems or other churches. There is the *militant* church that is trying to grow in numbers, power, and prestige at the expense of all other church groups. Far from having a "live and let live" policy, its leaders are out on a mission to persuade the whole community to their way of thinking without calculating the social effects of their militancy. And there is the *cooperative* church that, though strongly believing in the correctness of its message and organization still conceives of itself as being part of a larger system in which churches of different types have different purposes to perform. The minister of such a church usually joins the local ministerial union, participates in community events, and is willing to see the church building used by the Boy Scouts and other groups needing a regular place to meet.

It is necessary to identify and classify the church bodies in this fashion if one is to see the part each plays in the total religious system of the community.

Church attendance, which is only one measure of the importance of religion in the life of a local community, had leveled off by December, 1974, according to a Gallup Poll.[5] The poll showed that the weekly attendance of American adults was being maintained at the 40 per cent level since this was the same figure found in 1971, 1972 and 1973. Between 1958 and 1971, however, attending church or a synagogue had dropped from 49 to 40. Most of this decline was due to the falling attendance among Catholics from 71 per cent in 1964 to 55 per cent in 1974. In contrast the Protestant figures were 38 per cent in 1964 and 37 per cent in 1973. Attendance among Jews at synagogue has also shown little change over the last decade.

LOCAL GOVERNMENT

Regional Differences in Local Government

The study of American community life is complicated not only by the number of administrative units in a given area but by the fact that there are differences from region to region. Luke M. Smith (1949) in an early study of this regional distribution sought to discover what types followed trade and social areas. He found:

> In New England the territory of the State is divided into townships, most of the local government functions being performed by them, although they are grouped into counties as State court, sheriff, and land-recording districts; the boundaries of the townships coincide rather closely with the trade or other social areas; legal separation of the social-trade centers from their rural hinterland is rare . . . the township hall is almost always in the largest, sometimes the only, urban center of the township. The Middle Atlantic States are transitional between New England and the Middle West. (p. 351).

In the Middle West, on the contrary, the townships are the basic units as in New England, but the counties perform more local functions. The townships, having been laid out into areas six miles square, have little correspondence with trade or other social areas

---

[5] As reprinted in *The Boston Globe*, January 13, 1974.

(Hoffer, 1964). Furthermore, the social-trade centers become incorporated, legally separating themselves from the rural areas, to a greater extent than elsewhere in the United States. In the Far West the county assumes nearly all the functions of local government, the townships having been almost entirely abolished.

> In the South, especially in the Southeast, the townships are reduced to justice-of-the-peace districts and the counties are made virtually the sole units of local government; the counties are smaller than they are elsewhere in the United States and coincide more nearly with the trade or other social areas, although not so closely as in the case of the New England townships; the social-trade centers legally separate themselves from their rural hinterlands more frequently than in the Middle West; the county seats are often in the social-trade centers of their counties, although they are more likely to be toward the easily accessible geographical centers . . . than they are likely to be in the largest social-trade centers. (p. 351).

Principal Organs of Local Government (the "Official" Subsystem)

In view of this variety and regional distribution, what, then, are the kinds of groups through which the governmental machinery conducts its business? Some kind of body must exist with powers to act. In every state except Rhode Island there is an elective county board (in Louisiana the parish is equivalent to the county). Most counties have boards consisting of three to five members, often called commissioners, whose duties and powers relate to finance, maintenance of highways, bridges, and other public works, charities and corrections, appointment and supervision of county officers, control of elections, and a large variety of other matters.

Cities, on the other hand, have one of three possible types: the mayor-council type, which still is the most prevalent form; the commission type; and the council-manager type.

In the mayor-council system, the councilors and mayor are elected, with the councilors representing the legislative side and the mayor the executive side of government. The work of the local government is carried out not by the council but by administrative departments, which vary largely in number but will include at least the following six:

> . . . (1) a law department headed by the corporation counsel or city attorney, and charged with giving legal advice to the mayor, council, and

all city departments, prosecuting and defending suits brought by or against the city, drawing up or approving city contracts, and drafting municipal ordinances; (2) a department of finance, commonly including the offices of city treasurer, city comptroller, auditor, and tax assessors or collectors; (3) a department of public safety, including the machinery of fire, police, health, and building administration; (4) a department of public works—usually the largest of all—with subdivisions or bureaus attending to streets, public buildings, parks and playgrounds, sewerage and water systems, and practically all the engineering work of the city; (5) a health department, charged with enforcement of the sanitary code; and (6) a department of education—although in numerous cities the administration of school and library affairs is handled by more or less independent school or library boards, chosen by popular vote or appointed by the mayor.[6]

In some cities the mayor may appoint the department heads, while in others they are popularly elected.

Under the commission plan, instead of a mayor and a council, one finds a small commission, usually of five members, elected on a general ticket. All of the legislative and most of the administrative authority is concentrated in their hands. Each member of the commission usually serves as the head of one of the five departments into which the administrative work is divided.

The third plan, the council-manager system, works through an elected city council or commission whose members have no administrative duties as they would under the commission plan but who turn such work over to a professionally trained city manager (Floro, 1955). He is supposedly a nonpolitical, highly competent, well-paid individual who follows the policies set by the council. He has general administrative charge over the work of the departments.

In the case of the New England town the authority for decision rests with an assembly composed of the town's qualified voters, although in areas of heavy population concentration this assembly is made up of duly elected representatives. It has an elected board of selectmen who serve as an executive committee between the annual town meetings. There is no mayor or chief executive. The townships of the Midwest have either a committee or board of supervisors or trustees, and in some states the township has a well-defined head called the supervisor. But as was noted earlier, in these areas the role of the township is much less important than in New England.

[6] Frederic A. Ogg and P. Orman Ray, *Essentials of American Government* (6th ed.; New York: Appleton-Century-Crafts, Inc.), pp. 669–70.

In addition to these formal organs of local government (county board, city council, board of selectmen, supervisors, or trustees) one finds in many communities other governmental agencies or groups with considerable power. These are such state agencies as the county court, a part of the state judicial machinery; there are state welfare agencies and numerous units of the Federal government administering agricultural and other programs. Thus, not all government in a local community is local government, but it is all part of the resident's experience of government.

The political machine, under a recognized "boss," may, when it exists, be considered part of the official system. Since the 1968 Democratic Party Convention in Chicago, much attention has been focused on Mayor Richard Daley and the role of his organization in the governing of Chicago. As Lowi (1967) has shown, such political machines were eliminated in most cities during a reform period through a combination of populism and stress on efficiency. Populism, viewing the evils of the city as due to bigness, urged decentralization and sought to rid local elections of "politics." Nonpartisan elections were thought to be more desirable than partisan elections. The stress on efficiency calls for centralization and rationalization of government activities and services, which in turn leads to large bureaucracies. These Lowi sees as the New Machines:

> Sociologically, the Old Machine was a combination of rational goals and fraternal loyalty. The cement of the organization was trust and discipline created out of long years of service, probation, and testing, slow promotion through the ranks, and centralized control over the means of reward. Its power in the community was based upon services rendered to the community.
>
> Sociologically, the New Machine is almost exactly the same sort of an organization. But there are also significant differences. The New Machines are more numerous, in any given city. They are functional rather than geographic in their scope. They rely on formal authority rather than upon majority acquiescence. And they probably work with a minimum of graft and corruption . . . The New Machines are machines because they are relatively irresponsible structures of power. That is, each agency shapes important public policies, yet the leadership of each is relatively self-perpetuating and not readily subject to the controls of any higher authority. (pp. 86–87).

Thus the modern city has become well-run but ungoverned, according to students of local government. The bureau chiefs and the career commissioners will often be loyal only to their agency, its work, and related professional norms.

To offset this bureaucratization some mayors attempt to set up "little city halls," so located throughout the city that people with a problem can go nearby, air their grievance, and hopefully find redress. Under the Old Machine, such people would have gone to the ward boss, who would have helped them out if he felt sure of their vote. Lowi points out that under the new bureaucracies cities are well-run in terms of the interests that these large-scale structures serve, but are poorly run as far as interests which lie between them are concerned.

By now the official structure of local government in the community should be somewhat more clarified. If the community extends beyond the corporate boundaries of a town or city, as it usually does, one must include the county as well as the town or city government, identifying each agency connected with either body. To these must be added the district school boards, the state and Federal agencies represented locally, and the connections, if any, between the county or city governments. Since some serve only a part of the community and others the rest of the community, these governmental units may tend to divide rather than unite the people in joint undertakings of mutual benefit.

The "official subsystem" consists, then, of the chief organ (council, etc.) and the departments and agencies connected with it, as well as its connections with other "official" agencies (county, state, Federal, etc.). The interaction within this "official" subsystem can be studied in great detail, including the behavior of the police department toward the fire department, the public works staff, or vice versa. It is important to know how the members for the subsystem are recruited: by merit examination, by the spoils system, or otherwise. Such a study would also trace the flow of power as originally outlined in the charter provided by the state legislature and would try to determine to what extent the locus of power resided in spots other than that legally intended. The study of this subsystem would show whether the city and the county welfare workers shunted clients back and forth between them; how taxes were assessed differently in the county, township, and the city; and a number of other features involving two rival jurisdictions in the same community. Since the school board as well as other elected boards also appertains to this "official subsystem," its role must be fully understood. Here, then, is a network of social relationships consisting of many, many groups marked by hierarchies of status throughout which power is supposed to flow.

The "Party" Subsystem

But setting down the formal structure of government, with its official organs and numerous departments and agencies, is only the beginning of the story of government. There is also a "party" subsystem consisting of local organizations of national political parties through which candidates for office are chosen, campaigns conducted, and rewards redistributed to those who supported the winning ticket. Such rewards may include appointment to official position or the grant of lucrative contracts.

Noel P. Gist and L. A. Halbert (1956) have this to say about such organizations in the city:

> Supplementing the bureaucratic structure of formal government is the party organization, which in a large city, and even in smaller ones, may be complex. At the base of the organizational pyramid is the precinct worker whose responsibility is to get out the vote in his political division. A little higher up the political pyramid is the ward committeeman, usually a precinct executive who has been promoted because of his diligence and success. His duty is to supervise the precinct workers who operate within his political domain. At the apex of the political pyramid is the boss, the generalissimo of the party. . . . The local party organization is, of course, an integral part of a bureaucracy that is national in scope. (p. 374).

More and more, elections to local government are being conducted on a nonpartisan basis, but even then mechanisms must be found for drawing up nonpartisan slates and publicizing these candidates so that the voters can make an intelligent decision.

One study of 198 American cities for the period 1934–1960 indicates that the ethnic impact on voting turnout has declined in cities with partisan slates but not in those with nonpartisan elections. The parties, Democrat and Republican, take ethnicity into account in rounding out their list of candidates for office, but the nonpartisan cities have no local party system to build in ethnic interests. So, when an election is held in nonpartisan cities with large ethnic groups the turnout is greater so that people can support their own ethnic candidates. (Gordon, 1970). A study of social and political participation by blacks in Indianapolis and Detroit provides a consistent finding that, with socio-economic status controlled, participation rates for whites decline while those for blacks increase in every activity investigated in the two cities. (Olsen, 1970).

The "Citizen" Subsystem

In many communities one finds a third governmental subsystem in operation, and it might be termed the "citizen" subsystem. This includes voluntary joint efforts by citizens' groups to improve the quality of governmental services, to increase the honesty of elections, and to call forth a greater sense of civic responsibility on the part of the members of the community (Greer and Orleans, 1962). In one way this might be thought of as a pressure subsystem that arises in response to other pressures brought to bear upon officials to show favoritism, split fees, and divert public funds for the private gain of themselves or others.

The League of Women Voters, a national group with local branches scattered in most major American cities, is a good example of associations dedicated to good government and more intelligent citizen participation. (Tannenbaum, 1961).

The "citizens" subsystem is not so closely knit as the other two subsystems, but when local leaders do mobilize opinion and unite local groups into a network for "good government," the "official" subsystem begins to respond. Should it get to the point of actually selecting and campaigning for candidates the "citizens" subsystem turns into a unit of the "party subsystem." This does not inevitably occur, because many of the citizens' groups realize that their chief contribution comes when they maintain strict political neutrality as far as candidates are concerned and speak out only on the issues involving better government.

Within this network, when it does come into existence, there is likely to be stress and strain, since many groups who support such a move do so for a variety of different reasons. They find that they can unite on this one issue at this particular juncture of time, although they may otherwise constitute rather strange bedfellows (e.g., the Tax Reduction League, local branch of American Association of Social Workers, Ministerial Association, Freethinkers' Society). This explains to a large degree the nature of the instability of such a subsystem and shows why a new beginning has to be made periodically to correct recurring governmental abuses.

There seems to be a stratum of leaders who hold the three sub-systems—official, party, and citizen—in some working relationship. This at least seems true of four middle-sized Wisconsin cities (Alford and Scoble, 1968). A set of formal leaders was identified: (1) mayors, other city officials, aldermen, school superintendents and school board members, (2) political party county chairmen and precinct committeemen, and (3) formal heads of non-governmental organizations. These totaled 380 and were compared in various ways with 1621 nonleaders from the same four cities.

The study shows that the leaders work much harder in organizations and in keeping abreast of what is going on in the community. This holds true for the noncollege leader in comparison with the college-trained nonleader. Leaders such as these, connected as they are with different governmental subsystems, through their interaction relate the official subsystem to the party subsystem, and the citizen subsystem to each of the others. And even if the leaders do not interact personally, their awareness of what others in the community are doing helps guide the measures they take in the groups and subsystem for which they have responsibility.

SYSTEMIC LINKAGES

The major community systems that we have just been describing are linked to each other as well as to systems outside the community.[7] What is the nature of this linkage and what does it tell us about the way the community is put together?

Systemic linkage, according to Charles P. Loomis (1960), who has written most on this topic, is "the process whereby one or more of the elements of at least two social systems is articulated in such a manner that the two systems in some ways, and on some occasions, may be viewed as a single unit." (p. 32.) We shall note in what ways the major community systems and their subsystems become thus articulated, although the terms we use will not correspond in phrasing to those in the more complex model that Loomis uses.[8] There

[7] A full treatment of the local institutional order would have included the economy, education, recreation, health, and welfare. Those included here, however, are sufficient to show the persistence of the community as a social system. See Chapter 19 where various programs related to local institutions are discussed as part of a community action field, with numerous linkages indicated.

[8] The Loomis model is described by its author as "The Processually Articulated Structural Model (PASM)."

are at least five points at which the systems in which we are interested can be so joined as to seem to act as one. (Hassinger, 1961).

Nature of Linkage

1. *Ideological commitment.* The aims and goals of two systems, which are otherwise quite independent, may be so identical that they tend to act as one when a particular situation arises in the community. Groups of the extreme right may be so opposed to certain trends that they discern in American society that they take similar actions to thwart these trends; likewise, groups of the extreme left may be so zealous in battling evils that they perceive in common that they may also behave similarly in trying to correct them, although there is no linkage other than the ideological between the groups. This holds true when one compares local groups of the right or left with national groups of the same persuasion. The pronouncements at one extreme may be so similar in many localities throughout the nation that one assumes a more thoroughgoing linkage than actually is the case. The point is that the sharing of a common ideology means that these groups and larger systems will define the situation alike, and thus, act alike.

The matter of ideological commitment comes to the fore in the school dropout problem. Alvin L. Bertrand (1962) has shown that the functional requirements of family, the local school, and other primary social systems can be dysfunctional to the national educational system.

2. *Personnel.* A common form of linkage is the appointment of one or more people to positions in two different systems. Even though their roles may vary in the two systems—that is, they are supposed to carry out different kinds of tasks—the persons involved do aid in the articulation of the elements of the two systems. The functionaries who champion a particular major system may not often be involved as functionaries in two local systems, but they may very well have positions in systems outside the community that influence them in the direction of giving a local system many of the traits of the national system.[9]

Although functionaries may not serve dual capacities locally, one does find in every community some people who are serving on

[9] For the role of functionaries, see Art Gallaher, Jr., *Plainville Fifteen Years Later* (New York: Columbia University Press, 1961).

two or more boards of directors. A prominent religious layman may be active in an association of businessmen; a woman active in politics and with national ambitions may be serving on the local school board. This kind of linkage is often welcomed, and because it is visible in most cases, it is watched by the community leaders who want to be sure that the linkage is not used to the advantage of one system and the disadvantage of the second.

Then, too, there is common membership of the rank and file in large organizations serving two or more major systems. They may try to avoid role strain by seeing to it that the two organizations react in the same way to some issues before the community. The educational system, through the PTA, may link with recreation, through the Little League of Baseball, with the same sets of parents involved in each. An issue might be the closing of school playing fields to Little League use because the school board does not have enough money to maintain these fields during the summer.

3. *Program.* Important community programs often receive the support of the networks constituting more than one local community system. In fact, the two systems may each officially adopt the same program as its very own and work diligently toward its implementation, conscious that other systems are doing the same. An example could be the beautification of the town in which the economy and local government would both be actively engaged, to say nothing of the women's garden clubs.

Then, too, a local organization not otherwise affiliated with a system outside the community might take over as a major part of its program some line of activity developed outside. There may be lively correspondence and even visitation between the local and extralocal systems about the program, but no other type of linkage is appropriate or carried out.

4. *Finances.* The contribution financially on the part of one system to another may mean that there is a similar allocation of funds within both systems; it may also mean that administrative arrangements governing budgeting, accounting, and personnel policies may result. Although it is often true that "he who pays the piper, calls the tune," the articulation of the administrative procedures may take place without any dictation to program by the donor organization. There are two striking examples of the extracommunity financial linkage in American communities today. One is the contribution by state and local governments to a variety of programs under the

auspices of the educational and governmental systems. The influence of the outside system increases as higher and higher standards of performance are set and as the local community is rated by its rank according to state or national averages. A second example is in the health field, where one finds local fund-raising campaigns, the income from which is sent for the most part outside the community. In the event of some urgent local need, the health authorities may lay claim to the national fund, but relatively little may be retained locally as a reserve. Some health organizations, of course, have very active local programs as a part of the national policy of the outside association. It is true, however, that both within the community and between local and outside systems there is systemic linkage through the use of funds derived either from a common source or given by one system to the other.

5. *Combined linkages.* Perhaps the most common kind of linkage among social systems is not single but multiple articulation. Program, personnel, finances, and ideology—or at least a combination of two of them—are interwoven to the point that the two systems seem to behave in common in these respects. The danger is, however, that if one system penetrates the other on a very large scale, the identity of the second system may be endangered. Where too many features of the systems are merged, the independence of the two as systems is in question. But without some linkage, no major community system could operate effectively in the modern American town or city. And these linkages have to be with other major systems in the same community and with state or national systems outside the community.

Irving A. Spaulding (1959) views many of the changes occurring in rural communities in terms of their reintegration into the larger, urbanized society. This reintegration, he says, is taking place most thoroughly at the present time in the governmental, economic, and educational systems:

> Of these three, the governmental institution is the one in terms of which the agricultural population has the most stable relationship to the national system; by virtue of citizenship and contingent legal rights and obligations, the agricultural population has an institutionalized position in the governmental power structure. . . .
> The economic institution is the one with respect to which the involvement of the people in agriculture with the industrial-commercial gesellschaft integration is not stable. The reintegration which is taking place

necessitates, among other changes, a change in the level of living and the use of goods and services which are available to the agricultural population only through the use of money or credit. . . .

The educational institution is involved in the reintegration since there is increased emphasis on scientific commercial farming, for which technical training is useful. In addition, many people leaving agriculture use education to get the training for employment within the industrial-commercial integration of the social system. (p. 220–21).

To understand the meaning of systemic linkage, however, another dimension must be added, namely, the organizational level at which the articulation occurs. The major system as a whole never acts totally with another system; the linkage is selective. This means that it may be at the level of the individual, or of the social group, or at the network or subsystem level. We need more studies to show us in what respects different levels are used for specified kinds of linkage. Every reader can supply his own illustrations of how some system with which he is acquainted is tied in with other systems at the various levels listed above.

The nature of systemic linkage becomes clearer as we note examples of interconnections among some of the major systems.

The Family and Other Major Systems

No family, particularly if it consists of lively, adventurous youngsters who wander into many parts of the community, can remain aloof from community influences. Even those parents supposedly "set in their ways" are not immune to the nonfamilial forces at play about them. As these new ways become accepted by the parents, they incorporate them into their child-reading practices or into the system of beliefs that they transmit to their children, thereby producing within the community new members whose orientation is different from that of the previous generation (Inkeles, 1955).

What are some of these influences that have a bearing upon family life? One area of close interdependence is that between family and religion. Lee G. Burchinal (1957) has noted that earlier marital prediction studies indicated that success in marriage was associated with "premarital participation in church actvities, a church-sanctioned marriage, being a church member before and during marriage, and attending church regularly." He also observed contradictory findings in some of these studies and therefore set out to check on them. But at the end of his research he concluded that the association between church activities and marital satisfaction generally held true.

But some studies suggest that the contemporary family is declining as a religious force, and they consider this trend as an urban rather than a rural phenomenon, one that affects various religious bodies differently. Although John L. Thomas (1951) made a careful, extensive study of religious training in the Roman Catholic family to find out whether this decline was real or not in that religious body, he was unable to discern any trends that could be stated with confidence. Regional differences as well as rural-urban differences did assume a significance when the religious training of the preschool Roman Catholic child was analyzed. Until more evidence to the contrary is available for other religious groupings as well, it is possible to assume that family life is becoming more secularized in the United States and that parents are increasingly leaving what might be called specific religious training to the Sunday Schools and other types of instruction, such as parochial schools provided by church authorities; but even such trends can experience reversal if parents should decide to play a more active part in these matters.

The effects of transition in national economies upon family life are too well known to need much elaboration. But these seem to differ in different cultures (Tambiah and Ryan, 1957; Willems, 1953). In Japan, according to Irene B. Taeuber (1951), where industrialization and urbanization occurred on a broad scale, the family system rather than the individual worker became the unit that responded to and guided the changes under way.

> The process of economic readjustment . . . was achieved primarily through the reallocation of youth, and that reallocation occurred through the family system. The movements for employment and for marriage that created one of the most rapid urbanizations in the modern world were controlled through a household system whose ancient roots and modern formation were alike components of a feudal social structure. . . . Industry and commerce become added functions of a family whose cohesiveness in the metropolis became in some ways even greater than it had been in the village, and monetary values permeated a culture sizeable portions of whose people worked without wages. (p. 151).

The pre-eminence of the family in the Japanese economy is shown by the fact that it also served as the function of a social security system. Anyone losing his job in the commercial economy could rejoin his original family, secure subsistence, and work in the family enterprise whether it was a farm, small shop, or piecework. Furthermore, women entered the labor market in ways consistent with their family role; that is, they worked within the home or in the family enterprise, not outside it, even though they were gainfully employed. Changes were being fashioned, however, by the migration of young people to industrial centers, and additional changes were introduced by the democratic reforms set up during the American occupation of Japan. These legally abolished the responsibilities and obligations of the household head. Women were given independence of action not known before. In short, individualism was to replace familism, equality to replace feudalism. Western-type social welfare services by the state were to replace those of the family. Whether these imported ideas will win out over the entrenched traditional family system is a contest that social observers are watching with keen interest. It is significant that the Japanese response to industrialization and urbanization was different from that of the Western nations. In Japan the family persisted as the important economic unit; in the West, where individualism developed, the family tended to lose some of its economic functions, especially those having to do with production.

The family and government as major systems interact at many points. Family dependents figure prominently in the fixing of individual income tax rates, since allowable deductions are permitted for each dependent. In the United States child welfare and old-age assistance programs, parts of the Federal social security legislation administered through state agencies reveal the effect of government upon family life. For example, does the existence of such provisions for elderly people mean that grown children feel less responsible for their aged parents? Are they more apt to think that the community, through the mediation of the government, should take care of their parents, comforting themselves with the thought that they need to spend what income they have on their own children? With increasing urbanization the trend toward a lessened sense of responsibility for parents was becoming pronounced even before the old-age assistance provisions were passed as part of the Social Security Act of 1935. At any rate, government has an important influence on such family relationships today.

Government has long been involved in the registration of marriages and in the premarital health tests required by some states, chiefly in the interests of preventing the spread of venereal disease. When divorce is contemplated or carried through, the government too is closely tied in with the fate of the members of the family unit being dissolved, since it determines whether or not the wife receives alimony and what provisions are to be made for the children. Even the services of marriage and family counselors are provided by some units of local government, chiefly the larger cities, where there are Courts of Domestic Relations.

The family, as one of the major community systems, is therefore closely tied in with the other systems, and its changing character must be seen against these interrelationships. Not always, however, does a family system contribute positively to the community as a going concern. Sometimes its behavior is dysfunctional to the system. In their study of a South Italian village, L. W. Moss and S. C. Cappannari (1960) concluded that the cohesive nature of the family, close kinship ties, and godparent-godchild bonds set limits to the social participation of the individual and to any feeling of community responsibility. E. C. Banfield (1958), who studied another South Italian village, has termed this characteristic of stressing the nuclear family as the sole source of individual security as "amoral familism." In such villages it is almost impossible to enlist support for projects that benefit the community generally and not one's own family particularly.

Functional Interdependence of Government and the Economy

In its original form local government existed to maintain law and order, protect property, and perform a limited number of services, such as repairing bridges. But as society has grown more complex and individuals have been less and less able to control many influences affecting their lives, government has been called upon to assume functions that it did not formerly have. Much of this is done under the general welfare clause in the first paragraph of the Constitution of the United States, for there the purposes for establishing the constitution are listed as being "to form a more perfect union, establish justice, insure domestic tranquility, provide for the common defense, *promote the general welfare* [italics added], and secure the blessings of liberty to ourselves and our posterity." This meant that government was no longer primarily interpreted as a protector of "property" but was rather the supporter of what was good for the general public. This latter shift was strengthened by the broadening of the franchise, under which the poor man's vote counted as much as that of the rich man. The shift was certainly accelerated by the breakdown of most of the economy in the depression of the 1930's and the need for government, particularly the national government, to step into the breach.

The connection between local government and the economic life of the community must be seen in historical perspective. Many businessmen hold firmly to the belief that the least government is the best government and believe that the fewer and lower the taxes the more efficient the government. Officials in the governmental hierarchy, on the other hand, often hold that they are "the servants of the people" and that the more they can do "for the people" the better they are carrying out their jobs. In the case of such contrasting points of view some accommodation is usually worked out: The businessman increasingly recognizes a responsibility for those in his community who need some form of help and the government officials admit that businessmen also are part of "the people." But, while many businessmen argue that relief should be given through voluntary, private organizations and not through the government, others argue that only the government is capable of handling the needs of our highly mobile population.

In spite of wide divergence in point of view, it is well to remember that many of the government officials themselves, such as councilmen and school board members, are apt to be active in the economic affairs of the community and that many businessmen have often held contracts with some branch of government. But to indicate the nature of the interaction of these two systems and their dependence upon each other, a few examples might be listed:

> To attract new industry to the community, the Chamber of Commerce may persuade the local governmental council or commission to give such new industry a tax-free status for a specified number of years.
> To erect a new school building, the local government may need to borrow money by selling bonds, which the business community is asked to buy in large amounts.
> To avoid unfair competition through the "cutting of too many corners" in some businesses, such as the food industry, local govern-

ment is asked to make periodic inspection to be sure that all competitors are measuring up to the sanitary code.

To gain an upper hand in a labor dispute, both labor and management seek to use court decisions as a weapon for their cause.

To increase local revenues, businessmen may have to cooperate in the added red tape involved in a sales tax or a payroll deduction for an "occupational tax."

Such illustrations only begin to scratch the surface of the great number of ways in which the government and the economy are mutually self-supportive. These do not preclude the periodic "economy drives in government" by tax leagues nor an effort now and then to elect to the local council a slate of officials who will understand the businessman's problems.

Were one to include what the state government does in the way of public utility commissions or the granting of alcoholic beverage licenses, or what the Federal government does in its program of social security, one would find the ties between the economy and government numerous indeed.

These suggestions about posssible connections between the government and the economy do not begin to exhaust the list of those that might be discovered; they simply indicate some of the types that have community-wide significance.

*　*　*　*

This chapter has only partially answered the question as to why and how communities persist through time as on-going social systems. Later chapters will consider various operations of the system that maintain and bring about adaptive change. It is a good starting point, however, to realize that so many of our daily activities are related to institutionalized complexes or major systems, which in their totality tend to perpetuate a traditional normative system (what is right or wrong, desirable or undesirable, appropriate or inappropriate.)[10] Furthermore, a strain toward consistency of conduct, which seeks to discourage deviance, results from the close interlocking of the major institutions with each other. This systemic linkage can be both a deterrent or a facilitator of social change: a deterrent in the sense that innovation is frequently discouraged, but once

[10] Terry N. Clark has correctly called attention to the existence of non-institutionalized activities which may have much importance for community behavior. See his "Structural-Functionalism, Exchange Theory, and The New Political Economy: Institutionalization as a Theoretical Linkage," *Sociological Inquiry* 42 (1972), 275–298.

accepted in a single major system it can then spread to other systems, or areas of life.

Here, as elsewhere in the discussion of the community as a social system, it is important to recognize that we have been using abstract concepts as shortcut characterizations of actual social life involving community members in everyday behavior. In reality, only the people act and interact. Yet the totality of their actions does take certain patterned forms, which we can label as familial, economic, religious and then discuss as a type of generalized behavior.

9

Recruitment, Socialization, and Social Control

Three operations must occur in any community if it is to persist through time: (1) new members must be recruited so that the population is maintained in sufficient numbers to make community life possible; (2) the new members must be trained to play the proper roles expected of them in the various positions (statuses) they will occupy in the course of their daily affairs; (3) certain types of social control must be brought to bear upon those who deviate too far from standards of conduct.

These three operations can be made specific in terms of a single community—West Roxbury, a part of Boston, Massachusetts, which is facing its share of problems.

THE CASE OF WEST ROXBURY [1]

The 1966 sedan barrels down the construction road into West Roxbury's Billings Field, past a group of workers to a patch of turf at field's edge.

[1] Courtesy of the *Boston Globe:* "Trouble Finds West Roxbury," by *Globe* Urban Team: Anne Kirchheimer, Ken Harnett, and Bob Sales; and Doug Brown and Mike Koetting, September 16, 1973.

192

Then, in low gear with engine racing, the car begins a series of slow circles, tires gouging the earth, dirt and grass flying.

"Hey, I'm responsible for that grass," says the man in charge of the work crew. He begins walking stiffly toward the car, which then heads back in his direction. As the car shoots by, one of the young men in the front seat looks back and makes a vulgar gesture.

"This is how murder happens," the crew chief says.

Occasionally, in white and well-to-do West Roxbury, the kids play destruction as casually as they play touch football, doling out the damage with light hearts and even hands.

Usually, the toll is minor—a fence, a street light, a patch of grass.

It's the kind of damage inflicted in any town, in any neighborhood, the kind people have learned to expect.

West Roxbury, like everywhere else, has learned to live with that kind of vandalism, shrugging it off as a byproduct of youthful high spirits. Usually.

But not always. Sometimes it's a different kind of damage, the kind you might see in a badly neglected public housing project or in the worst sections of a slum neighborhood, the kind that goes beyond pranksterism, the kind that's marked with rage.

"These kids are the new barbarians," says The Rev. Kenneth Murphy, pastor of Holy Name Church. "They have no values at all."

Damage to Holy Name runs in the thousands of dollars and the church is not the only institution in town to feel the pressure.

At the YMCA someone has been kept on the premises around-the-clock, with one exception, in the past two years. The exception was Christmas Eve. Vandals ransacked the place that night.

Now there is a policeman each night at Friendly's Ice Cream parlor on Centre street and steel screens guard the windows of commercial establishments.

It is an unusual merchant who can report that he's had no window damage, no vandalism in the past year.

It's such a nuisance," says Bill Aronson, vice president of a carpet and linoleum store hit by vandals four times in a five-week period.

"I'll tell you how bad it is," said Anthony (Tom) Critsley, another Centre street merchant. "Let's go back to the Memorial Day weekend. In that three-day period, there was $500,000 damage to this community."

Most of the damage was inflicted on the Congregational Church, a West Roxbury landmark that had endured since the first half of the 19th Century.

Arsonists destroyed it.

"Churches are big, formidable, easy targets and the kids know there's nobody in them and they're not wired with alarm systems," said The Rev. Charles Separk, pastor of the ruined church.

"It's just an easy way to say to hell with everything," said the Rev. James Kelly of St. John's Roman Catholic Church. "They can make their point and aren't likely to get caught."

Schools are also prime targets.

Vandals did a $25,000 wrecking job on the Ripley School this summer—an incident that precipitated a short-lived crisis over police response.

A year ago, vandals went on a window smashing spree at the Robert Gould Shaw Junior High School. Now each window at the school wears protective screening.

"This is not an isolated thing. It's universal but it's particularly noticeable here because in West Roxbury we never had it before," said former State Sen. Robert Cawley of West Roxbury.

Despite all the incidents and the concern, most people in West Roxbury appear reluctant to do anything beyond placing blame, which means coming down hard on drug pushers, City Hall, the police department, indifferent parents, television and the young people themselves.

The community has yet to unite on even a definition of the problem, let alone a course of action.

"It's tough to get people off the ground here," said a Centre Street businessman.

The most ambitious attempt—a three-year-old effort to create a Boy's Club—is foundering, despite generous support from foundations and neighborhood bankers. Donations from West Roxbury residents are simply not forthcoming.

"Those involved with kids and youth problems know there's a need for it," said Paul J. Kilgarriff, Boys' Club president.

"Some people will tell you now is not the right time. But there's never going to be a right time. The problem exists right now."

Why now in West Roxbury? Many say it has to do with change, in the city, the region, the world, societal change.

Others say—and the 1970 census tracts do not bear them out—that the community is becoming more blue collar, less white collar and middle class.

Still others say that the entire problem is being blown out of proportion, that only a handful of the community's youths are involved and that the problem could be cleared up overnight if the police and the parents really cracked down.

Few youths will be specific about their grievances—though a frequent target for verbal abuse is black people, so little in evidence in the neighborhood.

Most youths don't pretend to have any answers either. They grumble about the boredom, about the hassles from the police, about the disagreements with the adults in their lives.

"All the attention goes to the politicians and no attention goes to the kids," said a young Vietnam veteran.

"Everything is done here to make the politicians happy. . . . The only thing they have in West Roxbury is churches and supermarkets."

"There's no communication," said a college student home for the summer. "If people talked to each other there would be no problem."

At times, it does appear, communication breakdown or no communication breakdown, that there is no problem.

On the surface, little has changed. The neighborhood appears suburban and serene.

West Roxbury—as most of its people will tell anyone who asks—remains one of Boston's most favored places, a neighborhood where most people would be delighted to raise a family.

It is safe, secure (the crime rates are among the lowest in Boston and comparable to those of a suburban community) and comfortable, perhaps even a stodgy place of green lawns and tall trees and spacious housing that can accommodate a class of upwardly struggling people they used to refer to as the "two toilet Irish."

Now there are not only two but sometimes two and a half baths and two and sometimes three cars in the driveways. There are also air conditioners and wall-to-wall carpets and kitchens with automatic ice cubes.

There are color televisions and swimming pools and a few fur coats.

But the prosperity is flawed. At least 300 West Roxbury families are on welfare and almost 1500 of its 8500 families earn less than $7,000 a year.

Many of those low income families comprise elderly households. Although over 10,000 of West Roxbury's 35,000 people are under 23, nearly as many are over 55.

If a certain conservatism comes with age, then a certain conservatism is built into West Roxbury where the elderly not only reside in large numbers but where they also vote.

They are a constituency to be reckoned with.

As far as young people are concerned, West Roxbury offers organized sports and a wide range of recreational facilities. Certainly, it offers far more than was ever available to the adults when they were growing up.

If there are a handful of malcontents, a few gangs of the alienated smoking marijuana and drinking Southern Comfort with Schlitz chasers, there are hundreds of the others who never get in trouble, who never step out of line.

"There are a lot of good kids here; in fact, the troublemakers are only a minority," said a receptionist in a Centre street shop. "First thing you know, people come to think of this as a bad neighborhood."

West Roxbury remains a neighborhood where property values are strong and prosperity deep (the average family is earning about $13,000 a year). It is a neighborhood where one of every three eligible boys is a Boy Scout or Cub Scout, a neighborhood which supports three Catholic churches, a synagogue and one of Boston's most bustling neighborhood business districts.

But it's also a neighborhood that's locked in myth, including the one that says it's stacked with people with "heavy connections" downtown. West Roxbury isn't that deeply stocked in powerful men.

Mayor White grew up there and still has kin there, but the mayor lives on Beacon Hill. Only one of his commissioners—Police Commissioner Robert diGrazia—makes his home in West Roxbury and only one member of the City Council.

The community is heavy in government workers but many of them are policemen and firemen. Long known as a white collar community, West Roxbury is also heavily blue collar with homes within the price range of a moonlighting factory worker or a working couple.

The occupation mix is real. On one block of prosperous Corey street, for example, clerks, chauffeurs, carpenters and laborers own homes beside doctors, lawyers and social workers.

Some of the blue collar workers were able to move to West Roxbury from Dorchester or South Boston or Mission Hill only because they worked all the overtime that came their way or held two jobs or married a working woman.

In more stable times, they might be able to cut back on the supervision of their children, banking on the school, the church, or some organized youth activity to pick up the slack.

But the school and the church seem to have lost much of their leverage with young people, and some people in West Roxbury believe the community banks too heavily on organized youth activity, particularly sports.

"People are always looking for someone else to do it for them," said Commissioner di Grazia. "That's why there are so many kids playing Little League baseball. It's cheap babysitting."

If few have a definitive answer to what may be going wrong in West Roxbury, most suspect it has something to do with change.

West Roxbury has changed. It is the only neighborhood in Boston to have added population between 1960 and 1970. It has grown bigger (from 28,000 to 35,000) and more urban.

If it remains a place for people from the more densely populated sections of Boston to settle as their income swells, it is no longer a place where one can go and leave the urban problems behind.

More and more people in West Roxbury seem to be discovering that such havens no longer exist within the city or outside its boundaries.

"I sure don't know what the answer is," said Albert Van Wagenen, editor of the weekly newspaper, the West Roxbury Transcript. "But I know the problem isn't limited to West Roxbury. They've got it in Needham, Dedham, Westwood, and you name it.

"There are a lot of people screaming for more police, but I really don't think that's the answer. It has to be something like having the kids learn about respect for people and property.

"But we're all living in a vicious violent society—nobody gives a damn."

There are those who do. Kilgarriff is determined to push ahead with the Boys' Club; Father Murphy is talking about ways of getting his parish more involved; William Holland, the manager of Little City Hall, is looking for ways to strengthen that elusive concept called community.

Ultimately, what West Roxbury is facing is a crisis of values.
"Our whole society is breaking down," says Joseph W. Praught-of
Park street. "It's not just neighborhoods. It's a complete collapse of
morals and standards and it's not just in one city, it's all over.
"You don't give your kids or their problems to the teacher, the police
or the church. You handle them yourself. This is the big problem.
People are asking where's the clergy, where's the teachers, where's the
police. But where the hell are the parents?"

RECRUITMENT

Before taking up the question of vandalism in West Roxbury it
is useful to notice some aspects of the recruitment of new members
in this community. The operation has certainly been successful, as
witness the growth from 28,000 to 35,000 between 1960 and 1970,
an increase accounted for by people who shifted from the more
densely populated sections of Boston in the future hope of leaving
urban problems behind. The recruitment has resulted in an occupational mix, with blue collar workers coming into what was once
thought of as a white collar community. Such a move is financially
possible for the blue collar family if the family head works at two
jobs, known as moonlighting, or both husband and wife work. In
any event, West Roxbury has recruited more than enough newcomers to hold its own in population numbers. As Chapter 4 has
shown, a town may grow in three ways: natural increase through a
surplus of births over deaths, in-migration on a greater scale than
out-migration, or the annexation of surrounding areas that were formerly part of some other locality or political unit. The ability to attract and then to hold people depends on the sense of satisfaction
that living in a given community affords, a point made at the very
beginning of Chapter 2, on the ways of viewing the community.
There we noted that people in Greensboro, North Carolina, were
more satisfied with their community than were those in Durham,
North Carolina. Charles M. Grigg (1965) used the same method in
his study of Brevard County, Florida, which is part of the Cape Ken-
nedy area. The three communities in that county have expanded
greatly through in-migration as workers have come to take the many
new jobs opening up in the area. Community satisfaction is highest
in the community where the influence of the old residents is minimal;
it is lowest in the community where the old residents have managed

to keep a comparatively tight-knit society that the newcomers find difficult to enter.

From the standpoint of the community as an operating unit, recruitment need not be aimed solely at attracting individuals, although this is the net result. Formal efforts may concentrate on attracting a new industry, with the negotiations being conducted with company managements rather than with the rank and file of those who might follow the company into the community. Recruitment also takes a second form of "going out after" an educational institution, a state hospital, a defense installation or another kind of large-scale unit that will bring recognition (and a payroll) to the community. Residential recruitment, a third form, is directed at families whose breadwinners work within a given area but, because of the possibility of driving some distance to work, can live in any one of several adjacent communities, finally settling in the one they think has the most to offer.

The significance of recruitment lies more in replacement than in expansion of the population. Community services require a minimum amount of support if they are to continue; where this support is lacking, they shut down. The closing of churches, business establishments, branch libraries, or neighborhood schools because of insufficient demand may indicate that the recruitment operation has failed, although in some cases it may really mean shifts in ways of rendering the particular service through larger units than heretofore. The shifts may also reflect the preferences of types of people different in tastes from those who used to live in the community, since the recruitment may have brought in a large proportion of a single ethnic or occupational group that was numerically unimportant before.

SOCIALIZATION

West Roxbury provides an interesting illustration of the process of socialization as well as its partial failure. The nature of socialization and how it comes about, as well as its significance for any social system, has already been discussed in Chapters 5 and 7. At this point we might first focus on the need to equip children and young people to play their social roles in keeping with accepted norms and values as essential to the functioning of a community. Then, we can turn to socialization of adults, who might be new arrivals in a community.

The vandalism in West Roxbury is interpreted by many people as more than the byproduct of youthful high spirits. "These kids are the new barbarians. They have no values at all," says a pastor of the Holy Name Church. Obviously, the relatively small number who participate in these acts of destruction do have values, but not the ones that the older generation expects them to have, nor are they values around which a community can be built, (Lerman, 1968). What happened to the socialization process? It is easy enough to place blame: the drug pushers, City Hall, the police department, indifferent parents, television and the young people themselves. The particular form of deviance (vandalism) chosen by these young people, in a fairly well-to-do community hits targets such as churches and schools. Damaging them is "an easy way to say to hell with everything. They can make their point and aren't likely to get caught."

One way to become aware of a community operation is to note its failure. Otherwise, it is taken for granted and people may not understand how it works. What the West Roxbury case should illustrate is that many young people do not engage in vandalism and the fact that even those who do, function in other areas of life (within the family, on the job, in school) in expected ways.

But what about adult socialization? Adults frequently experience some socialization when they move into a new community, particularly if there are marked differences between how things are done in the new community and how they were done in the one from which these people have come.

But there is a tendency for adults to eliminate this socialization or relearning experience as much as possible by selecting those communities where they are apt to feel at home. One resident of a suburban community that attracts upwardly mobile junior executives commented on his observations there as follows:

> These young corporation executives, who expect to be transferred every year or so like army or navy officers, have gotten moving down to a fine point. In fact, they take great pride in so organizing the movers that every piece of furniture is placed just right, all china and silverware are unpacked, the lamps and bric-a-brac are in their proper place by the end of the day. And it is considered a fine accomplishment to have

guests in the very first evening, thus showing that you can entertain without the interruption of a moving experience.

But even more interesting, all of these corporation executives look, dress and talk much alike. New arrivals can attend an affair at the Country Club and seem as much at home as if they been a member for years; the wives fit into women's organizations or else pursue some hobbies that they continue from place to place. They fall into the routine of driving the husband to catch the morning commuting train, deliver the children to their appointments during the day, and then meet the husband upon his return from the city.

It's a standardized existence and it seems that whole communities, like a chain across the country outside the big cities, have been created just to cater to this kind of living.

This social commentary is saying that frequent moves would require too much psychological wear and tear if each move took one into an utterly different kind of community where new social rules had to be learned and observed. To the extent that one can take one's way of life with one from place to place, problems of adjustment are easier. But one should not gloss over too quickly the impact of a move. Young people, especially, find severing of friendships painful. When this has happened two or three times, the formation of intimate, deep associations is much more reluctantly carried out, for fear that a sudden move will bring about a painful interruption. This explains why so much of the association in some communities is at the acquaintanceship rather than the friendship level, and why the conversation one hears reveals very little of the actual thoughts of those involved.

William H. Sewell (1963), in reviewing studies of socialization, correctly points out that we have very few studies of adult socialization. He writes that there is practically no good research on socialization into the marital role, but some good beginnings in studies on socialization of occupational roles. The only other good studies in the field of adult socialization have been on the adjustments of old age and on the adjustments of patients and inmates to hospitals, mental institutions, prisons, and homes for the aged. Obviously, a much neglected area is the study of how adults modify their behavior in moving from one community to another.

Some communities are more proficient than others in indicating just what is expected and not expected. The Welcome Wagon hostess, now advertised as available in 4000 communities represents some local merchants and may be an initial source of some informa-

tion; neighbors may provide more; children may bring back em-
broidered tales of how different the children are in this new community; and the husband's employer may provide helpful leads.
Churches have newcomers' groups, as does the League of Women
Voters. These operate on the assumption that the new residents
have some interest in learning about the community to which they
have been "recruited." But there are many arrivals who avoid much
organizational affiliation, either because it is not customary at their
socioeconomic level or because of personal aversion to too much involvement. From the standpoint of the community at large, they
may behave properly without ever becoming active participants in
community affairs. Their social antennae may bring in enough guiding signals to help them make an adjustment that, while not necessarily the most satisfying to them, interferes little with the activities
of those around them.

Not all in-migrants are easily assimilated into the community, for
some do not respond to the subtle efforts at socialization of neighbors
and work associates. Indeed, they may even take action counter to
the accepted standards. John C. Leggett (1963), in his study of
Detroit blue-collar workers, concludes:

> Contrary to Marx's expectations, uprooted workers are found to express
> a higher level of class consciousness than the prepared, partially because
> the uprooted bring with them fewer skills and experiences that might
> help them to deal effectively with their new environment. Consequently,
> they are readily exploited during part, if not all, of their work lives. This
> exploitation, coupled with insufficient skills, effectively limits their
> chances to obtain secure working-class positions or to move into the
> middle class. Marginal economic position linked to blocked mobility in
> turn creates grievances and sometimes engenders collective protests de-
> manding an alteration of their condition. These protests function so as
> to solidify and strengthen the class consciousness of the uprooted, espe-
> cially those who both derive from rural backgrounds and presently
> belong to labor unions. (p. 692).

SOCIAL DEVIANCE

American communities to function as social systems today must
not only learn to recognize but to deal with social deviance. Several
municipalities, for example, have passed ordinances making it illegal
to discriminate in employment or otherwise against someone who is
admittedly a homosexual. These "gay laws," as they are called, are

designated to recognize and legitimize what has heretofore been considered a deviant, or even a way of life dangerous to the established order. There is also increasing acceptance, in certain urban areas at least, of living arrangements involving both sexes outside of marriage. This is still a form of deviance, but hardly considered the threat to the community that it was a decade ago. Increasingly, the community members are asked to distinguish between those forms of deviance which affect only the individual or individuals who participate and those forms of deviance which obviously endanger many others. A major problem in West Roxbury is that "the community has yet to unite on even a definition of the problem, let alone a course of action." How does one define deviance?

There has been a shift in sociological studies of deviance from an attempt to explain deviance solely in terms of *characteristics* of those defined as deviant. Instead, some writers see social relations (rather than individual characteristics) as key determinants of deviant behavior and deviant situations. Schur (1969) writes:

> The important point emphasized in this approach is simply that identities are always in flux, that statuses may be conferred and withheld, that deviance is to a considerable extent an ascribed status. It reflects "what other people do" as much as what the deviating actor himself does. (p. 312).
>
> . . . the "establishment" of deviance is crucial in promoting social cohesion and serves as a boundary-making device. . . . It is from this standpoint that one appreciates the impossibility of completely eliminating deviance, although certainly it may be possible to develop functional alternatives to some of its forms. (p. 313).
>
> None of the reactions theorists would maintain that the acts we commonly label homicide, stealing, homosexuality, and mental disturbance would never occur if they were not defined as "deviant." Rather, these theorists are insisting that since these behaviors inevitably are defined and reacted to in various specific ways in a given social order, it is meaningless to try to understand the behaviors without taking such definitions and reactions into account . . . What is made of an act socially—indeed, one could say the very "reality"—is crucially dependent on, or constituted of, the diverse social constructions individuals and groups place upon it. (p. 315).

Put another way, some communities seem to produce more "deviance" than others because they have more rigid definitions of what is and what is not acceptable behavior. This is especially true when the social controls of the community weaken and individuals do not fear the sanctions which might be imposed for their deviant acts.

At the same time, while some deviant behavior is permissible, though discouraged, other deviant behavior (murder) is considered such a threat that it is dealt with immediately and seriously.

This, of course, leads into the consideration of how a community reacts to deviance of various sorts. What social controls can its members bring into play?

SOCIAL CONTROL

Any group, to survive for long, must have regularity and order. George C. Homans, (1950) points out that control over persons who threaten to depart from the norms of the group is often exceedingly effective but is not imposed from without. Instead it is implicit in the system of relations in the group. This finding applies to the community whether it is viewed as a group or not. Indeed, the mere fact of moving into a community implies a willingness to conform to its prevailing patterns or accept certain consequences, even though these may be no more than the obvious disapproval of one's immediate neighbors.

The Processes of Social Control

Figure 9–1 shows the major processes of social control. Of course, these four processes occur in every community; however, the more totalitarian the society, the greater the emphasis on the fourth process, coercion. Communities, like whole societies, differ in the emphasis they place on these four processes (Etzioni, 1957).

But why should any control be necessary? Cannot individuals do what they want to do and each man take care of himself? Obviously, they cannot, for the result, as social philosophers through the centuries have pointed out, would be anarchy or at best the rule of only the physically strong. Thus each individual has to sacrifice some of his own individual longings for the security provided when social stability is maintained by various methods of control.

Some individuals do "get out of line" in the views of many people living in a community. They do not conform. They may be eager to flaunt the social conventions and behave in ways considered by others around them as quite improper. They may violate the sex mores, proclaim political ideas that are considered treasonable, or assert religious views thought to be heretical. Many people in the

SOCIALIZATION	SUGGESTION
To so control the social environment that the child while growing up incorporates into his own personality structure as attitudes the values set forth by the community; accepts as "natural" the hierachy of community statuses; and learns as "proper" the officially prescribed norms, or rules, governing the behavior of those occupying the various statuses, together with the reinforcing explanations as to why the social world is as it is.	To set up as copies to be imitated those whose behavior best conforms to the values of the community, indicating the rewards which follow such emulation. To initiate thoughts which will cause community members to think that they have arrived at conclusions on their own.
PERSUASION	**COERCION**
To gain concurrence by appeal both to emotion and reason, using both formal media and informal, face-to-face discussion.	To gain acquiescence to community demands, using nonviolent psychological pressure to induce compliance (threat of punishment) and violent physical force to bring about submission.

Figure 9–1. Types of control (from the standpoint of those exercising control). *Source:* Adapted from Earle Edward Eubank, *The Concepts of Sociology* (Boston: D. C. Heath & Co., 1932), p. 234.

community consider them troublemakers. By the time their behavior has become recognized as "irregular," it is obvious that the processes of socialization and suggestion no longer are effective controls. At this point, persuasion is brought into play. Their relatives or others who supposedly have influence with them are asked "to talk some sense into their heads." This appeal, as the chart indicates, is both to emotion and to reason. They are reminded of the shame they are bringing upon their loved ones and of the ways in which their action is jeopardizing their own future. Appeals may also be made in the name of religion or in the name of justice and fair play. With many people, persuasion is effective. The weight of social pressure of this sort is sufficient to make the individuals agree to conform more fully than in the past. They may still think what they were doing or saying was perfectly right and proper but consent to keep such "dangerous" matters to themselves.

In spite of all of these pressures, however, some individuals cannot be dissuaded from the course they have set for themselves or into which they are drifting. Persuasion, whether by a juvenile-court judge, a clergyman, or a grown son or daughter, seems to be of no avail. (Matza and Sykes, 1961; Reiss and Rhodes, 1961). The community then brings into play the techniques associated with the process of coercion. At first, there may be social ostracism. People whom the deviant counted as friends pass him by; doors that were once open to him are now shut; pastimes he once enjoyed no longer are fun, because of the reaction of those about him. Whatever occupation or profession he is pursuing in the community becomes affected, so he can measure the ostracism in dollars and cents. But added to the effect on himself is the effect such community behavior has on his wife and children, who are made just as much the targets of this nonviolent psychological pressure as he is. He may know that in the larger society there is general approval of what he is doing or of the ideas he is championing (race relations, religious tolerance, citizen responsibility), but the community, with its present structure and set of traditions, finds this deviant irritating and unwelcome. If the deviant is obviously breaking the laws (the criminal code), then violent physical force in the form of the police is brought into play, and the individual may even be restrained against his will behind bars until his case is heard in court and he is freed or given some other punishment, varying from probation to the death sentence—the supreme form of control in the hands of the state (Goode, 1972).

But these processes of social control do not operate mysteriously; they are incorporated in the interaction one can observe on every hand. In other words, it is not necessary to try to keep a weather eye on the whole community all at one time in order to see these processes at work. The neighborhood gossip who relates some choice bit about the young widow down the street is setting herself up as a sort of "community conscience." Sunday-morning sermons may be directed at her kind of bearing false witness and community meddling, but she continues blithely on her course of trying to structure public opinion to her way of thinking, often successfully when the object of her attention is particularly vulnerable and defenseless.

Turning again to the case of West Roxbury, we note that all of the processes of social control shown in Figure 9–1 have been brought into play or at least recognized. First of all, there was the admission that the socializing agencies—particularly the home—were failing in their tasks. There is also the belief that the Boys' Clubs, church groups, and local government can help in the suggestion and persuasion processes. Nevertheless, there are also those who feel the need for more police protection, the coercion process. Underlying the whole community concern is the readiness to admit that no one really seems to know how to deal with the current crisis of values, which is confined not just to West Roxbury but runs through American society.

Yet, most members of the community are sensitive to what others in the community think. Each segment of the community is apt to have particular *reference groups* (Shibutani, 1955) whose approval is most desired and who therefore tend to represent the whole community in the sense that they pattern the behavior, within limits, of those sensitive to them. A businessman will ask another businessman he admires, "What kind of a new car are you going to buy?" and may be influenced accordingly; a woman will ask another woman whose approval she seeks, "Where do you buy your clothes?" and may be seen the next day in that store. The individuals to whom these questions are addressed are important not so much as individuals to the ones putting the questions but rather as symbols of the "type of people" upon whom the questioners want to make the greatest impression. And when these "symbols" speak disapprovingly of certain actions or of certain people, those seeking their approval are quick to note these points and remember them in future social situations. Before returning to reference group behavior, let us first note the importance of informal groups and neighborhoods in the socialization and social control processes.

INFORMAL GROUPS AND THE COMMUNITY

In a simple society represented by the rural villages of Europe and Asia, life goes along chiefly on a face-to-face basis without the help of numerous formally organized groups (associations) to mediate in behalf of the individual. The family, the kin group, the neighborhood, and the play groups are definitely structured in that they possess recognized statuses to be respected or accepted; yet the groups are not set up in the same way and for the purpose that the numerous societies and clubs of a modern American city come into existence. A description of one such community will illustrate the importance of the informal groups.

Informal Groups in Pelpola, Ceylon

Pelpola is an agricultural village of four hundred households situated in the lush lowlands thirty-five miles from the city of Colombo, the capital of Ceylon, a member of the British Commonwealth just south of India. Although the majority of its households depend upon paddy (rice) cultivation as their primary economic activity, the more prosperous ones own small rubber holdings, while the poor supplement agricultural income by labor in the nearby absentee-owned rubber estates. Within the village there are no telephones, although mail service, a school, temples, and retail traders are present. The village boasts four radios. About fifteen newspapers are delivered daily, a number of them to retail shopkeepers.

Most of the people of Pelpola are closely interrelated by blood, are members of the "cultivators' caste," and live in homes set in small highland gardens, seldom more than a quarter of an acre in extent. Given such a setting, what connections does one find between the informal or primary group and the community?

Bryce Ryan (1952) provides some answers to this question. The strongest unit of social life is the patriarchal marital family, whose household is typically both a production and a consumption unit. In addition to the immediate family household, the kinship group is very important. The vast majority of household heads live in physical proximity to their siblings, many of whom are also married householders, although wives are more frequently isolated from their blood kin. As a matter of fact, the multiplicity of daily contacts with kin is so great that its statistical expression would be extremely difficult.

A third type of a primary group that looms in importance is the neighborhood. In the intimate circles of those who chat and gossip together—Pelpola's most frequent form of interhousehold social life— 43 per cent of the household heads specified groups composed exclusively of relatives, while 89 per cent described groups composed exclusively of neighbors, many of whom were also kinsmen. The significance of the neighborhood within village life does not detract from earlier observations as to the importance of kin. Kin tend to be represented within the neighborhood, and in many instances blood and "in-law" relationship is, no doubt, fundamental to the bonds of personal intimacy. The neighborhood appears, however, to be the most critical boundary of personal interaction.

For the vast majority of villagers, it is the chatting in the village lanes and similar unspecialized forms of interaction that encompass the adult individual's primary social life outside the home. Participation in the few secondary or special-interest groups is limited. Less than a fourth of the household heads attend a cinema, and even of the literates only 37 per cent are regular newspaper readers. Insofar as the evidence goes, the kinship and neighborhood bases of intimate social life are entirely congruent and harmonious with the village special-interest group. It is quite possible that kinship and neighborhood cliques are the nuclei upon which successful interest groups are organized.

Thus, Pelpola maintains a strong primary group life on the basis of the neighborhood and kinship, neither of which seems threatened by the coming in of special-interest groups. But what of the American city? Do informal groups exist there too?

Informal Groups in the American City

One study of Lansing, Michigan, indicates that there is much local intimacy in a middle-sized city (Smith, Form, and Stone, 1954). The investigators asked a sample of 573 people to give the location of their three "best friends." Only 15 per cent did not report as many as three and only 4.5 per cent reported none. All the rest indicated that they had these intimate associates and could tell where they lived. Whereas in Pelpola, the Ceylonese village, the neighborhood was the chief basis for intimacy, in Lansing most of the friends named lived outside the neighborhood of the person interviewed. This means that the city is a place where the person finds it possible to develop a sense of intimacy, both city-wide and locality based.

However, an analysis in terms of degree of intimacy of the friendships that are locality based shows that the highest intimacy scores of Lansing residents are found in areas of high socioeconomic position. Also, local intimacy develops as a result of residential stability. According to those making this study, there are two reasons why greater local intimacy will be found in high-income areas than in middle and lower economic areas: first, low economic groupings are more often subject to economic pressures demanding changes of residence than are high economic groupings; second, low economic groupings occupy a greater share of the city's space and have more spatial alternatives for moving. As a consequence, friendships in this stratum tend to be dispersed more widely through the city's space than friendships among urbanites in higher strata. The Lansing study concludes: "Thus, urban social integration is contributed to by the fact that urbanites derive social satisfaction from informal relationships both within and outside of their local areas of residence. Spatial mobility makes for city-wide ties; stability makes for local area ties; and most urban residents have both." (p. 284).

A study of New Haven, Connecticut, which concentrated upon the patterns of voluntary association of working-class families there, showed that three-fifths of the men and four-fifths of the women and children in the families studied did not participate at all in formally organized associations (Dotson, 1951). However, there was widespread informal contact of three types:

1. *Acquaintanceship and friendship*. According to Floyd Dotson, who reported on the study, the acquaintanceship category is large but vague. It embraces people known in childhood, former neighbors, and fellow workers. Such contacts may give a superficial sense of broad participation, but their role in day-to-day activities is a marginal one. Since organized social life must rest upon a firmer basis than acquaintanceship provides, the loosest type of informal, voluntary association that can be profitably recognized is the friendship group. The study showed that the majority of working-class husbands and wives did have friends outside their own families and relatives, but *two-fifths did not*. (In Lansing, Michigan, the study covered all occupational groups and not just working-class families.)

2. *Kin cliques*. Dotson defines a clique as "a psychologically intimate relationship which involves frequent and regular interaction." In New Haven, which is a relatively stable community, family and kin groups played an unusually important role in providing for the companionship and recreational needs of the persons interviewed. Even the two-fifths who had no friends did have rela-

tives in the community, for until recently, working-class families have been typically large, thus providing a large enough social circle to make possible a self-sufficient social life.

3. *Nonkin cliques.* Such cliques, founded upon neighborhood propinquity, are nearly universal among children and adolescents. As noted above, strong adult cliques of nonrelated persons are less common than those among kindred, but they nevertheless appear in appreciable numbers. A note of particular interest is the fact that although most of these adolescent cliques break down and disappear with the coming of adulthood and marriage, most adult clique relationships found in this study could be traced back to childhood and adolescence.

Other studies have dealt with nonkin cliques, particularly the adolescent cliques, some of which are delinquent and others not. The Dons, a delinquent gang, react to the response of the conventional community to their action (Jansyn, 1966). The boys are often rejected in school and in other areas of contact with the adult world. They make up a marginal group which is not well-integrated into the life of the neighborhood.

> The boys saw many of the people whom they considered enemies to be a threat to them, to the group, to the neighborhood and even to their way of life. It is partly in regard to these threats that the group is important to them. They see the group as a defense . . . Altercations frequently arise between them and Negro and Puerto Rican groups, and groups from other locations in the neighborhoods . . . Finally, in the existing situation, there was a likelihood that a boy who did not belong to a group was always eligible for harassment by any of the numerous groups in the area. (p. 614).

The solidarity of such a group goes up and down but two-thirds of the membership is relatively constant.

Neighborliness in the Town or City

Most neighborhood visiting patterns arise spontaneously as people meet casually over the back fence or as the person next door drops in to call. In many parts of a community such patterns may be rare, and in such a case an effort may be made to *organize* a neighborhood club. But the very fact that it has to be organized consciously, frequently by an outsider, means that it takes on the character of the formal or secondary association and seldom captures the spontaneity of the informal neighborliness pattern (Fellin and Litwak, 1963).

In one approach to the informal locality group, Peter H. Mann (1954) considers neighborliness as a twofold concept. On the one hand, there is what he calls "manifest neighborliness." This is characterized by overt forms of social relationships, such as mutual visiting in the home and going out for purposes of pleasure. On the other hand, there is what he terms "latent neighborliness," which is characterized by favorable attitudes to neighbors that result in positive action when a need arises, especially in time of crisis or emergency. After a study of two British housing projects, in which he tested out his ideas of neighborliness, Mann concluded:

> This paper has stressed the importance of latent neighborliness as the basis of social solidarity and how a high degree of manifest neighborliness can be mistakenly taken to be indicative of social solidarity for all the inhabitants of a neighborhood. At times sociologists overestimate the significance of manifest forms of action, while the underlying attitudes are neglected. The modern neighborhood is not a functional unit in the older sense of the isolated agricultural village. In many cases all the people have in common is the fact that they happen to live near to one another. Community centers, clubs, and other such groups cater largely to special interests; they rarely attract the whole population of a neighborhood. Nevertheless, if, at first visit, a neighborhood appears to be sleepy and apathetic, with absolutely nothing happening at all, this is no reason for thinking that the inhabitants lack neighborliness. If the observer can go below the surface to discover the latent neighborliness, he may well find a very definite attitude expressive of social cohesion. In the modern urban neighborhood this may well be the most important factor of all. (p. 168).

Neighboring is important for the successful American middle-class male. Ruth and John Useem and Duane L. Gibson (1960) have interviewed 75 men, aged 25 to 50 years, holding middle management positions within bureaucratic structures in the Midwest, about the neighborhoods in which they live. All but one of the men were married, and 60 per cent had lived in their present neighborhoods less than two years. Apparently, they use the word neighborhood in two senses: the immediate neighborhood, or the locality of close neighbors, and the larger neighborhood, or the geographical area distinguished by the characteristics and style of life of its inhabitants—its reputation, so to speak.

In characterizing what it means to be a good neighbor, the

respondents gave answers that stressed the following: 1) *emergency aid*—a neighbor can be counted on for help in times of crises; 2) *mutual aid*—a good neighbor is one with whom mutual aid patterns can be established; 3) *borrowing*—a good neighbor is one from whom one can *borrow* and to whom one can *lend;* 4) *perimeter of privacy*—good neighbors respect the privacy of each other; 5) *friendly—but not friends*—good neighbors are friendly with each other—but they are not friends.

When the men were asked to describe the neighborhood in which they lived, none of them spoke in terms of interpersonal interaction, e.g., friendly, cooperative, interesting people, and the like, even though these terms were used in describing the neighbors. Instead, the men, in referring to the larger neighborhood, spoke either of its name, social class ("upper middle class"), price range of homes, age of neighborhood, or occupations of the residents. From this study one may conclude:

> . . . the residential neighborhood has become, for upwardly mobile men stripped of kin and whose values stem primarily from the work role, the *locus* for working out the supporting framework for the functioning of their nuclear family and the basis for entrance into other supporting institutions of church, school, clubs, etc. The high preoccupation of the men with the social and status characteristics of their neighbors and neighborhood is understandable, for it stems from their need to have consistency and mutually reinforcing life segments. . . .
>
> Residential mobility, so characteristic of this segment of American life, is not then *per se* a stressful process leading to anomie, as it has sometimes been claimed, but is actually a resource for occupationally upwardly mobile men; for moving enables them to activate the supporting neighborhood functions appropriate for their changing occupational role. If the men can meet the cultural norms of neighboring . . . neighbors and neighborhoods become limited but tangible resources; if the men and their families cannot meet these norms, they become a potential source of stress. (p. 76).

Further Observations About Informal Groups

The informal group in every society comes about spontaneously and in a comparatively unplanned fashion. It continues as long as people follow some traditional behavior pattern or pursue some common interest; it lasts as long as it continues to provide the satisfactions that its members expect from it. The informal group serves numerous functions in the community, though both the group activity and the functions will vary as society moves toward greater complexity. An analysis of data from Hungary and the United States leads two researchers to conclude that technological development contributes to new forms of primary group structure. Because technology permits rapid communication over distance and enhances rapid group indoctrination, extended family kin can maintain contacts despite breaks in face-to-face interaction; neighborhoods can exist despite rapid membership turnover; and friendships can continue despite both of these problems. The study suggests that because of differences in structure, neighbors can best handle immediate emergencies; kin, long term commitment; and friends, heterogeneity (Litwak and Szeleny, 1969).

Earlier, mention was made of reference groups which are not groups in the sense that they are formal membership structures but are rather the construct of an individual (a social actor) who is trying to decide on some course of action. As we have seen, informal groups often can serve in this influential fashion.

A systematic treatment of reference groups has been provided by Theodore Kemper (1968). Table 9–1 indicates three types of reference groups. The normative groups "provide the actor with a guide to action by explicitly setting norms and espousing values. The normative group expects the actor to comply with these norms and values and makes quite plain its expectations." Examples of normative groups may be the family, one's religion, or one's nation.

Comparison groups "provide the actor with a frame of reference which serves to facilitate judgments about any one of several problematic issues." There are various types of comparison groups: the *equity group* is used as a frame of reference for judging whether or not one's situation or fate is fair or equitable; the action or opinion *legitimator group* is employed by the actor when the question arises as to the legitimacy of his opinions; *the role model* demonstrates for the individual how something is done in the technical sense; the *accommodator group* provides the individual with a cue for complementary response in cooperative situations or a parallel response in competitive situations.

The third main type of reference group is the *audience*. The actor attributes certain values to an audience group and attempts to behave in accordance with these values.

As Table 9–1 shows, each type of reference group has specific functions and appropriate sanctions.

TABLE 9-1

Characteristics, Functions and Sanctions of Reference Groups

Type of Reference Group	Defining Characteristics	Function	Sanctions
Normative	Provides norms and values	Assigns individuals to roles; specifies standards	Punishment or negative reinforcement
Comparison	Provides:		
	(1) Equity Standard	(1) Basis for satisfaction with one's fate.	None
	(2) Legitimation	(2) Legitimates actions or opinions.	None
	(3) Role Model	(3) Exemplifies how role should be played.	None
	(4) Stimulus for action	(4) Basis for accommodation to behavior of others.	None
Audience	Values imputed	Creates pressure for achievement	Reward

Source: Theodore D. Kemper, "Reference Groups, Socialization and Achievement," *American Sociological Review* 33 (February 1968), p. 38.

The occurrences just described are called the *informal* mechanisms of control. Kimball Young (1949) characterizes them as largely symbolic means, since they occur chiefly through talk and writing. Some of these devices, as he lists them, include praise and flattery, indoctrination, advertising, propaganda, slogans, rewards, badges, medals, uniforms, insignia, gossip, satire, laughing at others, calling names, commands, and threats.

But, in addition to being aware of these informal or chiefly symbolic means of control, one must be aware of the means whereby force in one of its forms is actually applied. This resort to force often finds expression in the decisions of official bodies, such as a school board's dismissal of a school principal, a labor council's calling of a strike, the banning of a motion picture for the members of a particular religious group by its board of censorship, a jury's verdict of guilty, a reduction by the local fiscal court of the recreation budget because of some unfavorable publicity given to one of the amateur-night programs staged two months before. Each of these might at first seem to be an isolated event involving only a few people, but, on closer examination, one finds that any one of them has wide community implications in that these decisions will in the future influence others in positions of responsibility to act in such ways as to avoid the censure of such groups.

Who Controls the Processes of Community Control?

Knowing about the processes of control is not enough. For a real knowledge of a community, it is also necessary to know who guides or controls these processes. Three considerations are involved in answering this question. First, the past still plays an active part in the present; second, each individual exercises some control, particularly in face-to-face contact; and, third, most communities have what is usually termed a "power structure" whose upper echelons may make many important decisions of community-wide scope.

1. The Controls from the Past. Every now and then one becomes acutely aware of the "dead hand of the past" in learning about some conditions set by a person long since dead. For example, a leading family of a Massachusetts town in a truly generous gesture donated an excellent beach to the town many years ago but stipulated that no man could use the beach unless he was wearing a two-piece bathing suit, a provision difficult to enforce in these days of bathing trunks. Other communities have to wrestle with problems growing out of large bequests set aside for the use of foundlings or to take care of horses too old to work any longer. These exceptional instances are often cited as illustrations of how the past, through specific legal documents, controls the present.

But the past, as the discussion of socialization has shown, makes its greatest contribution in that it has worked out such satisfactory solutions to many problems that these have been incorporated into the lifeways of the society and passed on from generation to generation. To the extent that these are accepted by each new generation, people are free to devote their attention to other problems. The problems solved in the past cover a vast variety of human behavior ranging all the way from the development of techniques of medical care to the small details of etiquette, such as the custom of gentlemen standing when a lady enters a room. Thus, in the development of American society, to which all American communities are inevitably bound, there is a unique approach to the meeting of economic needs, a system of public education worked out long ago and continuously implemented through the years, a pattern of the separation of church and state, as well as the formulation of a distinctive American political credo, which, though not always obeyed, still remains an important social force in our lives.

Whenever some part of the social heritage is considered sacred by most of the members of the community (such as the practice of monogamy) or even highly desirable (such as the owning of one's home), the traditions and socially inherited values may be said to be generally in charge of the processes of control. This would be particularly marked in the tradition-directed society, as described by Riesman (1953), but would hold true for any surviving society, since no generation is capable of starting anew to solve all of the problems that arise before it. In most matters, it accepts the controls from the past, leaving its own imprint upon them as it transmits them to a succeeding age group.

It is in this sense that the dominant institutions of a community discussed in the previous chapter provide basic controls. Those seeking to strengthen or maintain an institution, whether they realize it or not, are actually promoting and perpetuating in their own lifetime the formulas for living, the accepted practices, and the systems of rewards and punishments that long ago were built into the institutional complex. Thus, religious leaders and the men of science are each, in turn, attempting to stress solutions worked out by predecessors. In the case of religion, it may involve ways of establishing relationships with the supernatural and of living with one's fellow man; in the case of science, it may mean applying the scientific method, whose lineage is ancient, to wider and wider areas of life. As skillful adjustments are made to new situations, culture lag is avoided; on the other hand, when the past is in complete control, serious lags develop between the solutions provided by the past and the needs of the present. But the fact remains that in many matters the past provides ready-made solutions, and, to the extent that these are followed, the past is exerting social control.

2. Control Exercised by the Individual. An individual, simply by being present in a social situation, exercises control over others. "Two's company, three's a crowd" is often quoted to show the impact that a third person can make. Or the woman who jokingly says that she had better go to a bridge party or a church supper "just so they won't talk about me" recognizes that her presence is apt to have at least an inhibitory effect upon those about her. If she belongs to some minority religion, out of politeness to her the others will not make that subject a topic of their discussion; if her husband is a politician, people will be reserved in their remarks about those in public office; if she brings an out-of-town visitor along, the other women will be even more restrained in what they say until they learn a little more about the visitor.

In addition to mere presence, however, an individual by his actions can encourage or discourage behavior on the part of others. Showing a readiness of response, an eagerness, can stimulate others to continue some course of action; expressing indifference or disapproval can cause others to shift to different behavior patterns. Furthermore, the registering of apathy by followers can lead to frustration by self-appointed or even elected leaders, with the result that group activity weakens.

Nevertheless, those individuals who go into some social situation with a conscious purpose to fulfill are truly agents of social control. Whether they have tickets to a hospital bazaar or a firemen's ball, their persuading of others to buy and attend is a simple case of control. Or the pressures may be more far-reaching in that they seek to influence some community decision (the location of the new waterworks, the advisability of keeping out any additional industry, the curtailing of advertising support for a newspaper whose editorials are considered "meddlesome" or "troublesome" by those whose activities are affected).

Thus every individual in his own social space, in his network of acquaintances and associates, is in a position to exercise some kind of social control. The more intimate the relationship, such as in the family, the greater the likelihood of control; the more active and respected a person is in a social group to which he belongs, the greater his influence there; the greater a person's access to the chief means of communication, the more likely he is to influence others. The businessman through advertising, the judge through interpreting the law, and the worker by influencing other workers to better or poorer standards of performance exercise control within their individual spheres.

Most people of the community, however, live and move in a relatively restricted social space. They are concerned chiefly with making a living, having a good family life, enjoying their leisure;

they feel no great urge to control the whole community. In many ways, they do control more than they realize: It is they who are the ultimate consumers to whom the business appeals; it is their actions that raise or lower the standards of morality for the community as a whole; and it is their vote that settles many matters of wide importance. But this control is a byproduct of their reaction to the world about them and represents little in the way of a drive toward control.

3. The Role of the Community Power Structure. Power, or the ability of an individual to control others, is distributed in unequal degree throughout the community. Parents have more authority than their children; an employer, more power than his employees; and the police, more power than a rowdy individual disturbing the peace. Each of these, however, is exercising a type of power derived from a different source such as the family, the economic sphere, or the government. These are institutional networks, or major community systems, which serve as means of distributing power throughout the community. But what has come to be called the *community power structure* refers to the informal decisions made by people at the top of their respective social and occupational hierarchies about matters of community-wide concern. These are the people "who run the town," or who are considered the "most important people." They are "the people to see" if a person is interested in promoting some big program in the community, for without their help no large-scale undertaking is likely to succeed. Who are these people who have such control? How did they gain it? How do they use it? These questions will be taken up in Chapter 15.

This discussion has shown that the three operations of recruitment, socialization, and social control are essential to the continuity of any community. A glance at Figure 7–1 (page 133), which shows the components of the community, indicates the different levels at which these sets of activities can be carried out—at the personal, group, subsystem, and major-system levels. It also suggests that no one agency or intergroup network has sole responsibility for any single operation of the type described here.

10

Division of Labor, Allocation, and Communication

A community is a service center. At the same time, it is the place where most of the adults earn a livelihood unless, of course, the community is of the suburban type, where the job holders make the daily trip back and forth to the metropolitan center. But even in the suburbs the stress continues to be on the provision of adequate services.

The use of these services depends, of course, upon the financial ability to pay for them, which goes back to the level of employment, the average wages and salaries received, and the degree of occupational specialization found in the community. To understand this economic structure and its social overtones, one can look at a particular city such as Oshkosh, Wisconsin, described so fully by John W. Alexander (1955), who writes:

> A city is like a living organism. It has a shape and a form—a skeleton, so to speak, of streets, city limits, blocks and buildings. But a city is more than that. A city has life. It has people circulating in, through, and around those features which constitute its skeleton. Without people Oshkosh would be dead. To be sure, the streets would still be there; the factories, the stores, the schools, the parks would all be in their same location. Perhaps from the air, it would still look like Oshkosh. But it

219

would not be Oshkosh. It is the people who make the city. They constitute the life that ebbs and flows through the inanimate framework.

Life flows through a city primarily because people cannot secure all the things they need within the bounds of their own property. They must "go to work" to earn money for purchasing the things they need. They "go to the store" to spend that money. They "go to school" to learn about life and things. They seek relaxation by going to the park, or to the library or other places for recreation.

A city is a group of people on the go. The one most important factor lubricating such complex activity is *money*. This medium of exchange frees a man from growing all his own food and making all his own clothes and equipment, or from the wasteful and time-consuming necessity of barter. Every citizen in a city is engaged in some form of economic activity, either earning money, or investing money, or spending money, or perhaps all three.

A city then is an economic organism through which the life blood of commerce, money, is continually circulating. The flow is an endless cycle. The factory worker receives his pay check which goes to the landlord for rent, to the grocer for food, to the clothier for clothes, to an auto dealer for a car. These businessmen in turn use the money to make purchases from others to satisfy their own needs. Much of the money goes right back to the factory in payment for goods which the businessmen have purchased in wholesale lots. And so it goes, a continuous flow of money is the life blood of a city's economy. (pp. 23–24).

This flow of money, this specialization of labor, this social interaction leads to the formation of groups which in turn are linked to other groups. The economy that we usually think of in terms of impersonal factors is also based on social factors. Like the family, it is made up of people in relationship to each other. Without such predictable, relatively permanent relationships a complex economy could not operate; people would not know what roles were expected of them in a given business situation. In addition, if a community is to persist, certain operations must be carried out. The previous chapter has already referred to the importance of recruitment, socialization, and social control. Equally important are the operations leading to division of labor, the allocation of people to the jobs and other positions that are required in the community, and the distribution of goods and services to the people of the community. (See Figure 7–2).

DIVISION OF LABOR

Division of labor, or the tendency of people to specialize in one task at which they can become expert, is found in nonindustrial communities as well as in the highly industrial ones. Some tasks carry more prestige and are taken over by those in the upper statuses with greater power; other tasks are considered "inferior" and are performed by those having the least advantages. Emile Durk- heim, a prominent French sociologist, argued that this division of labor, since it made people dependent upon each other, actually led to social solidarity, which would not exist if everyone were self-sufficient in an economic sense (Simpson, 1933; Kemper, 1972). One advantage of studying the job classification and the numbers employed in each job is the picture one gains of the interdependence on which community life is based.

There are many ways of listing the occupations of a community as a reflection of the division of labor found there. One of the most common classifications was worked out by Alba M. Edwards. It divides occupations into six levels or strata called "socioeconomic groups":

1. Professional persons
2. Proprietors, managers, and officials:
    2-a. Farmers (owners and tenants)
    2-b. Wholesale and retail dealers
    2-c. Other proprietors, managers, and officials
3. Clerks and kindred workers
4. Skilled workers and foremen
5. Semiskilled workers
6. Unskilled workers:
    6-a. Farm laborers
    6-b, c. Laborers, except farm
    6-d. Servant Classes

Some sociologists criticize the Edwards classification on the ground that it puts all occupations into too neat a vertical rank, whereas some might very well be equal even though in different socioeconomic groups set up by Edwards. Richard T. Morris and Raymond J. Murphy (1959) have worked up a classification, taking into account horizontal comparisons, by the use of the term *situs*, or a category of individuals or positions placed on a level with other categories, all of which are given the same evaluation. They have described ten civilian occupational situses as follows:

1. *Legal authority*—All occupations primarily concerned with the formulation, arbitration, interpretation, or enforcement of the law, including those primarily concerned with the custody of law-breakers.

2. *Finance and records*—All occupations primarily concerned with the handling of monetary affairs or the processing of records, accounts or correspondence.

3. *Manufacturing*—All occupations primarily concerned with the fabrication of articles or the processing of raw materials on a production-line basis.

4. *Transportation*—All occupations primarily concerned with the movement of persons or goods from one location to another.

5. *Extraction*—All occupations primarily concerned with the extraction, procurement, or production of raw materials.

6. *Building and maintenance*—All occupations primarily concerned with the construction of buildings or other nonmass-produced units, or the installation, maintenance, or repair of equipment, property, or facilities.

7. *Commerce*—All occupations primarily concerned with the buying, selling, exchange, or marketing of goods or persons.

8. *Arts and entertainment*—All occupations concerned primarily with the creation of art forms or with the provision of entertainment, recreation, information, or aesthetic satisfaction for the public.

9. *Education and research*—All occupations primarily concerned with formal instruction or training or with the acquisition of knowledge as an end in itself.

10. *Health and welfare*—All occupations primarily concerned with the detection, prevention, or alleviation of illness, hazard, or distress. (pp. 236–37)

Furthermore, they have done some pilot studies that ranked various occupations found in the ten situses. Figure 10–1 shows the result of one such ranking.

The division of labor in a community goes beyond economic specialization, for it also includes a number of positions that people fill as an avocation, often with little financial remuneration. In a New England town, the three selectmen who direct local governmental activities are paid very little. They must continue to work at their business or profession for their livelihood but devote large blocks of time to affairs of the town. Certainly, a community needs to set up mechanisms, such as town elections, to fill such a post. A detailed look at any community would show that there are a number of important offices, organizational and governmental, which people hold without pay. Why people seek such posts depends upon their own personal goals: to use the office as a stepping stone to something else, to render public service, to be in the limelight, to get away from a disagreeable situation at home, and many other rea-

SITUSES

PRESTIGE RANK QUARTILES (Student Ratings) / STRATA	1 Legal Authority	2 Finance & Records	3 Manufacturing	4 Transportation	5 Extraction	6 Building & Maintenance	7 Commerce	8 Aesthetics & Entertainment	9 Education & Research	10 Health & Welfare
1	Supreme Court Justice Lawyer	City Manager	Owner of a Large Factory	President of a Railroad		Architect		Conductor of a Symphony Orchestra	College President	Physician Minister
2		Banker	Biologist for a Pharmaceutical Company	Airline Pilot	Geologist in an Oil Company	Building Contractor	Advertising Executive Commercial Artist		Philosopher County Agricultural Agent	Welfare Worker
3	Policeman	Bookkeeper	Machinist		Farmer Forest Ranger		Manager of a Hardware Store	Radio Announcer Singer in a Night Club	Music Teacher	Fireman
4	Prison Guard	Cashier in a Restaurant	Restaurant Cook	Mail Carrier Truck Driver	Coal Miner	Waiter in a Restaurant Garbage Collector	Milk Route Man	Barber		

Figure 10–1. Theoretical situs location of selected occupations and empirical location made by sample of student raters.

sons. From the community standpoint, however, the motivation is less important than the effectiveness with which the job is carried out. The fact that some people will give concentrated attention to a line of community activity means that others in the community can specialize in something else. Some fathers manage Little League Baseball, others direct United Way Campaigns, while still others serve without pay on a School Board or a Library Committee.

The discussion thus far has indicated ways of looking at the division of labor in the community. As an operation of a social system it relates to the specializations, economic and non-economic, whose practitioners carry out the tasks necessary for life in the community. Without such specializations the high standard of living in modern society would not be possible.

One effect of division of labor is the increased interdependence of units in the system upon each other. In fact, it is this very interdependence that causes some sociologists to view the community as if it were a system. Cataloging lists of occupations highlights the differences, but the longer the list the greater the dependence of those in one occupation upon others. This interdependence, however, is not limited merely to occupations. Neighbors develop a pattern of mutual aid; various local groups make use of church and school facilities; courts adjudicate civil suits among businessmen; radio and television carry public service announcements about community events. In other words, the systemic linkage described in Chapter 8 illustrates the reliance one social unit has upon another. In a social system, as in other systems, differentiation necessitates interdependence.

ALLOCATION

In addition to differentiation, or a division of labor, every community has a system of distribution, which is more complex than one might expect. First of all, as pointed out in Chapter 7, goods and services must be made available to those who require them. Yet, these are not distributed equally; some get more than others. This results from the ability of those with the most income to pay higher prices for the scarce, most desired goods. Such allocation usually is determined through the market place.

Behind this, however, is a more fundamental allocation: namely, to the statuses within the community. We have already noted that some occupational statuses provide much more income than do other statuses; How do people get assigned to these? A simplified answer would be that in traditional societies the part played by kinship in such allocation is paramount; in industrialized societies bureaucratic procedures, based on job specifications and competence, provide the route. Yet we know that people do not all have an equal start in their efforts to comply with the demands of the job they seek, a topic which we will explore in Chapter 13. What needs to be stressed here, however, is that a community to survive as a social system must make use of various mechanisms to get capable people into the jobs that must be filled, both the highly desirable and the undesirable jobs. One observing this operation at work may approve or disapprove of the assumptions underlying it as well as its results. Yet, in some way it must be carried out.

Much the same holds true for another kind of allocation: namely, that of prestige. Some people are honored; others are not. Sometimes this honor, often called prestige, is *ascribed*. In the past, a person from an old-established family may have been born into a position of honor. Or the honor may be *achieved* through outstanding contributions to the community, success in one's profession or occupation which corresponds with the dominant values of the community, the use of wealth in socially-approved causes, as well as in a number of other ways that reflect the local way of evaluating performance.

Another "good" to be allocated within a community is power. Obviously, this is not the same thing as prestige. A very rich man may have great economic power (a slum landlord) but not enjoy any honor or prestige; a political boss may have much power but not the respect of those who work closely with him, though he may enjoy their loyalty; a professional man at the apex of an institutional complex may have a form of power. As we shall note in Chapter 15, one way of looking at power is in terms of the exploiter and exploited or the consequences of unequal distribution of power. In viewing a social system, however, it is necessary to discover where the positions of power lie, how people are allocated to these positions, and under what circumstances abuse of power or even failure to exercise it become dysfunctional for the system.

These forms of allocation are treated briefly here because they will be discussed in much greater detail within the conflict paradigm. They are just as important a feature of social systems analysis as for any other approach but to treat them at length in two places would be redundant. For example, every community has some stratification pattern, even though the people may refuse to admit that they have a "class system." "Everybody is equal around here," they often tell a researcher from outside. In viewing the community as a social system one inquires into the functions of a stratification pattern for the community as a whole, how people are "assigned" to social classes, and how willingly they accept their social position. From the conflict, or dialectical point of view, as we shall note in later chapters, one may look at the same stratification pattern as a demonstration of class antagonisms, as evidence of instability in the community, and as an example of concentration of power.

In closing this discussion of allocation, we might note that knowledge is a form of social good, which also is not equally distributed. This leads into a consideration of communication, which is another important operation in a community viewed as a social system.

COMMUNICATION

One corollary of interdependence is the need for communication, another important operation of the community viewed as a social system. This requires the physical transportation of people and services, the ability of people to come together in physical proximity when they so desire—either through private or public transportation. It means delivering the milk, the bread, the newspapers, the hundreds of kinds of items that have to be at a certain place, often at a stated time, if they are to be of use. The other kind of communication is sociopsychological: people talking intelligibly and meaningfully to each other in an individual capacity or as representatives of local groups and institutions.

The communication of ideas and other forms of social interaction occurs through informal communication networks as well as through formal channels.

The Informal Communication Network

Baker Brownell (1950) in his discussion of "Communicability and the Community" indicates that communication arises from the fact that people are many and different and still establish contact with one another:

> Communication is also a function of the identification of people with one another. In this is the substance of community. Men behave not only as if they were separate; they behave also as if they were identified with one another. . . . Through communication we confirm the basic unity of our common life and try to convert it into intelligent or at least successful action. By means, either direct or indirect, we identify our experience with another's. We try to live together in a fairly coherent world, share in its values and bring about mutual cooperation. . . .
>
> Through communication we enter more fully into the knowing and assimilating process of living. We identify our experience more fully with that of another thing. (pp. 240–41).

Morris Freilich (1963) views the community as a set of inter-related centers within a town or city where people encounter each other, where they pool information, and then distribute it more widely. In more complex terms it is that group of people that share (1) a unique set of information which could be called local-inter-action culture, (2) a unique set of rates of dispersing particular kinds of information, (3) a unique hierarchy of centers, and (4) a unique proportion of fixed (e.g., a store) as against moving centers (e.g., private homes, any one of which might be a center of com-munication to those visiting it at the time). It is in these centers that one can trace the important patterns of interaction.

Numerous other studies of large collections of people, whether in factories, in universities, on the police force, or as sports enthusi-asts, would reveal similar clusters of people who are interrelated as part of a large "gossip chain" that stretches through much of the community. Some of those in this chain get many details of a news story from the formal media, but as the story spreads, it becomes more personalized, frequently more vivid, and even altered in its essentials.

These informal channels operate wherever social cliques gather and wherever conversation becomes free and easy and intimate (Cleland, 1960; Gumperz 1964; Lionberger and Copus, 1972). Word gets passed around at filling stations in the short period while the gas tank is being filled, at the courthouse where hangers-on congregate to learn what is new, at the feed store where farmers gather to discuss crops or politics, at the union hall, on the job, or in the beauty parlor or barber shop where no formal pattern of con-versation is determined in advance.

The gossip chain operates at most recreational functions—at the bridge club, the church supper, the after-theater party, or during a golf game. Topics may relate to events as well as to personalities. They may range from the cause of a recent fire to the behavior of the minister's wife. Men just as much as women are part of this informal system of communication, which deals not only with matters in the day's headlines but with affairs that could never be printed or broadcast without fear of libel suits.

To understand then how people communicate with each other in a given community, one needs to be aware of more than the bus, streetcar, or subway system. One also needs a familiarity with the formal media of spreading news and ideas as well as with those informal means that any community develops long before it is fully equipped with telephone, press, radio, and television (Riley and Flowerman, 1951). "Word sure gets around!" is the surprised statement that people often make when they discover just how rapidly segments of the community can learn of something that has just occurred (Larsen and Hill, 1958).

Rumor.   The role of rumor in this whole process of informal communication deserves careful study. For a well-documented case we turn to the account by Warren Peterson and Noel Gist (1951) of what happened in a community as an aftermath of an unsolved crime involving the rape and murder of a fifteen-year-old baby sitter. These authors define rumor as "an unverified account or explanation of events, circulating from person to person and pertaining to an object, event or issue of public concern." [1] They also point out that rumor "opinion" differs from other forms of public opinion in that it is not verified through customary channels. "A social setting conducive to rumor occurs when a public is interested and concerned about a past or anticipated event, when authoritative information and explanation are lacking and when social controls relevant to the situation are external to most members of the public." (p. 160)

Peterson and Gist indicate that people who were never interested in nor informed about the situation were drawn into the informal discussion of the murder which had occurred. They observed:

---

[1] Warren A. Peterson and Noel P. Gist, "Rumor and Public Opinion," *American Journal of Sociology* 57 (September, 1951), 159. Copyright, 1951, by the University of Chicago.

"As persons move from one discussion group to another, speculation tends to be passed as rumor; and rumor comes to be represented as fact, often supported by citing supposedly authoritative sources. Typically, the rumor public is more emotional than other publics." (p. 162). In the beginning, the opinion about the event is unstructured with many differing views being expressed. "The communication of rumor tends to reduce the divergence in attitudes and to produce a common definition of the situation and a common feeling or mood. Rumor is one means by which a collectivity, albeit a temporary and unstable collectivity, emerges from an aggregate." (p. 160).

The central theme of a set of rumors that circulated for three or four days about this crime was that Mr. X, the baby sitter's employer, had left a party that he and his wife were attending, returned home, entered the house, committed the crime, and subsequently returned to the party after changing his clothes. According to Peterson and Gist:

> The numerous variations which developed from this central theme indicate interpretation, speculation and creative imagination on the part of the public in the direction of coordinating the story with previous conceptions of the murder, of attributing stereotyped sex-criminal characteristics to Mr. X, of constructing a basis for sympathizing with his wife, of supplying authentic verification and of generally molding a sensational account. (p. 162).

Other types of rumors, such as those preceding race riots or a run on a bank, although ephemeral in character, have grave community consequences, since the misinformation and doubts that are spread are never fully counteracted by correct stories of what actually occurred. In fact, the National Advisory Commission in Civil Disorders (1968) reports:

> Rumors significantly aggravated tension and disorder in more than 65 percent of the disorders studied by the Commission. Sometimes, as in Tampa and New Haven, rumor served as the spark which turned an incident into a civil disorder. Elsewhere, notably Detroit and Newark, even where they were not precipitating or motivating factors, inflaming rumors made the job of police and community leaders far more difficult. (p. 326).

The Commission suggests that police, public officials, and community leaders quickly and effectively circulate the facts, with loudspeakers available to police at the scene of an incident. Also, many people can be reached by radio and television announcements as well as by special telephone networks. Obviously, rumor is one form of communication that can prove dysfunctional for the community as a system.

The Formal Channels of Communication

Communication has become big business, both in the local community as well as nationally. The written and electronic media not only convey messages within the social system, but they also seek to strengthen or create a sense of community. Up to 1930, according to Thomas Cochran (1972), only one-quarter of the advertising revenue was national and "local news had a chamber of commerce or booster character; what was good for the city was played up; what was likely to hurt local business was carried on back pages or not at all." (p. 69). Although newsmagazines appealed to a national audience it was the radio and television which sought for business reasons to build a national community whose attention would be focused upon characters playing parts in the programs they presented. Cochran also notes:

> The number of daily newspapers reached a peak of 2,500 in 1915, and then gradually declined to about 1,700 in 1970. The drop in numbers was not caused so much by the competition of the new media for disseminating news, such as the radio after 1920, as it was by the spread of chains and mergers . . . By 1950 very few small cities had competing dailies, and only about half of the cities with over 100,000 population had such competition. (pp. 68–69).
>
> As would any system of ownership, this business pattern of control introduced its biases into the news . . . (p. 69).
>
> . . . the electrical mass media of the twentieth century came to be powerful influences for a uniform national culture, a culture not specifically planned to satisfy business needs, but one subject to subtle business influences and censorship, since these media reached children as much as, if not more, than adults, they gained enormously as social conditioning forces. (p. 71).
>
> . . . Mass media may inform, but in general a person will not accept the idea or change his role-playing until he has tested it by conversation with influential people in his role-set . . . (p. 79).

A central question in the effectiveness of communication as an operation of the community system is the flow of news from source to reporter and into the press. Walter Gieber (1960) observes:

News is a product of the mediation by communicators who in turn are influenced by psychological and social forces. Activity in our society is under constant surveillance by individuals who may or may not communicate to others. In a more formal sense, the event is communicated to a community (or large groups) through the press; the event becomes news. In the majority of instances, news events come to the attention of the press when a source decides to "tell" the community. The two communicators, the source and the reporter, are "gatekeepers" in the channel of news: that is, they make the decisions controlling the flow of news to the community. (p. 77).

Somewhat the same approach to news is taken by Molotch and Lester (1974) who see the news content of mass media "as the result of practical, purposive, and creative activities on the part of news promoters, news assemblers and news consumers." These authors view the power of newswork as that of closing off possibilities at each of the above points.

The social effects of the mass media can be seen at both the individual and community level. Much concern has been expressed, for instance, as to the influence of television upon children. This, in turn, affects the socialization process which was discussed in the last chapter. There is general agreement that studies on this question are still inconclusive. One effort by DeFleur and DeFleur (1967) to see the contribution of television to children's knowledge of selected occupations found that children scored significantly better on the televised occupational roles than those for which "general culture" was the principal learning source. Nevertheless, the roles learned from television appear to be stereotyped, leading to a homogenization effect, which reduces the individuality among the members of the audience. They conclude that television does appear an important agency of socialization but that it presents information which is distorted in a variety of ways. One example is the misleading information about the labor force in our society.

The mass media can also affect social structure (Harrison, 1972). Godwin Chu (1968) divides the networks of social interactions which comprise the village structure of the Taiwanese village into three broad functions: *economic,* or filling the economic needs through exchange of goods and services; *affiliative,* meeting affiliative needs through exchange of affective support and esteem; and *instrumental,* which fulfills cognitive needs through the seeking and acquisition of information and advice. The author found that media information had an impact upon rank distribution in the instrumental hierarchy. It also provided a balancing function, which helped restore the equilibrium of the social structure, through the process of "selectively channelling advice-seeking toward those individuals already relatively high in the affiliative and economic hierarchies, and who had better access to information. By giving social reward to some and withholding it from others, the disequilibrium caused by the introduction of mass communications in a traditional social system can be reduced. At the same time, the necessary function of instrumental interactions is fulfilled." (p. 199).

DIFFUSION OF IDEAS AND PRACTICES

Within the past few years two traditions of communication study have been converging. One tradition has dealt with persuasion through mass communication and the other has dealt with the acceptance of new farm practices. They finally discovered each other with mutual enrichment for both (Katz and Lazarfeld, 1955). Over the last two decades, for instance, rural sociologists have conducted several hundred studies of the communication and acceptance of farm practices (Lionberger, 1960; Spector et al, 1971). Other sociologists have been studying the rate of acceptance of innovations by school systems and the adoption of new health practices, while marketing specialists have been studying the acceptance of new products.

Elihu Katz and Martin L. Levin (1963) define the sociological approach to diffusion as the (1) *acceptance*, (2) over *time*, (3) of some specific *item*—an idea or practice, (4) by individuals, groups or other *adopting units*, linked (5) to specific *channels* of communications, (6) to a *social structure*, and (7) to a given system of values, or *culture*.

Katz (1960) lists three major findings that have grown out of diffusion studies as defined above. First, in both urban and rural settings, personal influence appears to be more effective in gaining acceptance for change than are the mass media or other types of influence. Second, when decision making is broken down into phases, the mass media appear relatively more influential in the early informational phases, whereas personal influences are more effective in the later phases of deliberation and decision. Third, those who accept an innovation first are more likely than those who accept later to have been influenced by agricultural agencies, mass media, and other formal or impersonal sources. Those who accept later on are more likely to have been influenced by personal sources than those who accepted first. Furthermore, the personal sources to which the early adopters respond are likely to be outside their own communities or at a greater distance than are the personal sources influencing later adopters. (pp. 439–40).

Table 10–1 also relates the diffusion stage to source. On the left

TABLE 10–1

Communication in Diffusion of Information to Farmers

Diffusion Stage	Order of Importance of Sources
1. Awareness 2. Interest	a. Mass media b. Agricultural agencies c. Neighbors and friends d. Agricultural salesmen
3. Trial 4. Acceptance	a. Neighbors and friends b. Agricultural agencies c. Mass media d. Agricultural salesmen

Source: Adapted from Agrisearch (October, 1955).

it shows the stages through which diffusion of information or the spread of a new practice goes. First, people become aware of the new practice, then they become interested; after this, they are ready to try it and accept it if it works. On the right are listed the sources of information about the new practice in their order of importance.

One of the most interesting recent findings about diffusion has been the discovery by C. Milton Coughenour (1964) that, in the case of twelve Kentucky localities which he studied, there is an underlying rate of diffusion for each locality. In other words, the same communities rated high in the case of all five practices studied while other communities rated low. This substantiates the observation that communities differ in the readiness with which they accept change. The role of communication as an operation of the system is important in this connection.

THE LARGER COMMUNICATION STRUCTURE

If a community is to remain a part of a larger society, it must be in touch with what is going on elsewhere in that society (Hassinger, 1961; Rogers, 1969). Even the internal system of communication, which we have just discussed, depends for many of its features upon media operating outside even the largest centers. Not even New York City is self-sufficient, since it, more than smaller places, is subjected to a daily barrage of new ideas and fresh information because of its worldwide contacts. The ordinary citizen today travels more often and over greater distances than formerly. The number of Americans traveling abroad has also substantially increased. Through such travel members of the community absorb new ideas from the world outside their community. Television, with its advertising appeals, comes very intimately into the living room. Movies are imported into the community from Hollywood, and the nationally circulated magazines arrive in large bundles from outside distribution points. Such an obvious fact need not be belabored, but the results of such extensive outside communication should be noted.

First, mass communication is leading to standardizing of our material life. People in New England want ranch-type houses. People in the Southwest put up prefabricated Cape Cod cottages. A supermarket in California is like one in Georgia: the same brands are on display and packaged in much the same way. Each home town is intimately involved because of the dynamic nature of the capitalistic economy. In an industrialized society, mass production is necessary to take advantage of the heavy investment in capital equipment; accompanying mass production must be mass distribution or getting products to every potential customer; but mass distribution depends upon mass advertising, which leads to the development of and heavy support of mass media.

But in addition to the standardization of material life, the *social organizational* aspects of community life are being standardized. A Rotarian from Shreveport, Louisiana, should feel at home in a club in Boise, Idaho—so standardized is his membership role. The same holds true for the numerous other local religious, civic, welfare, educational, and cultural organizations that have national affiliations, since the central office of each is trying to get the local groups to follow certain programs of action to emphasize the same creed and ritual and to send in adequate financial support.

The most thorough study of the connection between a small community and the larger society describes a rural New York locality called Springdale by its two authors, Arthur J. Vidich and Joseph Bensman (1958). Three thousand people live in Springdale township and about 1000 of these in the village of Springdale. The residents have a strong commitment to the rural way of life, thinking that it offers them the best of two possible worlds since they can choose what they want from the city and not become concerned with the acute urban problems. Few of them realize, however, how closely their daily life is linked with the outside world. In their chapter on "Springdale and Mass Society," the authors trace the many importations by Springdale, summarizing the situation as follows:

Springdale is connected with the mass society in a variety of different forms. The cumulative effect of these various connections makes possible the continuous transmission of outside policies, programs and trends into the community, even though the effects of the transmission and the transmitting agents themselves are not always seen. Outside influences can be transmitted directly by a socially visible agent such as the extension specialist who lives in the community for the purpose of acting upon it. Outside interests and influences can also be expressed indirectly through members of the community: Policies and programs of relatively invisible outside interests are transmitted by *heads* of local branches of state and national organizations, by *heads* of local businesses dependent on outside resources and by *heads* of churches attached to larger organizations. In some instances the community is affected by the consequences of decisions made by business and government which are made with specific reference to the community, i.e., the decision to build a state road through the community or the decision to close down a factory. Plans and decisions that refer directly to the community are made from a distance of invisible agents and institutions. Perhaps most important are the mass decisions of business and government which are transmitted to the rural scene by the consequences of changes in prices, costs and communications. These affect the town even though they are not explicitly directed at it, and they comprise the invisible social chain reactions of decisions that are made in centers of power in government, business and industry. The invisible social chain reactions emanating from the outside no doubt alter the life of the community more seriously than the action of visible agents such as the extension specialist. (pp. 81–82).

In further elaboration of these points, Vidich and Bensman describe how cultural importations from mass society are brought in through formal importing organizations such as the Farm and Home Bureau, Boy and Girl Scouts, and the American Legion. Mass media, including press, radio, and television, reach Springdale in all of their variety. Even courses of instruction in Sunday schools are prepared in denominational headquarters far removed from the community. Very important, too, are the individuals who, because of their occupation roles, serve as gatekeepers. As such they are recognized both in the community and by representatives of the mass society. First, there are the professional people, most of whom have a college education. They have "contacts" with outside agencies and they can understand and interpret "official" documents, and can supposedly accomplish things for the community that no one else can.

Shopkeepers, businessmen operating on a franchise, and the feed mill and farm implement dealers are all dependent to varying degrees upon outside sources of supply and local farmers are dependent upon them. But there are two classes of farmers: the rational and the traditional as shown in the way they organize their production in relation to the mass market and government regulations. Because of this tie-in with the market, any price upheavals can drastically change the status structure of the local community.

It is in political life, however, that there has been greatest surrender to the mass society. Many important decisions are made for Springdale by outside agencies because the programs and policies of local political bodies are determined largely by acceptance of grants-in-aid offered them and by facilities and services made available to them by outside sources. Thus the most influential person politically on the local scene is the person with access to the sources of decision in the larger political unit. Nevertheless, it is in the area of politics that Springdalers can respond to the mass society, thus through voting exerting a reciprocal influence.

Although Springdale is caught up so fully in the mass society, there is little likelihood that in the foreseeable future it will lose its identity as a community. Its political units or village and township will probably continue and the local institutions, though based on outside sources, will keep on helping local people meet their daily needs. One way of describing this retention of community identity is *boundary-maintenance*. As the term implies, any social system to persist must keep a boundary between itself and other systems, larger or smaller, so that it does not merge with another system to the point that it no longer exists as a separate entity. Boundaries can shift, of course. Nor do they refer basically to physical boundaries but to social boundaries as defined by responsibilities that one system has vis-à-vis another, by a sense of identification and belonging on the part of members (whether individuals or groups), by an ability to carry out the operations being described here.

But if Springdale is able to maintain fairly clean-cut social boundaries, some other communities find it increasingly difficult to do so. One such is Intercity, a New England city of 25,000 that was studied simply because it is located in the midst of larger centers pulling its residents in several directions, thus weakening the hold of a wide variety of institutions that we ordinarily associate with a given community. Intercity is atypical—it is at one end of the spectrum of boundary-maintenance—but its problems of even keeping a semblance of a bona fide community illustrate many of the forces at work in modern society.

Leo Bogart and Frank E. Orenstein (1965) directed the study of Intercity. Their main research interest was the role of the mass communications media, particularly the daily press, in attracting people to shop and pursue recreational interests in the communities where the daily papers are published. Intercity has no daily paper, but its inhabitants are served by mass media emanating from five big cities no more than forty miles away. Some of the interesting findings about Intercity are the following:

Intercity comes close to being an average kind of town. The 1960 Census gives the median family income as just short of $7,000. 17% of the families had incomes between $10,000 and $25,000; 7% reported less than $3,000 a year. Over half the wage earners are employed in manufacturing, mostly in metals, machinery or machine parts, and the most common jobs are held by skilled workers or operatives. Half the respondents in the survey had completed high school or gone beyond, and another 28% had had at least some high school education. 21% had not gone beyond grade school. On the other hand, only 7% were college graduates, and another 12% had some college education.

Like any interurban area, Intercity is characterized by a high degree of personal mobility. 18% of the respondents had lived in town for less than two years, less than half had been in the town for over ten years. Most of those who had been born elsewhere came from one of the other towns in the area, but no one city accounted for any preponderant number.

Intercity, in spite of its interurban location, is an independent community rather than an appendage or suburb of any other big town nearby. This is shown by the high proportion of its principal wage earners who work in Intercity itself—37%—and also by the fact that the remainder are spread among a great many of the surrounding communities, and not concentrated within any single one. 12% work in Central City, 11% in Naborcity, and eight other cities and towns account for between 1% and 6% each.

The automobile makes mobility a daily commonplace in Intercity, and it is by no means confined to the principal wage earners who commute to out-of-town jobs. Nearly everyone interviewed (97%) had been out of Intercity for some purpose within the previous four weeks, and 89% had been outside within the previous week. Almost everyone left town by car; only a handful had used the bus or train.

People travel out of Intercity for a considerable variety of reasons, and there are remarkably small differences between men and women. During the past half year, over a third have gone out of town for medical or dental treatment.

In the past seven days over half have gone shopping in other towns. In the past seven days nearly half of those interviewed have visited out-of-town friends or relatives; over a fourth have gone elsewhere for a snack, drink or meal; one in ten has gone to a movie or show; one in ten to a religious service; one in eight has gone to a meeting of some out-of-town group or club.

Sports teams or clubs represent the principal voluntary association activity outside of Intercity. However, most of the athletic teams which people report that they follow with interest are teams from one of the major national centers rather than from one of the nearby cities.

Mass Media in Intercity

Most people in Intercity are exposed every day to both daily newspapers and television. On a "yesterday" basis, 89% read one or more papers, an average of 1.8 per reader, mostly home-delivered. All but 17% of these people also watched TV, and an additional 9% watched TV "yesterday" though they did not read a newspaper.

In general, those people who read *only* a paper published in one of the larger, more distant cities of the group show a more cosmopolitan outlook than do those who read a paper from one of the smaller, more nearby cities (*regardless* of whether they also read a paper from the more distant metropolis).

Intercitizens report themselves to be more interested in national and international news than in local news. However, individual dailies show substantial variation in the extent of their appeal to people who have a national or a local news orientation. One of the Central City papers appeals strongly to readers with a cosmopolitan orientation and one does not. Conversely, one of the Elm City papers appeals strongly to readers with a parochial orientation and one does not. In short, the character of the individual newspaper seems to shape its audience regardless of where that newspaper originates.

We may draw a few other conclusions from this study:

1. The reader's choice of an individual newspaper may reflect his politics, his cosmopolitanism, or his ethnicity. But in an area where people have a range of choices, the cities of origin of the newspapers they read reflect their patterns of mobility and orentation.

2. In an era of interurban sprawl, people seem to be able to think of different towns accessible to them as having differentiated functions, much as a resident of a metropolis may look to specialized districts or neighborhoods for different services or facilities. There may be a town to work in, a town to play in, a town to shop in, a town where friends or relatives may be found. Each place may evoke a different set of associations with movements that take place at a different time of the day or week.

3. Media do seem to define a market, not only in the national sense, as specialized magazines do when they single out people who share an occupational or social interest, but also locally, spatially in the traditional sense. The relation between the newspaper and its market appears to be a two-way affair. People go from Intercity to Plant City, River City or Central City precisely because they see the ads in the papers describing the specials of the day. But they are drawn to read those papers because they are the voice of the very towns where they are accustomed to shop. And the day-after-day, month-after-month exposure to the news minutiae of a particular town inevitably creates a sense of identity with its people and institutions.

4. This study adds to the body of literature which shows that media serve complementary rather than competing functions for the public. People do not think of the media as possible substitutes for each other. They perceive them as serving unique and distinctive needs. The weekly paper of the local community is not in competition with the surrounding dailies. It provides a different kind of coverage and focus of interest than the dailies do. Television, with its aura of show-business glamour and the national hook-up, represents a different kind of experience to the consumer than the daily newspapers which reflect primarily informational needs that reflect the individual's local orientation.

5. Increased personal mobility in America's growing inter-urban regions may make meaningless the classical designations of community and society as terms defined in space which determine social allegiances and social ties. In Intercity, there is a crisscrossing of mobility patterns, orientations and allegiances from one community to the next. The areas dominated by each central city interpenetrate with those dominated by others. Each of the surrounding larger centers reaches into Intercity for part of its human traffic and loyalties, and in turn Intercitizens borrow from each.

This study offers a modest demonstration of how people may experience identifications at many different levels—with the larger society of which they are a part, with role segments or strata in that larger society, with the local neighborhood community in which they live, and at an intermediate level with the cities or towns whose affairs they follow through the mass media, and to which they are drawn by work, shopping, friendship, or entertainment. Their actions as consumers in the marketplace are inseparable from their other social roles. (pp. 179–88).

In closing this discussion of communication as an operation within a community and—as in the case of Springdale and Intercity—as an operation of the larger society, it is important to stress again the role of interpersonal relationships as a part of the communication channels. Mass media, as we have seen, play a vital part in the flow of information, but social contacts have much to do with individual decisions. This chapter also highlights, as did the concluding section of Chapter 7, the interplay between community and society and how the needs of both social systems are articulated to fulfill the needs of individuals, who claim membership in both systems—as a Springdaler and as an American.

11

Adaptive Change to Internal and External Pressures

A community persists through time because it changes. Without adaptation to internal and external pressures its organization and institutions would become so rigid and outdated that it would break down as a social system. This becomes clearer as we inquire into the nature of social change, the kinds of adaptation that occur, and the extent to which a community social system can approach integration (Ryan, 1969).

THE NATURE OF SOCIAL CHANGE

Change itself is neutral. To describe it is to state what has occurred without necessarily telling whether this seems good or bad to the investigator. This is why social scientists do not try to *measure progress* but attempt to *describe change*. What seems progress to one group in the community, such as banning the sale of liquor within the city limits, may seem a step backward to those who are engaged in the activity. Any individual should be able to read the description of change, and then, from the standpoint of his own values, judge whether progress or retrogression has occurred.

241

The Temporal Aspect

Furthermore, change has a time dimension, since it indicates differences in relationships between two points in time. To trace the changes occurring in race relations would require comparing the situation as of a given date with the relations at a later date. The original description of relationships from which change is traced is often spoken of as the "bench mark" for measuring social change.

There are many communities which have been studied over a period of time by social science research groups. Some of the best known, however, have been done by one or two investigators. For example, Robert and Helen Lynd (1929) pioneered in community study by a survey of Middletown, an Indiana city, in the 1920's. In the 1930's they returned to make a resurvey, which they published under the title *Middletown in Transition* (1937). Another trail-blazing community study was done of Tepoztlan, Mexico, by Robert Redfield (1930), an anthropologist. This was restudied in 1943–44 and during shorter periods in 1947 and 1948, by Oscar Lewis (1951), twenty-five years later. The later study showed not only that the community had changed but also that social science methods and perspectives had matured considerably. A New England town labeled "Indecisive Hamlet" by Carle Zimmerman (1938), in his work *The Changing Community*, was restudied during the 1940's by David and Mary Hatch (1949), and called "Hilltown" in their published account. More recently Art Gallaher, Jr., restudied a Missouri Ozark community called Plainville by James West (1945), who observed it in the 1940's. Gallaher (1961) found major differences in the stratification system when comparing his results with those noted fifteen years before.

As those who study the community develop better-defined methodologies, the restudies, known as *replications*, will be increasingly more valuable, especially if care is taken to follow the same methods and to work within the same conceptual orientation. The general tendency, however, is for the author of the restudy to incorporate new approaches and supplementary methods in the hope of making a more significant interpretation than would otherwise result (Sewell, 1949).

Types of Change

What do these studies and many others like them show about the meaning of the term "social change"? First, they illustrate at least three kinds of social change (Washburne, 1954). One kind is *cat-aclysmic* as represented by a revolution, an earthquake, or some other social or natural catastrophe. Such events shake and some-times topple the community social structure (Form and Nasow, 1958). Another kind of change is *planned* (Holmberg and Dobyns, 1962; Lippett, Watson, Westley, 1958). A group of people consciously set out to modify segments of community life. A third kind, *sociocultural drift*, may be illustrated by the fact that dating and courtship practices over a period of time adjust to and even influence new economic patterns, the community value system may shift somewhat, or the role of local government may shrink or expand. Since these results are not necessarily sought in themselves, such change comes about in a haphazard way. Roland L. Warren (1972) has listed seven aspects of what he calls the "great change" taking place in American communities:

1. Division of labor
2. Differentiation of interests and association
3. Increasing systemic relationships to the larger society
4. Bureaucratization and impersonalization
5. Transfer of functions to profit enterprise and government
6. Urbanization and suburbanization
7. Changing values

Most of these are treated, if not in this chapter, elsewhere in this book. Such a list serves the useful purpose of stressing the impor-tance of change in modern community life, and of showing its many aspects and the need for further inquiry into the nature of social change.

Nor must one assume that all change is external to a community. There is immanent social change (Sorokin, 1947) that is inherent in the social structure of the community and is a reflection of the var-ious strains to which it is subjected. Wilbert E. Moore (1960) cites three kinds of strains: the first is demographic imbalance. As was shown in Chapter 4 populations do change in numbers and in com-position through time resulting in adjustments in the family system, the economy, and other parts of the social structure (Mayer and Marx, 1957). A second strain mentioned by Moore is that of uni-versal scarcity situations. He writes, "Not only are goods and ser-vices, or their monetary representation, likely to be scarce relative to human 'wants,' but so are time and loyalty (or 'affective energy'). These three scarcities are often interrelated, so that allocations of loyalty may be indicated by allocation of time or treasure or both."

(p. 814). Therefore, strains are set up in a community due to un-equal distribution of wealth or unequal political support (Phillips, 1963). A third strain is the "dialectic" conflict between normative alternatives. For example, should a person be judged and given social prestige on the basis of birth or of what he can achieve as an individual? This question is never fully put to rest no matter what the answer to it may seem to be at a given moment. Many such questions involving normative alternatives (what should and should not be) produce strains within the social structure (Cancian, 1960; Parsons, 1961).

Thus a mature theory of social change holds that a community as a social system is not simply pushed around by the larger system of which it is a part, but that much change finds its source in local conditions that reflect strains in the social structure. But this having been said, it is also necessary to describe forces generated from with-out which act upon the community (Ogburn, 1950).

Selected Change Processes

Many communities feel the impact of numerous features of dom-inant metropolitan areas. The young people of a community be-come attracted to the city and move there in search of work, thereby leaving the older people and children behind to carry on life in the home community; or the conveniences of city homes have such a fascination for those in smaller communities that they, often at con-siderable sacrifice, seek to install them too. With these conveniences come many other patterns of city life, so that one can correctly speak of the process of *urbanization* as covering not only the movement of people to the cities but the movement of city ways to rural areas where they are taken over by the people still living there (Hauser, 1955).

When factories come to a community, they introduce the process of *industrialization* to that town, which is making an adjustment in the interest of what its people hope will prove to be greater eco-nomic gain (Bertrand and Osborne, 1959; Black, Frederickson and Maitland, 1960; Kahl, 1959; Wilkinson, 1960). This process involves mass employment, but also the possibility of mass unemployment; it increases the social heterogeneity as far as occupational strata are concerned; it is usually accompanied by unionization, or the mass organization of workers into labor unions, to deal with those guiding the mass production of our economy. Alex Inkeles (1960 and 1969) has studied industrialization, urbanization, and the development of large-scale bureaucratic structures in order to test the proposition "that men's environment, as expressed in the institutional patterns they adopt or have introduced to them, shapes their experience, and through this their perceptions, attitudes, and values, in standardized ways that are manifest from country to country [one might add from community to community], despite the countervailing randomizing influence of traditional cultural patterns." (1960, p. 2). Thus, the industrial worker in one place will be much like the industrial worker elsewhere simply because of the character of industrialization.

Still another process of change is *commercialization,* which means that more and more aspects of life are brought under the influence of the businessman. Recreation, which may at one time have been cost-free, since it took place in informal groups and involved participation by the people themselves, becomes a business, and people pay to enjoy activities that fill up their leisure.

Another process of change necessitating adjustment is *secularization,* or the tendency to substitute rationality for tradition, to apply the scientific inquiry to areas formerly considered sacred or taboo (e.g., the Masters-Johnson studies in sex), to vote for the candidate one prefers rather than for the party to which one's father belonged, to accept some impersonality in social relationships without feeling that one needs to know all of the intimate details about one's associates.

Maurice R. Stein (1960), who has made one of the clearest expositions of these transitional processes, adds to urbanization and industrialization a third process of bureaucratization. He bases his analysis of urbanization primarily upon the work of Robert E. Park (1952) and his associates at the University of Chicago, the analysis of industrialization upon the two studies of Middletown by the Lynds, and the analysis of bureaucratization upon the studies of Newburyport, Massachusetts, which was written up by W. Lloyd Warner (1941) and his associates as the Yankee City Series. One indication of this bureaucratization is the passing of the control of local factories from people living in the community to corporation boards whose members live outside the community and may reveal little interest in its welfare.

These processes—urbanization, industrialization, commercialization, secularization, and bureaucratization—are part of the American and Western European way of life and few communities avoid their impact. These not only characterize areas of life in which change is occurring but they also typify certain major adjustments that the people of a community make to dynamic forces about them.

On the assumption that one is trying to understand the community as a social system, to figure out how it operates as a totality of interacting persons, the study of social change can be limited in scope to cover the area of social relationships. If these are the focus, then such a study would concentrate upon changes in status and role, in values and norms. It would be concerned not just with persons as social actors but also with groups and subsystems as partners in interaction. There are four levels at which this change may be analyzed, according to Nelson, Ramsey, and Verner (1960).

One is that of the total community where we see, for example, the process of secularization at work with its shift from a sacred-folk to a secular-prescribed structure. A second level is that of the pan-community, or the shifts in relations between a given community and other area-bound social units such as the school district or even the Great Society. A third level involves community-wide elements of community structure, such as the stratification system or the relations between the family and the school. A fourth level of change may occur in a component such as the family or the organization of the school itself. This last level is not community change per se, but it may be significant in producing community-wide change.

Obviously, attention would have to be paid to ecological and demographic influences, to the importance of economic and psychological factors, and certainly to historical continuity. But the starting point of the inquiry would be: What is happening to the relationships (in both structural and dynamic terms) among the social units of this community?

Attitudes Toward Change Within the Community

A social scientist may carefully trace numerous changes within one community, publicize his findings, and create a ripple of interest that soon subsides; in another community, his report is greeted with great consideration, becomes the topic of animated discussion, and eventually proves the focal point for some planned community action. Such experiences indicate marked differences in attitudes between communities toward the introduction of new ideas and ways of doing things.

A community may be characterized by the way its leaders, who are responsible for deciding about matters of joint concern, react to social change as they try to establish what to them seems an equilibrium (Tumin and Rotberg, 1957).

In the first place, they may resist change in all its forms to the best of their ability. They may feel that what they have is so good that it ought to be preserved; they may fear any alteration in their own position or situation if new forces begin to work within the community. To such people, the coming in of additional factories may seem undesirable. They fight their coming, frequently in open meeting, so that industrialists who may have originally thought of locating there shift to some other place. Such leaders may also resist a school bond issue that would help the community meet its educational needs. The reasons they give for opposition are complex, involving more than the objection to additional taxes that would have to be levied; they may even reveal an attitude that "ordinary people" should not be educated too far out of line with their social expectations. Not all of the people of the community agree with these leaders; yet they have little voice since they are not involved in the major decisions unless some issue is put to public vote.

In the second place, and much more commonly, one finds that the leaders are selective in their approach to social change. They recognize that change is inevitable; they have a philosophy of progress and lean toward the idea that a certain degree of social planning will help the people of the community arrive at goals considered desirable. Such leaders may also fight the coming in of what they think undesirable; they may also try to retain for the community some plant or government establishment that is about to be transferred elsewhere; they may also contribute generously to the development of an over-all metropolitan plan for the area in which they live. These leaders differ from that type of innovator, a few of whom are found in almost every community, who seem to think that any change is good and thrive on the excitement of a crisis situation.

Many communities, to mention a third reaction to change, seem to be apathetic or indifferent to change. In such cases, the leaders are often found to be deeply immersed in their own personal affairs and turn to community problems only when some acute difficulty has arisen and demands immediate attention. They have no real understanding of the nature of social change nor of its operation in the community; they seldom try to see the community as a whole or to think of its potentialities five or ten years hence. The rest of the community accepts conditions as they are, is little concerned about changes under way, and gives only token support to those members of the community who try to take positive action about housing, health, unemployment, or youth activities.

The attitude of the leaders toward change need not be just a matter of conjecture. It, too, can be studied, as shown by Marvin Bressler and Charles F. Westoff (1954) in their analysis of the reactions of leaders to increased industrialization in a semirural area of Pennsylvania (Bucks County). They were able to make the following inferences:

> The attitude towards social change in Lower Bucks County did not appear necessarily to be either stable or unidimensional, but instead frequently fluctuated between extremities of enthusiasm and vigorous opposition in the course of a single interview in accordance with the respondent's assumptions of one of his multiple roles. . . . Thus while as a businessman a leader might evince great enthusiasm for the impending changes, he might be less enthusiastic as a homeowner, somewhat apprehensive as a father, and positively distressed at the thought of the disturbance which the anticipated influx of new residents might impose on his ordinarily tranquil Sundays. (pp. 236–37).
>
> However, the roles which seemed to assume the highest priority for the respondent and appeared characteristically to be most influential in determining the direction of this attitude were those roles which involved current responsibility for his impending changes and entailed redefinition of his function. . . . (For example, a local official might realize that his duties would increase tremendously, so he would be gloomy about the prospect of industrialization.)
>
> Both the advantages and disadvantages accruing to Lower Bucks County as a result of the industrialization and urbanization process were perceived in tangible and material terms, primarily as it affected the economic sphere and the condition of community facilities and only secondarily in terms of expected alterations of cultural-ideological patterns and anticipated changes in the community as a result of the personal characteristics in the incoming population. (People thought concretely in terms of money, taxes, sewage system, crowded hospitals.)
>
> Certain words and phrases seemed to possess the quality of independent symbolic imperatives so that they seemed capable of requiring responses which sometimes appeared to be at variance with the respond-

ent's "real" attitude. (Such words were progress, planning, big-ness.) . . . . (p. 237).

[Furthermore]. . . . the more powerful group manifests a higher degree of favorability than the less powerful group. . . . This suggests the possible existence of a general mechanism by which an institutional role subtly influences individual cognitive and perceptual processes; those whose position in the social structure is vulnerable perceive any sort of change as still another threat to their security, while the strong and the powerful having already inherited the earth confidently expect that altered conditions, except those directly and specifically threatening them, will simply extend the range of their blessings. (p. 243).

One of the clearest examples of the ways in which communities differ in their approach to social change was provided by the comparison of Rimrock and Homestead already cited in Chapter 5. The Mormon village of Rimrock, which would be considered by some as conservative theologically and socially, was receptive to economic change and had a social organization geared in with the development of such change; Homestead, many of whose members would be considered much less conservative in social conventions, was indifferent to the available changes.

Leaders must act within this value orientation or else run the risk of losing their following. If they possess certain economic or political controls, and are not immediately and directly dependent upon prompt approval by the rest of the community for everything they do, they may feel that occasionally they can run counter to the value orientation or, to put it more correctly, rise above it and set it aside.

The differential attitudes toward change within a community may prove a source of local conflict. A *pro* and a *con* group arise to fight for or against some proposed change. Such disagreements may become bitter and result in impaired social relationships affecting community life for years to come. Oftentimes the *con* or *anti* group is fighting a losing battle, since it may be trying to resist some impersonal change that is already well under way in the larger society and is beginning to make its impact upon the local community.

On the other hand, the need to meet some crisis or community problem may draw many of the people of a community together. They may feel that they have had something to do with guiding change for their locality. Whether this is a correct interpretation or not, the fact that the people believe it, affects their relationships with each other and the zeal with which they will deal with future problems.

Before leaving the topic of social change it is important to draw attention to the fact that those who use the social system paradigm are often accused of ignoring social change because of their preoccupation with the relationship among the parts of the system, thereby seeming to defend the *status quo*. Lauer (1971) notes:

> . . . Sociologists, then, have been far more concerned with structures than with processes, and, even where they have dealt with processes, they have tended to delimit them within structurally legitimate bounds. Persistence and regularities have been viewed as the normal state of affairs; change has been viewed as a kind of social deviance. (p. 881).

Parsons (1961) has taken the position that social system theorists are not oblivious to change, and so the debate is joined. The issue revolves around the question as to whether one must have a picture of the structure so that one will know what it is that changes versus the belief that a knowledge of structure is not necessary but rather gets in the way of understanding social change.

ADAPTATION

The previous discussion has highlighted both the fact of social change and something of its nature in the community. We still must deal with the question of how the community as a system changes, since the change processes already described relate not only to the individual caught up in them but also affect the relationships among the various groups and subsystems of the community. Furthermore, a community's connections with other communities and the larger society shift through time. These, too, must be understood.

At least two operations within the community relate to its response to change and its efforts to keep going as a social system. One of these has been termed *adaptation* and the other *integration*. When each of these has been looked at individually, we shall then note the interplay between them.

Where conditions are relatively *static*, behavior patterns within the community undergo minor modifications but remain essentially the same through time. However, where dramatically new forces come in to shift the accents in human motivation or create new value orientation, the behavior patterns, or roles, change too. Groups such as political parties or business enterprises that will not change their methods to meet new conditions lose out in the struggle for support of the public; however, the fact that such groups do usually change means that their competitors must also change, and the changes carried out by these rivals in turn stimulate other change. Under such conditions of change and counterchange we have a *dynamic* society. Change becomes built into the social structure and is accepted as one of the normal expectations of social life.

One of the most helpful ways of viewing the change within any community or segment of the community is to think of it as an adjustment by people to what they may consider new circumstances. William H. Harlan (1954), in studying what has happened in St. Petersburg, Florida, under the influx of many aged people, makes use of the term *community adaptation.* He says:

> The functional relationships among the individuals and institutions of a community may be altered as a result of changes in demographic, economic, or social processes. As one segment of a community undergoes change, adaptive or adjustive modifications are to be expected in others. Distinctly social changes are described by the term "social adjustment," which has been defined [by E. W. Burgess] as "the adaptation to social change by modifications of social institutions." The term "community adaptation" . . . is more inclusive, covering both ecological and social changes. (p. 332).

One of the most common examples of adaptation is the development of a specialized group to deal with the new problem being encountered. As communities move from the simpler to the more complex forms, this process of *differentiation*, as it is called, is a key to understanding how change occurs. In the economic sphere we see new specialists open up shops to repair all kinds of electronic equipment that were not even dreamed of by the average person a generation ago; in recreation, new forms arise to interest the person with more leisure due to a shorter work week; in religion, various ministerial and lay councils come into existence to work out more harmonious relationships among those of different faiths; in civil rights, human relations councils are created to advise the mayor and other officials on ways of reducing racial tension and of extending to all the people of the community the benefits to which they are entitled. Thus the community is never a closed system; it is open to its environment and must respond to innovation through its various components. In recent times specialized groups have been set up primarily to deal with innovation as a fact of life.

Adaptation, according to John E. Bebout and Harry C. Bredemeier (1963), can refer to the procurement of things from an environment, and the disposal of things to the environment. They write:

> It follows from this that if we want to understand a social system such as a city or a region, we first must specify what its parts are and what its environment is. Second, we have to discover what the city or region needs from its environment, what it offers its environment, and by what mechanisms it seeks to effect those transactions with its environment. Third, assuming that we have identified the city's or the region's inputs and outputs and the mechanisms governing them, we have to discover how *well*-adapted it is—whether it is suffering from procurement difficulties or disposal difficulties, or both. Fourth, assuming that we discover there is something wrong—as we know we will, since everyone is complaining loudly about aches and pains—we have to find out what it is about the city's or region's bargaining power or legal position or loyalty-relations that is responsible for its maladaption. Fifth, we must ascertain what changes would be necessary in order to *improve* the bargaining, or solidarity position of the city. At this stage, we will almost certainly find that the changes that would have to be made will hurt someone or some group. That is, it is probably nearly always the case that whatever the distribution of bargaining power or legal rights and obligations or loyalty-solidarity sentiments, *some* units or *some* systems are making at least short-run profits out of that distribution.
>
> In any case, assuming we have ascertained the changes that would have to be made in order to correct the disequilibrium, the *sixth* step is to decide how to persuade those persons or groups to accept the pain that will be necessary if adaptation is to be improved; and this step will involve us precisely in either bargaining with them, coercing them, calling upon their sense of duty, or calling upon their sympathy and solidarity. Having thus explored the adaptations of the city or region, we must consider its integration. This will involve discovering which persons and groups within the city are maladapted, in what ways and to whom; what is wrong with their respective bargaining, legal, or solidaristic; positions; and what can be done, through bargaining, coercion, or other mechanisms to improve their positions.[1]

But not all adaptation is as rational an operation as the above passage would indicate. Very few people are taking the overview of the community as a whole. Most of them, even while making an adaptation that in the long run benefits the system, are thinking

---

[1] John E. Bebout and Harry C. Bredemeier, "American Cities as Social Systems," *Journal of the American Institute of Planners* 29 (May, 1963), 66–67. Reprinted by permission of the American Institute of Planners.

along two lines: (1) how can I solve this immediate problem connected with my job, my organization, my community responsibility; and (2) what possible solution will cause me least trouble from others in the community (my competitors, the city fathers, my neighbors, etc.) who might be affected by the solution accepted. Thus selfish short-run interest is tempered by the knowledge of community reaction. It might be cheaper for a factory to let all of the fumes from its furnaces float into the atmosphere, but those affected by these fumes call for a different adaptation; it might be simpler for a community to dump all of its sewage untreated into a nearby river, but the communities below would raise such a hue and cry that the first community is forced to treat the sewage before releasing it. Such decisions are being made continuously about many matters in the community, many of them by people trained and paid to make such decisions. The totality of what they individually decide and are able to carry out makes up the overall community adaptation at any one time. Now and then, some official organ such as the city council may make a decision which cancels out or modifies the decision of most householders (say an adaptation to a water shortage) or businessmen or any other group. What is significant, however, is that the innovation or adaptation affects and is affected by the community environment in which it occurs.

INTEGRATION

Werner S. Landecker makes a helpful distinction among four types of integration, each of which has a bearing upon the community as a social system.[2] First, there is a *cultural* integration, or a relationship "among traits which constitute cultural standards in the sense that they require adherence." This takes one back to the cultural factor in "The Setting," p. 43. If the values, beliefs, and standards are full of inconsistencies (not integrated), then the social system that shares that culture is beset with difficulties. To illustrate, there may be contradictions in certain standards required of everyone (that is, "universal" traits). People may be expected to be both altruistic and competitive and may have these two standards

---

[2] Werner S. Landecker, "Types of Integration and Their Measurement," *American Journal of Sociology* 56 (January, 1951), 332–40. A main theme of this article, not touched upon here, is the problem of selecting indexes whereby these various types of integration can be measured.

drilled into them without being shown under what circumstances they are to be one and not the other. Or again, there may be inconsistencies among the standards required of special groupings within the population ("specialties") that have societal references, such as those shared by labor on the one hand and business management on the other as to the proper place of labor in the business enterprise.[3] It is clear that what is being integrated in this cultural type are the traits of culture themselves, a topic touched upon in Chapter 5. A community whose members inherit many of these unresolved contradictions in their thought-ways has difficulty in achieving community solidarity.

Although a social scientist can study the consistencies or inconsistencies existing among these cultural traits, such matters only become a part of the community system as people react to them and accept or reject them as norms of conduct. Landecker terms this second type of integration *normative*, for its central question is the extent to which conduct is in accord with the norms. There could conceivably be genuine cultural integration but little normative integration if the people failed to abide by the norms supposedly in force. This occurs in those communities of rapidly industrializing societies where old standards no longer seem to apply, at least as they have been customarily interpreted, to the new situation. Some young people in particular are apt to reject most of the traditional traits and seek earnestly for what they would consider more modern substitutes.

A third type of integration is *participative*.[4] As Landecker indicates "the more comprehensive the network of interpersonal communication, the smaller the number of isolated persons" and in his interpretation the degree of isolation is an important clue to breakdown in communication. Isolation can be social as well as physical. Being present with a number of other people does not necessarily imply participation or overt interaction with them. This kind of integration is central to an understanding of the community as a

---

[3] Landecker points out that the third of Ralph Linton's types of cultural traits ("alternatives"), in terms of which people have a choice and face no moral dilemma, is not as relevant to the problem of integration as are the "universals" and "specialties." See Ralph Linton, *The Study of Man* (New York: Appleton-Century-Crofts, Inc., 1936), p. 282.

[4] The term *participative integration* has been substituted here for Landecker's term *communicative integration* as more nearly descriptive of the type under discussion and as more suitable to the analysis of the community as a social system. After all, what is meant here is the integration of social actors (persons, groups, etc.) into the over-all system, and not the integration of symbols used in communication.

social system, since it deals with the degree to which people are involved actively in community life. As earlier chapters have shown, this interaction is through groups, most of whom at times take on communal characteristics in that something they do or stand for has a community-wide influence. Not only does the study of this type of integration deal with the breakdown of barriers of communication, but it also involves the means by which community members are encouraged to express themselves with reference to matters of social concern. Along with this goes the process of identification, which Nelson Foote (1951) views as an important element in the understanding of motivation. As people participate, they develop a sense of belonging but at the same time derive a heightened sense of their own identity, for "identification is the process whereby individuals are effectively linked with their fellows in groups." (p. 21)

The fourth type of integration is *functional* interdependence, with special reference to the division of labor in the community. How are the social components of a system dependent upon each other? Who exchanges functions with whom? Many who approach the study of society from the standpoint of ecology (see page 43) use this particular type of integration as an important tool for analysis (Hawley, 1971) and try to arrive at a community description without using the value system as a guide to the interpretation of community behavior. But no matter what the approach and despite varied preferences for terminology, the fact remains that if a social system is to exist its components must be interrelated—that is, function—for the benefit of the system. This is closely tied in with the operation of differentiation and allocation of status, with the emphasis upon what holds the system together once people have been distributed to many specialties.

In viewing integration as an operation of the community as a system we therefore find it useful to distinguish among the various kinds of integration. But when we have studied each of these by the use of varied indexes, we can probably express a net judgment as to whether the community is becoming more or less integrated and can list any obstacles to further integration. [5]

Albert J. Reiss, Jr. (1954), in one of the most incisive monographs evaluating research on the community, sets forth four tentative

---

[5] E. A. Wilkening effectively states the need for greater attention to studies of integration in "Some Perspectives on Changes in Rural Societies," *Rural Sociology* 29 (March, 1964), 1–17.

postulates on change within the community; one of which deals with the level of integration:

1. Certain institutions, e.g., sustenance and residential institutions, primarily exist on a communal basis and function with respect to local orientations and actions.
2. Change always requires overcoming institutionalized resistances.
3. Communities may have certain institutionalized modes of change, unique to communal systems.
4. The orientation of residents of a community to change is a function of the level of integration of the communal system.

To illustrate the fourth point he cites the writings of Burton W. Kreitlow and Roland Koyen, who have studied the way Wisconsin communities accepted reorganization of their elementary school districts, and have indicated those factors that led to acceptance of and resistance to change.

Bebout and Bredemeier (1963), quoted earlier in connection with adaptation, link it closely to integration:

> The "integration" of a system, then, is a matter of the mutual adaptation of its parts. A system is well integrated to the degree that its parts procure from one another the things they are specialized to need, and find acceptance from one another of the things they are specialized to produce. Integration and adaptation, then, are the same thing looked at from two different points of view. What is an adaptive problem from the point of view of a unit, is part of the integrative problem of the system of which that unit is a part. For example, the mutual adaptive problems of the City of Newark and of neighboring if not "suburban" East Orange are part of the integration problems of Essex County, of the state of New Jersey, and of the New York metropolitan region. In the same way the mutual adaptive problems of whites and Negroes are part of the integrative problems of the United States. (p. 64).

Put in social system terms, the expected result of adaptation is the maintenance of the system as an *integer*, or whole. Adaptation is change, to be sure, but of a sort that tends to offset disintegrating trends.[6] Some of these trends are within the system and must be

---

[6] In analytical models of social systems, frequent mention is made of stable and unstable equilibriums and of static and moving equilibriums. These concepts have deep theoretical interest and deserve expanded study and research. At the present time, their utility in concrete community studies is questionable. Dealing with different kinds of adaptation and different levels of integration holds more promise just now. Eventually, computer techniques may make it possible to deal effectively with community equilibrium models and the large number of variables that would have to be included. See Everett E. Hagen, "Analytical Models in the Study of Social Systems," *American Journal of Sociology* 67 (September, 1961), 144–51; Parsons, *op. cit.*, pp. 221–25.

corrected in the normal course of the system's ordinary behavior. This correction, or internal adaptation, does not effect significant structural changes within the system or alter its characteristic properties. But there are disintegrative trends from outside, such as some of the change processes described earlier in this chapter, which can only be countered by some structural or operating changes in the system itself. This systemic change may occur in the modification primarily of one major system (the economy, for instance) with some slight adjustments on the part of other systems (such as the family). Or, the modification may extend through several major systems, with much more drastic effect on the community as a whole. In the face of such an event, the responsible community leaders try to keep the community behaving as a unit of action, achieving whatever integration they can, although they realize that the community will not be restored to the condition it had prior to the drastic change. Some of their followers, however, may not accept this fact and keep pressing for a restoration of the *status quo ante*.

COPING

Adaptation and integration can be viewed as operations describing a community's reaction to change. Within the social system paradigm which has been presented, it is permissible to speak of the community as an acting unit, as a totality of social relations which has consistency and form an entity. Thus, at an abstract, theoretical level the analysis is well-founded and proves useful in classifying the observed data, and in indicating various interrelationships which may be found. To use the social system metaphor is a convenient way to talk about communal behavior.

What is troubling at the everyday, practical level is the fact that a community very rarely acts as a unit. Relatively few problems are of the sort that go before duly constituted local governmental bodies for decision and these obtain only when the community boundaries are made to coincide with the political unit. They hold for the statutory community, not the natural community.

If the community as a whole does not act, how does a community cope? It does so through the formation of various coalitions when new problems are defined and have to be dealt with. Such a coalition is made up of those people who are concerned with a particular problem (wetlands control, abortions in the local hospital, type of sex education in the school, provisions for low cost housing, lessening conflict between two religious bodies, declining values of a business district, halting a highway extension through a populated area, control of local campaign expenses, dealing with a teen-age drug problem or adult alcoholism). Often they are self-appointed champions of some cause in behalf of the community without any official legitimation of their role; they may or may not by their actions bring into being an opposing group, so that an issue is joined at the community level. Frequently, these coalitions are able to get favorable action without ever raising the problem to the level of a community issue. Integration of a system concentrates upon ways the various parts relate efficiently to each other; coping stresses the ways various coalitions arise to deal with what to them are real personal concerns.

Coping, like integration, seeks to broaden consensus among members of the community by providing a rationale within the existing value and normative systems. This is because problem-solving proceeds much more quickly if there is consensus (Scheff, 1967). At times, however, coping introduces conflict and tries to create a new consensus about a problem, rejecting the past ways of viewing the problem. The more successful coalitions often are able to work out accommodation at the friction points between two agencies, organizations or institutions. To do this, they help reinterpret the organizational domain so that the feeling of threat is reduced on the part of organizations affected; they may help social units with whom they deal to reinterpret their goals so that there is closer correspondence between stated aims and what is actually being carried out; and they may seek a redefinition of the authority of the leaders involved. The coalition is not consciously concerning itself with system properties but with the actual social network related to the specific problem it is trying to resolve. Some forms of coping, as we shall see in the next chapter, run counter to the consensus, accommodative model in favor of the conflict model. This happens when the coalition is not merely seeking to carry a project or limited goal to a successful conclusion but where the coalition is striving to change the systemic properties of the community itself. It chooses not to work through the established value system and established channels. Often such efforts fail because those involved do not realize the persistence of the community as a system and the difficulty in changing its institutionalized patterns.

To summarize, the community from the social system standpoint continues generation after generation because it has a local institutional order, inherited from the past, which continues to operate with a momentum that is sometimes hard to stop; it has a series of operations designed to maintain its continuity: recruitment, socialization, social control, division of labor (differentiation), allocation, communication, adaptation and integration. Viewed at the level of the individual actors, their formation into coalitions to solve particular problems also provides a coping mechanism which under many circumstances reinforces the perpetuation of the community as already constituted.

IV

THE COMMUNITY IN PROCESS: INEQUALITY AND CONFLICT

Part Four deals with conflict and sets forth some of the views of those who either see conflict as an inherent and, in some respects, useful part of an on-going social system or who view it as an inevitable consequence of existing inequalities in society and a prelude to drastic, radical social change.

People with different perspectives and social philosophies ask different questions about a community and social change. The vast majority accept the community as it is for that is the way they have been brought up. They are conditioned to prefer its way of doing things in comparison with that found in other social systems around the world. Quite a few, especially those in favored positions, are apt to ask:

How can we keep unwelcome change from upsetting our community?

By this they mean discouraging the entry of large-scale industry that would bring in labor unions and thereby upset the current wage scales, the opposition to construction of low-cost housing that they think might encourage poor people to settle in the community, and obstruction of legal measures that would "disturb" existing relationships among various ethnic and minority groups. This, of course, means the solid support of the *status quo*.

Others who view the community in a favorable light may nevertheless be conscious of some of its faults. They frequently ask:

How can we make this community a better place in which to live?

They face up to the existence of long-tolerated social problems and urge the promotion of social justice for all people, better education for the underprivileged, the elimination of various forms of pollution, and the adoption of numerous programs that hopefully ameliorate conditions they deem undesirable. They are often called *reformists*. Committed to the present system, whose advantages in their opinion outweigh its disadvantages, they want to make it better.

A smaller number of people, whose ranks are apparently increasing, are becoming more aware of the fact that they are not getting as many benefits from the community as other people derive. They talk about their rights. Not content with the accepted fact that *education* in the community is today a *right*, they are saying that *health services* should be a right and that *having a job* should be a right. They have moved away from the traditional concept that such benefits should be an individual responsibility to the idea that provision of these "goods" is a collective responsibility. They ask:

How can I get more of what should be coming to me?

Such people may accept the social system of which they are a part, not as reformists who seek to improve the system, but as recipients who want to benefit more fully from the system. On the other hand, some of them may have given up the idea that they and their kind will ever benefit sufficiently from the community as it now stands and that the only recourse is to overthrow the system. They and others who do not accept the basic operating premises of American society, and therefore of its communities, may ask:

How can we weaken the existing power structure to the point that another system greatly modifying economic and political relationships can be constructed?

This is, of course, the *radical* perspective. Conflict is therefore not to be lessened as the reformers would hope; it is to be encouraged because through conflict one can weaken the present system in order to bring about a revolutionary change.

The chapters immediately following deal with the matters posed by the questions noted above.

12

The Conflict Paradigm

Some community sociologists prefer to view the community in terms of conflict rather than as a stable social system. They argue that basic social change comes about primarily through conflict and, if one wants to know how and why a community changes, one should analyze the conflict which occurs there.

The purpose of this chapter, therefore, is to provide a conceptual scheme with conflict as the central theme and then show how a community appears if seen in terms of this scheme. Since there are so many kinds of conflict and these are associated with so many factors, no comprehensive coverage will be attempted. Yet a consistent approach will be presented. Although some conflict theorists refer to whatever unit they are describing (society, community, group) as a social system, we will not make use of the social system paradigm here. Instead, one should think of the community as an aggregation of people, pursuing their own self-interests; they join into groups to further these interests (family, lodges, churches, labor unions, business concerns) and these groups interact with each other. At any given time, some of these interpersonal and intergroup relationships will be antagonistic and lead to overt conflict. What the conflict is about, what efforts are made to contain it, and its effect will depend upon many social characteristics of the community, some of which will be spelled out in this and the next four chapters.

The conflict point of view has a long tradition in sociology. Most of its proponents have thought in much broader terms than the local community. Those in the evolutionary tradition, such as the "social Darwinists" viewed struggle for existence as conflict among fit and less fit individuals; Ludwig Gumplowicz saw such struggle as being primarily between hordes, leading to racial conflict and the enslavement of the weaker by the stronger; while Jacques Novicow considered eternal struggle as a universal law basic to human society but thought that in time the more deadly types of struggle (war) would be replaced by milder forms.[1]

Karl Marx and Friedrich Engels claimed in *The Communist Manifesto* that the history of all hitherto existing society was the history of class struggles. In addition, they held to a dialectical theory of social change which claims that every value or social fact (thesis) has its opposite (antithesis) with which it eventually clashes, resulting in something new (synthesis). These contradictions can exist at three levels: first, between values, ideologies or scientific or philosophical theories; second, between institutionalized principles or forces arising out of the social structure, as evidenced in latent internal contradictions; and, at the third level, between groups which have different interests, often conflicting (defined by sex, education, wealth, etc.) (Van den Berghe, 1963).

Lewis Coser (1956), basing his work in part on that of Georg Simmel, deals with numerous sociological aspects of conflict. Some of his major points are the following:

> Social conflict . . . may be taken to mean a struggle over values and claims to scarce status, power, and resources in which the aims of the opponents are to neutralize, injure, or eliminate their rivals. (p. 8).

Coser also indicates that such conflict may be between individuals or between collectivities; or there may be opposition between an individual and a collectivity. He reminds us that social conflict is not always a negative factor but may actually contribute in many ways to the maintenance of groups and collectivities.

Two writers (Lyman and Scott, 1970) have used the term "the Sociology of the Absurd" to highlight their belief that the world is essentially without meaning. The idea of a social system is repugnant to them. Instead, they assume a "model of man in conflict— with others, with society, with nature, and even with himself

---

[1] For a good discussion of the early "conflict" theorists see Pitirim Sorokin, *Contemporary Sociological Theories.* New York: Harper and Brothers, 1928; Lewis A. Coser, *The Functions of Social Conflict.* New York: Free Press, 1956.

. . . By beginning with the assumption that social life is one of conflict, it follows that every social situation is problematic for those involved . . . The sociologist must view man as the maker and remaker of social existence, as the producer and reproducer of stable engagements, as the craftsman of society and the ever-renewed social order."

(p. 6)

As one can see, the Sociology of the Absurd draws its inspiration from existentialism and phenomenology.

COMPARISON BETWEEN THE SOCIAL SYSTEM AND THE CONFLICT PARADIGM

Before turning to the details of the conflict approach it is useful to compare it in very general terms with the social system or integrative approach. For this we draw upon the writings of Ralf Dahrendorf (1959), who views conflict in terms of coercion. Some people are "kept down," they do not have free expression, they experience an element of constraint in almost every relationship.

TABLE 12–1

Contrasts in the Integration and Coercion Theories of Society

Elements	Integration Theory	Coercion Theory
Stability or Change	Every society is a relatively persistent, stable structure of elements.	Every society is at every point subject to processes of change: social change is ubiquitous
Integration or conflict	Every society is a well-integrated structure of elements.	Every society displays at every point dissensus and conflict; social conflict is ubiquitous.
Functional coordination or disintegration	Every element in a society has a function, i.e. renders a contribution to its maintenance as a system.	Every element in a society renders a contribution to its disintegration and change.
Consensus or coercion	Every functioning social structure is based on a consensus of values among its members.	Every society is based on the coercion of some of its members by others.

Source: Adapted from Ralf Dahrendorf, *Class and Class Conflict in Industrial Society*, Stanford: Stanford University Press, 1959.

Dahrendorf (1959) recognizes, of course, that these are extreme and incompatible characterizations of the social system and conflict models. The truth obviously lies somewhere in between. In his application of the coercion theory he writes:

> . . . In institutional terms, this means that in every social organization some positions are entrusted with a right to exercise control over other positions in order to ensure effective coercion; it means in other words, that there is a differential distribution of power and authority. One of the central theses of this study consists in the assumption that this differential distribution of authority invariably becomes the determining factor of systematic social conflicts of a type that is germane to class conflicts in the traditional (Marxian) sense of the term. The structural origin of such group conflicts must be sought in the arrangement of social roles endowed with expectations of domination or subjection. (p. 165).

THE COMMUNITY CONFLICT PARADIGM

A schematic presentation of conflict is difficult. In contrast to a social system which by definition has a unity, a consistency, conflict is sporadic, mercurial, episodic. Yet it does have a subterranean quality in deep-rooted antagonistic relationships, which at any moment may express themselves in unpredictable social forms and lead to unanticipated social effects. Figure 12–1 attempts to summarize some of the major aspects of conflict in the community and will serve as the organizing basis for the treatment of conflict in this and the following four chapters.

Conflict in any community, as the figure shows, involves three important elements. It consists of antagonistic relationships, differential power allocation, and some actual expression recognized by people in the community. The antagonistic relationships may be of two kinds: first, structural, which are built into the institutionalized patterns usually in the form of inequalities; second, issue-related, which are usually referred to as community controversies. Power is connected to the first of these—structural antagonistic relations—in the form of coercion, or the invoking of various kinds of social control to maintain the inequities by keeping "people in their place." Power is tied to the second kind of antagonistic social bond—issue-related—in terms of resource mobilization. Parties to a dispute bring to bear any resources at their disposal in order to have the controversy decided in their favor.

Types of Antagonistic Relations	Differential Power Allocation	Community Expression
Structural: Based on Sex Race Economic criteria Residential pattern Social criteria (e.g., religion, social class)	*Coercion:* Based on differ- tial allocation of Jobs and income Goods and services Prestige Network resources	*Channelled:* e.g. collective bargain- ing; political cam- paign *Unchannelled.* e.g., race riot
Issue-Related: Fluoridation School Busing School bond Issue Sex Education Low-cost housing etc.	*Resource Mobilization:* Legal action Finances Media Organizations Leadership Volunteers	*Stages:* (See Chapters 16 and 17)

Figure 12–1. Aspects of community conflict.

The expressions of conflict within the community also vary by type of antagonistic relationship. The structural may go through channelled forms, such as collective bargaining between labor and management, or through unchannelled protests, such as race riots. A controversy can be viewed as a series of stages which are accompanied by factionalism and disrupted social relations within the community, although resource mobilization also leads to the creation of new forms of cooperative relations among the partisans of a given side to the controversy.

Any paradigm is based on certain assumptions which should be made explicit. Some such assumptions are the following:

The community is viewed as a set of social relations.

A social relation has both integrative and dissociative tendencies.

At a given point in time a social relation may be characterized as being antagonistic or not.

The study of the community in terms of a conflict paradigm is the study of the antagonistic social relations, usually intergroup relations.

The kind, intensity and frequency of such relations in a community reflects and in turn affects the social characteristics of the community.

The Setting

The *conflict situation* consists not only of the antagonistic relations under study, but the setting in which they occur. Three kinds of setting features are included:

The ecosystem. There is competition for and frequently conflict over the choice physical sites in a community; there are "desirable" and "undesirable" places in which to live (see Chapter 3). Furthermore, the economic system favors some people and puts others at a disadvantage. Who will gain and who will be deprived is influenced by the type of economic system. Yet, any economic system will tend to lead to some inequality, which can be a fertile ground for conflict. Changing technology, especially in means of communication, is another factor bearing on conflict situations.

Demographic characteristics. Although conflict is expressed in social relations, these in turn are influenced by such matters as age and sex distribution of the population; the proportion of old residents and recent migrants; the ethnic and racial mix; the proportion who are well-educated and uneducated. To what extent, for instance, is the higher birth rate among the poor in some communities and their unwillingness to use birth control a way of expressing antagonism, subconscious though it be, at a society that mistreats them! Such points have been indicated in Chapter 4.

Historico-cultural factors. There may be a legacy of conflict between two factions or groupings in the community; excessive competition, which shades into conflict under the guise of "win at any cost," may be a pervasive value in many areas of community life; the tendency to oppress or exploit certain groups may be a tradition little questioned by present residents in the favored or majority status; the interaction between the major institutional complexes (termed the institutional order in Chapter 8) may promote rather than deter conflict. Communities differ, then, in the evaluation placed upon conflict, which is a part of the local cultural heritage (Chapter 5).

One could also list *personality* as a setting factor, but in the discussion here we are not concerned with *intrapersonal* conflict, or the case where the individual has to choose between antagonistic roles. We do recognize the fact that certain persons in key community statuses, through the way they exercise their roles, may heighten or limit conflict. Most of our analysis, as already indicated, will treat the interaction between groups and between groupings rather than that between individuals.

Throughout, however, the antagonistic social relations have a connection with their setting and must be so understood.

Discovering Antagonistic Relationships in the Community

As already indicated, important clues to these are structural inequality and differential allocation.

Structural inequality. If one starts with a theory which holds that most people in a superordinate position exploit those in a subordinate position, then one only need locate the superordinate-subordinate relations in a community. With exploitation one would expect to find conflict. Brand (1951) describes the case of a Mexican municipio, named Quiroga, where there were numerous antagonistic relations: the town opposed the rural people, the landed were against the landless and the *ejidatarios* (those farming cooperatively), the "whites" vied with the "Indians," the lower part of town (El Centro) contended with the upper town (El Calvario), and the *sinarquista* Roman Catholics were against the agrarian agnostics and atheists. (p. 104).

Indeed, since such unequal relations are built into the social structure, some conclude that the only way to make them more equal is to rebuild the system, once it is torn down, into something better. Some inequality, such as that between old and young, admittedly will continue to exist in any system.

Differential allocation. Along with structural inequality one finds social processes which bring it into existence and maintain it. Communities, as pointed out in Chapter 10, assign the best jobs to some kinds of people and the worst jobs to others through an employment mechanism that does not give everyone an equal start; through the market place rich people procure for themselves more goods and services than others. This distributive mechanism continues to favor the haves against the have nots.

There is also unequal allocation of power. Some conflict theorists seem to hold to conspiracy view of society, which claims that only a very few people run every community. They have gotten control in their hands and manage the affairs of the town so that they get even more control. Although numerous recent studies have shown that this conspiracy theory does not uniformly apply, it is still an appealing—though oversimplified—view to those who are trying to assess blame for the evident injustices found in any community.

To summarize, one main approach to the location of antagonistic relations in a community is to find evidences of social inequality and to assume that those who are subordinate feel antagonistically toward those above them. Much of the time the feeling may be latent, pent-up and not expressed; some of the time it bursts out into the open. One's search for such relations is often guided by one's ideas of what a good community should be or of a theory of history that sees social life as a struggle among differentiated groups. In the Marxian view, of course, once the masses of the people take into their own hands the means of production (operated in their behalf by the state), many kinds of inequality will be eliminated. According to the dialectical argument, however, new kinds of inequalities (the antithesis) may then arise which in time have to be dealt with, leading to a new synthesis.

Community controversies. A more frequent method used by community sociologists to identify conflict is to find out what controversial issues have rocked the community in the recent past. A reconstruction of what occurred reveals much about the nature of antagonistic relations and the effect of such conflict on community life. Such controversies may or may not be related to the social inequalities mentioned above. Many times sociologists have an opportunity to study a conflict situation while it is happening, thereby having a chance to test some of the hypotheses developed earlier. Because this "controversy" or "issue" approach is quite different from the two cited above, it is treated in a separate chapter (Chapter 16).

Characteristics of Antagonistic Social Relations

Antagonistic social relations may be analyzed in terms of six characteristics, the first of which is awareness of antagonistic interests.

Awareness of antagonistic interests. There are three degrees of awareness: in the first case, neither party in the relationship may be aware of an antagonistic feeling toward the other. However, an observer outside the relationship may impute much antagonism to it. One young sociology instructor spent much of a class hour explaining what he considered to be the exploitation in the typical doctor-patient relationship in the United States. He described the expected behavior in the two roles, citing the almost total subservience of the patient. Were this same instructor to be engaged in a community study he would probably wish to study the doctor-patient relationship as one of the more fundamental examples of interaction in the community supposing that it would illustrate a conflict syndrome. What he would probably find is that most of the people interviewed, who have a regular doctor, express much confidence in him or her: they feel no antagonism. Yet, they might have very harsh things to say about the medical profession, the costs of medical service, the unwillingness of medical practitioners to do this or that. The instructor would find antagonism but not necessarily in the specific relation where he most expected it.

There are instances, however, where one of the parties is aware of antagonism, though the other partner is not. Community studies often bring to light, through interviewing, many examples of individuals or groups feeling anger toward other groups but without letting this feeling become public knowledge, or even denying it if pressed too far by their superiors. It is commonplace that in communities with black or brown minorities the white majority may assume that little antagonism exists, that real progress is being made in racial understanding, and that the local minorities recognize how "fortunate" they are. However, conversations with the minority reveal quite a different picture: one of antagonism and bitterness.

In most cases, however, both parties are aware of the existence of antagonism, though each may provide different explanations of why it came about. Workers who are out on strike know very well that they and their employer are caught up in a conflict situation.

Goal Orientation of the Social Relation

Competition supposedly describes a situation where two people are moving toward the same goal, each conforming to the rules of the game. From time to time, one competitor may ignore the rules and thereby gain the animosity of the other competitor; the situation may deteriorate to the point that each is out after the other, both having lost sight of the original goal. A local political campaign may provide an instance of such a case. The uncomplimentary remarks two candidates make about each other may stir up the community to the point that each candidate feels that upholding his personal honor and putting down the opponent is more important than winning the election. Families of each candidate stop associating with each other; relatives, friends and work associates begin to take sides and the rancor generated lasts far beyond election day.

Antagonistic relations may result when two parties interfere with each other in obtaining different goals. Sometimes an organization is trying to further the goals of a group outside of the community; often the antagonism is within the local arena of action. The Woman's Garden Club may launch a community beautification effort, with the local junk yards as the first target. The junk dealers, including those owning second-hand car cemeteries, may resist either relocation to another place or the cost of putting up high, concealing fences around their property. The goal of the junk dealers is to make what profit they can without becoming involved in extra expenditures; the goal of the Garden Club is to close down or modify the present operations of the junk yard. The situation becomes more complex when the junk dealers go to the husbands of the members of the Garden Club and talk to them in terms of economics rather than aesthetics, urging that beautification endeavors concentrate elsewhere.

A third possibility is that there is hostility, perhaps on both sides, even though there are no explicit goals. This can happen with the influx of outsiders who differ from the residents of the neighborhood into which they move. Nobody tries to organize any movement to stop the newcomers, but there is an uneasy air and talk of moving out by the established residents. Of course, such a situation can become goal-oriented if some course of action is proposed and accepted by one of the groups involved.

Normative Aspects of Conflict

Since all communities have experienced conflict over and over again, their members have developed ways of trying to reduce it or contain it. This can apply more to some forms of conflict than to others: e.g., labor-management disputes, land use disputes, or family disputes.

The parties to the antagonistic relation may both recognize and accept what seem to be the community norms. They may avoid extreme behavior, such as violence; they may listen to third parties trying to adjudicate or arbitrate; they may agree to have the matter if of community-wide significance decided by referendum; they may try to avoid involving other parties in the dispute. Such an instance might be the furor created in one part of town when it becomes the proposed site for a new incinerator. Opposition arises, but the antagonistic relations operate within the accepted norms of the community for such kinds of controversies.

There are numerous occasions, however, when one party fails to abide by the norms. A racial or student riot demonstrates the overthrow of what any community would consider acceptable behavior. The destruction of property—and even of life goes far beyond accepted standards for conflict. Yet, those who flaunt these standards may feel that they have been driven to them because the community at large may have ignored their needs, exploited them unmercifully, and left them no recourse but violent action.

Another possibility is that neither party accepts community norms. Juvenile gangs in their "warfare" with each other draw up their own norms and seem to have little regard for the standards of the adult or of the middle class society. In some communities there have been clashes between one rejected group (such as a motorcycle group dedicated to a rough way of life) and another rejected group (politically extreme groups of right or left). For neither does the normative patterns of the majority of the society hold much importance, at least at the time of the conflict hypothesized here. The same held true for Chinese communities within the United States, according to an account of Valley City, California (Weiss, 1974):

> . . . conflict became an endemic factor in Chinese overseas life in America. Yet its presence does not indicate community disorganization . . . Individuals and groups engaged in struggles for wealth, power, status, and women; yet custom and tradition dictated how the conflict should be resolved. Conflicts were initiated, prolonged, and finally resolved by a shared set of sentiments common to all participants; *American values and precepts rarely entered into Chinatown conflicts.* (italics added). (pp. 40–41).

This illustration shows the pervasiveness of in-group and out-group norms, where one standard of conduct holds toward the in-group but quite a different standard toward the out-group.

Duration of the Conflict

Some conflict is obviously continuing; it never really lets up. This would be true of the underworld and the police, though this might have its rhythms in a particular community. For example, police activity might increase markedly prior to an important local election in order to gain the "law and order" votes for some incumbent candidate. Where two almost equal groups are struggling for the major seats of power, they may keep at it from year to year, despite the ups and downs of fortune.

Much community conflict is episodic. It occurs once and then is resolved. A school bond issue for the purpose of enlarging an already palatial high school in a suburb; the fight over a local ordinance saying that all dogs must be leashed when outside the house; the conflict over whether the city and county governments should be consolidated into a single unit—all of these may be decided at one point in time. Once in a while something that was thought to have been put to rest, may be raised again. But there are numerous conflicts which occur only once. The way they were decided definitely influences the way future conflicts are treated, but they have been dealt with.

Some conflict is recurring. One can predict that every two or three years the labor union at the local plant will be involved in negotiating a new contract, either as part of a national effort or simply on the local level. Antagonistic talk increases, threats of strike or lockout are hinted at, and local merchants try to get themselves ready for what may be a stormy period. Or, one can predict that certain ethnic groups will display hostility toward each other on a particular holiday when one of the groups has a parade; or when a high school championship match is played by teams from schools in sections of town which feel unkindly toward each other and rioting has come to be an expected aftermath—to such an extent that authorities seriously question the advisability of continuing the championship series.

Resource Base.

Perhaps one of the most crucial questions of all is the relative extent of the resource base of each partner. When one member of the relationship has strong economic and political support and the other does not; or when one partner has strong public support and the other does not; or when one is an experienced master in dealing with conflict and the other is not—then the relation is obviously unequal.

There are cases, however, when the relative strengths are not very different or when one kind of support (economic) may be outweighed by another kind (political). When an administrative agency is a party to the conflict, the legal authority provided the agency to intervene is another type of resource. Related to this is the definition that relevant important people in the community give to the conflict: is it important or unimportant; is it apt to damage the community if it goes too far; are the protagonists using their resources correctly. At times, depending upon how the above questions are answered, support can swing from one side to the other in the relation. Cost to the community, whether measured in an increased tax rate or otherwise, is one factor which influences public reaction to the various positions of those in an antagonistic relationship.

Intensity of Antagonism

The major differentiation is between violent and non-violent behavior. Mention has already been made of riots as a form of violence and of the kind of antagonistic relation that stays within the bounds of community norms. Berelson and Steiner (1964) in drawing up a list of findings from various writers about social conflict say that it is *more intense*

1. the less adjustable the goals or the more fixed the rewards being sought by the disputants.
2. the less the contact or openness between disputants.
3. the less integrated the community involved in the conflict.
4. the more that ideology is involved.
5. the more committed the participants to the organizations involved in the controversy.
6. the more uncertain or unstable the rules by which the conflict is supposed to be resolved. (pp. 619–23).

To conclude, in the study of community conflict one is made realistically aware of the close connection between the local community and the national society. Conflict is often introduced from outside rather than spontaneously arising from within the community, though there may be local conditions with potentials for conflict. Outside agencies, with funds and prescriptions for local problem-solving may be totally unaware of local conditions and introduce a divisiveness that did not exist before. Although Figure 12–1 does not encompass it, the antagonistic relations may very well be with units external to the community; these, too, can be analyzed according to the characteristics discussed above.

The discussion thus far indicates a straightforward approach to conflict: that is, the antagonistic relations discerned in the locality under study. First, one can see the interplay between the antagonistic relations and the setting; second, one notes that conflict is not an abnormal but an anticipated part of human experience since there are scarce resources to be distributed among many people. This does not mean that in looking at one's community in the conflict perspective one necessarily accepts the theory of biological determinism which claims that aggression is a built-in characteristic of man's biological heritage; nor does it mean that conflict is the only way of resolving differences. It does recognize, however, that in every community some conflict is a recognized part of daily life. Third, antagonistic relations also occur as a society shifts from rural to urban, as some of its groups move from immigrant to native status, and as many relations become more impersonal. It is, in fact, closely linked to social change. Finally, the understanding of conflict prepares one better to deal with social problems, community disorganization, and social deviance.

13

Structural Inequality: Selected Relations

A visitor interested in what is going on around him soon notices that people in a community use many labels in speaking of each other. These labels may be based on biological criteria, or economic or social criteria, but they designate groupings of people who are lumped together because they possess some characteristic or characteristics in common. Poor people living along the river may be contemptuously referred to as "river rats," whereas those occupying some choice residential heights may be said to be from Snob Hill. Other labels may be much more neutral in that they describe distinctions without carrying condemnation or approval: Republicans, Democrats, Independents; Catholic, Protestant, Jew; Irish-American, Yankee. Of course, the one using the label may have his own private opinion about groupings of which he is not a part and he may even use epithets in referring to them. An Italian-American in New England may speak of WASPS (White Anglo-Saxon Protestants); an ardent proponent of fluoridation for his community may refer to the antifluoridationists as "antis," suggesting by his inflection and tone of voice that he considers them to be not to his liking. One hears, too, the commonly used terms of "working class," "middle class," and "upper class."

THE NATURE OF GROUPINGS

Such collections or categories of people are called *groupings* to distinguish them from *groups,* which are units characterized by face-to-face association and a more discernible leadership hierarchy than one usually finds in a grouping. However, various groups quite often serve to protect the interests of a grouping (National Association for the Advancement of Colored People for the Black grouping; Knights of Columbus for the Catholic men; Chamber of Commerce for the businessmen of the community). But the grouping is a social unit that has meaning to the extent that it is socially relevant to some issue before the community. Some groupings can be nothing more than statistical units. For example, those aged from 20 to 24 can be termed a grouping, a collection of residents with a specific characteristic in common. It may become socially meaningful on occasion, particularly where all drivers in that age bracket are required to pay a higher automobile insurance premium. In a grouping, people may react individually to political or community fund appeals. In this sense, they are a public, or a target for advertising media or for those wishing to win support for some community undertaking. Should the individual seek to respond with the support and backing of others in the same grouping, he would move into a group situation and no longer be merely a statistical unit; he becomes socially involved even if the group be informal in nature. To illustrate, some grouping, such as residential property owners, may have had no sense of identity with each other although appearing as a statistical category in all economic analyses of the community; but with some threat to their interest on the horizon a number of them may organize (form a group) to protect their interests, soliciting contributions if not memberships from all others in the same category willing to cooperate in this collective action.

It is not necessary here to describe all of the hundreds of possible groupings that one might find in a community. Figure 13–1 provides some guide to the criteria that might be used in the classification of people into various social divisions. It can also provide us with a way of looking at various kinds of social inequality. This is why we will take up each of the criteria for differentiation into groupings. A selection of one or two illustrations for each kind of grouping can demonstrate how a community sociologist, sensitized to conflict potential, can make use of this approach.

BIOLOGICAL CRITERIA
AGE: children, youths, adults, aged
SEX: males, females
RACE: Negroes, Semites, Eurasians, etc.
NATIONALITIES: Americans, Mexicans
OTHER PHYSICAL TRAITS: paraplegics, blondes, etc.

ECONOMIC CRITERIA
POSSESSIONS: home-owners, radio owners, stockholders, etc.
OCCUPATION: farmers, unskilled workers, skilled workers, managers, professional people
RESIDENCE: city-dwellers, villagers, townspeople, suburbanites
INCOME: upper fifth income bracket; below poverty line.

SOCIAL CRITERIA
POLITICAL ORIENTATION: Republicans, Democrats, Independents
RELIGIOUS ORIENTATION: Christians (Catholics, Protestants, Orthodox), Moslems (Shiites, Sunnites), Jews, Buddhists, etc.
FAMILIAL STATUS: single, married, divorced, widowed, parents, childless
SOCIAL VIEWS: left wing, right wing, moderate

PERSONAL ACHIEVEMENT CRITERIA
EDUCATIONAL ATTAINMENT: illiterates, university graduates, etc.
FORMAL HONORS RECEIVED: Phi Beta Kappa, Nobel Prize Winner, etc.
RANK: presidents of civic organizations

CRITERIA OF COMMON INTERESTS
SPORTS: football enthusiasts, hunters, chess players, etc.
ARTS (AS AVOCATION): music lovers, museum-goers, etc.
RADIO and TELEVISION: listeners to baseball broadcasts, devotees of a popular news program, etc.
HOBBIES: stamp collectors, amateur carpenters, tourists, etc.
"CAUSES": antivivisectionists, "Women's Libbers," Advocates of Planned Parenthood, Esperanto enthusiasts, etc.

Figure 13–1. Types of groupings in a complex community, with examples.

Before we turn to an examination of specific types of inequality we should be aware of the debate in social science literature about the types of equality which exist and the different policies that flow from a concentration upon any one type. S. M. Miller (1974) calls attention to the fact that there are four types of equality (and inequality) and we paraphrase him as follows:

First, there is equality of opportunity. Through social mobility and the reduction of barriers to its operation people rise through merit to preferred positions. "The equality of opportunity approach does not attempt to change the rewards to position but to give everyone a similar chance of getting to desirable positions." A fundamental problem in this approach to equality is that all people do not start with equal chances.

Second, there is representative equality. This means that inequality exists if certain categories (Blacks, women, youth) are not adequately represented in desirable positions in a particular community. Efforts to overcome such inequality lead to practices variously termed affirmative action, compensatory opportunity, positive discrimination. This type of equality sorts people, not positions.

Third, there is resource equality. It seeks the reduction of economic differences among occupational positions. Here the stress is on utilizing taxes and public transfers to bring about a narrow band of resource differences. Such measures do not, however, "touch upon the bases of selection for position nor the distribution of tasks among individuals. It affects the rewards to position but not access to position; nor does it affect non-money aspects of position. Jobs may be still very hierarchical in power and status, even if income differences have become narrowed."

Fourth, there is task equality. This position recognizes that there are some prestige jobs which are viewed positively, there are other jobs which are viewed negatively: dirty work, debilitating routine, narrow tasks. "Task-resource equality seeks to reduce resource differences at the same time that it aims at redistributing the tasks which now make up occupations so that individuals do not have mainly satisfying or mainly unsatisfying tasks to perform."

With these approaches to equality-inequality in mind we can now look at specific kinds of inequality arising out of such criteria as shown in Figure 13–1.

INEQUALITY BASED ON BIOLOGICAL CRITERIA

Discrimination on the Basis of Sex

Looked at in national terms, women still face discrimination. Table 13–1 makes this quite clear. In a 1973 Supreme Court Decision the Court said that women in military service must be granted the same dependency benefits for their husbands that military men receive for their wives and that they do not have to prove that they

TABLE 13–1
Discrepancy Between Earnings for Men and Women

WOMEN MAKE UP A GROWING SHARE OF THE WORK FORCE

	Male Workers	Female Workers	Women as a Percentage of Labor Force
1955	44.5 mil.	20.5 mil.	32%
1960	46.4 mil.	23.2 mil.	33%
1965	48.3 mil.	26.2 mil.	35%
1970	51.2 mil.	31.5 mil.	38%
1972	54.1 mil.	34.1 mil.	39%

. . . BUT FALL FURTHER BEHIND MEN IN PAY

Median Earnings of Full-Time Workers		
	Men	Women	Women's Pay as a Percentage of Men's Pay
1955	$4,252	$2,719	63.9%
1960	$5,417	$3,293	60.8%
1965	$6,375	$3,823	60.0%
1971	$9,399	$5,593	59.5%

. . . AND EARN LESS IN ALL KINDS OF JOBS

Median Annual Earnings of Full-Time Workers	Men	Women
Professional, technical	$12,518	$8,312
Schoolteachers	$ 9,913	$8,126
Managerial	$12,721	$6,738
Clerks	$ 9,124	$5,696
Salesmen	$10,650	$4,485
Craftsmen	$ 9,627	$5,425
Factory hands	$ 7,915	$4,789
Laborers	$ 6,866	$4,548
Service workers	$ 7,111	$4,159

Source: U. S. News and World Report, May 28, 1973. P. 69.

provide more than half of their husband's support before collecting benefits as housing and medical allowances for the husband. In the Court's majority opinion Justice William J. Brennan, Jr., wrote:

> There can be no doubt that our nation has had a long and unfortunate history of sex discrimination. Traditionally, such discrimination was rationalized by an attitude of "romantic paternalism" which, in practical effect, put women not on a pedestal but in a cage . . .
>
> It is true, of course, that the position of women in America has improved markedly in recent decades.
>
> Nevertheless, it can hardly be doubted that, in part because of the high visibility of the sex characteristic, women still face pervasive, although at times more subtle, discrimination in our educational institutions, on the job market and, perhaps most conspicuously, in the political area.

Although sex discrimination is a national problem, its effects are usually seen at the local level. It is here that some of the national women's organizations promote what they call "consciousness-raising sessions," designed to make women more aware of the discrimination they face and of the responses they can make to this. For instance, a group of women may stage a sit-in at a bar which has exclusively served men up to that time, picket a bank which does not give women loans on the same basis as that extended to men, or stage a silent demonstration at a church whose top hierarchy opposes the admission of women to the clergy or priesthood. Some of these conflict situations are evanescent in the sense that once the point is made and accepted, the protest ceases; underneath, however, there is the antagonistic relation that comes into play whenever the women's group senses what it believes to be excessive male chauvinism. Through time many of the women in the community begin to take a different view of the feminine role under various conditions, which reciprocally causes shifts in the masculine role. For instance, suburban women in the middle years are increasingly going back to work, once their children are in the teens. Nanette E. Scofield (1960) has some observations on this point:

Changes in the Life of Women

> Living conditions in the suburbs and the place of suburbia in life in the United States are in flux for suburban residents. For women, there are even added complexities.

Married women have been going back to work at a greater rate than ever before. Since 1950, says the National Manpower Council, the largest source of new workers in the labor force has been women in their middle and later years. This trend changes the climate of opinion for the return to work of women of all economic levels.

Women continue to be haunted by their education. Margaret Mead reports "We have the striking paradox of women who are educated like men and who can do most of the things men do but who still are taught to prefer marriage to any other way of life. . . . In this paradox lies much of the confusion for women today."

In addition, for women who moved to the suburbs ten years ago, a new level of life is beginning. Now, for the first time, they can see a future where the family plays a diminishing role. At the same time, society encourages them to cut apron strings once that family is grown.

Women's middle years cause speculation and conflict among many authorities. Theodore Caplow, a sociologist, feels that while the housewife in her middle years may have no personal economic need, she has the psychological need to justify herself, for our culture emphasizes striving and economic productivity. The Department of Labor in its *1958 Handbook on Women Workers* suggests that "very few women are working just for the satisfaction of having a job." David Riesman sees women ". . . being driven out of many of the areas in which they formerly occupied their leisure with amateur competence."

Guides to a Survey

With these statements in mind, a questionnaire was mailed to more than 200 women of an upper-economic group (annual income over $25,000), college-educated, ranging in age from 25 to 35, living in the suburbs with children and husband.

A high-income community was used to minimize economic need; the age range of 25 to 35 would offer a cross section of residents who are feeling the impact of change.

More than half of these women plan to go to work: 13 per cent immediately, the rest in 5 to 15 years. Sixteen per cent do not know their plans; 32 per cent know they will never work.

Of those expecting to go to work, 75 per cent feel they are inadequately prepared, and of these, more than 80 per cent plan to go to school; some are there now. Many plan to change from original major fields, especially in the arts and social science fields. One social science major says: "I have always felt that graduating from college with a degree such as mine prepared me for no special work."

These women will change their fields if they find no vocational outlet; they will change their fields if a change of interest has taken place over the years, as evidenced by one comment: "Although I enjoyed the world of fashion as a younger person, I find that it has no interest for me now as far as careers go. I want to be in a field that will help the world, if only a little."

No one who majored in education planned to change her field.

It is significant that 50 per cent of these women, from an upper-economic group, see themselves in remunerative work. In other generations, these were the women who carried the brunt of charitable work. Charity depended on them, and they themselves felt a moral obligation. This moral obligation now has apparently disappeared, replaced by the psychological need to be economically productive.

In making their choice, women are reflecting the social attitudes of our time: (1) we are an economic society, and all things are valued in terms of money; and (2) women, educated as men are educated, have been given the same objectives.

The liberal arts colleges, which used to specialize in the humanities and whose objective was the educated person, have tended to become vocationally oriented. The courses that flourish are those that are economically geared, while philosophy and the classics languish. Given a man-sized education, women begin to feel that the only proper use of it, in this dollar-conscious economy, is a paid job.

Conclusions

It is clear that the traditional volunteer activities of women are no longer of interest to them. Women desire to be paid for what they do, because they want the social status that money brings. This supports Mirra Komarovsky's statement that ". . . generally low status is accorded unpaid hobbies and volunteer activities . . . being important in our society is being professional, not a dilettante." For this group, the ability to earn money is a way of distinguishing oneself. There are exceptions: some unpaid jobs have more status than paid ones. A state board position with the League of Women Voters has more prestige than a doctor's assistant.

When families moved to the suburbs ten years ago, they were looking for a good way to live life, for a place where child raising would be simplified and expenses minimized, and where small-town life, in its happier aspects, would be realized. If father is to spend two hours a day commuting, let it be counterbalanced by an idyllic existence for mother and the children. However, the equation is not equating. Taxes have skyrocketed; child rasing has not been simplified, but rather has become more complex than in the city. Mother is bored and counteracts lonesomeness with too much belongingness. She, who sought freedom in the move to the suburbs, finds more demands on her time and, with it, more responsibility.

How will she carve out her future? Will she "sink back into indifference" or, striking out in all directions, hope to stumble on one right way? Or will she find a sensible solution, unique to her? To accomplish the latter, she must be firm of purpose, for society, as it now stands, offers little help. For society to help, it must alter the framework built around and into the situation. Given proper status, volunteer work could be an answer; given proper cultural outlets, many women would not feel the need for a job; given an understanding society, more and better part-time jobs could be made available. (pp. 451–57).

Inequality on the Basis of Race

We can take residential discrimination as only one of many possible measures on which racial inequality manifests itself.[2] Table 13–2 below shows the segregation index for 14 large SMSA's for

TABLE 13–2

Segregation Indexes for Selected Cities [a]

Metropolitan Area [b]	Blacks			All Nonwhites		
	1960	1970	% Change	1960	1970	% Change
New York	.30	.29	−3	.30	.28	−7
Los Angeles-Long Beach	.37	.31	−16	.35	.27	−23
Chicago	.37	.45	22	.36	.44	22
Philadelphia	.39	.44	13	.38	.44	16
Detroit	.47	.58	23	.47	.56	19
San Francisco-Oakland	.46	.52	13	.36	.40	11
Pittsburgh	.54	.59	9	.54	.58	7
St. Louis	.50	.57	14	.49	.56	14
Baltimore	.35	.44	26	.34	.43	26
Dallas	.15	.29	93	.15	.28	87
Atlanta	.38	.51	34	.38	.51	34
Birmingham	.20	.30	50	.20	.30	50
Greensboro-Winston-Salem-High Point	.37	.40	8	.37	.40	8
Boston	.62	.66	6	.59	.61	3
Average, 14 large SMSAs	.39	.45	15	.38	.43	13
Boston	.62	.66	6	.59	.61	3
Providence-Pawtucket-Warwick	.60	.65	8	.57	.60	5
Hartford	.60	.68	13	.59	.66	12
Springfield-Chicopee-Holyoke	.56	.59	5	.54	.56	4
Worcester	.32	.48	28	.29	.35	21
Average, 5 New England SMSAs	.54	.60	11	.52	.56	8

[a] The higher the value of the segregation index, the greater is the degree of residential concentration.

[b] Because of data limitations, the indices for the San Francisco-Oakland, Atlanta, Birmingham, Greensboro-Winston-Salem-High Point, and Dallas SMSAs were calculated from Census county subdivision, rather than municipal, data. Census county subdivisions are generally larger than individual municipalities, and this probably results in a downward bias in the values of these indices.

Source: Frederic B. Glantz and Nancy J. Delaney, New England Economic Review, March/April 1973, p. 6 (a publication of the Federal Reserve Bank of Boston).

[2] Bonacich (1972) relates ethnic antagonism to a split-labor market where businessmen seek to displace higher paid by cheaper labor, leading to exclusion movements and "caste" systems.

1960 and 1970. There would be an absence of segregation, or a score of zero, if the proportion of black population to the total population were the same in all municipalities as it is in the SMSA itself. Cities such as Boston, Pittsburgh, Detroit, St. Louis have the highest segregation indices, whereas the greatest increase in the segregation indices over the ten-year period occurred in Southern cities such as Dallas, Birmingham and Atlanta.

Some of the most spectacular instances of community conflict occur when the public becomes excited over what is termed "blockbusting," or the attempt by real estate dealers who are active in white neighborhoods to use scare tactics when black families start moving in. They try to panic the white families into selling. An interesting series of articles appeared in the Cleveland Press in 1961. The articles were based on interviews with people in a neighborhood which was integrating, and the headlines or titles of each article tell something of the contents: Reveal How White Residents Panic as Negroes Seek Homes on Street; Admits Using Subterfuge to Buy Lot; Realty Dealers' Calls Stirred Panic on Eldamere Ave., Negroes Pay More in Buying Houses; Activities of Some Brokers Blamed for Neighborhood Panic; Bi-Racial Harmony; What Is Solution? An editorial which concluded the series opened with these paragraphs:

> Two groups of people are equally deserving of sympathy and understanding for the unhappy roles they play in the drama of changing neighborhoods.
> One group includes those white homeowners, most of them decent and fair-minded people, who are caught up in the emotional storms which the movement of Negroes onto new streets touches off.
> The other group is made up of the Negroes who must face these storms simply to exercise the simple and basic right of acquiring decent homes for their families.
> A third group, which also figures heavily in the "Is It Blockbusting?" series . . . deserve nothing but contempt for the melancholy role they play.
> These are the greedy opportunists, a small group of real estate salesmen, who whip up the storms, and who loot their profits from the confusion they generate.[3]

Moving from the early 1960's (when the word Negro was still in wide use) to the 1970's we read in the *New York Times* the head-

---

3 "Blockbusting: An Editorial," *The Cleveland Press*, Aug. 21, 1961.

line "Westbury, Now 30% Black Seeks to Stay Middle-Class." [4] This Long Island community, made up chiefly of professionals owning homes in racially mixed neighborhoods, is faced by the fact that the Westbury School District, which has different boundaries than the village, has become 54 per cent black. So some white residents are seeking to force an amalgamation, through the court, of the Westbury district with other predominantly white districts. They fear that educational quality will decline while the black president of the Westbury School Board says: "We've got good education in Westbury."

Thus the stage is set for a conflict situation arising out of the fact that some members of two races, biologically determined, are being forced into an antagonistic relationship. This is in spite of the findings by Hermalin and Farley (1973) to the effect that nationwide there is an attitudinal receptivity and economic potential for extensive residential integration.[5]

In addition to sex and race, which have illustrated biological criteria, there is also the fact of age. There is an emerging theory of age stratification which helps one understand the potential for age conflict. (Foner, 1974).

SOCIAL INEQUALITY BASED ON ECONOMIC CRITERIA

Occupations

The most revealing statistics on social inequality—namely, income distribution—will be taken up in a discussion of poverty and its treatment at the community level (Chapter 19). Here, however, it is important to notice the relationship between occupational differentiation and prestige as related to the kind of society in which they occur (Faunce and Smucker, 1966; Haller et al., 1972). Three countries can be compared: The United States (Figure 10–1) the Philippines (Table 13–3 below) and Poland (Table 13–4 below).

---

[4] *The New York Times,* article by George Vecsey. November 15, 1973. pp. 43, 65; © 1973 by the New York Times Company. Reprinted by permission.

[5] A detailed study of a "community" within the city of Chicago shows conditions which lead to integration and those which help maintain segregation. See Harvey Molotch, "Racial Integration in a Transition Community," *American Sociological Review* 34 (December, 1969), 878–893. See also Rainwater, 1970.

TABLE 13–3

Ranking of Occupations, The Philippines, All Respondents Evaluating Eleven to Thirty Occupations

Occupation	Final Rank [a]	Occupation	Final Rank [a]
Physician	1	Owner of a *sari-sari* store	15.5
Congressman	2	Salesman	17
Lawyer	3	Tailor	18
Engineer	4	Fisherman	19
University professor	5	Carpenter	20
Priest	6	Farm tenant	21
Manager of a business company	7	Construction worker	22
Officer in the armed forces	8	Factory worker	23
Intermediate schoolteacher	9	Sugar-cane-plantation worker	24
Professional artist	10	Barber	25.5
Farmer	11	Bus or jeepney driver	25.5
Midwife	12	Gasoline-station attendant	27
Office clerk	13	Road repairman	28
Policeman	14	Produce peddler	29
Enlisted man in the armed forces	15.5	Domestic servant	30

[a] To obtain the mean rank value of a given occupation, the total sum of ranks was divided by the number of respondents rating the occupation; the final rank represents the position of the mean rank of a given occupation relative to all other mean ranks.

Source: Edward A. Tiryakian, "The Prestige Evaluation of Occupations in an Underdeveloped Country: The Philippines," *American Journal of Sociology* 63 (January, 1958), 394.

Table 13–3 lists the ranking of occupations by both rural and urban Filipinos. Two of the occupations deserve a word of explanation. In the Philippines a "jeepney" is a surplus jeep used during the military occupation of 1944–45 that has been converted into a taxi accommodating as many as eight people. *Sari-saris* are small, independently owned, retail stores found throughout the Philippines where one can buy canned and baked goods, soft drinks, and a host of other household items.

Turning now to a city in Eastern Europe where a Communist regime is in control—Warsaw, Poland—we find a somewhat different ranking of occupations. Two Polish sociologists, Adam Sarapata and Wlodzimierz Wesolowski, asked Warsaw inhabitants to rank a set of occupations three times: on the basis of social prestige, material rewards, and job security. Table 13–4 shows the ranking based on these three considerations.

TABLE 13–4

Ranks of Occupations, Warsaw, Poland, on Basis of Social Prestige, Material Rewards, and Job Security

	Rank According to		
Occupation	Social Prestige	Material Rewards	Job Security
University professor	1	7	2
Doctor	2	5	1
Teacher	3	22	4
Mechanical engineer	4	12	8
Airplane pilot	5	8	12
Lawyer, attorney	6	3	7
Agronomist	7	16	9
Minister of national government	8	1	20
Journalist	9	9	11
Skilled steel-mill worker	10	10	3
Priest	11	11	6
Nurse	12	27	10
Machinist	13	13	5
Factory foreman	14	17	13
Small farmer	15	15	14
Accountant	16	19	15
Shopkeeper	17	2	27
Tailor with own workshop	18	4	19
Locksmith with own workshop	19	6	21
Office supervisor	20	18	24
Army officer	21	14	16
Railway conductor	22	26	17
Policeman	23	21	18
Office clerk	24	24	28
Typist	25	25	29
Sales clerk	26	20	26
Unskilled construction laborer	27	23	23
Cleaning woman	28	29	25
Unskilled farm laborer on state farm	29	28	22

Source: Adam Sarapata and Wlodzimierz Wesolowski, "The Evaluation of Occupations by Warsaw Inhabitants," *The American Journal of Sociology* 66 (May, 1961), 583–85.

An interesting feature of Table 13–4 is the use of three criteria to rate occupations: prestige, material rewards, and job security. Some interesting variations appear when one compares the prestige rankings in Warsaw with those for the Philippines. Different classifications for occupations were used but relative positions of a number of occupations can be noted in the two countries.

Sarapata (1974) finds that over the past fifteen years there has been a stable occupational hierarchy in Poland. Certain occupations from time to time come into conflict, particularly in industry.

Industrial Conflict

In an excellent summary statement on industrial conflict and its mediation Clark Kerr describes, among other points, the nature of industrial conflict, responses to conflict, and tactical and strategical mediation. A review of some of his main points should prove helpful to anyone who wishes to understand the labor disputes that occur in a rapidly industrializing society.

In treating the nature of industrial conflict, Kerr points out that it is inevitable for four reasons:

1. The desires of the parties are more or less unlimited, while the means of satisfaction are limited. Wages can never be as high as workers desire or profits or salaries as high as owners or managers might wish. . . .

2. Someone manages and someone is managed, and this is an eternal opposition of interest, which may be made bearable but can never be eliminated in a complex, industrial society. . . .

3. Industrial societies are dynamic. Even if a certain distribution of income and power could be devised which, in a given situation, was not subject to controversy (though this seems unlikely), the situation itself would change—because of new regulations by the state, changed expenditure patterns of consumers. . . .

4. If management and labor are to retain their institutional identities, they must disagree and must act on the disagreement. Conflict is essential to survival. The union which is in constant and complete agreement with management has ceased to be a union.[6]

Furthermore, some aggressive conflict is even acceptable. According to Kerr, there are three positive gains that may outweigh the injuries inflicted:

1. Out of aggressive industrial conflict or its latent possibility comes the resolution of many disputes . . . the parties find the bases for continued association and acceptance of each other. . . .

2. Conflict, and particularly open conflict, reduces tensions. In modern industrial society the sources of unrest and hostility are enormous. The strike provides an outlet for them when they are so severe as to require forceful expression. . . . The chance to rebel against the other party on occasion establishes the independence of the group and of the

---

[6] Clark Kerr, "Industrial Conflict and Its Mediation," *American Journal of Sociology*, LX (November, 1954), 231. Copyright, 1954, by the University of Chicago.

individual, makes acceptance of the surrounding social system easier, and, therefore, can make a net addition to satisfaction and production. . . .

3. Out of the conflict of management and union . . . the worker is better served. As the two parties compete for his loyalty, his interests are advanced. (pp. 232–33).

While not advocating violence for violence's sake, Kerr does argue that limited antagonism serves a social purpose. However, he points out that conflict can be destructive as well as constructive and thus needs to be guided if the social fabric is to be protected and serious injury to individuals and groups avoided.

Responses to conflict may be of three broad alternatives: A party "may withdraw; it may seek to destroy or dominate the other party; or it may accept the adversary more or less permanently, adjust itself to the fact of conflict, and adapt itself to live with it." (p. 235) In labor-management conflict only the third alternative is the realistic response.

Of particular interest is what Kerr calls strategical mediation, which concerns itself with the manipulation of social situations and thus with factors quite external to the parties themselves. He writes:

> From one point of view, society is a huge mediation mechanism, a means of settling disagreements between rival claimants—tax-payers and recipients of benefits, buyers and sellers, proponents of opposing political ideologies—so that people may live together in some state of mutual tolerance. Some societies mediate their disagreements, through their markets, their courts, their political processes, more effectively than do others. Society in the large is the mediation machinery for industrial as well as other forms of conflict. (p. 243).

Kerr then lists six conditions that are most favorable to the non-violent industrial conflict. These have much importance for any community where industrial plants operate:

> 1. Integration of workers and employers into society. To the extent that workers and employers consider themselves primarily citizens with roughly equal status, privileges, and opportunities, the sting is taken out of their relationship. The greater the social mobility, the more mixed in membership the various social associations, the more heterogeneous the community's occupational composition, the more accepted the institution of workers and the greater their participation in general community life, the more secure the worker in his job and the higher his skill—the less violent will be the industrial conflict in the long run.

2. Stability of the society. The incidence of strikes is directly related to major changes in the operation of the society—particularly to the business cycle and to wars. . . . The parties normally can adjust more peacefully to gradual than to precipitous change.

3. Ideological compatibility. . . . Where people believe in brotherly love or the equality of man, for example, their disagreements will be fewer, less sharp, and more amenable to easy compromise. Where, however, they believe in the inevitable opposition of classes, in the rapacity of other men, then violent industrial conflict is more likely. . . .

4. Secure and responsive relationship of leaders to members. For the minimization of violent industrial conflict, it is desirable that leaders be (a) relatively secure in their position and (b) responsive to their constituencies . . .

5. The dispersion of grievance. The mass grievance, one which is held by many people in the same place at the same time against the same antagonist, grows and feeds on itself. Society can more readily accommodate and adjust the small grievance. . . . If the grievance is directed against several individuals and groups—the merchant, the landlord, the state, for example—rather than against an employer who provides housing, retail facilities, and law enforcement—it can have additional outlets . . .

6. Structuring the game . . . Rules which reduce the risks of the parties and limit the means they may employ, without unduly stifling the conflict, can make a substantial contribution to non-violent resolution of controversy or can mitigate the destructive consequences of violent conflict. [The employer, for example, may forego the use of strikebreakers, the discharge of strikers, or the blacklist. The union may forego sabotage, the boycott of products, or violence against officials of the company.] (pp. 243–45).

Britt and Galle (1972) relate degree of unionization and size of union to such variables as proneness of conflict, extensity of conflict, and intensity of conflict. Their interest is in developing a model which will "decompose" the overall measure of industrial conflict with theoretically distinct dimensions. Hill (1974) finds that industrial unionization is conversely related to black–white income inequality in urban labor markets in the contemporary United States.

Social Inequality According to Residential Pattern

The examples cited for racial inequality have already led us into the problems of residential patterns, where it is clear that economic factors are certainly one type that come into play. Yet, even with sufficient income members of a minority group find it difficult to have free choice in selection of a home. To illustrate further the existence of groupings based on residential location we turn to a Muslim village in Lebanon, along the Eastern Mediterranean. A contrast with American communities is often helpful. In this village the 1,100 people are divided into four main categories of people. As the accompanying map of the village shows (Figure 13–2), these groupings tend to be in the same residential areas.[7]

The first group speaks of itself as the *Learned Families* and represents one-fifth of the total population. The men of these families bear one of two titles—either Shaikh (Sheik) or Sayyid. The title of Shaikh rests theoretically on the acquisition of religious knowledge, over a very long period, at the Shi'ite Muslim University in Najaf in Iraq. Very few earn it this way, but are accorded the title of Shaikh by virtue of their birth. These Shaikhs are the recognized authorities on legal and theological matters; they officiate at marriages and at funeral and mourning ceremonies, and conduct public prayers. They capture all administrative and teaching posts in the village. The Sayyids, distinguished by their green turbans, because of their descent from a famous religious-military Muslim leader, are accredited with a special power to bless. Thus, they say prayers for the dead. They supposedly do not possess the religious knowledge of the Shaikhs, but are always present at religious ceremonies. They, like the Shaikhs, receive religious dues for their services, and own relatively large areas of land in the village.

The second grouping in the village is composed of shopkeepers, all of whom are petty traders. All the senior men in this category wear the red fez but otherwise dress in European-type suits. As a group they are better housed and enjoy a higher standard of living than the peasants. Although many of these shopkeepers are related to each other and sell virtually the same goods, they compete fiercely. They and their families make up less than one-fifth of the total population.

The peasants, the third grouping, usually wear felt hats, shirts, and trousers with baggy seats and narrow legs, although the younger men are turning more and more to wearing European clothes. The womenfolk, gaily dressed in colored clothes, walk about unveiled, gossip in little groups on corners and move freely to and from their gardens, though they do avoid the village square. Their behavior

[7] Emrys L. Peters, "Aspects of Rank and Status Among Muslims in a Lebanese Village," in Julian Pitt-Rivers (ed.), *Mediterranean Countrymen* (Paris: Mouton & Co., 1963). Adapted from pages 167–71.

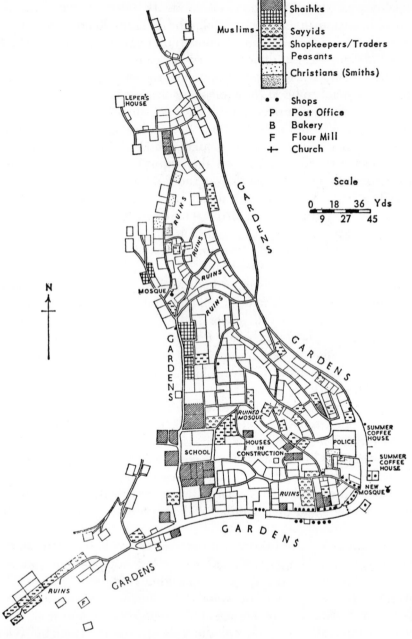

Figure 13–2. Groupings in a Lebanese village. *Source:* Emrys L. Peters, "Aspects of Rank and Status Among Muslims in a Lebanese Village," in Julian Pitt-Rivers (ed.), *Mediterranean Countrymen* (Paris: Mouton & Co., 1963), p. 168.

is in contrast to that of the wives of the Shaikhs, who wear the veil and black clothes and leave the house only in company or with an escort. The peasant families constitute more than three-fifths of the total population.

The Christians, numbering only twenty-three in all, participate as a fourth grouping in political life but are not strong enough numerically or economically to exert significant influence on it. The fact of being Christian is a bar that has the effect of proscribing their relationships in a number of fields. Thus their population has remained static for the past two or three generations; any increases in population seem to have been curtailed immediately by emigration.

SOCIAL INEQUALITY BASED ON SOCIAL CRITERIA

Numerous illustrations could be presented of conflict related to social inequality based on social criteria: political orientation (revolutionary versus conservative ideology), familial status ("gay" or homosexual movement), social views (those wishing to preserve agrarian values versus those favoring industrialization). Religious conflict will here serve as the example.

Religious Conflict

In some countries religious conflict has been heightened by wars between members of two faiths (Catholics and Protestants, Muslim and Hindu), with a legacy of antagonism which persists in almost every community. There are other cases in which one religion was associated with an upper ruling, aristocratic class and another religion with a subordinate class, with the result that religious feeling entered strongly into any movement to change the class structure. This happened in the case of Poland which was partitioned among neighboring powers: Prussia (Protestant Lutheran) and Russia (Eastern Orthodox) held political sway over the Polish people who were predominantly Roman Catholic. Again, there are religious groups who maintain a strong sense of their own identity, a separateness in some areas of community life, and who therefore tend to be misunderstood and are suspect because they are different. The Amish or Hutterites are often given as illustrations of this. Jews have often suffered through the centuries because of their attempt to preserve their own religion and culture, becoming victims of anti-Semitism at the local level.

Life in a Welsh Countryside (Rees, 1961) dwells at some length on the role of religious conflict in the parish of Llanfihangel, near the English border. There the antagonisms between the Established Church (Anglican) and the Non-conformists (Chapel people, such as Methodists) were of long-standing. The former was identified with the conservative ruling group. This religious schism permeated every area of local life, even at times serving as a barrier to business transactions or marriage alliances. With the gradual disappearance of the landed aristocracy and the declining political influence of those adhering to the Established Church, the religious cleavage has become less marked and people of the two groups are mixing much more freely now. Yet there are still many villages and communities in many countries where one's religious affiliation means that by that very fact one is supposed to feel unfriendly toward those of another faith, even to the point of not associating with them and at times hating them. In almost every case, one religious group is in a more favored social position than the other, exemplifying a structural inequality.

Sociologists since the days of Max Weber, who related the rise of capitalism in England to the Protestant work ethic then prevalent there, have been studying the connection between religion and occupational aspirations and achievement. There exists in some local communities a resentment on the part of one religious group because its members believe that they do not get fair treatment in gaining an education or a job. They see religious discrimination. What the actual facts might be will have to be determined at the local level because national studies are still somewhat inconclusive. One study by Glenn and Hyland (1967) notes:

> At the end of World .War II, Protestants in the United States ranked well above Catholics in income, occupation and education; since then Catholics have gained dramatically and have surpassed Protestants in most aspects of status. (pp. 84–85).

One possible explanation offered is the fact that Catholics for the most part live in the larger urban centers where "earnings, occupational distributions, educational opportunities and rates of upward mobility are more favorable."

Another study (Jackson, Fox and Crockett, 1971) four years later found:

> To summarize, the data analyzed in this paper suggest several moderate religious differences in occupational achievement: (1) Protestants are more likely than Catholics of the same occupational origin to enter professional and business occupations; (2) Catholics are more likely than Protestants of the same origin to enter white collar occupations; and (3) Protestants are more often sharply upwardly mobile; Catholics are more often sharply downwardly mobile. (p. 60).

The authors do find that some Protestant-Catholic differences probably can be attributed to religious factors, but then they point out the difficulty of interpreting why this is so. (Also see Schuman, 1971).

Another researcher (Featherman, 1971) in the study of white metropolitan native males from five religio-ethnic backgrounds has discovered that there is no evidence of occupational and income discrimination on purely religious or ethnic grounds. He noted that Jews, regardless of ethnic ancestry, attain higher levels of education, occupation, and income than all other subgroups, while Roman Catholics of Italian and Mexican heritage achieve the lowest levels.

As one would guess, the disagreements as to findings which these three references exhibit may be due to the questions asked, the methods used, and the population studied. In actuality, the reason may be lack of education, lack of skills, or lower class background but the perception is that of religious differentiation and inequality.

At times, however, the conflict becomes so overt that there is no question about latent antagonisms. Wayne, New Jersey provides an illustration of conflict between Christians and Jews. Two sociologists (Weinberg and Williams, 1969) have reported on their attempt to find out the effects of this conflict. A few pertinent facts set the background:

> (Wayne) has grown from a community of 11,522 in 1950 to a population of 29,353 in 1960; 42,000 in 1965; and 47,000 in 1966. These recent migrants included a large number of Jewish families that split the community into Jewish and non-Jewish sectors. In 1958 Wayne had only 15 Jewish families; by 1967 the number of Jewish families had increased to an estimated 850. (p. 171).

Although there were a few incidents that indicated some latent antagonism by some Gentiles toward the Jews, there was a prevailing belief that all parties were tolerant and behaved in brotherly fashion toward each other. This belief was shattered at the time of a school board election, where the central issue was whether or not to increase the school budget. The electorate generally opposed the increase but community leaders supported it.

Of the five candidates for election to the school board, four favored the budget proposal; of these four, two were Jewish . . . The vice-president of the school board, Newton Miller, was opposed to the budget increase, although all the other members of the board favored it. (p. 171).

Just before the election Miller attacked the two Jewish candidates in the local newspaper on two grounds: first, that most Jewish people were liberal, especially when it comes to spending for education. Two more Jewish members added to a Jewish incumbent with one more year to serve would give three Jewish members on a board of six. Their votes could thus swing a majority vote in favor of spending, thereby putting Wayne "in real financial trouble." Secondly, he said: "Two more votes and we lose what is left of Christ in our Christmas celebrations in the schools. Think of it." Such statements led to vigorous denunciation of Miller by civic and religious leaders and attracted the attention of the national press. Miller was asked to resign but refused to do so, nor did he retract his original statement. In the election, the two Jewish candidates were defeated by a two to one margin and the school budget was disapproved by a three to one margin. The follow-up analysis was designed to study the ethnocentrism and anomie which affected the Jewish residents. Needless to say, many were badly shaken by the incident.

It is often assumed that religious conflict is confined to those churches of widely divergent views such as the Roman Catholic and Protestant or between different faiths such as Christians and Jews (Middleton, 1973).

The traditional religious conflict in America, however, has not been limited to that between Catholics and Protestants but there has been much schismatic conflict within a particular denomination, resulting in divisions or splintering off by those wishing to establish a new religious organization of their own. (Laumann, 1969). The story of such a split in one South Carolina community has been told by Gus Turbeville (1949). It involves a Methodist church whose members refused to endorse the unification agreement of 1939 in which the Methodist Episcopal Church, South, joined with the Methodist Episcopal Church and the Methodist Protestant

Church to form the "Methodist Church." This case illustrates the fact that often what may seem to be religious conflict really has other than religious roots and that what is frequently called heresy is not the cause for a schism but an excuse for it.

The Turbeville community had in 1945 a population of 653, of whom 150 were Negroes. The inhabitants have, for the most part, been traditionally Methodists and for a living depend largely upon crops of tobacco and cotton:

> Some families have been more prominent than others. The Summerville family had been instrumental in getting a church, school, and post office for the community. As other families, chiefly the Browns, Newberrys, and Bettors, began to come into the community, some of them began to resent the dominant role being played by the Summervilles. . . . Neither side showed much inclination to cooperate with the other and, as a result, on almost any debatable issue that would arise, the Summervilles and their followers could be found on one side, and the Browns, Newberry's, and Bettors on the other. (p. 32).

When the question of unification was brought up in Turbeville at the Pine Grove Church, the Summervilles seemed to think that it was a forward step in the advancement of Methodism. The Browns and their coteries could do nothing else but come out vociferously against it and advanced every possible type of argument to support their stand. They gained a larger following than did the Summervilles. Then matters began to happen in dramatic fashion.

On November 8, 1938, when it was time to appoint a new pastor, the stewards wrote to the bishop asking that the Conference not send them a preacher, since they were not a part of the newly formed "Methodist Church." This letter was ignored and a Mr. Williams was sent about the first of December.

The "antis" (the Brown group) began holding their services at a different time from those of the regularly scheduled services. They had to take any kind of preacher they could find.

On April 13, 1939, the "antis" posted notices, signed by the church stewards, calling for a conference on April 23. This notice was posted after the "antis" had requested the minister to call such a conference but he had refused.

At the April 23 meeting the three dissident trustees, who formed a majority out of the five, deeded the Pine Grove Church property to three of its own members for the sum of $5.00 with the provision that the latter were to hold the property in trust for the benefit of the members of the Pine Grove Methodist Episcopal Church, South.

The "antis" then wrote a letter to the preacher forbidding him to use or trespass on this church property.

By the next Sunday the bishop who had been consulted helped the district superintendent and the minister get in touch with a lawyer who was able to have an injunction drawn up forbidding the dissident group from interfering in any way with the regularly scheduled service of the Methodist Church. The injunction did not forbid them from using the church at the other hours.

This was the beginning of a long legal battle with the Methodist Church on one side and the self-styled Southern Methodists on the other. Since this was something of a test case of the unification arrangement, the former body had six lawyers and the Southern Methodists had two lawyers. The Methodist Church finally won on all points before the Circuit Court as well as before the State Supreme Court and the United States Circuit Court of Appeals.

This so-called religious conflict has been accompanied by considerable social upheaval in the community. Both parties to the controversy have spread malicious gossip about the other; family relationships have been strained due to differences within the family over supporting the Summervilles or the "antis"; no social progress has been possible in the community, and even such matters as school board elections have been affected. An indication of the seriousness of the cleavage is shown by the fact that the "antis" have constructed a $25,000 church as well as a brick parsonage. Thus this small community is well churched but not prone to practice some of the cardinal Christian principles enunciated in the pulpits on Sunday morning. The conflict remains unresolved.

The other two types of Groupings shown in Figure 13–1 will be illustrated later. For example, a vivid case of conflict surrounding personal achievement criteria is that over the busing of school children in order to desegregate a school district. The inequalities in our present educational system (Sewell, 1971) and some of the antagonistic relations engendered by these inequalities will be the subject of Chapter 19. The last major category—common interests— flashes to the fore as one group of people with common pursuits (sportsmen for right to own guns) conflict with law enforcement bodies trying to outlaw private possession of firearms. Of particular interest is the clash between two groups promoting contradictory "causes."

PERCEPTIONS OF GROUPING CHARACTERISTICS

The divisions within a community become socially important in terms of how a division is perceived by those within and without that division (Alexander, 1972). It is here that stereotypes become important for they are the symbols or concepts we use in classifying persons or groups. As we grow up, we accept uncritically the evaluation that our parents, teachers, and close associates ascribe to people with certain labels; whenever we hear about or meet someone with that label his actions may confirm the stereotype unless we get to know him well as a person. If we like someone from a group to whom we usually apply an uncomplimentary stereotype, then we may assume that he is an exception and proceed to enjoy him as an individual.

Since one cannot get to know individuals from all community groupings on such an intimate basis, we tend to continue with our use of stereotypes. These become very much in evidence when there are demonstrations about civil rights, presumed police brutality, labor disputes, reorganization of school districts, or when there is a bitter local political campaign. Not only will people react in a hostile way when others publicly ascribe undesirable traits to them, but they will use stereotyped replies that can become catchwords on picket signs, scribbled on walls, or repeated over and over again in fiery speeches by leaders of an embittered grouping.

Thus, it would seem that one needs to know not only what groupings exist in a community but how community members "size up" each grouping. Here is a description someone has given of the stable American worker, excluding the "lower class," irregular working people. The reader may well ask whether this description conforms to that prevailing in his own community or whether it is just another stereotype.

The stable American worker, according to Miller and Riessman (1961), is:

. . . traditional, "old fashioned," somewhat religious, and patriarchal. The worker likes discipline, structure, order, organization and directive, definite (strong) leadership, although he does not see such strong leadership in opposition to human, warm, informal, personal qualities. Despite the inadequacy of his education, he is able to build abstractions, but he does so in a slow, physical fashion. He reads ineffectively, is poorly informed in many areas, and is often quite suggestible, although interestingly enough he is frequently suspicious of "talk" and "new fangled ideas."

He is family centered; most of his relationships take place around the large extended, fairly cooperative family. Cooperation and mutual aid are among his most important characteristics.

While desiring a good standard of living, he is not attracted to the middle-class style of life with its accompanying concern for status and prestige.

He is not class conscious although aware of class differences. While he is somewhat radical on certain economic issues, he is quite illiberal on numerous matters, particularly civil liberties and foreign policy.

The outstanding weakness of the worker is lack of education. Strongly desiring education for his children, he shows considerable concern about their school work, although he feels estranged and alienated from the teacher and the school, as he similarly feels alienated from many institutions in our society. This alienation is expressed in a ready willingness to believe in the corruptness of leaders and a general negative feeling toward "big shots."

He is stubborn in his ways, concerned with strength and ruggedness, interested in mechanics, materialistic, superstitious, holds an "eye for an eye" psychology, and is largely uninterested in politics. (pp. 90–91).

Almost every characteristic mentioned holds implications for community involvement, positively or negatively. The same would hold true for similar descriptions of any other significant grouping we might study. The grouping is truly a community component not to be taken lightly; particularly when seen as an illustration of social inequality with a potential for conflict.

14

Structural Inequality: Social Classes

In all communities residents rank some people and groups higher than others. This has been demonstrated in the discussion of antagonistic relations among groupings taken up in the last chapter. In the Lebanese village, for instance, there were distinct social strata.

Stratification is the term that describes this social expression of inequality and carries with it the image of strata or layers such as one would see in the rock walls along a highway cut through a mountain. A *social stratum* is actually a grouping of people of similar social rank—having functions, accomplishments, and possessions of similar value. Tied in with the idea of stratum or rank is that of *status*, or position, within the social structure. As Harold F. Kaufman (1952) has remarked, "One's community status is a composite of the statuses in the various groups in which he participates and of the evaluations of his personal qualities, accomplishments and possessions." (p. 431). It is obvious that in the smaller primary community, where people know each other quite well, there will be considerable agreement about the community status of each individual. In the metropolis, where people are not nearly so well known to each other, the concept of community status is more difficult to define. Kaufman gives three reasons for the greater difficulty. First, there is a lack of status equilibrium in the metropolis, which is another way of saying that an individual's characteristics will not have similar value and will not be consistent (congruous) with each other with respect to rank—for example, the underworld operator who resides in the exclusive residential district. When incongruity in status becomes the rule rather than the exception, the conception of community rank tends to lose its scientific usefulness. Second, there is differential perception of status in the urban world. The person being ranked will not only differ with observers concerning his status, but the observers will also disagree among themselves depending on the stratum to which they belong. Third, whereas in the small, primary community the individual is the unit that is ranked, in the metropolis it is formal positions, such as occupation or organizational memberships and possessions.

Social *classes*, the customary way of referring to those individuals who occupy a broadly similar economic rank in a status hierarchy, are traditionally accepted as the upper, middle, and lower, although sometimes each of these has been divided into two groupings (Gordon, 1949; Gross, L. 1949; Gross, N., 1953). A *caste* system is one in which those in an inferior status level are prohibited in various ways from moving upward. They are not allowed to marry into an upper level (endogamy), cannot practice vertical mobility (or the movement from the lower status level to the higher by educational, occupational, or other attainment), and are segregated (Berreman, 1960; Pohlmann, 1952; Srinivas, 1959).

These definitions—stratification, status, class, and caste—are necessary for any useful discussion of the social ranking present in a community.

VARIOUS APPROACHES TO SOCIAL CLASS

One way to delineate a class system for a community is to make use of certain objective indexes such as type of house, dwelling area, occupation, and source of income in ascribing a class position to individuals. This has been the method developed by W. Lloyd Warner (1949) and his associates and worked out as an Index of Status Characteristics (I.S.C.). Supplementing this I.S.C. is the subjective evaluation of a person by his associates to get at what might be called his social reputation. This Evaluated Participation (E.P.) is determined by the individual's social acceptability in formal organizations and informal cliques—as judged by others and not by himself.

When this method is applied, with the use of the Warner (1949) five-fold division of upper, upper-middle, lower-middle, upper-lower, and lower-lower, the class structures can be diagrammed. Figure 14–1 shows the stratification pattern for "Yankee City."

In a study of "Georgia Town," Mozell C. Hill and Bevode C. McCall (1950) found the distribution set forth in Figure 14–2.

Figures 14–1 and 14–2 describe the total community without making any distinctions on the basis of racial or ethnic lines. If whites and Negroes are considered as separate social groupings,

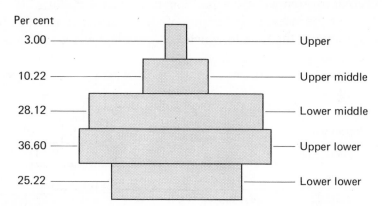

Figure 14–1. Class structure of "Yankee City" as presented by W. Lloyd Warner and associates. *Source:* See W. Lloyd Warner and Paul S. Lunt, *The Social Life of a Modern Community* (New Haven: Yale University Press, 1941), p. 88.

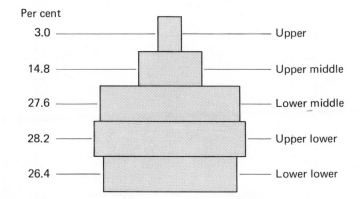

Figure 14–2. Class structure of "Georgia Town." *Source:* Mozell C. Hill and Bevode C. McCall, "Social Stratification in 'Georgia Town,' " *American Sociological Review* 15 (December, 1950), p. 724.

"Georgia Town" would have the caste-class structure shown in Figure 14–3, with the vertical line denoting the caste barrier.

W. Lloyd Warner employed a different type of diagram to show the caste-class structure of a Mississippi community that he calls "Old City." This is illustrated in Figure 14–4.

Figures 14–3 and 14–4 show that within each caste there are class lines, although the lower caste has a much larger proportion of the total lower class members of the community.

A second approach to social class makes use of an individual's subjective awareness of his position in a class structure. It seeks to discover the individual's feelings of identification and on this basis to assign him to the rank to which he thinks he belongs. This is the

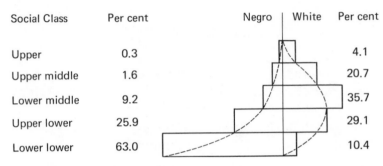

Social Class	Per cent	Negro | White	Per cent
Upper	0.3		4.1
Upper middle	1.6		20.7
Lower middle	9.2		35.7
Upper lower	25.9		29.1
Lower lower	63.0		10.4

Figure 14–3. Relation between the caste–class structures of "Georgia Town." *Source:* same as Figure 14–2.

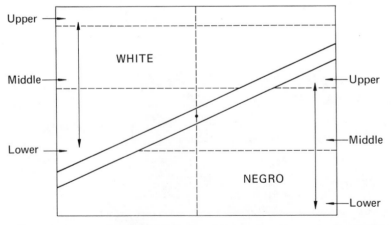

Figure 14–4. Relation between the caste–class structure of "Old City." *Source:* W. Lloyd Warner in the *Introduction* to Allison Davis and Burleigh Gardner, *Deep South* (Chicago: University of Chicago Press, 1941), p. 10.

approach employed by Richard Centers (1949). The two methods have been compared by John L. Haer (1955) as follows:

> The approaches of Warner and Centers, then, differ with regard to the units of stratification, indices employed, and general orientation. Warner focuses on communities taken singly, Centers on diffuse publics which may be nationwide in scope; Warner obtains a ranking of individuals in terms of a composite of objective socio-economic symbols, Centers in terms of verbal designations of affiliation; Warner perceives social classes as a function of disparities in objective status symbols, Centers as a product of the subjective aspirations or interests of large aggregates distinguished by their relationship to the means of production and political structure. (p. 690).

Haer also conducted a study to find out if the two approaches measure the same thing. He found that the two agree quite well in the case of high position. Disparities develop, however, with differences in size and heterogeneity of the cities; also, cities varied in the perceptual differences in the evaluation of status characteristics. Jackman and Jackman (1973) have also compared the two approaches and conclude that the data tend to support the Centers approach.

Many adaptations of these two approaches have been made. A. B. Hollingshead and Redlich (1953) have made use of the objective scale, having constructed an Index of Social Position applied to New Haven, Connecticut. They use ecological area of residence, occupation, and education as the items for the index. What is particularly interesting is the series of five classes that they delineate for New Haven:

> *Class I.* This stratum is composed of wealthy families whose wealth is often inherited and whose heads are leaders in the community's business and professional pursuits. Its members live in those areas of the community generally regarded as "the best"; the adults are college graduates, usually from famous private institutions, and almost all gentile families are listed in the New Haven *Social Directory*, but few Jewish families are listed. In brief, these people occupy positions of high social prestige.
>
> *Class II.* Adults in this stratum are almost all college graduates; the males occupy high managerial positions, many are engaged in the lesser ranking professions. These families are well-to-do, but there is no substantial inherited or acquired wealth. Its members live in the "better" residential areas; about one-half of these families belong to lesser ranking private clubs, but only 5 per cent of Class II families are listed in the New Haven *Social Directory*.

Class III. This stratum includes the vast majority of small proprietors, white-collar office and sales workers, and a considerable number of skilled manual workers. Adults are predominantly high school graduates, but a considerable percentage have attended business schools and small colleges for a year or two. They live in "good" residential areas; less than 5 per cent belong to private clubs, but they are not included in the *Social Directory.* Their social life tends to be concentrated in the family, the church, and the lodge.

Class IV. This stratum consists predominantly of semi-skilled factory workers. Its adult members have finished the elementary grades, but the older people have not completed high school. However, adults under thirty-five have generally graduated from high school. Its members comprise almost one-half of the community; and their residences are scattered over wide areas. Social life is centered in the family, the neighborhood, the labor union, and public places.

Class V. Occupationally, Class V adults are overwhelmingly semi-skilled factory hands and unskilled laborers. Educationally most adults have not completed the elementary grades. The families are concentrated in the "tenement" and "cold-water flat" areas of New Haven. Only a small minority belong to organized community institutions. Their social life takes place in the family flat, on the street, or in neighborhood social agencies. (pp. 165–66).

Further light on class behavior is given in a study of Evanston, Illinois, by Leonard Reissman (1954), who divides his informants into high and low classes. These two divisions contrast with Hollingshead's five, although Reissman used occupation, income, and education as objective indices to assign his ranks. He found that the higher class (which he equates with the middle class) showed a higher degree of participation and involvement in the community. As one would expect, individuals in this class read more books and magazines, attend church more frequently, belong to more organizations, and more often hold office in those organizations. They tend to dominate the organizational activity, the intellectual life, and the leadership of the community. Also this class is more realistic in its aspirations and knows just what steps to take to move upward. The lower class, on the other hand, shows a startling lack of ideals in this matter. Not only are they less active in the life of the community, but they are also more willing to sacrifice their personal views to take advantage of an opportunity for upward mobility. They seem unwilling to become involved in community affairs, a point of considerable political importance.

Still another approach to the description of stratification in American communities is demonstrated in the case of Detroit. Werner S. Landecker (1960b, 1963) in collaboration with Gerhard E. Lenski, makes use of the idea of "class crystallization." Their informants, highly diversified in cultural background and ancestry as well as in economic pursuits, were ranked in terms of occupation, income, education, and ethnic-racial descent. These investigators note that a major rank system, such as the ones they use, must first, provide a place for virtually every member of the population; second, be one in which it is possible for all members of a family to hold identical status (though of course this situation does not necessarily obtain); third, in relation to any major rank system already selected, another major rank system must have a reasonable degree of conceptual and logical independence. These researchers devised a method of computing a "crystallization score" for each person that indicates the degree of equivalence among the ranks held by that person. Table 14-1 shows in an approximate fashion the equivalent rank levels in the four rank systems.

Although Landecker does not try to diagram the class structure as it emerges from his approach, he does observe that the community as a whole seems to constitute a class system to a rather limited degree and that the highest status level constitutes a class to a greater extent than does any other status level in the community.

Here we see that certain occupational groupings (bankers, engineers, industrialists, physicians, school principals) rank higher than other occupational groupings. We also note with no surprise that those with the highest annual income rate highest in the rank system based on income, that those with 15 and more years of schooling stand highest in the educational rank system, and that those of English stock are far higher on the ethnic-racial rank system than the in-migrant hillbillies, who are also of English stock. Werner S. Landecker, who has done this study of Detroit, uses the term stratum for each status gradation in a single-rank system (income, education, etc.). Thus a stratum is the same as a grouping, but implies some ordering in a ranking system. The term social class applies to composite groupings whose members tend to have relatively the same position (high, medium, low) on all of the ranking systems. The term status inconsistency is used to describe those

TABLE 14–1

Approximately Equivalent Rank Levels in Four Rank Systems[a]

Status Percentiles	Occupa-tional Rank System[b]	Income Rank System (Annual)	Educational Rank System (in Years Completed)	Ethnic-Racial Rank System[c]
91–100	A	$8,000 and over	15 & over	English
81–90	B	6,000–7,999	13–14	Scandinavian French
71–80	B	5,000–5,999	12 (diploma)	Scottish Finnish
61–70	C	4,000–4,999	12 (others)	German
51–60	C	4,000–4,999	11	Irish
41–50	C	3,000–3,999	10	Greek Italian
31–40	D	3,000–3,999	9	Polish
21–30	D	3,000–3,999	8	Hungarian Russian
11–20	D	2,000–2,999	7	Negro
1–10	E	1,999 and less	6 & less	Mexican Hillbilly

[a] Upper and lower percentile limits of each rank are rounded to the nearest tenth percentile.

[b] Major occupations illustrative of each level are the following: A—banker, engineer, industrialist, physician, school principal; B—building contractor, electrician, newspaper reporter, registered nurse, toolmaker; C—auto mechanic, bricklayer, policeman, secretary, real estate agent; D—barber, machine operative, salesclerk, truckdriver, typist; E—dockworker, gas-station attendant, janitor, maid, waiter.

[c] The ethnic-racial categories listed constitute major examples. Each status decile is represented by its largest component if the latter fills more than half of that decile; otherwise it is represented by its two largest components.

Source: Werner S. Landecker, "Class Crystallization and Its Urban Pattern," Social Research, 27 (Autumn, 1960), 314.

groupings that may be high on one or two ranking systems but not high on others (Hodge, 1962).

In this approach to social class, the importance of groupings as an analytical concept is shown by the fact that the individual resident is first assigned to a membership in a stratum (grouping) and it is these strata that are combined to make up a social class. This corresponds to the way most local residents would go about delineating the stratification system of their community. Even when they mention the names of individuals, they think of them as representative of various groupings that have meaning for that particular community.

These meanings, however, may differ from community to community according to size. This was borne out in an exercise by Thomas E. Lasswell (1959) in which he asked introductory sociology students at Grinnell College over a period of years to describe the class stratification pattern of the community in which they had lived most of their lives. The communities were divided according to size into five categories: I—less than 15,000 in 1950; II—15,000–50,000; III—50,000–250,000; IV—suburbs of metropolises of over 250,000; V—metropolitan centers over 250,000. Then Lasswell ranked in order the frequency with which major categories of values were mentioned, as shown in Table 14–2.

This study bears out the findings of previous studies (Ellis, Lane and Olesen, 1963) that the values stressed do differ in order of importance in communities of different size. The larger the communities the more important type of housing and residential area become and the less important are community activities and choice of associates. Occupation is closely related to social class in communities of all sizes, but material possessions are believed to be more closely related to social class in communities of 50,000–250,000 than in either larger or smaller communities. Also, notice in the table how much more important ethnic group identification is in the largest metropolitan centers than in the smallest communities (Glazer and Moynihan, 1963).

Many recent studies of stratification in the United States have been drawn from national statistical samples rather than based on the investigation of a single community. In this connection Jessie Bernard (1973) reminds us:

> . . . At the societal level a major emphasis is on power; at the community level ranked status is emphasized. Class at the societal level is abstract; what the upper classes do at work or at play is not immediately visible to people in the local community (or was not before television). What the upper classes in the community do is more conspicuous . . . Social class is therefore more meaningful, more personal, and more immediate at the local level . . . (pp. 52–53).

As one would expect, one of the problems addressed in the national studies is that of locating certain occupational groupings in the stratification system. Glenn and Alston (1968) studied the distances among occupations and concluded that skilled manual workers in the United States, considered as a whole, are more appropriately considered part of the working class than of the "middle

TABLE 14-2

Community Stratification Patterns—Rank Order of Values

Rank Order of References	Category of Community by Population Size				
	under 15,000	15,000– 50,000	50,000– 250,000	over 250,000 (suburbs)	over 250,000 (metropolis)
	I	II	III	IV	V
1	Occupation	Occupation	Material possessions	Housing	Housing
2	Community activities	Income	Occupation	Occupation	Occupation
3	Education	Material possessions	Housing	Material possessions	Residential area
4	Housing	Community activities	Residential area	Leisure activities	Income
5	Income	Housing	Leisure activities	Residential area	Material possessions
6	Associates	Attitude to others	Education	Income	Education
7	Residential area	Residential area	Income	Education	Leisure activities
8	Material possessions	Associates	Community activities	Attitude to others	Attitude to others
9	Respect	Leisure activities	Respect	Community activities	Respect
10	Lesiure activities	Respect	Attitude to others	Associates	Ethnic group
	(11) Attitude to others	(11) Education	(14) Associates	(11) Respect	(11) Community activities
	(23) Ethnic group	(16) Ethnic group	(15) Ethnic group	(17) Ethnic group	(14) Associates

Source: Thomas Ely Lasswell, "Social Class and Size of Community," *American Journal of Sociology* 64 (March, 1959), 507. (Numbers in parentheses refer to rank order of that value.)

class" or a "middle mass." Farmers have attitudes and behavior that would locate them in the lower levels of the working class, although farmers' political attitudes and attitudes toward labor unions are "middle-class." Hamilton (1966) reports that in his study of the lower middle class over half of the clerical and sales group identify themselves as working class. Ordinarily, these white collar workers are thought to be a step above the working class. Hamilton indicates that the working class origin of these white collar workers is related to their continued identification with the working class.

The most searching examination of the middle class has recently been done by Bensman and Vidich (1971) where they explain changes in American society in terms of the revolution of the middle class. This class has been revamped by "the development of the service professions, the bureaucratization of business with its proliferation of managers and paid executives, and the growth in numbers of the academic intellectuals." Many of these are not likely to have the perspective of the traditional small-town businessman; in fact, they are apt to oppose it in towns and cities where it exists. This is because the new middle class is interested in education, cultural consumption, and is committed to liberal planning institutions for local affairs. This runs counter to the businessman's traditional ideology expressed in low taxes.

Kohn and Schooler (1969) find class consistently related to values. They define class as multi-dimensional (power, privilege and prestige) and not simply economic. The men in higher class position are more self-directed whereas those in lower class position conform more to external authority. Such a distinction, in their opinion, is explained by the cumulative effects of education and occupational position.

Although our focus is upon the local community, to understand the workings of stratification in a particular town one must realize that patterns have societal overtones. Archie Bunker, and the kind of class position he illustrates as the main character in the popular television program "All in the Family," is not confined to any single community but is a prototype found throughout the United States.

SOCIAL MOBILITY

Before turning to the question of the meaning of social stratification for the community sociologist and the treatment of class conflict, we might notice in passing the phenomenon of social mobility. In our discussion of migration in Chapter 4, we were talking about horizontal or geographic mobility. For instance, the

U. S. Census Bureau announced that 31.8 per cent of all Americans changed their residence during the three-year period ending in March, 1973.

A second form of mobility is vertical, with people moving up and down the social scale. Occupational mobility is one type of this. Before looking at the *fact* of occupational mobility, or whether people really do move up and down on an extensive scale, let us note the ideology people in Muskegon, Michigan, have about opportunity to improve one's situation. Rytina, Form and Pease (1970) interviewed 354 heads of households or their spouses, dividing up the respondents into poor, middle, and rich. They asked questions about the chance of an average man to get ahead, likelihood of occupational inheritance of top positions, chance of young people to go to college, equal treatment before the law, and why the rich are rich and the poor are poor. They found that there is no universal acceptance of the tenets of the American ideology of opportunity, though the support is strongest among those who profit most from the system—the rich in this case. The data also revealed that people from various economic strata differed in their belief about the effectiveness of different institutions to implement the ideology of opportunity. The authors found also that some of the people interviewed faced the dilemma of giving support to the prevailing ideology of opportunity in the face of massive intergenerational poverty.

But what are the *facts* of occupational mobility? First of all, as the occupational structure changes (more white collar jobs become available) we expect upward occupational mobility. People tend to move to the next higher position rather than jump to occupations several steps higher in prestige. To the extent that education is the means used toward higher mobility (and it does seem important), the lowest groupings suffer most because of their inability to take advantage of education. Porter (1968) is optimistic about the new occupational opportunities in the coming post-modern period which will be available to the opportunity-minded. But working against such occupational mobility are the "low levels of motivation, working class culture, educationally deprived areas, and outmoded educational arrangements and curricular content for societies based on the culture of science and technology." The evidence from one developing society (Thailand) seems to indicate that the opportunities Porter cites for the highly industrialized societies may not hold true for all countries. Evers (1966) concludes that in formerly loosely-structured societies, such as Thailand, there may originally be more occupational mobility with the start toward modernization, but that a bureaucratic group comes into existence which takes on class characteristics, one feature of which is to close mobility opportunities to those in other classes.

Another study based on six cities in the United States shows that there is a significant city effect upon the relationships among son's occupational prestige, son's education, and father's occupational prestige. The connection among these three variables seems to be stronger in smaller cities (Lane, 1968).

Social mobility is broader than occupational mobility, although the study of the latter often leads to conclusions about the former (Lopreato, 1961; Warner, Meeker and Eells 1949). One can frequently hear people discuss social mobility, perhaps without realizing it, when they charactrize mutual acquaintances. Carson McGuire (1950) has selected the following comments to describe the types of mobility orientation in Jonesville:

> *The Climber:* "He's really getting along in the world." "Oh! She made a good marriage and finally got out of that mess at home."
> *The Strainer:* "He's really trying to get ahead—but I don't think he's got what it takes." "She's doing her best to get in . . ."
> *The Static* (non-mobile): "Like father, like son." "She's a nice, quiet person like her mother." "He'll follow in his father's footsteps." "She's not much interested in things—stays at home."
> *The Clinger:* "He's trying to follow in his father's footsteps but he's not doing so well." "Her folks didn't leave much—she's going to have a hard time." "They're just managing to hang on."
> *The Decliner:* "Just a backslider." "She's dropped out of things—we never see her anymore." "The family's hit the skids—the kids are delinquent." "Maladjusted." "Alcoholic." (p. 200).

Just as there are different types of mobility orientation, so there are special channels through which mobility may be effected. Harold F. Kaufman (1952) has described these channels as follows:

> Major channels of mobility are occupation and the job, entrepreneurship, education, formal associations and marriage. Most studies of mobility have used as an index either the change in occupation or in years of schooling from one generation to the succeeding one. Demographic conditions which set the stage for rapid mobility are (1) the upper occupational groups do not replace themselves and (2) the great reservoir of rural youth together with the continuing expansion in industrial employment. . . .

The absence or closure of channels which facilitate upward movement might be considered as obstructive of mobility. Some major barriers would be: (1) lack of continuous economic expansion, especially in industrial employment; (2) restriction of membership in professional, business, and workers' group on any basis except competence; and (3) limitation of educational opportunities and other aids to acquiring the knowledge and skills necessary for higher ranks. If the channels for vertical mobility are absent and if a large number of people possess a strong desire for improved status, they either greatly modify their aims, or tensions are created which threaten the social order. (pp. 436–37).

The above considerations abundantly indicate the complexity of job advancement. Many kinds of barriers—sex, race, social class— impede its free exercise, and a variety of incentives—prestige, material rewards, and job security—combine to keep it working even though imperfectly (Davis and Gardner, 1941; Jackson and Crockett, 1964; Miller, 1960).

SOCIAL CLASS AND CONFLICT

The description of social class thus far has demonstrated that there are structural inequalities in most societies. Though methods of defining and measuring social class may vary widely, there seems to be little question that in a complex society social gradations are very real. What are the implications of this for social conflict in the community.

Karl Marx viewed society as divided into *hostile* classes. This conflict will continue until a classless society emerges which would be true communism. Antagonisms between classes result, he held, as long as there is private property. Those with the most property continue to exploit those that have little or none at all; this inequality is based on the modes of production which characterize a particular economic system. Under capitalism, according to Marx, the worker through his labor adds value to the products he makes and for which he is not fully compensated; instead, such surplus value accrues to the capitalist. Through revolution the class-conscious workers, or proletariat, will rise up, take the means of production into their own hands, and set up a mode of production free from exploitation.

Since Marx's ideas were formulated over 100 years ago, the economic systems have changed in ways that he did not foresee; the social revolutions he championed occurred in agrarian rather than in industrial societies; and the economic factors he stressed, though of major importance, are not necessarily the only ones involved in social conflict. Furthermore, the growth of the middle class in the Western world ran counter to his expectation that there would be a polarization of society into the capitalistic and working classes. Unpredicted, too, is the tendency of many members of the working class to identify with the lower middle class (Berger, 1960) even though, as pointed out earlier white collar personnel of workings class origins often identify with the working class. (Hamilton, 1966).

For the community sociologist, however, it is useful to test out in a given community some of Marx's basic premises. Where one finds antagonistic relations are they based on economic differentiation? have these, if they exist, moved into recognized class conflict? Put in other ways, is there dramatic economic exploitation which local community residents accept as the normal course of things? Of course, answering this question means using external value judgments based on some ideology significant to the questioner.

A second approach to stratification and conflict was proposed by Max Weber. He distinguished between *class* (determined chiefly along economic lines) and stratification (*status*) based on honor and social prestige. The community members judge status according to life styles, patterns of consumption and good taste, and accept distinctions of prestige and deference among social groups. According to Weber, a community sociologist would have to understand the class system, economically determined, as well as a social hierarchy, based on a series of statuses, which co-exists with the class system. However, the relative importance of class and status hierarchies, as well as the individuals within them, fluctuates with changes in economic, social and political power.

For the understanding of the local community a major contribution of Weber is his distinction between the *class situation* and *class organization*.[1] A class situation may exist in which by the standards of an outside observer real exploitation exists and it may be recognized as such also by those within the oppressed group. But this does not assume social importance until the class members organize themselves to correct injustices inherent in the situation.

[1] For a particularly helpful clarification of this point see Reinhard Bendix, "Inequality and Social Structure: A Comparison of Marx and Weber," *American Sociological Review* 39 (April, 1974), pp. 149–161.

Thus, an important consideration from the standpoint of the conflict model is the extent to which people who feel they are exploited (grape pickers, consumers, coal miners, tenants, the urban poor) have organized themselves to set up antagonistic relations with those exploiting them, a fact which any detailed community study would bring to light.

In this connection Jencks and Riesman (1968) see little change in the class situation, indicating that the income distribution remained *relatively* unchanged over a twenty-year period even though actual dollar figures increase.

❖ ❖ ❖ ❖

The fact of social inequality in American communities, as well as in those in other countries, seems beyond question. There are many different groupings, some of them described as social classes, whose members have unequal access to the scarce goods around them. Not unexpectedly, antagonistic relations come into existence and even color the life of the community. Thus, a community sociologist who set himself or herself the task of dealing only with perceived antagonistic relations would have much to do and would learn much about the community in the process. More and more he or she would be made aware of the allocative mechanisms within the community, seeing in their operation the manifestations of power and prestige. This will be the topic of the next chapter.

One explanation given for the absence of heightened class organization in the United States is provided by Wiley (1967) who holds that different kinds of groups occupied the lower rungs of the various economic hierarchies.

> . . . the farmers and workers both had inconsistent sets of class attributes, for the farmers lacked a clear interest in the labor market and the workers lacked interest in the credit market. This individual inconsistency was so widespread, and structured in such a way, that there was a clash between debtor and worker needs. . . .
>
> This conflict was not entirely clear at the time [late 19th century] for both groups identified themselves under the heading of "producing classes" and both identified their opponent as big business, the plutocracy or the "money power". Yet the two sections of the producing class were quite distinct in their relation to property; and the concessions they wanted from their common enemy were also distinct, if not incompatible. (p. 534).

Ransford (1972) in his study of blue collar anger shows that a class situation obtains among blue collar workers but there is little class organization. More specifically, though the white working man is overstereotyped as a narrow-minded bigot, his anger is rooted in the actual or perceived social situation. Some of the tangible strains, independent of personal bigotry, are: lack of decision making power on the job, the fact of hard earned dollars going for tax programs to aid blacks with no comparable programs for working class whites, a power structure unresponsive to the needs of the workingman. The white workers who feel politically powerless are especially antagonistic toward student and black protestors. "Apparently the potential exists for black as well as white militant action when individuals perceive a distributive injustice and, in addition, feel blocked in gaining redress through institutional channels."

15

Differential Allocation: The Use of Power

Power has a central place in the conflict paradigm. Coercion, not consensus, holds a community together. Since power and its accompaniments are distributed differentially in the community there can be no real knowledge of a community if power is not fully studied.

William Ryan (1971) in *Blaming the Victim* states the conflict case well:

> The signs are everywhere that the focus on power as the major issue is absolutely correct; the only meaningful way to change the prevailing American system of liberty for the free, justice for some, and inequality for all is through shifts in the distribution of power. Here a genuine community group gets itself together and deals, and manipulates, and gains control of a piece of poverty money; there a black legislator is sent to the state capitol; up on the hill a group of wild students demands, and *gets*, a voice in the affairs of the university. (pp. 240–41).

Ryan also observes that the primary cause of social problems is powerlessness and the cure for powerlessness is power. Power, he thinks, must be redistributed and this will permit the redistribution of income.

Another writer (Hurst, 1972) concludes an article on "Race, Class, and Consciousness" in a somewhat similar vein:

> The class and colony models are both systemic views of society. In the extreme class model, social institutions largely reflect the economic

institution, and the ruling ideas in society come from the top class. Similarly, in the colony model, the institutional ideologies resemble each other in encouraging a colonial relationship, white over and against black. That blacks by and large feel both politically manipulated and economically subjugated, as well as discriminated against, suggests that they see all institutions as intertwined and in the hands of a group whose efforts are against them. But, as with most research, these conclusions are tentative, and their verification must await more refined research. (p. 668).

One quickly learns in a thorough-going community study that many kinds of social relations look very different to those who are subordinate than they do to those who are on top. (Form and Rytina, 1960). A community, however, consists of all the people.

The most important development in community study in the past twenty years has been the effort to describe what has been rather loosely called "community power structure."[1] Long before that, however, community studies made reference to community leaders and analyzed the nature of community leadership. Some of these earlier studies described the relationships between the leaders and their followers, indicating that a person was a leader because he embodied the interests of and spoke for the group that he led. Attention was also given to the methods that leaders used under such labels as autocratic, democratic, and the like (Nelson, Ramsey, and Verner, 1960). With few exceptions, the focus was on community structure and the position of leaders in this structure. Allocation of power was a secondary consideration.

One of the earliest full-fledged sociological studies of a community was *Middletown*, by Robert and Helen Lynd (1929). The authors restudied this Indiana city in the middle 1930's. Here the community leadership centered around a leading family of three brothers and their immediate kin who through the years had accumulated considerable wealth. This in turn meant that they became directors and officials of a major bank and could decide who should not have credit. The glass plant that they owned was a leading source of employment and became the biggest factory of its type in the world. Other business interests included the ownership of the largest department store in the city, much real estate and stock in a daily newspaper. Members of the family were directors in

---

[1] For some insights into the nature of power see E. Michael Bannester, "Sociodynamics: An Integrative Theorem of Power, Authority, Interinfluence and Love," *American Sociological Review* 34 (June, 1969). Also see Leif and Clark, 1972.

other businesses that they did not own. Furthermore, they were active politically, and they held positions on the local school board and other civic bodies as well as being prominently represented in philanthropic and charitable organizations. Part of their power lay in the generous contributions they made to various causes, since, because they were large donors, whatever suggestions they might make with respect to personnel would be taken much more seriously than the suggestions of others with less financial power.

In reading this study one does not gain the impression that this family was hungry for power or intent on exploiting the community. Its members as a rule seemed interested in community service, a fact definitely enhancing their community standing even more. As they prospered financially, the members of the family sought more and more outlets for their accumulated wealth, thereby gaining greater economic control. Thus the power held was a result of success in several lines and the tendency to take an active interest in what was going on in the community.[2]

There are still communities where a single family group exercises the type of control described here, but today this is much less common than it was thirty to forty years ago in American towns and cities.

The social stratification studies of Lloyd Warner and his associates, mentioned in Chapter 14, also dealt with leadership. By identifying individuals who were in the upper class they supposedly were identifying a leadership elite, although they also investigated organizational leaders and sought to place them in the class system.[3]

With the appearance of Floyd Hunter's *Community Power Structure* (1953) a new dimension was added to community study. This described a southern city and had to do with the behind-the-scenes leader, whose behavior could not be adequately treated under the ordinary leadership terminology, used in previous studies. Such a person was not "leading" in the customary sense of the term; he was exercising power, often in a manipulative way. Hunter has identified and described forty top leaders, pointing out that this power elite is divided into various cliques whose members interact in-

[2] For a critique of the Lynds' "theory of power," see Nelson W. Polsby, "Power in Middletown: Fact and Value in Community Research," *The Canadian Journal of Economics and Political Science* 36 (November, 1960), 592–603.

[3] Nelson W. Polsby is also critical of the stratification approach in "How To Study Community Power: The Pluralist Alternative," *Journal of Politics*, 22 (1960), 474–84.

formally, without publicity, and with no need of any formal structure for arriving at decisions. Once decisions are reached by these few (twenty-three executives of large manufacturing, financial, or commercial companies; five wealthy leaders of social or civic organizations; five corporation lawyers; four government officials; two labor leaders; one dentist), several hundred lesser leaders are called into action. These serve on numerous committees and boards and are called by Hunter the "executors" of policy. The Negro grouping is considered a subcommunity and has thirty-four top leaders of its own. Another point made by Hunter is the interlocking of some of the top leaders of this southern metropolis with the state and national power structures, which means that they have much to say not only about what goes on in the local government but also in the state capital as well, with some influence also being wielded in Washington.

Instead of asking, "Who are the leaders in this town?" many students of the community became more interested in asking "How is this town run?" Once the matter of power came under debate, the political scientists began to take a great interest, for the study of power is their stock in trade. Either jointly with sociologists or independently political scientists began to study the community (Banfield, 1961; Polsby, 1962), with several of them preferring to view the local scene in terms of decision-making rather than in terms of social structure or broad social process. Now there are hundreds of studies and articles in professional journals dealing with community power; there is healthy controversy over many aspects of the problem, and more and more social scientists are finding the local community an interesting research area.

THE STUDY OF POWER IN THE COMMUNITY

The different approaches to the study of community power are best reflected in the methods used to arrive at the wielders of power (Kadushin, 1968). These have been identified as the reputational, the decisional, and the positional approaches. In the *reputational* method local people, usually a selected number supposedly well informed about their community, are asked to name the most influential or the most powerful. These informants base their nominations on the reputation that the nominee has for leadership, although many times they have personal information about situations in which the nominee has wielded power. In the *positional* approach, the investigator assumes before entering the community that certain persons who hold important official positions in the institutionalized economic, political, or civic structures are by definition the most powerful and influential. One seeks them out and then learns from their behavior about the allocation of power in that community.

A third approach—the *decisional*—is based on the theory that power is revealed as one learns how major community issues are settled and important decisions made. If one knows the details of enough such decisions, and the part played by leading community members in these decisions, then one has an empirical demonstration of power (Rossi, 1957 and 1960).

Each of these approaches has its own defenders and critics. Noting the shortcomings attributed to each method is a good introduction to the problem of defining and describing the allocation of power. Charles M. Bonjean and David M. Olson (1964) have listed the following as the most frequently mentioned defects of each method. Criticisms of the *reputational approach* are: (1) It does not measure leadership per se, but rather the reputation for leadership. Critics do not feel that a reputation for power is a valid index of power. (2) It incorporates an a priori assumption of a monolithic power structure, whereas there may be several structures of influence. (3) It incorporates an a priori assumption about group structure. Critics say that the reputational leaders may be an aggregate of leaders rather than a ruling group, as some employers of the reputational method imply. (4) The reputational approach may not accurately identify leaders because (a) of inaccuracies in respondent perceptions; (b) interviewer and respondent may not agree on what is meant by power; (c) when nominations and rankings are tabulated, the arbitrary cut-off points may be too high and thus not include all of the leaders, or too low and thus include some of the followers.

The *positional approach* is criticized from numerous standpoints. (1) There is considerable variation in terminology characteristic of different associations in designating similar offices, so that one does not really know what influence a designated position carries. (2) There is some question about its basic assumption that those holding positions of authority actually make key decisions while those who do not occupy such positions do not make key decisions.

The *decisional approach* also comes in for its share of criticism, as noted by Bonjean and Olson. (1) Given certain issues, where does the investigator start? Observing committee and organizational meetings appears to involve accepting the same relationship between authority positions and decision-making assumed by the use of the positional approach. How does the investigator know whether or not the decisions have already been made informally some time before the meeting, and how does he know if the committee or organizational members who appear to wield influence are not themselves influenced by others who may, in fact, be covert? (2) To establish the rapport and gain the confidence necessary to be permitted to attend informal meetings (if they are part of the influence structure) is quite time-consuming. (3) By what criteria are the decisions or issues selected for study? If they are arbitrarily selected by the investigator, that presents a methodological problem; if local people are asked to pick the most important issues, one is then resorting to a reputational approach. (4) The study of decision making ignores those actors who may be able to keep latent issues from emerging into open controversy. The most important issues in a community may be submerged.

There is a basis for the debate that goes on among advocates of the different approaches because, when two approaches are tried in the same community, they often produce a different set of leaders. (Walton, 1966) Robert O. Schulze and Leonard U. Blumberg (1957) tested the reputational and positional methods. Using the first method, they drew up a list of 18 public leaders in a community they call Cibola, a midwestern industrial city of about 20,000 inhabitants. They obtained names from the formal heads of the local (white) voluntary associations by asking them to respond to five questions:

1. Suppose a major project were before the community, one that required decision by a group of leaders whom nearly everyone would accept. Which people would you choose to make up this group—regardless of whether or not you know them personally?

2. In most cities persons are said to be influential "behind the scenes" and to have a lot to say about programs that are planned, projects and issues that come up around town. What persons in Cibola are influential in this way?

3. If a decision were to be made in the state capital that affected Cibola, who would be the best contact man to get in touch with state officials (besides state legislators)?

4. Who (besides local members of Congress) would be the best people to get in touch with federal officials in Metro City, Chicago, or Washington?

5. Are there any other people whom these leaders work with and who have not been named so far, but who should be included in a list of community leaders? (p. 292).

Schulze and Blumberg found that all but one of the eighteen persons subsequently defined as public leaders ranked among the top nineteen in the responses to the first (major project) and second (behind-the-scenes) questions. Eliminating the answers to the last three questions changed individual scores but had almost no effect on the overall composition of the top eighteen. These investigators then used various ways of identifying positional leaders, such as taking the fourteen objectively defined public statuses selected by Samuel A. Stouffer (1955) as civic leaders: mayor, president of the chamber of commerce, chairman of the Community Chest, president of the largest labor union, county chairmen of the Republican and Democratic parties, commander of the largest American Legion post, regent of the DAR, president of the women's club, chairmen of the library and the school boards, the parent-teachers' association, the bar association, and the publisher of the largest locally owned newspaper. *Only 4 of the 18 public leaders were found to occupy any of the fourteen top civic statuses in Stouffer's list.* Schulze and Blumberg tried to draw up other objective lists of statuses, such as members of school board, top lay officers in the local churches, men's civic groups, etc., but obtained no better result. The conclusion is, therefore, that the heads of the voluntary associations in Cibola make a distinction between persons who occupy top formal positions and those who wielded most influence and exerted greatest public leadership.

Another effort at comparing the results of alternative approaches was made by a group at Syracuse University (Danzger, 1964; Freeman, et al., 1963). They conclude that the different methods help them locate different types of leaders. The methods based on the reputational, positional, and organizational participation uncovered what they call *Institutional Leaders,* or individuals who head up the largest and most actively participating business, industrial, governmental, political, professional, educational, labor, and religious organizations in Syracuse. They are not themselves active participants in community affairs, apparently have no direct impact on most decisions which take place, but they do lend prestige and legitimize the solutions produced by others. They provide access to the decision-making structure for their underlings: *the Effectors.* This second type is located by studying participation through the decisional approach for they are active in decision making. A third type of leader—the *Activists*—hold office in organizations and clubs and are involved in decision-making, but not as often as the Effectors. One locates the Activists by a study of social activity (organizational participation). This demonstrates the need to use a leadership typology that includes several types of leaders, the location of which may call for a variety of methods.

A different approach to the power structure has been worked out from the ecological standpoint by Amos H. Hawley (1963). He holds that power is an attribute of a social system rather than an individual. One way of viewing power in the system is to compute the ratio of managers, proprietors, and officials in the labor force (MPO ratio), assuming that the lower the ratio the greater the concentration of power. He further postulates that the greater the concentration of power in a community, the greater the probability of success in any collective action affecting the welfare of the whole. To demonstrate this, he has related the ratio of managers, proprietors, and officials in the employed labor force to the success of urban renewal and finds the two significantly associated. Put another way, the MPO ratios are lowest in urban renewal cities that have reached the execution stage and highest in cities that have never attempted urban renewal. Hawley points out, however, that this finding does not always hold for cities with mayor-council governments, with a predominance of service industry, with small proportions of college graduates among their residents, and with locations in the northeast and the west. Further testing by James M. Williams (1973) raises some questions about this method as an indicator of relative power distribution.

THE POWER GRID [4]

Norton E. Long (1958) has likened the community to an ecology of games. In a sense, these games compare with the subsystems

---

[4] Material in this section is drawn from Irwin T. Sanders, "Public Health in the Community," Howard E. Freeman, Sol Levine, and Leo G. Reeder (eds.), *Handbook of Medical Sociology* (Englewood Cliffs, N. J.: Prentice-Hall, Inc., 1972), second ed.) pp. 407–434.

mentioned earlier—banking, newspaper publishing, and the like—and they give structure to the community as well as goals, roles, strategies, tactics, and publics to the players. Players in each "game" make use of players in the other "games" for their particular purposes. Thus power is distributed throughout the whole community, with each "game" possessing power that other "games" must use. Functional necessity thus becomes an element in power because you have power if you are needed. Rather than thinking of power as absolute, we should think of it as *relevant* and *irrelevant* for a particular group or community purpose. Some players who are powerful in their own "game" have no power in another "game," for what they have to offer has no relevance to that "game."

Furthermore, power is often circumscribed. People trying to promote a community program often seek the help of a community leader who has no influence in the area with which the program deals; but even if he does have influence, there are definite limits to the power he can display in its behalf. He is involved in a whole set of obligations that he must take into account.

We get a clearer picture of how power is allocated if we relate it to a typology of leadership, recognizing that this serves as a sketch of the power grid. And in any one of the "games" that Long talks about there are levels of power shared by whatever hierarchy exists for that game.

Key Leaders

Long views the key leaders—or "top leadership," as he calls them—as largely confined to ritual and ceremonial roles and usually identified with status position rather than with specifiable roles in social action. In this sense, they correspond to the institutional leaders described in the Syracuse study. The key leader exercises power in more than one segment and derives dominance from one of the major segments of the type illustrated in Table 15–1 which shows the range of community components. Long sees these top or key leaders as giving the game a cross-system character, for the custodians of the symbols of top social standing provide goals that in a sense give all the individual games some common denominator of achievement. While the holders of top social prestige do not necessarily hold either top political or economic power, they do provide meaningful goals for the rest (Long, 1958). Key leader-

TABLE 15-1

A Typology of Community Leadership

Type of leader	Community frame of reference	Range—specific or diffuse	Duration
Key	Two or more major segments	Diffuse	Indeterminate
Dominants	One major segment	Specific	Indeterminate
Functionaries	One major segment	Specific	Indeterminate
Organizational	One formal association	Specific-diffuse	Determinate
Issue	One community realignment	Specific	Determinate
Spokesman	A grouping or locality	Diffuse	Indeterminate

Source: Irwin T. Sanders (see footnote 4).

ship is in fact a strange mixture of prestige, as well as certain kinds of system power (economic, religious, political) that can be applied to problems cutting across systems.

Delbert C. Miller (1958) has also developed a leadership typology that can be equated in part with Table 15-1. He sees community power structure as composed of key influentials, top influentials, the community power complex, and those parts of the institutionalized power structure of the community that have come into play when activated by a community issue (Hanson, 1959). He is making clear the fact that not all power exerted in a community (such as father over his children) is community power but only that which comes into play when the community is affected as a social unit. The key to his scheme is the identification of the top influentials, who compare with the dominants in Table 15-1, for they are drawn from various systems of power in the community. The key influentials, corresponding to the key leaders in the figure, are the top influentials who are sociometric leaders and tend to have some permanence at the top even though community issues change.

Robert K. Merton (1949) has used the term "influentials" for the leadership of Rovere, a town of 11,000 on the Eastern Seaboard. He divides these into "top influentials" (those mentioned by 15 per cent or more of the informants), the "middle influentials" (mentioned by 5 to 14 per cent) and the "rank-and-file" (mentioned by fewer than 5 per cent). He observes: "One first gains the impression that although a relatively few people—the top influentials—exert influence upon people on all levels of the influence-structure, there occurs a secondary tendency for people to be otherwise influenced by their peers in that structure." Because of the discrepancy in numbers "it appears likely that more personal decisions in a community may be the result of advice by the many people ranking low in the influence-structure than by the few ranked at the top." (pp. 410–11) Merton also notes that some of these top influentials exert influence in more than one sphere of activity (the key leaders in Table 15–1) while others exert influence in only one sphere (the dominants).

Turning now to Tijuana, Mexico, Orrin E. Klapp and L. Vincent Padgett (1960) have identified the top influentials there in keeping with the method used by Miller and Form (Hanson, 1959). In summarizing the integration of the Tijuana power elite they conclude: (1) business TI's (top influentials) feel apart from those in government, politics, and labor; (2) TI's in government, politics and labor tend to hang together as co-operating crowds; (3) relationships between the business and political-labor camps vary in effectiveness, depending upon who achieve power in the latter group; (4) within business there are a dominant clique, several independent TI's, and a number of other cliques, friendships, and coalitions; (5) "high society" is drawn mostly from business and mainly integrates it; and (6) churches do not seem to be important in the power structure or to have much function in integrating the elite. In general, the power elite of Tijuana is fragmented, and the term "structure" should be applied to it only with the above qualifications (p. 403). Interestingly enough, the authors find that Long's picture of the local community as an ecology of games is most applicable to the lack of integration of the Tijuana power structure.

Dominants

Some studies deal with specific kinds of dominants and try to assess their power in the total community system. Robert O. Schulze (1958) has dealt with the role of economic dominants in Cibola, a community already mentioned. He notes a bifurcation of power, stemming from the withdrawal of the economic dominants from active direction of the political and civic life of the community. The Tijuana study, already cited, bears this out. In many communities it appears that they do not hold central power but that they have to share power with other major systems, other "games," if you will. Donald A. Clelland and William H. Form (1964) tested Schulze's conclusions for Cibola in a study of Wheelsburg, located 60 miles west of Cibola, but an independent city of over 100,000 dominating a metropolitan area of about 180,000. They found a tendency for the economic dominants and the political dominants, which once were melded, to go their separate ways. This process in both communities parallels the integration of economic units into national markets and the process of governmental centralization. The economic dominants also withdrew from civic associations as absentee ownership increased, but more rapidly in the satellite city (Cibola) than in Wheelsburg. Apparently, too, in Wheelsburg the economic dominants still hold on to their decision-making role in community issues largely because they maintain an extensive network of economic ties with the political dominants.

A comparison of the dominants in El Paso, Texas, and Juarez, Mexico by William H. Form and William V. D'Antonio (1959) found more integration between the economic and political influentials and institutions in El Paso than in Juarez, but this does not indicate a simple centralized power structure in El Paso in the decision-making process. If one used the reputational technique for identifying influentials, then results would support the hypothesis that business interests dominate local government, but no ranking system appears that would place one type of economic leader (banker) over others (industrialists) or businessmen over governmental leaders. Questions are still left unanswered. In cases of community conflict, however, there was a difference between the two communities. In El Paso, a coalition of economic and political dominants joined to fight another coalition of economic and political dominants; in Juarez, such a cleavage would call for the resolution of local problems by one institution or the other. No coalition across community systems (politics, business, religion) would bring a broad range of organizational facilities to bear upon the problem.

Delbert C. Miller (1958) in comparing a Pacific City, a Southern City, and an English City finds that business men do exert a predominant influence in community decision-making in Pacific City and Southern City, but not in the English City. This is explained by the difference in occupational prestige factors in the United States and England. In the latter country captains of industry rank low in comparison with law, medicine, the universities. Furthermore, the form of local government differs in the two countries. In Pacific City, for instance, the city council has nine members, most of whom come from small business backgrounds. In the English City, the Council is composed of 112 members broadly representative of trade union members, business, and other segments of the community.

Robert E. Agger and Daniel Goodrich (1958) studied two communities in the Far West to see how the power structure affected political behavior. Valley City was a small retail trading center of about 2,000 adults and Boomtown, a rapidly growing industrial community of about 16,000. In each community self-identified Democrats outnumbered self-identified Republicans, but in both communities the partisan atmosphere on Main Street was predominantly Republican, although much more so in Valley City than in Boomtown. After testing a number of assumptions the writers conclude that control by the economic dominants in Valley City of the overlapping organizational membership and power structures discouraged Democratic activities in local politics. But in Boomtown, where economic dominants do not control the power structure, the Democrats were able to move directly into top leadership positions without a long apprenticeship in the Republican-dominated social structure.

Functionaries

Reference has been made in Chapter 8 to the community role of functionaries who manage the major local institutions. They have the power to determine many policies simply by the day-to-day execution of their job; they also can negotiate and work out arrangements with other local groups, which eventually get presented to the boards or other controlling bodies for approval. They are not treated as equals by the dominants of the segment of which they are a part, but rather as the professional help. From time to time, a functionary does emerge as a key leader because of his effectiveness in some areas of community life where he is not the paid professional. It is common for the key leaders and dominants to work through the functionaries and organizational leaders, although at times this process reverses itself.

Organizational Leaders

Organizational leaders, listed as a major category in Table 15–1, wield power to the extent that their organization has influence and is identified with the community project or action under discussion. Ideas for projects frequently originate with organizational leaders, who then must win the support of relevant dominants and some key influentials to move the projects ahead. Thus the power to originate, organize, and be the spark plug as it were for community improvement resides oftentimes in organizational leadership. Many more ideas grow out of organizational activity than the community could well absorb, so they go through the screening process of getting legitimized by the appropriate people in the leadership structure. Thus, power may be exercised in a negative way to keep some highly controversial or disruptive proposal from moving very far beyond the initiation stage. Thus, organizational leaders are so highly involved in seeking community support for various projects because the status of a given organization may rise considerably in public esteem if it can sponsor some undertaking that meets broad community approval. The alert organizational leader is always on the lookout for this kind of community service.

Issue Leaders

Another kind of leader is the issue leader, who is for or against some cause or proposal that has its strong adherents and opponents. Without the element of controversy it does not become an issue, but remains a project or worthy endeavor that interested people choose to support. One community that has been issue-ridden in recent years has been Levittown, Long Island.[5] It is a community artificially created on a potato field in 1946–47 when homes were constructed on a mass basis by the Levitt organization (Dobriner, 1963). Settlers came *en bloc* as each wave of construction was finished so that by 1961 the population numbered 65,000. When Levittown was established it inherited no ready-made institutions. It even had no local government for it was part of the large town of Hempstead, with little weight in this very populous political unit. The one institution that the community shared was the local school system, although the school district did not exactly coincide with the Levitt-built homes. Thus, it was inevitable that some of the frustrations felt by people in such a community would turn upon

---

[5] For details, see National Commission on Professional Rights and Responsibilities of the National Education Association of the United States and Ethical Practices Committee of the New York State Teachers Association, *Levittown, New York: A Study of Leadership Problems in a Rapidly Developing Community* (Washington: 1962).

the school, particularly when the Catholic residents—comprising 40–45 per cent of the population—also supported an elementary parochial school system. Many of the Jewish people, who make up about 20 per cent of the community, were very anxious for the schools to have the excellence that would guarantee college admission for their children. Many, irrespective of religious affiliation, were concerned about maintaining strict fiscal economy in school affairs for, as young married couples, they were having difficulty in paying for their homes and meeting other expenses. The Communism issue also was injected into the school picture as was the propriety of singing Christmas carols. The issues expressed themselves primarily in the election of school board members, with those for a conservative, economy-minded approach to education supporting one slate, and those seeking a number of changes supporting another slate. Over a period of several years, the composition of the school board in terms of educational philosophy changed, which meant dismissal of the superintendent and the threat of most of the teachers to resign and seek posts elsewhere. At this point the New York State Commissioner of Education ordered a special study to be made.

The Levittown experience is cited at such length to demonstrate how significant issue leaders can become in a community where there are no traditional positional leaders, where organizations are new and feeling their way, and where there are no dominants in major systems other than education. (Orzack and Sanders, 1961).

Spokesmen

Continuing the explanation of Table 15–1, we note that the Spokesmen is listed as a link in the flow of power. The more one studies the leadership behavior of the community dominants and the key leaders, the clearer it becomes that they are sensitive to the reactions of people up and down the power grid. There are people in every community who represent before the community at large the interests of some grouping or small part of the town. Those who bear the label of the grouping or who live in the distinctive geographical area have learned that the spokesman gives voice to their ideas or grievances; the community leaders, at least those who are wide-awake, have learned that the spokesman is usually correct in his assessment of how "his people" will react to some proposal before the community. There are many cases in every community where some key leader has changed his mind about supporting a program or a cause when he learned that some of the spokesmen took an unfavorable stand on it. This is particularly true where the cause may be caught up in the political process and tested by the ballot. These spokesmen serve another purpose as well. They are communicators, explicators of what is happening at the community at large, a role that other leaders may be quick to recognize. Obviously, spokesmen for racial and ethnic groups will vary in importance as their groupings are recognized by the community at large (Barth and Abu-Laban, 1959).

Before leaving Table 15–1 it is useful to note that some types of leaders play roles specific to some major segment, organization, issue, or grouping. The attribute of the key leader is that he crosses from one component to another, exercising diffuse leadership. Some leaders also hold their positions for determinate periods of time— especially the organizational officer and the issue leader. The latter drops from sight when the issue in which he has been interested is resolved or shelved.

It is also possible for a given individual to hold two types of leadership positions. A functionary can at times be a spokesman, an organizational leader may also serve for a time as an issue leader, and a dominant leader may move into a key leadership position for a while and then revert to exclusive interest in the major system where he is most important.

SELECTED CHARACTERISTICS OF POWER ALLOCATION

Attention has thus far been focused primarily upon the kinds of leaders to whom power is allocated within the community and the power grid of which they are a part.[6] Since the presentation has been largely descriptive of the characteristics of each kind of leader, one might overlook the fact that there is competition and conflict, cooperation and accommodation among these leaders. There are also various interpretations as to the nature of their power base.

One theory holds that power is a property of interorganizational ties, which can be described in terms of resource networks. Per-

[6] See Charles M. Bonjean's suggested typology of visible, concealed, and symbolic leaders in "Community Leadership: A Case Study and Conceptual Refinement," *American Journal of Sociology* 68 (May, 1963), 672–81.

rucci and Pilisuk (1970) in a study of a Midwestern community of 50,000 found that the following propositions were supported:

(1) There exists in communities a relatively small and clearly identifiable group of *interorganizational leaders*, or persons who hold high executive (policy decision-making) positions in "many" organizations.

(2) *Organizational leaders*, or persons who hold equally high positions in "few" organizations, will be less often identified on an *actual* community issue than will their counterpart interorganizational leaders . . .

(3) Interorganizational leaders will show greater homophyly [the tendency for people who are alike on some characteristic to share similar values] and primary or social ties among themselves than will organizational leaders.

(4) Those interorganizational leaders who are part of the same resource network will be judged more powerful by their peers and will show the greatest value homophyly and most frequent social ties. (p. 1044).

The key to the above is the resource base, through ties to many organizations as well as to other individuals who likewise have such access. In contrast to other groups in the community, this small elite could bring resources into play more effectively when it thought it important to do so. This approach is suggested as a test for the existence of ruling elites in community power structure not provided by the approaches previously described.

A different emphasis is found in the study of a small city in the Rhineland of West Germany. There Laumann, Verbrugge, and Pappi (1974) developed a causal model of the influence system. By the use of path analysis they attempted to show the dependence of Community Affairs Network on Predictor Networks. They claim as their most striking finding the absence of a direct path from the business-professional structure to the community affairs structure. In this community "the effect of the community's objective interest differentiation is exerted," according to the authors, "indirectly through its effect on channelling informal social ties and creating value homophyly." This stress on informal ties does not run exactly counter to the findings of Perrucci and Pilisuk (1970) mentioned above, but it does place less stress on interorganizational connections. The researchers do warn, however, that they are dealing with a comparatively small city where members of the elite do have a chance to know each other well.

Other students of community power are impressed by the importance of exchange behavior. Nix and Seerley (1973), basing their approach on that of Bates (1962), make use in their study of three Georgia counties, of the concept of interstitial, or "in-between" groups, which link interest groups. One type of interstitial group is the *exchange type,* in which actors relate to exchange goods or services (e.g., customer-merchant and client-professional relationship); a second type is the *coordinative interstitial group* (e.g. Chamber of Commerce, an informal decision-making clique) in which "actors from two or more different groups or organizations relate to coordinate functions or manage relationships among their varying groups which have differing and potentially conflicting interests." Nix and his associates conclude that individuals gain power through the exchange relationships but they exercise power and get the reputation for having power through the coordinative type. The Georgia study indicates that community leaders occupy a relatively greater number of positions in coordinative interstitial groups than do nonleaders, a point stressed by Perrucci and Pilisuk referred to above.

Studies such as those mentioned here are providing much new information about the nature of power and how it is exercised in contrast to many of the earlier studies which focused almost exclusively on the search for those who held power. We recognize that there are many subtle aspects to the wielding of influence in a community; that those who are powerful in one situation are not powerful in other situations. Furthermore, the unequal allocation of power in a community can be likened to a power grid, or hierarchies of power, with wide variations among communities as to the concentration of power (Clark, 1968). It is also clear that the kind of power structure one finds may be an artifact of the method used in its delineation, which explains why many recent studies use more than one approach. Studies also show that power does not reside in an individual alone but rather in his or her ability to mobilize and channel resources, both financial and non-material. It is true that some community positions (mayor, bank president, etc.) carry legitimized power (often referred to as authority), but this is frequently circumscribed. Although much power depends upon the possibility of tapping the resources of more than one important social network, it is also based on informal contacts with others who possess this possibility and who share a similar life style and view of the community. It is in this sense that one sometimes speaks of an *elite*.

Many other characteristics of power and its allocation could be mentioned. However, in terms of a conflict paradigm, one may ask how power becomes reallocated given the existence of a *power structure* in a community. One possibility, somewhat dubious in many cases, is to convince those whose decisions would be required to allocate more power to the group seeking the change. This might take the form of more adequate financing, better representation on important decision-making councils, or provision of better facilities.

Another possibility is the confrontation of the established leadership (or some segment of it) with a demand for reallocation of power. This is done by a public protest, such as picketing; by a strike—not just by labor unions, but by consumers who agree to buy no meat, parents of school children who refuse to send their children to school under certain circumstances; or by support of political candidates committed to a change. One form of confrontation is a lawsuit which seeks through legal means to force some reallocation of power in order to redress existing inequalities. Collective bargaining between employees and employers, though often couched in monetary terms and benefits, is basically a power struggle. James B. McKee (1953), in a study of Lorain, Ohio, with a population of 50,000, has listed three effects of the emergence of organized labor that have broken down the monopoly of decision-making once held by the upper stratum and created channels of influence for the low-status groups.

1. The alteration of power relations has disturbed the community's status system, since members of low-status ethnic groups, through achieving leadership in politics, local government, and the union, constitute a new elite in the community.
2. The union has taken over some decision-making once the prerogative of the upper stratum-managerial group, with the result that one group can no longer be considered the ruling group.
3. The organization of political power in the community contrasts with and contradicts the system of power and authority in the corporation. In the community, decision-making is more democratically structured than in the industrial bureaucracy where authority is located at the top, for those of low status can now have some share in community decision-making.

Additional information about organized labor's image of the community power structure comes from the study of Lansing, Michigan, by William H. Form and Warren L. Sauer (1960). Reminding us that "community power structure may be defined as that network of relations obtaining between individuals and organizations which affect decisions regarding issues or actions of community-wide importance," they then turn to a description of how this power is perceived by labor leaders. They find that only about twenty labor officials out of a union membership of 25,000 were actively involved in community affairs and seriously concerned about labor's place in the local power structure. They acknowledge management's general dominance of the local community, but they consider labor to be part of the power structure and not tangential to it. It initiates few projects, but does have a powerful voice when it enters a contest. Its goals are the attainment of a better social welfare system in a context of growing political power.

This study of Lansing, Michigan, also illustrates the importance of the concept of saliency in a power situation. Labor will become active when its own interests are involved. M. Herbert Danzger (1964) described salient goals as both the "pure" goals of an institutional order (wealth in economy, sacredness in religion, etc.) and the organizational imperatives of the different institutional elites (funds, members, physical plant, etc.). Unless these imperatives or system needs are met, the entire organization breaks down; or, if they are threatened by some outside action, the organizational leaders will respond vigorously. In this sense, Danzger feels that salience can be used to assess the relative power of elites in different institutional orders, despite the fact that a particular goal may have different salience for the contending elites.

LOCAL AUTONOMY AND POWER ALLOCATION

Community power can no longer be studied only in local terms in a dynamic society such as the United States. There are constant inputs from the larger society which greatly influence the behavior of local decision-makers. To trace these would require a description of American society itself. A diagram prepared by Terry N. Clark (1973a) sets forth some of the major variables to be taken

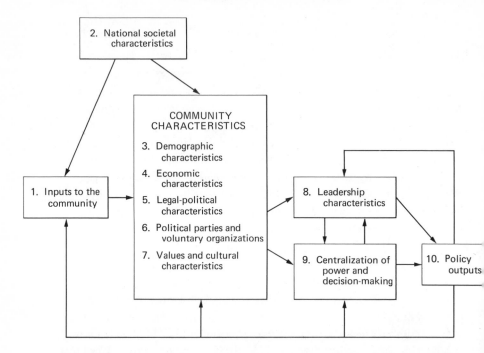

Figure 15–1. Ten fundamental sets of variables in community decision-making. *Source:* Terry Nichols Clark, *Community Power and Policy Outputs: A Review of Urban Research.* Beverly Hills, Calif.: Sage Publications, 1973, p. 3. Reprinted by permission.

into account in looking at local power allocation (Figure 15–1). One can assume that each of the "Community Characteristics" listed on the diagram has interconnections with extra-community structures of a similar type.

Clark, in reviewing recent literature, notes that in Europe community specialists earlier than in the United States focused on community-national relationships. With the increase in federal programs to be activated and managed at the local level, U. S. specialists have become much more aware of external factors.

Of course, the alienation of some community leaders may be the result of pressures from the larger society, as Ritchie P. Lowry (1962) indicates in his study of "Micro City, California." Such alienation may have positive features in terms of community social change.

This study of one small community experiencing rapid rural to urban change suggests that mass society trends and alienation are, indeed, re-

lated. However, alienation may take several different forms as far as
local community leadership is concerned. Leaders may withdraw socially
or ideologically from community life; they may participate primarily in
local community or extra-community activities; or a combination of these
forms may emerge. This multi-dimensional approach to alienation indicates that each type of leader has a specific function to perform in the
rapidly changing contemporary community. Alienation, then, becomes
the functional basis for providing the community with the varied leadership types necessary to maintain vitality in contemporary public life.
Problems arise only when certain leadership types predominate over
others or when alienation takes one rather than several forms. It is not,
therefore, alienation which becomes dysfunctional but the resulting disequilibrium in the total leadership structure.

In addition, the concept of function must be used as a relative term.
What is functional for the local community may become dysfunctional
for the larger society, and vice versa. It becomes mandatory, therefore,
for the small community in mass society to provide for an effective interaction between all of the possible leadership types. In this way a democratic confrontation of conservative and utopian and local and extra-
community interests can be maintained. (pp. 433–34).

A useful way of relating community leadership to the larger
society is through the typology of "locals" and "cosmopolitans."
Merton (1949) first used these terms in his study of "Rovere" to
distinguish between two types of individuals who exercised differential leadership. Sykes (1951) in a study of Plainfield, New
Jersey showed that "locals" had a knowledge of the community not
possessed by the "non-locals," most of whom commuted to New York
City regularly. Lowry (1968) also finds this a useful typology in
describing leadership in Micro City. However, he added to the
"local" and "cosmopolitan" typology a third type: the "mediating"
leader, who maintains overlapping memberships and informal relationships with both local and cosmopolitan groups. The ability of
such leaders to mediate is due to their place in the social structure
rather than to any particular ideological commitment; also, they
have multiple interests and activities, and may have roots both in
the local and national society.

As Warren (1970) indicates, much community development
literature holds up the ideal of community autonomy as very desirable. But he raises the question as to the price to be paid if a
community moves very far in this direction, concluding from recent
studies that autonomy and broad distribution of power are inversely
related. In other words, interdependence between the community

and national society leads to a type of competition among the leadership that moves away from a monolithic power structure. Looking at the community from the standpoint of viability, or the ability to confront its problems and take necessary action, Warren concludes on the basis of "sporadic" evidence that viability is inversely related to broad distribution of power.

To conclude, social conflict is explained in large part by the unequal allocation of power within a community. This inequality need not be based on conditions within the locality alone but is apt to reflect the inequalities expressed in the national society. At the same time, local communities (despite the limited autonomy which they possess) do occasionally act on their own to lessen the effects of this external maldistribution.

16

Community Controversy

Conflict in the community frequently takes the form of a controversy, which differs from other kinds of antagonistic relations in that it is issue-oriented. New coalitions tend to form for each new issue since only those who feel affected by that issue are apt to get into the act. In other words, the partisans on each side of the controversy may or may not reflect structural differences (class, ethnic groupings, etc.) but they do confront each other over an issue which has been brought before the public for decision. It is recognized as "community business." This distinguishes it from social protest which is an effort to call attention to what should be "community business" but which has not been put on the community agenda; or, if on the agenda the partisans think it is not being taken seriously enough.[1]

KINDS OF ISSUES

Various efforts have been made to classify and describe the kinds of issues that most often appear in a community. Some writers (Laumann and Pappi, 1973) distinguish between *instrumental* and *expressive* issues.

> . . . *instrumental issues* are concerned with controversies over the differing allocation of scarce resources, such as land, jobs, and money,

[1] For an excellent discussion of the meaning of protest see Ralph H. Turner, "The Public Perception of Protest," *American Sociological Review* 34 (December 1969), 815–831.

345

and find their particular locus in the adaptive and integrative sectors of community concern. . . . For such issues there is usually a fairly obvious calculus of costs and benefits to various interested parties. Conflict over such issues tends to be moderate, often characterized by bargaining and compromise among the contending parties. The specific outcome is the direct result of their relative power or influence . . .(p. 224).

In contrast, consummatory or *expressive issues:*

> are concerned with controversies regarding the maintenance or change in the organization of basic values, commitments, and orientations that shall guide or control community affairs . . . (they) are usually highly charged with emotional affect and have an "all or none" nature that usually precludes or makes very difficult negotiated settlements among the contending parties. (p. 224).

The authors indicate that the outcome and the level of community tensions connected with any issue depends upon how the issue gets defined: as instrumental or expressive.

Somewhat akin to the above is the classification suggested by Gamson (1966). In *conventional conflicts* people use established means of political expression to influence the outcome of issues. They may regard their opponents as mistaken or as pursuing different but legitimate goals; they are not seen, however, as representatives of evil forces. In *rancorous conflicts*, on the contrary, people believe that their opponents are violating the norms governing political conflict, and characterize their activities as "dirty," "underhanded," "vicious" and so forth. Gamson in his study of eighteen New England communities found that nine characteristically had rancorous conflict and nine had conventional conflict. Of the 54 issues studied, 18 concerned fluoridation, 11 concerned schools, eleven the development of some new community facility or service, eight were zoning issues, and the other six varied from change in form of government to urban renewal. One of Gamson's interesting findings was that political control was shifting in communities which had rancorous conflict but not in those with conventional conflict.

James S. Coleman (1957) in a classic work entitled *Community Conflict* concludes from his survey of many studies of local controversies that three criteria must be met if an event is to be characterized as community controversy: first, it must affect an important aspect of the people's lives; second, it must affect the lives of different community members differently; and third people must feel that local action can be taken to deal with the event.

STAGES OF A CONTROVERSY

Community sociologists find that community controversies tend to run through a series of stages from their initiation to their conclusion. Fluoridation can be one of the most rancorous issues and can quickly move into the expressive type as people's values become threatened.

If we assume that a fluoridation controversy goes through a series of stages from its inception to its resolution, we have a way of ordering events so that cross-community comparisons can be made.[2] In Surfside, Massachusetts, the fluoridation controversy went as follows:

Initiation. Mr. Burton, Superintendent of Water and Sewer Department, suggested to Dr. Vance, head of school dental clinic, that the town initiate fluoridation. These two consulted officials of the Massachusetts Department of Health, who sent literature which Burton and Vance studied.

Preproposal. Burton presented the idea of fluoridation to the water commissioners, who gave only perfunctory approval. Burton and Vance arranged for a panel of speakers at a PTA meeting; small audience; no objections. The proposal was prepared as an article for the next town warrant by Burton and Vance, although it was not clear whether it was officially sponsored by the Water and Sewer Board or the Board of Health.

Proposal. Article that town water be fluoridated appeared on the town warrant in advance of town meeting, indicating that it was to be a matter for town business.

Community action. The first sign of opposition after the proposal was published, was a letter by a dentist, Dr. Ames, to the *Surfside Gazette.* The Finance Committee discussed it at a committee meeting but took no action. The powerful Taxpayers' Association, which regularly meets before town meeting, withheld support. Dr. Grayson, a young physician, presented the Taxpayers' position against fluoridation. Those putting the proposal on the warrant did little to promote favorable action.

Decision. Article was decisively defeated in town meeting.

Aftermath. Dr. Grayson, who played a crucial role in defeating the measure, thinks that if the issue came up again he would support it for he was actually urging a "go slow" policy. (p. 56).

[2] The following material is taken from Irwin T. Sanders, "The Stages of a Community Controversy: The Case of Fluoridation," *Journal of Social Issues* 17 (1961), 55–65.

The six stages mentioned in the case of Surfside, which can apply to any community controversy, deserve somewhat fuller explanation:

Initiation. By definition we limit the initiation stage to that activity where (1) the initiator is seeking prmary group support, and (2) the idea is still in the discussion stage. . . . When the initiator is talking to those he knows on a face-to-face basis, and when these individuals mention the matter to their friends and colleagues, then the action is still being "initiated." This does not exclude the discussion of the matter in an official body or organization if the initiator happens to be a member of that body (a part of the in-group) and wishes to sound out his associates informally. . . .

It is also quite clear that many ideas, whether for fluoridation or other community measures, never go beyond the initiation stage. People talk about them informally, sometimes quite excitedly, but let the matter drop there. Later on, the issue may be raised again by the same people or by others who this time generate enough momentum to start the preproposal activity.

Preproposal stage. As already indicated, the initiation stage ends and the preproposal stage begins when those involved go beyond their primary groups and start making secondary contact. They call upon personages important to their cause but unknown to them on an intimate basis—newspaper editors, town or city officials, organizational leaders and professional people with career involvement in the issue. This preproposal stage is also reached when the initiators continue their discussion, but this time not to test their idea so much as to formulate a plan of action. At this point, they have developed a sense of commitment; they have decided to go ahead, at least to the extent of taking up the matter with secondary contacts whose approval is needed for a successful outcome. Strategy begins with (1) the decision as to what supporters are to call upon what personages and with (2) the agreement as to what they are to say and not say. Thus, a "pro" side has come into existence, with its self-conscious backers who may not yet be classed as partisans. It should be noted that the "pro" side may be the one seeking to throw out fluoridation, which is already in force. The "pro" here refers to the fact that support is being sought for a proposal to do something of community-wide significance.

At this stage open opposition may appear. In the initiation stage, some of the people with whom the idea was discussed may have been dubious or even antagonistic but the primary group relationship may have tempered their comments or they may not have sought a community-wide forum. But in the second stage, the opposition may become much more vocal. It faces the difficulty, however, that since the proposal has not been clearly formulated, it must argue against an idea or an incipient issue and not a concrete statement. At the same time, the proponents can now take the rising opposition into account and develop a program which may soften many of its objections when the proposal is at last formally before the community.

The proposal. This is the formal move for legitimation. The supporters conform to whatever requirements are necessary to bring forth a decision by those with authority to dispose of the measure. In the case of the ten towns in our sample an article on the town warrant was considered the proposal, since the town meeting itself (with one exception) was the legitimizing act.

The two prerequisites for this stage are (1) formal presentation and (2) necessity of action by the legitimizing body. In the formal presentation enough specific details are provided so that both the proponents and opponents know exactly what measure is proposed: it may be creation of a study committee, adoption of fluoridation, or holding a referendum, although in the legal terminology of the warrant the statement is phrased in neutral terms.

In other states where city councils can take effective action, the proposal would be presented to them. To arrive at this point, certain preliminary steps may have been necessary in the preproposal period, such as getting the approval and recommendation of the Board (or Department) of Health, or a statement of estimated costs from the city engineer. Unless the proposal is presented in the proper manner, so as to call for action, the issue has not yet moved into the proposal stage.

Community action. Up to this point—the presentation of the proposal before the proper legitimizing body—the issue cannot be squarely joined. There can be much argument back and forth on a number of related points, many of which in a fluoridation issue are basic points, but community pressure is not usually brought directly to bear upon the legitimizing agents (city councilors, water commissioners, voters, etc.) until the proposal has been formally lodged.

Controversy implies the existence of two conditions: (1) an opposition is active and (2) there is some general community involvement. Both of these are conditions of degree.

The decision. When a proposal is presented, a legitimizing body has four options: postponement, rejection, amendment, adoption. The appointment of a study committee or the request for an investigative report by the city or town engineer are two ways that postponement is sometimes effected. Simply to fail to put the matter on the agenda is one way of dealing with the proposal but cannot be considered a "decision" in the sense used here, for real proposals, as previously defined, cannot be long deferred in this fashion. Quite often the legitimizing body amends the proposals to take care of some of the opposition arguments and then approves it. Neither side is wholly satisfied, but the decision-makers feel that they have worked out the best possible compromise.

The sociological features of the decision stage do not relate as much to the type of decision taken as to the fact that (1) the legitimizing body acts and (2) somebody wins and somebody loses, with whatever social consequences this might have.

Aftermath. If a decision calls for execution, this would be part of the aftermath. But in the case of one town, for instance, official delay occurred because the town officers were afraid that they might be involved in legal difficulties if they carried out the will of the town meeting. A postponement or rejection by the legitimizing body would not require execution, which is why execution cannot be considered a major stage in a community controversy, although it is an integral part of a successful community action program.

Every community decision, by its very nature, has a bearing upon subsequent treatment of issues with any relationship to the one "decided." Something of a "community memory" does seem to operate as people try to recall what was done about an issue, why it was handled as it was, and why it won or lost. Mention is also frequently made of the names of people who were issue leaders and how this activity affected their community standing. Looked at sociologically, the aftermath is characterized by the fact that (1) the losing side may or may not consider the issue settled and (2) the partisanship surrounding the issue may or may not be transferred to other community activities or interpersonal behavior. (pp. 57–61).

The analysis of a community controversy must often go beyond the sequence of one set of stages as outlined here; the same controversy may be revived and go through two, three or more sequences. Figure 16–1 shows what happened in one community with respect to fluoridation. Although the pro-fluoridation proposal won the first time, the town water board failed to put in the necessary equipment and nothing happened. Three years later the pro-fluoridation forces put the same proposal to the town meeting and it was again passed. The opponents then took legal steps to prevent the installation of equipment again. Nothing was done. Three years later anti-fluoridation forces proposed that authorization be sought from the state legislature to hold a referendum which would be binding on local authorities. This proposal (that a referendum be held) was passed. The vote on that referendum was negative. Although not shown on Figure 16–1, recent information from the community states that another referendum was held in 1970, with 736 people voting "Yes," and 1161 voting "No." No further action to introduce fluoridation has been taken since that time.

This shows that some issues are never settled as long as there are partisans who set out to reverse the decision that is made. This is why controversies which are settled by a compromise are more

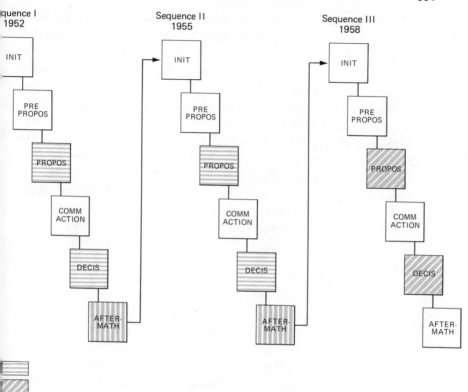

Figure 16–1. The fluoridation issue in a community: stages and sequences.

likely to stay settled than in the case where one side clearly wins and the other side clearly loses.

Several interesting facts have come to light in the study of fluoridation as a community issue. For one thing, the move toward fluoridation in the Massachusetts communities studied was made by dentists and other scientifically trained men. They sought to make their case on rational grounds, buttressing it with scientific arguments and stressing the approval of outside bodies such as the U. S. Public Health Service, the American Dental Association, the American Medical Association, and the like. But when the issue developed into a hot political controversy, the dentists were ill equipped to give the leadership that political maneuvering required. Furthermore, most of the leading figures of the community preferred to avoid entanglement in the issue, since it aroused so much heat and would lead to needless expenditure of whatever leadership "capital" they had. A further fact of interest is that, in those communities where an official study committee was set up to look into fluoridation, the committee reported out favorably in behalf of fluoridation even though some of its members had been originally opposed to it.

Maurice Pinard (1963), in a study of 262 communities, finds that the adoption or rejection of fluoridation referenda, as well as the degree of unanimity, is a function of the structural integration of the community. More specifically, he notes, it is a function of the attachments of community members to their power elites and of the interconnectedness between members.

Coleman (1957), whose work on *Community Conflict* has already been cited, has noted how an issue becomes transformed. It changes from a specific issue to a general one, such as a shift from an attack on books in the school library to a discussion of the whole educational philosophy of the educators. Another change is the appearance of *new and different* issues which are unrelated to the original one. Some of these are not brought out as long as stable relations exist but when the relations become unstable then suppressed topics come to the surface. Inhibitions no longer operate with the social networks. "I hesitated to mention this before but . . ." is one phrase used in the introduction of a new issue. A third change which may occur as an issue becomes more widely discussed is the shift from *disagreement* to *antagonism*. Where direct hostility comes into play by use of personal slander or rumor it can sustain conflict without regard to the issues. Original issues may have been settled but the controversy continues.

RESOURCE MOBILIZATION

While the issues are moving from one stage to the next, or being transformed, those involved seek to mobilize all possible resources to support their cause. From the conflict perspective, controversy illustrates the differential use of power, for only rarely do the contending parties possess equal resources. This relates specifically to what Coleman describes as the structure of authority. He notes:

> Decision-making power is political power; and in every community this political power is distributed in a certain way. Actually, the matter is considerably more complicated than a single distribution of power.

There are numerous *kinds* of decision, and numerous *stages;* power may be distributed differently for different kinds and different stages . . . (p. 15).

Within such a context it is appropriate to note the kinds of resources which can be brought into play in a local controversy. We will begin with the most obvious local resources.

The Financial Drive

Any kind of campaign to influence others costs some money: newspaper ads, spot radio and TV announcements, leaflets or flyers, travel of imported speakers, and a number of other incidentals. There are three sources of such funds. First, the contributions of affected businesses and agencies can be used to help swing the decision in the way best reflecting their interests. The contribution may not always take the form of cash, but may be in the nature of duplication of materials, freeing employees to work for the campaign on company time, or other benefits in the power of the company or agency to bestow. A second contribution may come from the exercise of a *quid pro quo.* Some active partisan may have in the past contributed to another cause which has been resolved. He may go to the former leaders of that cause and remind them that he at one time helped them out and that now they have a chance to help him out. The contribution is not in the nature of support of a given side of the issue but rather the return of a favor, which earlier was accepted with the tacit understanding that it would be repaid eventually when the donor wished to make a claim. The third kind of contribution is by individuals who have been motivated to want to help, preferably giving their time, or even a small amount of money in the hope that they would not be more fully involved. A small contribution can thereby buy non-participation in what may become a rancorous controversy. A fourth source of income may be the promotion of events to which people pay admission or the sale of baked goods or other merchandise to the profit of the cause. Fired-up partisans can find many ingenious ways of persuading people to help finance their side of the controversy.

Campaign Specialists, Amateur and Professional

A scarce item in any community is the person who really knows how to pull a variety of individuals, groups, and resources together to win a favorable decision about an issue. Those who can do this effectively are often quite well known and their help is sought. Now and then, a new leader with requisite skills emerges and becomes a good amateur campaign specialist. In issues such as fluoridation or other proposed changes for which there has developed a nationally organized effort pro and con, some outside campaign specialist may be brought in to organize the local partisans and to try to put opponents in disarray. Such scarce talent is often a resource, though no one is infallible in situations so mercurial as many community controversies. Over-organizing, over-spending, over-exhorting may have a negative effect in certain kinds of community.

The Mass Media

Coleman has shown that newspapers may often initiate controversy by uncovering some deal that would not otherwise be made public or reporting a proposed plan of action by a group to which other groups or people take immediate exception. The facts are, he points out, that in the community controversies he has studied the newspapers are not effective in persuading people to a point of view but they are more useful in reinforcing people in their pre-existing opinions. Media also play a part in the initial structuring of public opinion on an issue, particularly if the speakers who are first highlighted play upon fear or other emotions which influence an individual's alignment.

But who has access to the media? Obviously, those who can buy time in the form of paid commercials. But not so obviously are those who know how to manipulate the media. In one Eastern city, opponents of forced busing have every few months formed a new organization—each with a good local ring to it—in order to summon the press and tell about the inception of this new group and its program. Even very modest research has shown that the same people form each organization, but they know that by doing so they will have another chance to parade their point of view before the public.

The Organizational Network

Some issue leaders direct their appeal to individuals without realizing that an individual acts with reference to some group of people whose judgment he respects. Thus, a major resource to partisans in a controversy is the organizational network of a community.

Access to this, or parts of it, provides a forum for airing one's side of the controversy if one is invited as a speaker; it may strengthen the cause in the public's view if some organizations pass resolutions which appear in the media; financial contributions by formal groups is another potential asset. In addition, the role of the organizational leaders in helping structure public opinion is not to be overlooked. Coleman cites the technique of *cooptation*, of the bringing the opposition inside to voice its criticism, pointing out that some fluoridation controversies failed because leading community organizations were not coopted at an early· stage. Cooptation makes it possible for people to express opposition *within* a group without having to oppose it publicly to get their ideas across.

Use of Authority Figures

Authority figures connected with a community segment involved in an issue (schools, zoning, health measures) almost always are drawn into the fray. Their testimony may be interpreted as self-serving and not disinterested by many people trying to make up their mind about the issue. Consequently, the use of authorities who are either outside the community or connected with some other aspect of community life are sought as a resource to speak out in behalf of one side of the issue. Political leaders, religious leaders, economic dominants, socially prestigious persons—all may be approached to speak out on the matter before the community. The side with the best access to such people, whose leaders are a part of their network, may thereby have unequal access to them as a resource. Indeed, going back to Coleman's analysis the structure of the authority in the community and its use is one of the major factors in the outcome of an issue. If leadership is pictured as and believed to be unresponsive, too far removed from ordinary people its support will not necessarily help a cause.

Activation of Antagonistic Relationships and Community Cleavages

A resource, whose use is often deplored, is the activation of antagonistic relationships by those who would discredit the other side of a controversy. In some communities the cleavages run deep and result from earlier controversies and one only has to connect opponents with a particular segment and all the other segments will consider them to be opponents as well. Some of these fault-lines, mentioned in Chapter 13, are the oldtimer-newcomer split, religious and racial divisions, and political factions. Rancorous conflict is apt to be tied in with the use of this resource, which may be tapped fairly late in the progress of the controversy.

PERSISTING QUESTIONS ABOUT COMMUNITY CONTROVERSY

One fruitful approach to the study of community controversy focuses on the individual as the actor and tries to determine under what circumstances he becomes a partisan. This social psychological emphasis has gained increasing interest within sociology as symbolic interaction has become recognized as a more important subfield of the discipline. A different approach preferred by some sociologists is to relate characteristics of a controversy to characteristics of the community, thereby carrying out an analysis which focuses on the group rather than the individual. In this latter vein, we can ask two questions for whom we have only partial answers:

1. *Why do some community issues become controversial and others do not?* Every day a number of decisions have to be made by leaders in behalf of the community about the schools, economic life, local government, the health system, religious activities, and recreational opportunities. There are usually two or three sides to these decisions, with some arguing for and some against a certain course of action. Such arguments may take place informally among influential people in the community who reach a decision without calling the matter to public attention: they keep it submerged. Or, the issue may be debated within a formal decision-making body and resolved without the spotlight of much public attention. The issue frequently is not over the merits of a particular proposal; all may agree that it is desirable. But the choice involves whether the matter proposed is more or less important than something that would have to be changed or given up from the financial standpoint. Each such issue has conflict potential because those affected adversely by whatever decision is made may elect to bring the matter to public attention in an effort to have the decision changed. The conflict could then be *conventional*, in Gamson's term, (*instrumental* in

Laumann and Pappi terms) and go through accepted procedures toward a settlement. Or, it might build up to *rancorous* conflict in which the controversy overstepped the accepted community norms.

Against such a general background what can we say as to whether a specific issue really becomes controversial? Again we refer to Coleman, who finds that the content of the issue gives some clue as to whether it will lead to conflict. He identifies three general areas where this is likely to happen: *economic* issues are likely to produce strong response; *power* or *authority* in the community is a second area; *cultural values or beliefs*, illustrated by school and fluoridation controversies, constitute a third area. He points out that from time to time an issue which seems to be community-wide really reflects the continuing struggle between two groups over various issues or attitudes toward particular persons and groups.

In contrast to the above one might list conditions surrounding an issue which may keep it from turning into overt conflict. The first is *routinization*. If a routine for dealing with a type of issue is well-established then there is apt to be much less discussion of it. Second, the accepted *legitimacy of the decision-makers* and public *trust* in them is a factor (Gamson, 1968). In other words, *who* makes the decision is important. Third, if there is a *broadly-based, commonly-shared definition* of the issue there is less chance that it will be publicly debated.

Looking at the other side of the coin, we can find certain conditions which are very likely to make the issue controversial. First, if the decision taken (or about to be taken) involves *marked change in behavior* (putting chlidren on a school bus very early in the morning) it is more likely to meet some resistance. Second, a particular group may protest, if it suffers in *reallocation* of resources, particularly if it is called upon to make "sacrifices" that others do not have to make. Third, if the issue is of the kind that creates *fear or uncertainty* there is apt to be a demand for public discussion since a number of studies have shown that most people would rather stay with the troubles they have than embrace others whose effects they cannot properly forecast. Fourth, related to the above, is the appearance for the *first time* of an issue which cuts across different institutional segments. This means that no routinization is possible and no clear-cut mandate for any particular decision-making group to deal with it.

These generalizations just cited seem to be verified in the studies on community conflict but for each of them some exceptions could undoubtedly be stated. This indicates that even more precise statements are needed so that one can state under what conditions any of the above (such as *marked change in behavior*) will or will not become operative.

2. *Why do some communities have more controversies than others?* Some communities since their very founding seemed to have thrived on controversy. "Arguing things out" was an accepted way of reaching a decision. Other communities, whose members have valued cooperation and an avoidance of open conflict, seem to find ways of channeling controversy to a compromise. However, an explanation which relies on history and the value system tells but part of the story. What are other factors which might account for differences among communities in frequency of conflict? Some of them, but by no means an exhaustive list, are found in the studies which have already been cited in this chapter.

The degree of community integration supposedly influences the adoption or rejection of fluoridation referenda, as well as the degree of unanimity. (Pinard, 1963). This integration reflects the interconnectedness among the members of the power elites and the attachment of community members to them.

Another finding, also mentioned earlier in this chapter, was the strong connection between shifting political control and rancorous conflict. (Gamson). Neither the type of community nor its size provided as useful an explanation.

The difficulty of searching for correlations between conflict and community characteristics is shown in two interesting studies. Minar (1966) studied 48 suburban elementary school districts in Cook County, Illinois in order to get a better understanding of school system politics. He concluded that the communities whose members represented high socio-economic status had a low level of conflict over the schools. He thought that this finding could be explained on two grounds: first, the members of such communities had the experiences and abilities that made conflict management more feasible; second, they were more likely to grant latitude to hired technical expertise in the decision-making process.

Two other investigators (Crain and Rosenthal, 1967) came to a different conclusion: namely, that the greater the level of citizen participation (which occurs most in high-socio-economic communities) the higher the level of controversy. Their argument runs as follows: where there is greater citizen participation the community members have greater power vis-a-vis the local government and the elite and have a greater number of voluntary organizations and people who can be mobilized. The consequence of this is a decentralization of decision-making power, which in turn leads to immobility on the part of the government. Such immobility is fertile soil for controversy. The differences in the findings of the two studies may lie in the fact that they included a different sample of communities. Gamson's study supports the view that widespread citizen participation is not related to rancorous conflict, but again he was dealing with 18 New England towns.

Two other community traits which might possibly be associated with conflict are mentioned in these studies but were not proven to be unrelated: community homogeneity, or less internal difference due to class lines, and leadership characteristics. Later studies, using different hypotheses and different methods, might lead to modification in this finding.

It is clear that we do not yet have any decisive answer to the question posed at the beginning of this section. Under some circumstances and for some communities, we can say that certain social variables are correlated with conflict. Obviously, much more research needs to be done.

V

THE COMMUNITY AS SOCIAL ACTION

No study of community life would be complete without some attention to the problem-solving activities which go on in towns and cities across the country. Such problem-solving can be seen as part of a field of social interaction, one in which people combine, cooperate, coordinate to achieve common goals. Also, the community interorganizational network may be characterized by competition, conflict and accommodation at certain points in time, depending upon the forces at play in the social field.

Although a social field may have systemic qualities, such as social control, it need not be viewed as if it were a social system, thus distinguishing the field approach from the social systems approach. Nor need the field be seen as an arena of conflict, the approach of the second perspective just concluded. In fact, many of those using the field perspective are much more attracted to the patterns of cooperation, finding them more frequent than conflict, which becomes only one of the possible five or six types of interaction to be encountered.

In Part Five the Social Field Paradigm will be explained (Chapter 17) along with its varieties; it will be further illustrated in programs and plans centering around environmental problems and the physical aspects of the community (Chapter 18), and examples of economic end educational programs (Chapter 19); health and welfare programs (Chapter 20); and a concluding chapter to this section on community organization and community development (Chapter 21).

17

The Social Field Paradigm

One of the dilemmas in community sociology, as indicated in Chapter 6, is the choice of the theoretical perspective to use in studying one's community. This chapter seeks to set forth the third perspective presented in this book: namely, the social field, which emphasizes the community as social action and interaction. This can be best examined if we first note the characteristics of a social field, its utility and variations. Since community participation is a *sine qua non* of the local social field we will also see what factors influence activity of different kinds of people in community affairs.

THE SOCIAL FIELD

The concept of a social field received its major emphasis in social science with the work of Kurt Lewin (1951). He moved in his thinking from the study of psychological life space to the study of social space, which he saw as a social field. Therefore, the later application of the idea of a social field to the community was not a surprising development. This approach has become popular with a wider group of sociologists as the fact of change, the idea of a fluid, dynamic interplay becomes apparent at the local level, along with the difficulties expressed in Chapter 3 of fixing meaningful community boundaries.

The Social Field Defined

Rather than attempt a one-sentence definition of a social field one might look at four of its characteristics (Wilkinson, 1970a):

1. A *field is a holistic interaction nexus,* meaning that parts influence one another and include both causes and consequences of focal objects or events.
2. A *field is unbounded* in any strict sense, but is distinguishable from other fields according to its characteristic focus or core of field-relevant properties.
3. A *field is dynamic* in the sense that it is in a continuous state of change . . .
4. A *field is emergent,* meaning that its character is not governed entirely by the collective character of its parts, but is the outcome of the interaction of parts and is thus novel.

Some view the social field as a community arena or stage. (Kaufman, 1959). The players and the plays are guided by the ethos of the local society. Many engage in script writing and acting before very few spectators when the orientation is democratic and social contacts are primary. With large populations and less democratic leadership the same persons may appear over and over again while the rest sit as passive spectators or else are so busy with their own affairs that they pay no attention to the community drama. This analogy again stresses, as do the characteristics above, the unbounded, dynamic, emergent nature of the social field.

What gives the community character to the field is that in it is coordinated a wide variety of interest-fields (e.g., agriculture, industry, welfare, education); the social field generalizes across interest lines.

> The community field is manifested in the acts of generalized leaders which contribute to the accomplishment of goals in a variety of community projects over the course of time and is the structure and activities of groups and organizations which seek to coordinate and muster resources for these projects . . . (Wilkinson, 1972:45).

The focus of the social field may be an "activity which is concerned with the needs of the local population and with solving the problems of the local society" (Kaufman et al., 1975).

Types and Levels of Field

In addition to the interest fields (Wilkinson, 1969) already mentioned above, there are the polar types of the highly coordinated and the almost totally uncoordinated fields. Kaufman indicates that an example of the former is the overall long-range planning which would coordinate several areas of community life: new jobs with new schools and housing and other services. The uncoordinated social field could be found in the small town which acquired a factory but made no efforts to plan for the new workers and the needs of their families and themselves. This indicates that in a rapidly-changing social field "maladjustments, dislocations, tensions, and problems are the rule rather than the exception."

The social field must be distinguished, however, from other possible fields. One level of analysis is the ecological or demographic, the place and people; a second is the cultural or institutional, in terms of which a community is seen as a way of life, with a stress on fellowship and the sharing of basic beliefs and values. The third level—or the social field being described here—deals with "the collective action of a population in a given place as they meet the common needs and problems of life" (Kaufman et al., 1975).

A distinction is often made between *a community* and *a society* by those describing the social field. A community is a particular part of a society—its immediately common or collective life.

> *Community* is those parts of a resident society important to its unit or group concerns. Whatever developments require group decision or sanction, whatever happenings express unit loyalty or symbolize collective identity for a given resident population—these constitute *community*. *Community* is thus divested of its local connotation; its essence is not what is "local to," but rather what is "collective for" a resident population. (Sutton, 1970:59).

Utility of the Field Perspective

Before looking at the application of the social field perspective we should note claims made as to its utility:

1. It focuses on dynamics and change.
2. The conception of arena or field presents a pluralistic and open system as contrasted to a monolithic explanation and a closed logical system. It allows for convergence of various points of view . . .
3. It makes possible the treatment of both descriptive and normative data in the same context, thus orienting research toward action. (Kaufman, 1959:15–16).

Another argument advanced is the attention this perspective provides for the analysis of ends and goals important to the local citizen, leading to the discovery not just of what the community *is* but what the people think it *ought to be*.

Units Constituting the Social Field

Many researchers today are attracted to the concept of the social field but they tend to differ in their ideas as to its constituent units. Some see the social field as primarily a *network of individuals,* though these do occasionally combine into groups (Wellman and Craven, 1973). A second possibility is to define a *social action* as the constituent unit and a third is to make *organizations, associations, agencies* the chief units of interorganizational field.

In this presentation of the social field we will limit ourselves to the *social action* emphasis and the *interorganizational field*. Since they have much in common, distinguishing between them is sometimes artificial. Yet they do derive from somewhat different theoretical formulations, they rely on different methodologies, and even try to answer different questions.

COMMUNITY SOCIAL ACTION

Nature of Community Social Action

One of those who first systematized this approach described *action* at the observational level as consisting of projects, programs, activities or events. (Kaufman, 1959) Examples cited range from planning and building a community hospital to carrying out the annual community homecoming. The exact form of the action is not nearly as important as the fact that local people get together and do something in which there is community interest.

Another writer (Sutton, 1970) uses the phrase *complex action episode* to cover "any series of interaction events integrated and bounded by a common close relevance to some question, problem, or item of collective interest to a relatively numerous set of persons comprising the main decision-makers in the events." (p. 57). Of course, not all large-scale complex action episodes are related to the community but they do represent a field of interaction where something collective is happening.

In analyzing a complex action episode, Sutton (1970) uses three elements: the "value-goal component made up of the objectives and rationale governing actions taken in the events; an organizational component constituted by the social fabric of persons and groups participating in the events; and a temporal component comprised of the sequential and concurrent patterning of the flow of events." (p. 61)   These three elements would apply if one were studying the action focused on building a community recreation center or planning an anniversary celebration for the community.

Several people have provided criteria for judging whether an action is a community action as contrasted with one serving the private interests of individuals or groups.   Some such criteria are the following: (1) Degree to which it is locality related, as for instance trying to solve some problem connected with the locality where the participants live.   (2) Degree to which the people involved in or influenced by the event or activity are identified with the locality.   (3) Extent to which the local people participate in the activity.   (Sutton and Kolaja, 1960; Poplin, 1972)   An earlier formulation (Kaufman, 1959) included in addition to the above such criteria as the degree of comprehensiveness of interests pursued and needs met, relative number and significance of local associations involved, degree to which the action maintains or changes the local society, and extent of organization of the action.

Another way of posing the question is to ask when is an action locality-oriented.   Three conditions must be met (Wilkinson, 1970a): (1) the principal actors and beneficiaries are local residents; (2) the goals represent interests of local residents; and (3) the action is public, as opposed to private, in the sense that beneficiaries include other persons in addition to the actors (pp. 56–57). Put differently (Sutton, 1964:51), an action can be judged positively or negatively significant to the community to the degree it builds and maintains cohesion or belonging (identity-maintenance) and achieves or does things (policy-decision).

Such viewpoints, as indicated earlier, take into account the existence in any local society of what are termed interest fields, including education, religion, government, family life, economics, recreation and the like.   Each interest field has norms and values associated with it as well as actors, associations, and activities combined in the pursuit of the interests of the field. (Wilkinson, 1969; 32).   The community action takes place as there is overlap among the actors, and associations of more than one interest group, as well as coordinated activities crossing the fields. Such a field is emergent and has a multi-interest focus. Should a community-wide coordinating group be created and function effectively this particular community field may become institutionalized.

Both Kaufman and Wilkinson stress the "generalizing process" with its two facets: differentiation and elaboration on the one hand and integration or coordination on the other. This overall process links together differentiated interest fields, some of which may have been consciously developed to serve a particular private purpose, and gives them the character of community action.

In looking at the dimensions of the community field, Kaufman explains *differentiation* as the process by which community structure gains greater magnitude and complexity. He distinguishes between horizontal differentiation (that is, among recognized institutional interest areas) and vertical differentiation (social rank or class). *Coordination* is a second dimension; it refers to the cohesiveness of the structure, or how it is held together. Coordination, as a type of integration, describes how actors and associations are related to each other in order to carry out action effectively. Coordination is, according to Kaufman, perhaps the central community process. A third dimension of the community field is *openness,* which implies adaptability as expressed through representativeness or participation. "Openness means that community structure facilitates the movement of ideas, communication, as well as the mobility of persons from one position to another" (Kaufman et al., 1975).

The clue to the shift from an interest field to a community field lies in the study of the participating actors, the associations or groups, and in the actions themselves. Kaufman (1959) notes:

> The community actor or participant may be identified by who he is and what he does. Who the participant is depends on his position in the structure of the local society . . .
>
> In looking for what the community actor does, one investigates his behavior in organized groups and informal networks which are located in the locality. (p. 11).

One can even go so far as to use formal indices of participation for the actor, expanding those covered until one has a good index of the involvement of the local population in the interactional community. Of particular importance in the generalizing process described above is the behavior of leaders of the organized groups, the elites, the persons of influence in the different fields of interest.

Groups are important too. Kaufman (1959) observes:

> A great variety of groups may at one time or another be involved in community action. They range from the coffee-break clique through the civic clubs to the more institutionalized groups such as the board of aldermen. In addition to groups in which primary contacts are dominant, publics such as that of the local newspaper are important . . .
>
> At the association level the community may be seen as a network of interrelated associations, formal and informal, whose major function is problem-solving for the local society . . . (p. 12).

Kaufman then says that for the third element—action—the raw data are the sequences of observable events. Actions may be occasional, periodic, or continuous. They go through phases, to which we shall turn shortly.

Before leaving the characterization of the community social field it is important to note the nature of leadership found there. A role can be described as community action leadership if it contributes behaviorally in a community action process to accomplishing some task, developing some structure, or maintaining the process. (Kaufman and Wilkinson, 1967) In other words, one is a community leader if the roles one plays relate significantly to community social action as described here.

Thus far the discussion of the community as a field of social action has been dealt with at a very general level; references have continually been made to actors, associations, activities, complex action episodes. These theoretical considerations should become much more meaningful as we move to concrete examples. The most direct way to do this is to look at the phases or stages of community action as they relate to the social field.

Phases or Stages of Community Social Action

Through the years an extensive literature has grown up, particularly in rural sociology, to describe the steps through which some important community undertaking moves from initiation to completion. Much of it antedated the community field perspective being described here (Green and Mayo, 1953; Hoffer, 1958; Miller, 1952; Sower, 1957); it has been duly recognized by those who have built upon it. Since community social action is seen as a process, with a very definite temporal aspect, some way must be found to describe the flow of this process (Wilkinson, 1970a). It is here that

	Hospital Construction	"March of Dimes"	Special VD Diagnosis	Fluoridation of Water
(1) Rise of interest	General awareness of need	General awareness. State organization appoints county org.	USPHS unit decides to go to county. General awareness	Dentist talks to colleagues, city officials and state health department
(2) Sponsorship	Five business and professional men formed hospital corporation	County chapter (major), schools, civic clubs (auxiliary)	USPHS unit and county dept. (major), Negro professional leaders, white employers (auxiliary)	Dentist (major city council, civic org. and State Board of Health (auxiliary)
(3) Definition of objectives	Hospital Corporation created to build 4-bed emergency clinic	State and notional organizations and county president	State and national organizations	Dentist and State Board of Health
(4) Gaining participation	Personal and newspaper solicitation for funds	Extensive newspaper and poster publicity. Appointment of several chairmen and many solicitors; organization of "benefits"	Newspaper and poster publicity, movies, public blood testing clinics. Required of school children	Personal contact of dentist with groups concerned. No mass support requested
(5) Fulfillment of goals	In short time had reached nearly half of $75,000 goal; then goal abruptly changed to build 47-bed hospital and the beginning of a "new" action	Realized through contributions. Generally highly successful	Diagnosis and some treatment. Testing quota realized	Funds by civic organizations and city council; installation an engineering job

Figure 17–1. Four selected health programs in a southern town in terms of phases of project development. *Source:* Harold F. Kaufman and Kenneth P. Wilkinson, *Community Structure and Leadership: An Interactional Perspective in the Study of Community.* Mississippi State University, Social Science Research Center, Bulletin 13 (June, 1967), p. 33.

phases or stages come into play. The same holds true for a community controversy, such as fluoridation, discussed in the last chapter, where it was also necessary to indicate the stages through which the controversy passed.

Perhaps the clearest way of indicating the phases used in the field perspective (by some at least) is Figure 17–1, which shows the carrying through of four community health projects in a Southern town (Kaufman and Wilkinson, 1967). The comparison of the last column (on fluoridation) in Figure 17–1 with Figure 16–1 shows the differences which have to be taken into account if there is a serious conflict situation.

Figure 17–1 is self-explanatory. Those doing the study pointed out that the hospital construction program was nearer the center of the community field than the fluoridation project because it involved much greater initiative, decision making and responsibility on the local leadership. The fluoridation project was never put to public vote but was decided by the supposedly relevant and competent leadership in the community.

While the phases illustrated here exemplify an aspect of the community social field, it should prove useful to note that those working within the social system framework also try to elaborate steps, stages, or phases. One of the most complete list of stages, fifteen in all, has been prepared by George M. Beal (1964). No attempt will be made here to present each stage as a separate step, but use will be made of Beal's approach in a brief description of the sequence through which the social action passes.

Ordinarily, social action begins when a problem is recognized, articulated, and defined as a need by two or more people and a decision is made to act. This represents a convergence of interest, at which point the problem is tentatively defined, goals are selected, and means of action are discussed. But before any action gets under way, the most experienced change agents take a look at the prior social situation. They ask: "What other efforts at change similar to the one we are proposing have been made in the community?" They look for leadership patterns, power relations, and attitudes or beliefs that have resulted from previous efforts. They may find that some methods, appeals, and organizational structures worked, others failed. Some groups cooperated, others did not.

This analysis of the prior social situation helps the change agents next identify the community components relevant to the proposed project or effort at change. A component becomes relevant if its members are the chief target group. For example, if the goal is the construction of a new hospital, then the health system is relevant, for its personnel will be intimately involved. Other components are important too. A hospital costs much money. Relevant components, such as local government and the local financial interests, are those whose approval may be necessary if the project is to succeed. They legitimatize the undertaking in the eyes of the rest of the community. Other relevant components would be the social units controlling the chief communication channels or social units with whom the planned program would be in conflict. (For example, local hospitals having a hard time financially may not welcome another competitor).

Once those components that are in position to influence the course of action have been identified, then the change agents secure the help of "initiating sets," or people who have an inside track with the key leaders of these relevant components. They are asked to sound out a few of the leaders about the action under consideration. If the preliminary conversations work out satisfactorily, then the change agents take the next step of clearing or at least discussing the idea with all of the key power figures of the social units crucial to the success of the undertaking. In some cases, official action by formal bodies (such as city council) may have to be taken; in other cases, a favorable consensus from a wide variety of key leaders, based on informal conversations, may be sufficient. But this consensus not only must grow out of contact with the officers and functionaries of the components contacted; it also must involve the informal leaders as well.

After legitimation of the idea, the next task is that of publicizing it—if not to everybody in the community, at least to all of those who should participate in the decision. This calls for "diffusion sets," or people who can best formulate and diffuse the essential ideas of the new program to the relevant target systems. Since many kinds of components are involved, the diffusion sets will consist of a wide variety of people, each of whom is skilled in the interpretation and presentation. Before this can be done, however, a preliminary plan has already been drawn up so that there is something concrete to explain to the people who should be interested.

Once people are informed, it is hoped that they will become involved, and will participate. Therefore, many means are used to portray the project as a "people's problem" and therefore worthy of broad, public support. This occurs if there is an effective definition of need. When the target system or systems decide to act, one has the commitment necessary for later stages. This is followed by the formulation of goals on the part of the broader public. The goals emerging at this stage may be identical with or modifications of the preliminary goals that the change agents had in the beginning, but they are now the people's goals and not considered merely the change agents' goals. Likewise, once goals are set, alternative means and methods of reaching these goals—of accomplishing the solution to the recognized problem—must be selected.

After goals and methods have been chosen, it is possible for the representative of the relevant social systems (interest fields) to draw up a plan of work describing the organizational structure to be set up, how people are to be trained for the responsibilities they will be asked to assume, and a schedule of dates by which certain parts of the plan will be completed. Then follows the broad mobilization of resources, the carrying out of the plan, and its final evaluation. Throughout these later stages the leaders, who may or may not at this time be the original change agents, should be aware that they are modifying social systems (interest fields), both by direct action upon certain components and by changing to some degree its operations. Obviously, certain civil rights programs call for significant changes in the allocation of power in the community or in the allocation of scarce goods and services to groupings not previously sharing very fully in them.

THE INTERORGANIZATIONAL FIELD

Some community sociologists see much communal activity as manifested in an interorganizational field. That is, they select an organization or formal group rather than community action (as defined in the previous section) as the unit of analysis. The concept of the *field* is much the same in both cases in that it is unbounded since additional organizations can become involved in the field at a moment's notice; it consists of interaction among actors (in this case *groups*); and it is related to a number of properties of the community as a whole. A quick overview of the interorganizational field requires a definition, its rationale, and some suggested types of fields.

Definition

One characterization is provided by Turk (1970)

> Any large and complex social setting . . . may be viewed as an aggregate of organizations (associations), which appear, disappear, change, merge, and form networks of relations with one another. (p. 1).

Such a field can provide an independent level of analysis without reference to populations and status-role categories.

Another way of defining the interorganizational field in community terms (Aiken and Alford, 1970) is the following:

> Community systems can be conceived of as interorganizational fields in which basic interacting units are *centers of power*. A center of power can be defined as an organization which possesses a high degree of autonomy, resources, and cohesion. The linking mechanisms in a community system we call *interfaces*. (See Mott, 1970.) Interfaces are not only the current set of interorganizational relationships in the community, but more importantly include the historical accumulation of knowledge and experience among various centers of power. An *issue arena* is the organization set (Evan, 1966) of centers of power which must be activated on a given issue in order to effectuate a decision. (pp. 662–63).

Such a definition was reached as the authors tried to understand what structural conditions in a community led to innovation (urban renewal programs). They found that innovations could best be explained as a product of the nature and state of interorganizational networks in communities. Such networks, according to Aiken and Alford, "are properties of community systems that have developed historically through the interaction of organizational units and their leaders." (pp. 661-662).

The rich and extensive literature on interorganizational behavior contains many references to fields, but in relatively few cases do the authors apply the concept to an analysis at the local community level. The examples cited above show the direction such application would take.

Rationale for Using the Interorganizational Field

One of the most explicit statements of rationale (Turk, 1970:2) shows why groups serve as proper units for study:

> Our rationale lies in the assumption that individual behaviors depend upon the presence of organizations that encourage or accept them and

that organizations are primary determinants of regularities and uniformities in human potential for such behaviors. Organizations must be assumed to be both the formulators and the means of the individual action: organizations are the actors which comprise any large and complex structure.

The community action approach to the social field also argues in favor of studying interorganizational behavior; one adherent of this approach (Kaufman) even goes so far as to view the community primarily as "an association." Yet, when we look at the application made by the two approaches to the social field we note that the community action writers stress problem-solving or community events whereas in the interorganizational approach the stress is upon decision-making by groups legitimized for that purpose in a specific area of community life. In general, neither cites the writings of the other, probably because the community action theorists derive much of their background data from those concerned with social action (projects, programs) whereas those using the second approach quote almost exclusively the work of those dealing with large-scale organizations. Yet, the rationale of the two approaches is not very different: the individual is caught up in a network of interaction, which usually involves him in formal groups. To understand the group behavior is to understand much of community life.

Types of Interorganizational Fields

The real test of any theoretical approach, however, is its utility in understanding real life situations. Roland Warren (1967) has done considerable research in terms of the interorganizational field, particularly as community decision organizations (CDO's) are involved in the field. In looking at the CDO's of Boston he found four organizational contexts that accounted for the different behavior of the CDO's in the interaction process. These four contexts are shown in Table 17–1. What Warren means by the community decision-making organization (CDO) and the contexts is explained in the following statements:

> The *unitary context* is exemplified by a city health department or transportation authority. The units (divisions, bureaus, and so on) are deliberately organized for the achievement of inclusive goals. Decision-making, as to policy and program, takes place at the top of the structure and final authority over the units rests there. . . .

TABLE 17–1

Types of Inclusive Context

Dimension	Type of Context			
	Unitary	Federative	Coalitional	Social Choice
Relation of units to an inclusive goal	Units organized for achievement of inclusive goals	Units with disparate goals, but some formal organization for inclusive goals	Units with disparate goals, but informal collaboration for inclusive goals	No inclusive goals
Locus of inclusive decision-making	At top of inclusive structure	At top of inclusive structure, subject to unit ratification	In interaction of units without a formal inclusive structure	Within units
Locus of authority	At top of hierarchy of inclusive structure	Primarily at unit level	Exclusively at unit level	Exclusively at unit level
Structural provisions for division of labor	Units structured for division of labor within inclusive organization	Units structured autonomously; may agree to a division of labor, which may affect their structure	Units structured autonomously; may agree to ad hoc division of labor, without restructuring	No formally structured division of labor within an inclusive context
Commitment to a leadership subsystem	Norms of high commitment	Norms of moderate commitment	Commitment only to unit leaders	Commitment only to unit leaders
Prescribed collectivity orientation of units	High	Moderate	Minimal	Little or none

Source: Roland L. Warren, "The Interorganizational Fields as a Focus for Investigation," Administrative Science Quarterly, 12, No. 3, December, 1967.

The *federative context* for inclusive decision-making is exemplified by a council of social agencies (to a lesser extent by the newer type of community welfare council) or by a council of churches. The units (member organizations, rather than integral departments) have their individual goals, but there is some formal organization for the accomplishment of inclusive goals, and there is formal staff structure for this purpose. Decision-making is focused in a specific part of the inclusive structure. . . . Authority remains at the unit (member) level, with the exception of some administrative prerogatives, which are delegated by the units to a formal staff . . .

The *coalitional context* for inclusive decision-making is exemplified by a group of organizations cooperating more or less closely to attain some desired objective, such as persuading a new industry to locate in the community or developing a federally sponsored project. Each organization has its own set of goals, but collaborates informally and on an ad hoc basis where some of its goals are similar to those of other organizations in the group . . .

The *social-choice context* for inclusive decision-making is exemplified by the autonomous behavior of a number of organizations and individuals in the community as they relate themselves and their behavior to any particular issue which concerns more than one of them—as, for example, the issue of medicare or of housing desegregation, or highway location. . . . decisions are made at the level of the units themselves.

Table 17–1 indicates some of the characteristics not fully covered in the lengthy quotation above, particularly as to division of labor among the organizations, the leadership system and collectivity orientation of the units. Warren notes that, in a metropolitan community, people are not really organized for making centralized rational choices among values which cannot be maximized simultaneously. Instead, various values are allocated to specific CDO's for maximization; these organizations than compete as in a sociodrama for the available sources and their use, but always in ways acceptable to the large and important sectors of the community.

Various attempts have been made to adapt interorganizational field theory to the study of particular segments of the community. One such study (Allen, 1974) describes the cooptation by a corporation of the elites of other corporations, thus forming interlocking directorates. This tends to anticipate and control uncertainties that might be present through time in the interorganizational field. Similarly, the potential of organization theory for the study of citizen groups, political parties, and local governments has been pointed out (Elkin, 1974). In fact, one can think of a network of governmental organizations which has as its focus the local territorial unit.

Those groups within the network are dependent upon each other but the way each group manages its dependence becomes of interest to the student of local politics. Needless to say, this network of political groups must also be understood in terms of the more comprehensive network including the networks of other interest fields or community segments. This leads, of course, to the relations existing between any designated local networks and the external influences which play upon them.

Extralocal Orientation of Interorganizational Fields

It is easy enough to conceive of the community as an interorganizational field, but how does one go about studying it? Herman Turk (1970) demonstrated one way to do this when he investigated the local and extralocal linkages of the 130 incorporated cities in the United States which in 1960 had populations of more than 100,000 inhabitants. He computed one index to measure a city's extralocal integration and two organizational indices to measure its local integration. These network measures described the contractual relations among Federal agencies and local organizations in the War on Poverty during mid-1964 to mid-1966.[1]

Local integration was assessed in terms of (1) community-wide voluntary associations, since they show the presence of mechanisms for concerted action and the absence of highly organized cleavages within the city; and (2) 1960 municipal revenue, which signifies how much control a city government has over its own affairs for this is revenue that is generated locally.

Extralocal integration was based on the location of national headquarters of voluntary associations in each of the study cities. Such associations covered 21 categories ranging from business and health associations through religious and patriotic. Turk reasoned that any city which had such headquarters would be more integrated into the national society than those cities without such headquarters for their external connections would be less. Not only does action emanate from the headquarters to various parts of the country but there is feedback from elsewhere into the headquarters, strengthening the external links.

Other investigators have chosen different kinds of data to con-

---

[1] This article provides an interesting illustration of the use of multiple regression analysis in the comparative study of community phenomena.

struct their indices. One study (Harp, 1973) uses the term *vertical linkage* for an organization's affiliation with groups outside the local community. He found that in the 401 population centers of New York State, 82 per cent of the formal voluntary associations were linked with some organization located outside the center. Unlike Turk who used the national headquarters to show interorganizational linkage, Harp got the information from each of the voluntary associations as to their external affiliation. In addition to *vertical linkage*, Harp also studied four other properties of organizations and studied the patterns of relationships among these properties: *instrumental-expressive* character, measured by determining its prime beneficiaries: *accessibility*, or its openness to potential members; *stability*, demonstrated by its length of time in the center; and *organizational activity*, indicated by the frequency of its meetings. Such knowledge about individual organizations is helpful in understanding some aspects of their behavior in an interorganizational field, particularly the extralocal linkages.

SOCIAL PARTICIPATION BY COMMUNITY RESIDENTS

One assumption made by those using field theory is that communities will vary in the degree to which local people participate in formal group activities or in community events or episodes. (Rubin, 1971) Furthermore, such participation will be related to certain characteristics of the individuals.

Looked at from a national perspective, over half of all American adults report no memberships in formal voluntary associations (excluding unions) and 40 per cent are unaffiliated if we include labor unions (Curtis, 1971). Hyman and Wright (1971) placed the 1955 figure of non-participants at 64 per cent and the 1962 figure at 57 per cent, cautioning that these figures are based on secondary analysis of national sample surveys. Their results bear out the fact that those in higher socio-economic status affiliate more frequently than those in lower status, although they did find a trend between 1955 and 1962 of increasing affiliation among the lower status groups. Hodge and Treiman (1968) using 1963 data conclude that the parents' level of participation was as influential in an individual's membership in voluntary associations as was his socioeconomc status. As for church attendance, females but not males were influenced by parents' affiliation. Males' attendance is strongly affected by their spouses' attendance patterns.

Form in his study of auto workers in four countries (1973) found support for the proposition that there is a correlation between participation and higher economic status. In his sample, the skilled workers showed more community involvement than the unskilled, though the unskilled attended more faithfully the fewer organizations (chiefly religious) to which they belonged. One study (Hagedorn and Labovitz, 1968) also shows marked differences in belonging to community associations according to occupation. The sample was limited to employees of a large research organization in a metropolitan area and personnel in a school system. As expected, those who own their home as well as married persons are more likely to participate in community organizations than are tenants or single people. Likewise, long-term residents have more affiliations than do recent migrants.

Mention has already been made of differences in influences bearing upon church attendance by males and females. One study (Booth, 1972) shows that men exceeded women in number of voluntary association memberships but not in commitment of time to group activities. The writer classified voluntary associations by their instrumental (coping with external environment) and expressive (organized to prevent deviant behavior) objectives:

> Instrumental
>   economic—professional, trade and commercial associations
>   political—governing boards, protest groups and political parties
>   military—veterans organizations
> Expressive
>   educational—home-school associations and adult leaders of youth
>   programs
>   religious—altar societies, choir, missionary societies and other
>   church related groups
>   recreational—card clubs, bowling leagues and fraternal-service or-
>   ganizations
>   health and welfare—Heart Association, Red Cross, hospital volun-
>   tary societies and allied groups (p. 188)

Forty-four per cent of the men and only 13 per cent of the women belonged to one or more instrumental group; 61 per cent of the women and 53 per cent of the men belonged to expressive groups, with 35 per cent of the women compared to 25 per cent of the men holding office in such groups.

Minority group participation is an important goal of many leaders trying to deal with problems of the disadvantaged in the community. Hyman and Wright (1971) noted between 1955 and 1962 a sharp increase in memberships of blacks, to the point of possibly equalling that of whites in voluntary associations, though the available data are not conclusive on this last finding. Data collected in Austin, Texas (1969–70) showed that blacks had higher rates of participation than their Anglo counterparts (similar in rental paid); Mexican-Americans, however, had lower rates than either the Anglos or Blacks. (Williams, et al. 1973).

One measure of community activity is that of political participation, which has been studied by a number of social scientists. Olsen (1973) has drawn up a model of political participation stratification in order more carefully to describe the kind of participation that occurs. When he applied this model to Indianapolis, Indiana he found the distribution of political strata memberships as follows: leaders, 3 per cent; activists, 14 per cent; communicators, 13 per cent; citizens, 30 per cent; marginals, 18 per cent; and isolates, 22 per cent. Olsen (1973) also found that involvement by individuals in nonpolitical social organizations such as voluntary associations, community affairs, and churches serves to mobilize them to become politically active.

In these discussions of participation we have dealt with individual rather than group behavior. Nevertheless, such data show us not only proportions of people who through group affiliation engage in community activity; they tell us also what categories of people affiliate.

❊   ❊   ❊

This presentation of the social field perspective has set forth a very useful way of viewing the community. The approach described is not nearly as clear-cut as the summaries here might indicate, because a single investigator may at one time stress the social action field and at another time the interorganizational field. In other words, citing the name of an investigator in discussion of one emphasis should not label him as being limited to that emphasis. Furthermore, some students of the community who make use of the social field might see this as one aspect of social system analysis and feel very much at home with that paradigm; likewise, some conflict theorists might use the field approach to demonstrate their contentions about the community.

It would be misleading, therefore, to give the impression that every community sociologist can be assigned to one of the three perspectives and be expected to stay there. The situation is much more fluid. What is important is to realize that for a given study at a given point in time a community sociologist is stressing one perspective over another; understanding this perspective helps one much more readily appreciate and evaluate the study either when it is in progress or when its findings are reported.

18

Controlling Use of Space and Environmental Quality

As cities and towns grow, their residents become acutely aware of local problems connected with space and environmental problems. Traffic congestion and lack of parking facilities, arterial highways which divide local neighborhoods, and the need for improved mass transportation systems all highlight the importance of physical planning. The urban blight found in certain sections of the city, tied in with flight to the suburbs, and the concentration of massive housing, health, and safety problems in the rundown areas demonstrate again the need for urban redevelopment. The pollution of the atmosphere from automobile exhausts, and industrial fumes and the dumping of wastes into streams and lakes indicate the need for collective measures to halt further destruction of the natural environment. In this chapter we will provide some background information about these sets of problems and point out their relevance to the community as a field of social interaction.

PHYSICAL PLANNING AND ZONING

Types of Planning

If one forgets for a moment the technical definitions used by the specialists in various fields, one can divide the planning for the community into three types; physical, economic, and human-resource. These can be characterized as follows: *Physical planning* has to do with the spatial and material aspects of the community primarily. *Economic planning* has to do with the improvement of commerce and industry, with the raising of economic opportunity, with provision of more stable employment, with the training of a skilled labor supply, and with increasing the range of services, including professional services, available to the people of the community. It overlaps at many points with physical planning but is usually the concern of a different group (chamber of commerce, area industrial-development association, etc.) from that concerned with physical planning. *Human-resource planning* deals with the welfare problems of the indigent, the handicapped, and the delinquent and also with positive approaches to education and recreational opportunity. Its concern is with the human resources not viewed merely as economic assets. Many communities have welfare councils, bearing quite different names, which consist of representatives from all of the social-work and character-building agencies, as well as from other groups actively interested, as laymen and not professionals, in the welfare and human-resource field.

As one goes through the literature on planning, one finds many definitions that vary in details from the above. For instance, *public planning* is a comprehensive term that would include elements of physical, economic, and human-resource planning, but its chief trait is that it is carried out under *governmental* auspices. On the other hand, social planning may or may not be through the government, since it describes a general attack on social problems, no matter who seeks to carry it out. It is in essence what was formerly called "social reform." In some communities, social planning and human-resource planning are considered the same.

It is very significant, and perhaps an indication of a new trend, that the authorities of Providence, Rhode Island, in developing their Community Renewal Program for the late 1960's and early 1970's, also worked up a *Social Plan* to go along with the plan for physical and economic improvement. The Prologue to the Social Plan states,

> As urban renewal shifts people from place to place in the traditional relocation process, this handicapped segment of the community [those ill-equipped by virtue of their attitudes of hopelessness, lack of job skills, lack of satisfying social relationships] carries with it an infectious,

chronic, blighting behavior which is not changed because no one provides the help necessary for these people to deal with the problems which underlie their destructive actions. . . . Urban renewal must modify its objectives to include social goals and effective social measures must be developed as part of the urban renewal program.[1]

What is ordinarily called *city* or *urban planning* is claimed by its supporters to be over-all social planning, a meeting of the needs of the whole community. Yet, when one looks closely at what city planners actually do and at the organizations through which they work, one must conclude that, despite their profession of interest in the broad picture, they concentrate chiefly on physical planning. A review of the recent city-planning literature would indicate, however, a growing awareness of the social consequences of planned physical changes in the city and an increasing contact among social scientists, welfare planners, and physical planners.

According to one source, planning for a community has the following four steps:

1. Definition of the community's goals and values. A community's goals and values are merely the sum total of the goals and values of the individuals who make up any community. This is not an easy task since the desires of individuals are often diametrically opposed. Nevertheless, this definition is the starting point of good planning, and if it is passed over, this program will almost certainly fail from lack of community support.

2. Survey of physical and economic resources and future possibilities. The second step is the collection of information about the physical, economic and human resources of the community. If a community doesn't know what resources it has—population, business and industry, physical plant and financial resources—it cannot possibly formulate intelligent plans for present or future development.

3. Formulation of a master plan. The third step is the formulation of a master plan in two major parts—a future land use plan and a community facilities plan. By fixing the location of industrial, commercial, residential and recreational areas for future use, it is possible to determine in an orderly, attractive and efficient manner where people will work, live, shop and play. The second part of the plan, a community facilities plan, is concerned with services provided by public agencies. It should include a capital improvements program setting forth the order in which public projects should be undertaken.

[1] Rhode Island Council of Community Services, Inc., *A Social Plan for Community Renewal of the City of Providence, Rhode Island* (Urban Renewal Coordinator, City of Providence, 1964), p. 2.

4. Administrative machinery and controls to carry out the plan. . . . the desirability of having a special agency undertake planning functions is unquestioned.[2]

Needless to say, those engaged in any type of planning for the community would need to go through the first two steps, of determining the goals and values of the community and assessing its material and human resources. Some of them might part company at the third and fourth steps, preferring to leave to the physical planner the preparation of a master plan and ways of implementing it. Yet, every thinking person in the community should be seriously concerned about the nature of the plan and the steps proposed to put it into effect. Businessmen need to know about the recommendations for land use; recreational specialists, about the area set aside for parks and playgrounds; welfare workers, about the institutional facilities as well as about projects for slum clearance.

The tasks of preparing the master plan, keeping it up to date, and enforcing it call for people with specialized skills. Some cities prefer to employ those who have studied all aspects of physical planning and are generalists at this task; other cities such as Indianapolis, Indiana, prefer to get individual specialists in population, economic development, law, traffic control, and the like to work together as a team, with no one individual claiming greater proficiency in the field of the other. But, no matter how the work gets done, it calls for technical competence.

The Master Plan

The master plan, as we have already noted, is the third step in the planning process. It consists of two major parts: a future-land-use plan and a community-facilities plan. Such a plan must be based on intensive research. Although the planners give much attention to *space* and work out numerous maps, they must also be aware of *time* and estimate possible trends as accurately as possible.

For example, they not only must know the actual population count and composition of the community, they must also have some clear ideas of likely growth over the next ten or fifteen years, or even farther into the future, if that be possible. They must try to calculate the direction in which the expansion is apt to move and the utilities

---

[2] *A Report of the Greater Lexington Committee,* a citizens' committee of Lexington and Fayette County, Kentucky, April, 1955, pp. 118–19.

that will be demanded, as well as the types of subdivisions that will be created. In addition, they must have a detailed map showing the use of every plot of land in the area for which the planning is being done, whether it be a city, a county, or a wider unit. Then, in terms of expected growth, they must seek to work out, with the help of others, the kind of land-use pattern they want to see develop. The ideal that they will draw up will of necessity differ from real conditions, since, in the movement toward a better-planned town, some areas now partly business, partly residential may be set aside exclusively for business. This means that in the course of time the residences will no longer be occupied as dwellings, and no new residences may be built. The same will hold true for other types of zones where present land uses are considered undesirable.

The complexity of the city plan is shown in the following description (Black and Black, 1948) of what it includes:

In one sense, the city plan has been limited to those features that can be drawn on paper in the form of a map, such as streets, parks and public building sites. But the plan and its various projects must be supported by factual data justifying them and by figures as to their cost. Other elements of the plan, such as proposals for water supply and sewage disposal, can be shown only partially on a map. They must be accompanied by exhaustive reports and by tabulated data. Certain phases of the plan, such as zoning, are expressed, at least in part, by a written ordinance. Finally, improvement programs and budgets are essential to most city plans for completion of the operating machinery. These several elements properly related, broadly-speaking, may properly be called the city plan.

The city plan is ordinarily composed of three principal elements: Projects to be carried out by the municipality; things to be done by private corporations under more or less public control; and improvements to be made by the individual property owner. The first may be accomplished directly with public funds. The second must be approached through suggestion, cooperation and legislation. The third is largely a matter of guidance and education and, to an extent, legislation as illustrated by the zoning ordinance and by control of land subdivision.

The Planning Commission

The mayor, as the chief executive of the city, and the city council are the legally recognized authorities for city planning. The master plan is usually prepared by a planning bureau made up of specialists employed by the local government. The planning commission is the group of appointed, unpaid private citizens with legal powers to participate in the planning process.

There are three types of metropolitan planning agencies. One is the *multijurisdictional* type, which includes those agencies that cover two or more counties, plus some that cover cities and towns in states where county government is weak or nonexistent. More than half of this type serve areas with a population of over 500,000. A second type is the *city-county planning agency*, which cover a county and its central city. Two out of every three of this type serve areas with a population of less than 250,000. A third type is the *county planning agency*, in which the planning commission members are selected by the county board and receive all of their revenue from the county. Over half of these serve areas with a population of less than 250,000.[3]

The planning commission is in effect a policy-making group with authority to accept or reject plans and to recommend to the ultimate planning authority (mayor and city council). (Boskoff, 1962)

The connection between planning groups and other groups and agencies is shown in Figure 18–1, which diagrams a planning decision-making model. The Study Topics are actual problems that some people in the community think important; The Local Area Planning Team is charged with the responsibility of developing Planning Proposals, leading to Action Plans. But it should work out such proposals only in consultation with the governmental and nongovernmental actors. When ready, the plans are acted upon (the Decision) by the appropriate governmental actors, since the kind of planning being discussed here requires a political decision, hopefully based upon the recommendations of the professional planners.

The Legal Authority for Physical Planning

One of the interesting ways to trace the history of physical planning is to follow the steps by which men have agreed to surrender what would seem at first to be basic property rights in the interest of the common good. Arthur B. Gallion (1950) tells the story briefly and clearly, showing that, with the growth of cities and the growth of population, land took on other values than that attached to agricultural use. As he points out, special places were set aside for the

---

[3] U. S. Housing and Home Finance Agency, *1964 National Survey of Metropolitan Planning* (Washington, D. C.: Government Printing Office, 1965).

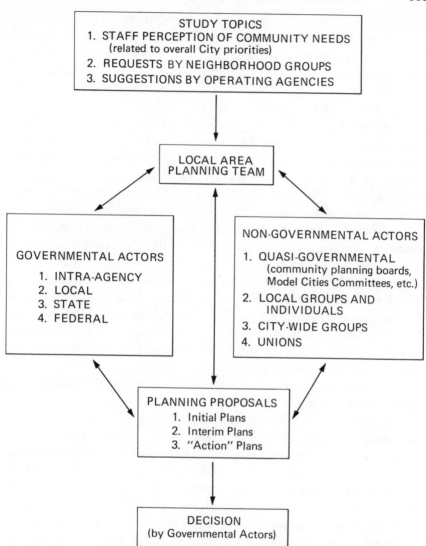

Figure 18–1. Planning decision-making model. *Source:* Jeffrey C. Stern, "The Determinants of 'Effective' Local Area Planning: A Case Study of New York City." Unpublished paper, 1973.

storage of explosives, for the slaughter of animals, and for the residential developments of the aristocracy. King Philip of Spain outlined procedures for establishing communities in the New World to the explorers before their departure in the sixteenth century, counseling them to lay out the streets in such ways that they would not be windswept. One of America's first recorded acts of zoning occurred in Boston, when a ban was placed on storing gunpowder in the center of the city. These and later measures relative to land use were the legal forerunners of the physical planning of today.

In the ancient cities, the ruling group enforced its wishes by the use of police power. Today we accept the principles that the source of all power lies in the hands of the people and that the people, or their representatives, have the power to pass laws to protect the welfare of all the people. This exercise of police power must be for a worthy purpose and with definitely stated objectives.

Thus, if residents feel that a junkyard burning rubber is a nuisance, they could bring suit and try to have the objectionable practice stopped. If the local government passes an ordinance, in keeping with the authority given to it in the state constitution or in state-enabling legislation, prohibiting the building of stores in certain residential areas, action can be brought against any individual violating that ordinance. Not to be confused with this police power, however, is the right of *eminent domain*, which means that land can be taken for a public purpose even when the owner does not want to sell. Under eminent domain, the property is condemned; the courts then establish a fair price to be paid to the owner.

More and more, the interpretation of physical planning has shifted away from merely the simple desire to eliminate nuisances and to protect the value of property that would deteriorate if undesirable invasion occurred. It has taken a much more positive view in its efforts to promote public health, safety, and general welfare and has even extended to such matters as "public convenience and comfort." This last interpretation, supported by Supreme Court decision, is the basis of our traffic laws that prohibit parking on certain streets where it would seriously impede the flow of traffic.

Zoning ordinances also bring ordinary citizens face to face with the fact that a planning body has tried to control land use in the community. They learn that they can or cannot erect a certain kind of building on their property or that their neighbor recently had his plans for a new subdivision on the edge of the city turned down by the zoning commission because he wanted to develop a residential subdivision in an area zoned for industrial use only. If they live in a medium-sized city, the planning and zoning commissions may be the same, but in any case citizens have the right to present their case to an appeal board if they think the decision of the zoning commission unfair.

But zoning is not only an urban phenomenon; there is rural zoning as well. Kenosha County, Wisconsin, is a good case in point (Marshall, 1964):

> Different types of rural zoning plans have been developed to meet varied land use requirements. Kenosha County has been zoned for agricultural-industrial purposes. All of Price County has been zoned for forestry-recreational purposes, while none of Lafayette County has been zoned for any purposes. . . .
>
> As early as 1955, a County Zoning Ordinance was proposed and a zoning map prepared in Kenosha County, Wisconsin. Before this ordinance became operative in any township, the local town government officials needed to approve its application to their area. . . .
>
> Examination of the County Zoning map revealed that in 1955 less than one-fourth of the total land area outside the city of Kenosha was zoned for commercial, industrial, recreational, and residential purposes and that the balance was zoned agricultural. Minor changes were made since then. . . .
>
> Another variation in zoning types is related to single or multiple uses of zoned areas. Exclusive zoning allows only a single designated use for a specific land area, whereas cumulative zoning allows land to be used for a specific purpose but does not exclude more restrictive uses for categories of less restricted areas. Kenosha County ordinances allow cumulative uses of land. Ordinances are not retroactive; that is, land used for a specific purpose at the time the zoning ordinance is adopted, or prior to that time, is not affected. Only as a new use for land is proposed do the regulations become operative. This can create problems during a transitional period. For example, an area may be zoned industrial but dwelling units already built there need not be removed. Or, the zoning ordinance does not prohibit a family from erecting a dwelling unit in an area zoned industrial, where cumulative type zoning is adopted. These situations could result in excessive costs for providing such services as streets or utilities.
>
> . . . It seems likely that urban growth will continue to reach out into the rural areas of Kenosha County. As this occurs, more land area will be withdrawn from agricultural production, either for other uses or because the increasing costs of land ownership make it less attractive for farming. Consistent and constant resource planning needs to be carried on in order to use the land most efficiently and to promote the social welfare of its inhabitants. (pp. 28–29).

The preceding examples show that during the past few years a new ethic regarding land use has been on the rise. It regards land no longer purely as a private commodity to be regulated by economics but as a national resource in which all citizens have an interest. There are two fundamental shifts of power;

One is the movement of the initiative in land use planning from individual owners and developers to the general public, acting through governmental agencies.

The other is a certain redistribution of wealth implied in large-scale land-use control: Individual freedom to maximize profits from land is replaced in various degrees by collective decisions about the disposition of land.[4]

Illustrations of these trends can be found throughout the United States. One issue which frequently is raised in communities by conservation groups is the preservation of wetlands and marshes on the grounds that these are needed to maintain an ecological balance. In contrast, developers who have acquired these properties want to drain them and put up apartment buildings or private homes. To settle such matters, political jurisdictions are more and more establishing conservation districts which cannot be used for commercial development.

Another issue is that of trying to control population growth. A law forbidding any new families to settle in a community would not stand up in court, but requiring that any new dwellings must be built on large houselots rather than small ones keeps down the number of houses to be built. More importantly for some, it means that those who buy and build must have more than an average income if they are to buy the larger lots and put up the kinds of houses specified. Such restrictive measures are counteracted in some states as the legislature passes laws favoring low and medium income housing.

Other questions relate to the effort to use suburban land for high rise apartments, thus adding to the rapidly growing population. One community managed to pass a local act which the courts upheld forbidding any further highrise apartments in their community. (Sanders, 1974) The fear among those sponsoring this act was that the apartment dwellers would add to the already swelling school costs, demands for police protection, and other local governmental expenses.

---

[4] Gladwin Hill, "New Land Ethic: Its Spread Raises Political and Legal Issues to Be Resolved by Public," The *New York Times*, September 4, 1973, p. 23. © 1973 by the New York Times Company. Reprinted by permission.

Heretofore, since the costs of local government were covered by revenues based on property taxes, the tendency has been to favor the use of land by anyone whose undertaking would bring in the most tax dollars, whether it be a junk yard, an industry, or an amusement park. But, as indicated above, this consideration is being questioned and the larger social good taken into account.

Further complicating the interactional field surrounding land use is the trend toward regional as opposed to local planning and the fact that several states have passed or are considering laws that would lead to statewide zoning for certain purposes, such as public recreation. These laws remove some of the control from the local community and thereby try to avoid the crazy-quilt pattern of land use that would otherwise result. There is a growing recognition, for instance, that the problems of a major city are tied in with the problems of the county of which it is a part, while both county and city tend to duplicate agencies in health, welfare, education, and other services which might possibly be more effectively handled on a joint county-city basis. The same is true of the problems of the central city and its suburbs. As long as the area of planning is seen as simply one or the other, because the tax base is computed on the political boundaries that are drawn, then the important problems cannot be tackled in a truly meaningful way. True enough, the definition of community must be drawn up to serve the purpose for which common effort is required and for which there is a legitimate sense of community. For many purposes the larger metropolitan area—not the central city or a single suburb—is the appropriate unit.

URBAN RENEWAL

Planning includes more than the development of a master plan and the decisions as to how land is to be used; it also must deal with the redevelopment of deteriorated parts of the city. Projects for this purpose have been supported by federal grants and usually call for the formation of a special local authority or recognized group; such projects are not under the direct supervision of the local planning commission. Yet the need for close coordination of efforts on the part of all of those seeking to change the physical aspects of the community is most apparent.

The ecological processes described in connection with the community as a place (Chapter 3) afford much insight into the past growth of blighted areas in cities. As was noted, there is competition for space in the downtown center, which is constantly expanding. As the center grows, it invades former residential zones that are no longer desired as family dwelling areas but rather for rooming houses and cheap apartments. According to this theory, such areas become transitional and run-down. Before being entirely taken over by business or some other land use, which may eventually happen, these areas are problem areas.

Elsewhere in the community, we find sections with large numbers of very cheap houses for the lowest-income groups. The houses are not provided with the ordinary conveniences, are not kept in repair, either by the tenant or the owner, and are in the parts of town many residents try to avoid. But these areas do exist and constitute a problem. Although city revenues from residential areas, in general, do not fully cover the cost of public services to these areas, we do know that a disproportionate amount of public funds is spent in policing and giving fire and public-health protection to the blighted areas. In other words, those who are making quick profits on a relatively small investment in such low-cost dwellings are actually making these profits at the expense of the other taxpayers of the community. These facts were brought to light in the 1930's and provided the arguments for a number of ameliorative programs prior to World War II.

The Housing Act of 1937, which placed primary responsibility on the local community, helped finance 191,700 low-rent housing units in 268 localities in thirty-seven states by 1949. The Housing Act of 1949 provided for the building of 810,000 low-rent public dwelling units over a period of six years. Local housing authorities were assisted by the federal government by loans and annual contributions. An effort was made to ensure the occupation of these low-rent housing units only by families of low income and to destroy unsafe or unsanitary dwellings equal in number to the number of newly constructed units. After the local housing authority had determined the need for low-rent housing, selected the site, appraised it, planned for the project through use of private architects, and estimated the costs of building and operation, the authority turned to private builders to get the work done. Once the projects were built and occupied, the local housing authority sought, through tenant and neighborhood councils, to draw the occupants into the mainstream of community life (Dean, 1949).

Other housing acts, in later years, sought to deal with urgent housing needs. The Housing Act passed by Congress in 1964 put added stress on neighborhood rehabilitation, authorizing projects consisting entirely of code enforcement. The cost of this enforcement was covered by federal grants. City ordinances to be enforced governed hygiene and sanitation, fire safety, and building-maintenance codes (Loring, 1956). Baltimore, Maryland, and Milwaukee, Wisconsin, provided good examples of concerted action by local authorities to enforce through court action the standards set. In this manner, landlords in blighted areas were compelled to improve their property if they wished to rent it and "stay clear of the law." Resulting from a process of education and strict enforcement, with specially designated "sanitarians" holding police powers, a remarkable improvement has been noted. In Baltimore, the tendency has been to go into the worst areas and, block by block, try to raise housing standards to minimum levels; in Milwaukee, the effort has been centered on chiefly those areas where blight is beginning and where proper measures now will prevent further deterioration.

In November 1966 an additional program, usually referred to as the Model Cities Program, was enacted. Cities could apply for funds to set up demonstration projects, not to cover more than ten percent of the people within their limits, to rebuild or revitalize slum or blighted areas. In addition, projects could improve job opportunities, educational facilities, recreational opportunities, as well as combat disease, and reduce crime and delinquency. The purpose, in other words, was to improve the living conditions for people in the selected area and the key strategy was to bring about more effective coordination of the federal, state and local public and private efforts.

The urban renewal programs often "redeveloped" a deteriorated area by tearing down the existing structures and building in their stead luxury apartments or office buildings. George Romney, when Secretary of Housing and Urban Development, observed:

> Take Detroit: As a result of the bulldozing of poor neighborhoods for urban renewal and highways primarily, the congestion in the 1967 riot area increased from 16,000 people in 1957 to 34,000 in 1967, when the riot broke out. What happened was that poor people who lost their homes to bulldozers simply moved in with other people, and units that

once housed one family began to house three and four families. This has been going on in cities pretty well across the country.[5]

The highway programs not only decreased the available housing for the poor but made it convenient for the more affluent to live in the suburbs with ready access to the downtown areas, leaving these areas as the now crowded residential sites of the poor. *Urban Villagers,* by Herbert Gans (1962), is a sociological classic which describes an Italian-American community in the West End of Boston which was "developed" out of existence. Another critique of urban renewal, particularly in New Haven, Connecticut, has been made by William Ryan (1971) in *Blaming the Victim.*

These shortcomings of urban renewal are mentioned to show that the early concentration of physical planners upon the elimination of slums and the building of profitable and at times aesthetically pleasing structures led to unfortunate social consequences. Those framing the Model Cities Program recognized this failure and sought to involve local people who would be affected by the program in the developmental plans. This step, as in the case of other programs calling for local citizens groups, for the first time brought about a confrontation between citizens and the professionals (often planners) who had been trained to tell citizens what to do rather than listen to what the citizens wanted and then try to negotiate with them the most desirable course of action. In other words, the social action field has become a much more complex one for the planners and the professional change agents for they are now dealing with representatives of citizen groups as well as with those holding political office.

PHYSICAL PLANNING AND THE COMMUNITY

Physical planning for any community may be carefully drawn up in keeping with the best scientific procedures, the recommendations may take into account the experience of many other cities, and the predictions about population growth may prove to be almost 100 per cent correct, yet the plan may prove a failure if it never receives social acceptance. To accomplish even the least important purpose for which the plan was prepared, private citizens must be

[5] *U. S. News and World Report,* July 28, 1969, p. 49.

willing to guide many of their actions by it. Earlier chapters in this book have taken up those elements of community life that have a decided bearing on such a question. Two of these can be reviewed with planning specifically in mind.

Social Values, Norms, and Public Opinion

The first step in planning, as we have seen, is to define the community's goals and values. What do the people of this community want most in life? What are they willing to pay for in terms both of taxes and of time? City planners are quick to recognize that various communities differ greatly in the way they respond to physical-planning proposals. This individuality among communities is thus a well-attested fact but one that is apt to be overlooked in the hurry to get on with the preparation of the more tangible aspects of planning, such as the graphs showing occupational distribution or the maps locating the recreational facilities.

Communities also differ in the way they permit the citizens to go about the realization of their goals. These "norms," as they are called, are the limits set upon the roles people can play. Take, for instance, the planner. What norms govern him? In some communities, people prefer not to be bothered with the details or even the processes of physical planning. They are willing to leave the whole matter up to the experts and wait for them to solve their traffic, sewage, or other problems related to space. The citizens appointed to the planning commission passively accept the recommendations made to them and then walk out of the meeting feeling that they have performed their job in a satisfactory fashion.

It is very different in other communities, where the expert is suspect to begin with and where the leading citizens want to know exactly what is going on. Their representatives on the planning commission ask a hundred questions and occasionally vote down a recommendation they do not feel is wise for their community. Here, the norms require the planner to be the adviser only, and not the one who, as a "lone hand," runs the commission.

Communities differ, too, in the means that they will accept for the remedying of some problem. Some will accept the direct approach. If a slum is to be torn down, the bulldozers are sent in to destroy the hovels or old tenements so that new structures may be erected or the place turned into a parking lot. It is not so with other communities. Some of the leading citizens there are sure to ask, "What is going to happen to those families whose homes are being demolished? Have you made provision for them before you move into action?" Once assurance can be given that each family is satisfactorily resettled, the task of clearance can proceed.

Some communities expect businessmen to be hard-boiled and respect those who can drive a hard bargain, even at the expense of the planning and zoning commission. Other communities require that their businessmen give at least a semblance of respect for the general welfare of the community and support the worthwhile undertakings that are periodically sponsored by local groups. Should the work of the planning commission be generally approved in the community, those individuals who want community recognition must cooperate with the work of the commission. In other words, understanding the norms that govern the behavior of the planner, the planning-commission member, as well as others in the community, is necessary for effective work in that community.

The third consideration, in addition to social values and norms, is that of public opinion. We must remember that physical planning is usually public planning, which means that it is connected with the governmental bodies dependent on public acceptance and approval. If the community gets aroused over too little planning or too much planning, it may change its local government at election time. This is why those who are involved in physical planning have a definite responsibility for seeking to keep the public informed about the nature of the problem and the possible means of alleviating the problem, together with pertinent information about cost and the benefits that are to be reaped as a result of positive action.

Response of Organized Groups

In spite of the existence of what seem to be general community values and norms, there are many individuals in the community who are ready to ignore them if some immediate personal interest is served. Physical planners are required to deal with these special-interest groups, as well as with the rather broad and vague general public. The identification of such groups is an important step in understanding the complexity of planning even in a medium-sized community.

Vested Interests.   In every community, there are some individuals whose business ventures might be curtailed if strict zoning practices were enforced. They may be reaping profits from substandard housing and may have little desire to bring these units up to minimum standards. Or, certain firms such as banks or even private individuals may have a great deal of money tied up in scattered real estate and may fear that too rigid enforcement of zoning ordinances might result in a decline in the value of this property.

Other vested interests may involve those homeowners who live in a small area that would be radically changed if the recommendations of the master plan were put into effect. They may collect money and employ lawyers to protect the interests they feel are being violated. If they are successful, their property may prove to be a little enclave surrounded by land used for very different purposes.

Not all vested interests are necessarily in opposition. Those who have vested interests in physical planning, such as realtors, banks administering trusts and estates, architects and builders, or utility and transportation companies, may be ardent supporters of the physical plan worked out for their communities. Vested interests need not be an opposition group. What their attitudes will be depends on how the plan is interpreted to them, how much they feel they have to say in its formulation, and the essential fairness and commonsense used in its preparation and application. The tempo at which it is being put into effect will likewise affect the attitudes of these groups.

One must also realize that these vested interests are often organized. The members may be held together quite informally simply by periodically talking over the situation and deciding what their individual action should be, or they may have their own trade or professional association that becomes the official spokesman of the vested interest. It is important to know the spokesmen for each vested interest, either as informal leaders or as organizational representatives. The city planner who sticks simply to his maps and his statistical tables fails to draw up the kind of reports and recommendations that take into account the feasible steps at a given time. Unless the planner makes a conscious effort to become familiar with these vested interests, he will be aware of only the vocal opposition whose members have no hesitation in expressing their dissent from the decisions of the planning commission; he also needs to know where he can look for support among those whose dollars and cents are likewise tied up in the decision reached.

Groups Pressuring for Change. Wide-awake communities usually have some individuals and groups pressuring for changes affecting the physical aspects of the city. They may not have much to gain financially from the proposed changes but will be rewarded with the satisfaction of seeing some cause won or in having contributed to what they consider the betterment of their community. These frequently include men's civic groups, women's clubs, church organizations, and a number of other widely diversified types, which for various reasons decide to push some community project. Many of these proposals would fit in excellently with the city plan; others would retard it. For example, residents in one part of a city may wish to have the city buy a few vacant lots and convert them into a playground; there is a pressure for the construction of a swimming pool, with little thought having been given to the problems of water supply and disposal. Other groups may be joining in a drive for a city auditorium and plan to use a site much better suited for another purpose. Still another group may be seriously and effectively agitating for more adequate public housing and may have gone so far in their plans as to suggest that present slums be replaced on the spot by new units, even though the master plan suggests that this area be converted into a warehouse district because of its close proximity to the railroad and through highways.

The obvious step, although some planners never consider this to be a part of their job, would be to meet with these groups and try to give them an over-all view of what their community could become if some rational, comprehensive physical plan were followed. It could be pointed out that even the best plan can be changed when better arguments are presented or when experience suggests the wisdom of a change, but that mere pressure for change alone is not sufficient reason for modification.

Resolution of Conflict

The discussion so far shows that physical planning cannot avoid involvement in conflict. The very fact that the planner seeks to help the people of a community move from present conditions to some conditions assumed to be more desirable is an open invitation to difference of opinion, running into vested interests and real conflict. The best planning provides sufficient information to avoid the opposition that arises simply out of misunderstanding. This assumes that the values and norms mentioned above are taken into account and that an expert job of informing the public is carried through. It also means that those responsible for planning are willing to listen to the ideas of the residents of the community, since in this way a better plan is usually brought about. Yet, no public-relations program is going to eliminate all conflict in physical planning, since people's pocketbooks are affected at many points. An individual property owner may feel abused and may rightly conclude that the plan would cause major shifts in his personal plans, or groups of taxpayers may rise up in opposition to the bond issues that might be necessary if certain recommendations in the plan are to be put into effect.

Fortunately, communities through the centuries have worked out ways of dealing with conflicts of this sort. Where it is a matter of determining community sentiment on a bond issue or some similar matter that can be put to the vote, the ballot is the means of resolving conflict—at least officially—although personal resentments may still remain. When, however, there is a question of an individual's rights versus the welfare of the community, a court decision resolves the conflict and the losing party must abide by the decision, although it may exercise its right of appeal until it has exhausted this possibility of having a decision in its favor.

These considerations bear out the facts that the community is a very lively arena of action and that the physical planner cannot hope to divorce himself, or his plan, from its influence.

IMPROVING ENVIRONMENTAL QUALITY

The passage of the Environmental Protection Act of 1970 created a federal agency to oversee, regulate and make recommendations to offset any negative impacts of industrial and technological developments. The Rural Sociology Department at Cornell University (Capener et al., 1973) was interested in the sociological implications of developing a program which would achieve the above objectives. Its staff interviewed leaders in twenty counties in the Hudson River Region in order to see their perceptions of environmental problems and to identify organizations considered relevant to such problems. The three most commonly perceived issues in the region as a whole were:

Water pollution (23.5 per cent of all issue mentions)
Land use (19.6 per cent)
Solid waste disposal (16.1 per cent)

Just under half of the informants (47 per cent) ranked environmental quality as a general concern in their county, but of less importance than other issues; one-quarter (24 per cent) thought it equally important as other issues; while 14 per cent rated environmental quality as the most important issue in the county. The more urban the area the greater the possibility of listing air pollution as a concern.

The leaders in addition to their perception of the urgency of the problems also held ideas as to what organizations are important in the environmental field. In these twenty Hudson River Region counties, the unofficial—environment specific organizations led, accounting for 26.8 per cent of all organizational mentions. These include the Sierra Club, Audubon Society, Scenic Hudson Preservation Association which were known to informants throughout the whole region. Governmental organizations—environment specific received 19.1 per cent of the mentions; civic organizations, 14.2 per cent; educational organizations, 10.7 per cent; and sports and recreational organizations, 9.1 per cent. In considering the organizational field, it is important also to see which kinds of organizations were not considered very important. Planning boards received only 5.1 per cent of the mentions, general government organizations, 3.3 per cent, business associations and private research organizations, 3.1 per cent, health organizations, 2.7 per cent, and agricultural organizations 2.7 per cent. Ranking even below these were general unofficial organizations, industrial and commercial firms, professional and single owner business, and mass media organizations.

The Cornell study found a definite relationship between population size and density and seriousness of perception of environmental problems, but the first two of these were not significantly related to the organization mention variable. This was a surprising finding and is being given further study.

We do not know, of course, whether or not the results from the Hudson River Region would apply to other parts of the United

States. The Committee for Economic Development (1974) is recommending that for each river basin or shoreline stretch there be a single agency for planning and executing or controlling all public water-quality programs. It also recommends setting up natural air-quality regions to formulate and implement pollution control programs in each region. This report prepared by a group consisting chiefly of businessmen stresses the reliance on cost-benefit analysis in determining the feasibility of control measures, but one member of the study team thought this an inappropriate guide. He wrote:

> Air pollution inflicts an estimated $16 billion a year in economic damages upon the people of the United States—in the form of illness, lost time, damage to materials, crops, livestock, structures, and so forth. Should consideration be given to how the cost of cleaning up the nation's air compares with the cost of *not* doing so. (p. 27).

Any long-term solution depends, of course, upon the weakening of the American's love affair with his automobile. "American drivers collectively log over a trillion miles a year in their cars and trucks and individually average nearly a month and a half of eight-hour days per year behind the wheel" (Erwin, 1974). Any student of community life knows the changes in social patterns which would be brought about with a shift of dependence upon mass transportation from the automobile.

As local communities attempt to deal with environmental problems they may find that they are being held responsible for the disposal of solid wastes, which are generated at an estimated rate of some 21 tons per person a year. But they will have to team up with other communities in regional authorities to control water and air pollution. This is another indication that, as problems become more complex, the local community as a unit of action is of insufficient size to cope with the total problem. Yet, how its members (and those of other communities) perceive the value of the solutions proposed and the costs to themselves in convenience, jobs, etc. will have much to do with the overall success of the broadly-based program (Buttel and Flinn, 1974). The local community may very well be the unit which has most to do with public opinion formation and with citizen participation in ways that give a program real effectiveness.

✿   ✿   ✿   ✿

There are various ways of looking at the social action field as far as land use and environmental control are concerned. One structured field is that surrounding the development of, amending, and enforcing the master plan. People in all areas of the community and in many occupations occasionally get caught up in the activities of this field. Related to this, but often with a distinct set of characters, is the complex of urban renewal programs which constitutes another social action field. External standards imposed by the funding agencies impinge upon the behavior within this field; professional people interact with citizens groups; economic agencies have close contact with social work agencies trying to relocate families to be displaced by the renewal; emotion runs high as some people are forced to do what they do not want to do and as some business interests gain advantage over competing interests. A third social action field dealing with space and its use is now part of the local scene: the environmentalist. Citizen and governmental groups dedicated to improving environmental quality enter into interaction with business and other interests whose deeds are considered by the change agents to be deleterious to the community. Many actors which participate in the planning or urban renewal interactional fields also become involved with the environmentalists. At any given point in time it is difficult for the local resident to follow closely what is happening in all three fields just as he cannot conveniently watch three rings in a circus. But the interested person can learn enough about each to see that they do bear a relationship to each other and to the totality of interaction that makes up the community.

19

Economic and
Educational Programs

The community as a field of social action includes, in addition to those programs that deal with the physical environment, others of an economic and social nature. They, too, have something of a life of their own (Greifer, 1974) but never in complete isolation from other collective efforts in the community.

To follow the progress of only one or two programs through their daily expressions is enough to convince anyone that the community is an arena or field of intense social interaction, some intended and much unforeseen, but invariably leading to new combinations and eventual change.

ECONOMIC PROGRAMS

The City, Economic Development, and the Businessman

Because of the growing interest in problems of economic development not only in the United States but also abroad, it is well to gain some historical perspective that will reveal the connection between this type of development and community life. It is hard for many people brought up in the western world to realize that 150 years ago their economy and communities resembled quite closely those now found in Asian countries where about 80 per cent of the people live in agricultural villages, and where what are termed "cities" are really population agglomerations characterized by relatively simple social organization. But with the rise of the industrial cities a century and a half ago, which, incidentally, sprang from villages or small towns more often than from previously established cities, new social arrangements came into existence. In the Western world these cities, according to Bert F. Hoselitz (1955),

> . . . adopted and modified the old institutions, but there was never any question that each of these rapidly growing entities formed a "corporation," a whole of some sort, that the inhabitants of the city were members of one and the same community and that they had rights and privileges in the community and duties towards it. . . . In spite of slums and low housing and sanitary standards in many parts of the industrial cities, the whole city formed a community. It was not merely altruism or beneficent self-interest which made some municipal reformers agitate for slum clearance and municipal improvement; an important role was played by the sentiment of community; i.e., the conception that any blemish in the city's landscape was a matter of concern for all its citizens. (p. 167).

Hoselitz points out two ways in which the sentiment of community was given expression. The first was in the tradition of self-government, of the city's taking care of its own present and evolving needs. The second was the attachment of the city's population to the urban way of life that led to a clearer distinction between the city and the country. It also led to the development of functionally specific areas in the city itself:

> The concentric arrangement of modern industrial cities, with their central business districts and their changing belts of industrial and residential areas, the location and function of district shopping centers, the pattern of intracity communications and many other features of a similar kind, show the interdependence of all parts of a city upon one another and are proof of the over-all unity of the urban community in spite of its internal wide diversity. (pp. 169–70).

Another characteristic of industrial cities is the fact that their growth was associated for the most part with the demand for labor; people moved there because employment opportunities existed. A third characteristic of the industrial city in economically advanced countries is the role that it plays in the process of cultural change. These points illustrate that the modern industrial city, as we know it today, developed sociologically as its economy developed.

The contrast between such cities and those in the underdeveloped countries is striking. For instance, the African is not loyal to the city in which he lives, but to his family, his kin, his tribe, and the village from which he originally came.

One of the great contrasts between the cities of the underdeveloped countries and those of the West is, therefore, the absence of "city-consciousness" in Asia and Africa and perhaps also in Latin America. This implies, at the same time, that the distance between urban and rural styles of life is less pronounced than in Europe; that the loyalties of the urban dwellers are frequently to groups whose center of gravity is outside the city; that sojourn in the city is regarded often as only temporary; that migrants to the city from one village or province not only tend to settle in clusters of their own, but that even when they have become permanent city dwellers they maintain some ties with the region from which they came; and that each district of the city forms a community of its own, often rigorously separated from the others. (p. 175).

Because of this historic sense of community, businessmen and industrialists in the Western world have supported civic enterprises by contributing generously of their time and money. A later and relatively recent development in their thinking, however, has been the realization that by their combined efforts they could do much more than as individuals to promote the physical well-being and economic welfare of their communities. Area development associations were set up at the end of World War II in many metropolitan centers for the purpose of dealing—through private enterprise, where possible—with problems of noise and smoke abatement, traffic control, urban renewal, and the attracting of desirable types of economic enterprises to the community. So successful were these efforts in a number of places that almost every community facing economic difficulties began to look upon "the bringing in of a factory" as a panacea. "If only we had larger payrolls," community leaders argued, "we would sell more merchandise, get more tax revenues, and balance our economy." Such thinking, however, frequently proved a snare and a delusion. A study of the experience of many communities and many industries has led to some sober second thoughts on the matter. But the gaining of new industry by no means exhausts the field of economic development in American communities. The dressing up of store fronts, the providing of free parking space for rural people, the creation of a shopping mall, the promotion of recreational facilities, which attract more people to town, and the insistence on good business practices by the merchants themselves tend to develop the economy to the point where more trade means more income.

Under the sponsorship of state chambers of commerce or of some other large-scale group, the businessmen of many communities have gone into what has been termed "community development" rather than economic development. This broader term is used, since the organization that they call into being may have an education committee, a welfare committee, a labor committee, as well as a tourist attraction committee, an agriculture committee, and the like. As set up, the focus is community-wide. If the community sponsors are chiefly motivated in economic terms, however, committees dealing with non-economic matters often consist of people poorly chosen for their tasks, or these committees are neglected for what the officers think are more important matters. Over a period of time, what has started out nobly as a community enterprise ends up as economic development alone, which in itself is a worthwhile and legitimate activity, but one that may have unintentionally and unfortunately misrepresented the true nature of community development. Any one segment that tries to speak for the whole community, no matter how noble its sentiments, is apt to set back the cause of community development. Where business leaders work out a truly cooperative approach with representatives from many segments and parts of the community, they are more likely to advance together in the promotion of activities that benefit the whole community as well as themselves. Economic interests can be welded in with other interests.

THE WAR ON POVERTY

Programs which are organized by and promoted for the benefit of the business interests (and indirectly the community at large) do not usually lead to any major changes in the economic system itself. This is why those who favor more equal income distribution organize different kinds of programs, often with the support of some local business and governmental groups, to bring about economic change. Outside funding from foundations or the federal government is usually available before such programs move into action. Urban renewal, which includes federally-financed housing programs, as well as the Model Cities Program have already been mentioned in the last chapter. For example, between 1969 and 1971 the Department of Housing and Urban Development's Government National Mortgage Association provided $12.5 billion in assistance for lower-income families. The tendency has been to move toward greater reliance upon municipalities to set their own priorities in the housing and development programs best adapted to their circumstances. Other federal programs designed for manpower training or to provide public employment are carried out in local communities and have a social as an economic impact.

The War on Poverty, however, was different from urban renewal, though both affected lower income people. In 1968, according to the Social Security Administration, a non-farm family of four with less than $3,553 income was considered poor (Downs, 1970). In that year 25.4 million Americans were classified as poor. By 1971 the poverty line was set at $4,137 a year, with 25.6 million people below the line. By 1974 the figure had risen to $5,357.

We need, however, to make a distinction between *relative* and *actual* poverty. Table 19–1 shows that between 1947 and 1968

TABLE 19–1

Changes in Income Distribution: 1947–1968

Type and Rank of Receiving Unit	Percentage of Aggregate Income (before federal taxes) Received by Each Group		
	1947	1950	1968
Families			
Lowest 20 per cent	5.0%	4.5%	5.7%
Highest 20 per cent	43.0	42.6	40.6
Highest 5 per cent	17.2	17.0	14.0
Unrelated Individuals			
Lowest 20 per cent	1.9	2.3	3.2
Highest 20 per cent	59.4	50.4	50.8
Highest 5 per cent	33.3	19.3	20.4

there has been little change in relative poverty. From 1938 to 1947 equality increased significantly in the U.S., but not so in the later period shown in the table. Though there was some decline in the share going to the top 20 per cent there was relatively little change in the share going to the lowest 20 per cent.

Tables 19–2 and 19–3 show the distribution of poverty according to location and race, using the figures of $3,553 as an actual measure of poverty. About 13 out of every hundred Americans are classified as poor, with almost as many living in non-metropolitan areas as in metropolitan areas. Yet, a larger proportion of those outside the

TABLE 19-2

Poverty in Metropolitan and Nonmetropolitan Areas: 1968

Area	Number of Poor Persons (Millions) [a]	Percentage of Persons in Poverty
United States	25.4	12.8%
Metropolitan Areas	12.9	10.0
Central cities	7.8	13.4
Suburbs	5.1	7.3
Nonmetropolitan Areas	12.5	18.0
Nonfarm [b]	10.4	17.2
Farm [b]	2.2	23.5

[a] Numerical subtotals may not add to totals because of rounding.
[b] Estimates.

TABLE 19-3

Poverty Among Whites and Nonwhites: 1968

Area	Poor Whites		Poor Nonwhites	
	Number (Millions)	As a Percentage of All Whites	Number (Millions)	As a Percentage of All Nonwhites
Metropolitan Areas	8.5	7.6%	4.4	25.7%
Central cities	4.4	9.8	3.4	25.5
Suburbs	4.1	6.2	1.0	26.0

Source for Tables 19-1–19-3: Anthony Downs, *Who Are the Urban Poor?* New York: Committee for Economic Development. Supplementary Paper Number 26. (Revised Edition). 1970. Pages 10, 14.

metropolitan areas were poor, almost 1 out of 4 of the farm population being so classed. Table 19-3 supports the well-known fact that much larger proportions of nonwhites than whites are in the poverty category, with the proportions for nonwhites being almost the same for central cities and suburbs. The table also shows that of the poor in central cities, 57 per cent are white (4.4 million as compared with 3.4 million nonwhite).

Figures such as these have driven home the fact that in the most affluent society in the world (the United States) poverty still exists and that social programs are needed to deal with it (Eitzen, 1974).

One of the most ambitious efforts was the Economic Opportunity Act, passed by Congress in 1964. By 1974 it had been repealed, no money provided for it in the Nixon budget for 1974, and it was thus an historical episode. Yet, the review of what happened during those ten years tells as much about community action as any other experience we might mention (Moynihan, 1969). First of all, President Johnson in his message to Congress on March 16, 1964 spoke of a total victory over poverty, but this was before the United States became so deeply embroiled in Vietnam and a quest for another kind of total victory. In summary, the Act created an Office of Economic Opportunity (OEO) which was to run such programs as newly created community action agencies, the Job Corps and VISTA (Volunteers in Service to America). The OEO established within the Labor Department a Neighborhood Youth Corps to help keep youths in school along with several other goals. Head Start, a preschool program, was also set up to take care of medical, nutritional as well as educational needs. The OEO also supported legal services for the poor as well as neighborhood health centers.[1]

The feature of the program which has proven most instructive to the community sociologist is the community action agency, which was a core concept (Greenstone and Peterson, 1973; Marris and Rein, 1973). By 1966 there were Community Action Programs in over 1,000 communities. These were public or private non-profit groups, usually bypassing City Hall, managed with the "maximum feasible participation" of the people to be helped. Hundreds of communities thus became battlegrounds as competing groups claiming to speak for the low income residents sought designation as a community action agency; once so designated they proceeded to take steps against slum landlords, local merchants, and even local governmental officials themselves. Many such groups seemed determined to restructure society and therefore promoted rent strikes, marches on City Hall, and sought to get more jobs for minority groups.

One city manager of a large western city graphically described what was happening in his city hall. On the first floor, in a rather dingy conference room, citizen representatives were coming together weekly to work out plans for carrying out the antipoverty program. They represented many low-income segments of the community as

---

[1] For an excellent brief overview see Mark R. Arnold, "The Good War That Might Have Been," *New York Times Magazine*, September 29, 1974, pp. 56–73.

well as some of the highest-income groups who saw in this approach a chance to make their community a much better place in which to live. Almost all of them were inexperienced in politics and even in this case thought of themselves as playing a social-planning welfare role rather than a political role. This group had been appointed by the mayor on the recommendation of those who knew the social structure of the community well and who wanted to constitute a truly representative body. But, when some vacancies occurred on the board, its members did not want the mayor to appoint the new people; the board members wanted to make the selection themselves. After much argument back and forth, the mayor finally capitulated.

On the third floor of the city hall, the city council regularly meets. It is so concerned with the specific details of running the city that it has had no time to consider broad social planning. In many ways, it is in poor communication with new forces at work in the community. The city manager mused that perhaps the first-floor body would in time unleash pressures and gain the kind of community support that would seriously affect politically the third-floor official council.

Such a frontal assault on the local power structure was causing so much consternation that in 1966-67 Congress enacted some restrictions to the Act, one of them permitting local governments to take control of the community action programs.

We can understand more fully the community action aspects of these programs and their political fate if we look at them in terms of their constituent stages, as set forth by one study (Metropolitan Applied Research Center, 1969).

> (1) an initial stage of evidence of *concern* and *protest* about some remediable problem adversely affecting the lives of human beings; (2) a second stage of *organization* and *mobilization* of the power of the victims for appropriate *social action;* (3) an intermediary stage of *confrontation*—the *initiation* and *sustaining* of the necessary action in spite of *controversy* and *conflict;* and (4) a final stage of obtaining and sustaining the desired *social change.* (p. 25).

It should be remembered that some of these local programs were being financed by the federal government—90 cents federal plus 10 cents local for every dollar expended. Furthermore, federal statements of the nature of community action programs remained ambiguous so that their definition varied considerably from city to city and even within a given city. Expectations of results also differed greatly, with the hopes of the lower income groups sometimes being raised to a point that would have been impossible to realize.

A major influence in the field of action was the established social welfare agency which traditionally had depended upon an agency-client relationship as the means for extending to the poor the benefits made available by the established order. The community action agencies not only bypassed City Hall in the beginning; they also bypassed or ran counter to the social welfare practices, moving beyond the agency-client stance to the demands of a protest group.

The heyday of the Community Action agencies also corresponded with the successful phase of the civil rights movement. The latter were characterized as middle class in orientation and leadership and therefore not centered in the neighborhoods of the poor. Furthermore, community action agencies, being dependent upon federal funds, were more subject to the local political structure than civil rights organizations customarily were (Helfgot, 1974). The role of the churches in the poverty program varied from city to city (Metropolitan Applied Research Center, 1969):

> On the whole, Protestant groups seem to have been the most conspicuous in such programs, in particular the Episcopal and Presbyterian—interestingly enough and probably not irrelevantly, those churches least active in the Negro ghettos and in the communities of the poor, where Methodists, Baptists, and storefront sects are the most prevalent . . . p. 175.

What the War on Poverty established in a sure way for the first time was the legitimate rights of the less disadvantaged—at whom many community action programs have been aimed—to have a say through organized groups in what is done for them and in their name. A sober evaluation of the Poverty Program, such as the one quoted just above, notes little economic change in the plight of the poor as a result of the Economic Opportunity Act. Yet, community life will never be quite the same again in those communities where a segment of the population not until then involved in decision-making got a taste of collective power and its political impact. Among the poor, as elsewhere in society, coalitions of divergent interests are fleeting and sometimes misdirected, but they can at times be right on target and thus influence a broader consideration of their needs.

EDUCATIONAL PROGRAMS

Education can be one of the liveliest fields of community action. One reason for this is its close connection with other aspects of community life.

The School System in Interaction with other Local Agencies

One of the most detailed studies of suburban life yet to appear, *Crestwood Heights*, was made after its three authors (Seeley, Sim and Loosley, 1956) had spent five years analyzing every aspect of daily living in the community studied—"from P.T.A. participation and wage-earning to dating and child-rearing." The community is located "somewhere in central Canada" on the outskirts of "Big City," but is typical of suburbia throughout North America. In Crestwood Heights the school is synonymous with the community for the two grew up together; also, the "massive centrality" of the school buildings makes the most immediate impact on any outside observer coming into the Heights. No attempt will be made here to summarize the kinds of education that go on in this community, which the authors discuss in detail; rather attention will be given the analysis of the relationships between education and other systems found in Crestwood Heights. The authors write:

> In the area of social development, the school finds itself partly co-operating, partly competing with other institutions: the church and its sponsored recreation programs, the community center and the program under its jurisdiction, and the families and their wishes. . . . The school, while it seems to view its recreational program as necessary to its aims—the inculcation of loyalty has a bearing on learning—still feels it proper to confer with church, community center, and family in any plans for extra-curricular activities. . . . The parents, imbued with the belief that it is their responsibility to provide recreational outlets for their children, and baffled as to the means for accomplishing their ends, turn, as usual, primarily to the school for help. Since the school, as a publicly supported institution, is in a more favorable financial and official position to initiate extra-curricular activities, it tends progressively to diminish the need for church and community center programs, which are supported more precariously by voluntary contributions and leadership. . . . The school, willing or unwilling, ready or unready, appears also, then, to be moving steadily into a position of dominance where the social development of the child is concerned. (pp. 238–39).

In Crestwood Heights the sphere of ethical and religious training, according to the authors, is not clearly assigned territory.

> As the institution invested with the major responsibility for transmitting the dominant cultural values, it (the school) is also expected to transmit a "religious heritage," without, however, espousing the position of any one of the competing "religions" or forms of religion. This necessity, together with the special care inevitably enjoined upon a school system encompassing two religious groups supposedly as widely divergent as Jew and Gentile, accounts for something of whatever may be peculiar in the religious instruction of the schools of Crestwood Heights. (p. 239).

Religion in this suburban community is characterized as a guide to a style of behavior rather than to any routine of conduct. It is against aggression and in favor of love and sympathy. It is not preoccupied with *ultimate values*, but teachers and parents alike view it as a *means* to other and much more important ends such as "happiness," peace of mind, or mental health.

> If the relationship of the school to the church is considered in this context, an interesting reversal may be observed. Formerly the views of the church dominated the parent who, in turn, dominated the child and the teacher directly—and the child again indirectly through the teacher. The existing configuration would suggest that the teacher now influences child and parent, who mutually influence each other, and these, in turn, unite to influence the church. The school, supported by the human relations experts and their institutions, has largely replaced the church as an ideological source, as the figure below suggests. (p. 241).

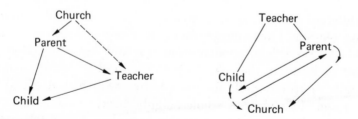

Such a complete reversal of traditional relationships may not be characteristic of most communities, but Crestwood Heights certainly reveals one direction in which the pendulum can swing. The writers also point out that the school is more and more being entrusted with the task of developing in the child an adherence to the emerging value system of health, happiness, and success, as well as the responsibility for his emotional well-being.

Considerations such as these come into play when opposition develops to proposed programs or actions by the school authorities. One community studied by the author (Sanders, 1974) was torn apart as never before by a planned program of sex education in the schools. Religious factionalism developed, parents differed over the desirability of the program and argued over specific diagrams of sexual anatomy that were to be used with the school children, candidates for the School Committee (or Board) used the issue to castigate the school administration and win votes. Such a program involved, therefore, both family and religion. A similar type of conflict occurred over the question of having a Christmas play in a public school in another community (Sanders and Orzack, 1969). Many Jewish parents protested the religious celebration and the issue became clouded over by accusations of Communism, unAmericanism and the like.

One of the very highly publicized cases of community controversy over schools occurred in 1974 in Kanawha County, West Virginia, where fundamentalist religious leaders and their followers protested vigorously, even to incidents of violence, over new textbooks which were being introduced into all of the county schools. Some of the content was thought by the opponents to be contrary to sound religious teachings and good American beliefs. After weeks of controversy, the school authorities decided to use some of the textbooks despite continuing vociferous denunciation by a group of parents.

A different kind of furor is created when the school authorities propose closing down one or more neighborhood schools on the ground that the school population in that area has dropped or that the cost of bringing the school up to required standards makes it financially more advisable for the children who had attended that school to go elsewhere. A whole neighborhood can mobilize to try to keep the school, with a variety of reasons being used to persuade the general public to support the opposition to the closing.

Education and the Economy

But education, chiefly as embodied in the school, is not only interacting with religion and the family; it is also closely tied in with

economic life. Since the employment picture grows more complicated all the time with increasing specialization, schools have for
many years been sponsoring selected activities and services, as the
following quotation shows:

> Practical arts courses are provided in junior and senior high schools
> covering general career areas, such as commercial, homemaking and in-
> dustrial. Among the purposes of these courses is the development of ap-
> preciation of the types and standards of work in these fields. . . .
>
> Guidance services for youth·are also provided in junior and senior high
> schools and include attention to the selection of courses that provide a
> foundation for adult life, keeping in mind both cultural and economic
> needs. . . .
>
> When the boy or girl is faced with the necessity of choosing a definite
> occupational aim, a course in occupations is often available. . . . Voca-
> tional preparatory courses are offered in many senior high schools and
> special vocational high schools. (Loomis and Moore, 1955, pp. 68–69).

Once the young person has had this instruction and guidance, many
schools help him register with the local employment service, or his
instructors in shop or laboratory may keep him in mind in their
contacts with prospective employers. Some schools even have developed an after-employment follow-up scheme, which keeps the
former student in touch with the school and also helps the school
officials learn about the effects of their training. But there is no
room for complacency in the matter of job training and job opportunity. James B. Conant (1961) writes:

> In conclusion, let me repeat my sense of shock as I contemplate con-
> ditions in our big cities with respect to youth in slum neighborhoods. To
> improve the work of the slum schools requires an improvement in the
> lives of the families who inhabit these slums, but without a drastic change
> in the employment prospects for urban Negro youth, relatively little can
> be accomplished. I urge that our large-city problems be analyzed in
> far more detail than in the past and with a far greater degree of frank-
> ness. Neighborhood by neighborhood we need to know the facts, and
> when these facts indicate a dangerous social situation, the American
> people should be prepared to take drastic measures before it is too late.
> (p. 169).

Education and Government

In a discussion of the need for coordination between government
and education, Eldon L. Johnson (1955) writes the following.

. . . No evil flows from the separation of school and government when
they have no, or few, problems in common. But that time is past. The
barricades will have to come down, somehow. The trouble arises when
problems are common, but the attack is separate, if not, indeed, rival or
competitive or possessively exclusive. Common problems call for common solutions, although the co-operators need not in any sense lose their
identity. The evil of separation is the propensity to build rival power
structures and to thwart the emergence, recognition and service of the
community of interest. (p. 136).

Johnson cogently argues that there needs to be a more realistic appreciation of the schools as a related part of the public enterprises of
the community, for they are not a unique entity, existing apart.
He points out that it is a basic misconception to assume that school
boards and districts, being creatures of the state government, are
somehow fundamentally different from all other civil government at
the local level. Johnson contends that coordination will prove more
likely if school administrators are trained more realistically in the
political processes and the nature of "the public" and its controls. He
advocates graduate training in the social sciences for school administrators and hopes that acquaintance with these subjects "will
enable the superintendent to see the problems of youth and schools
as they spin in their specialized orbits, held in place by all the forces
of the community; in other words, to see the schools in the context
of the community." (p. 140)

Good school administrators are aware of the extent to which the
schools become part of the community political process. School
bond issues are a good case in point. John E. Horton and Wayne E.
Thompson (1962) studied voters in two upstate New York communities shortly after the communities voted on and defeated school-
bond proposals. They conclude that the school-bond issue was the
outlet people had for expressing their protest and feeling of powerlessness.

> 1. In both towns defeat of the school-bond proposal was associated
> with the increased turnout among persons of low income and educa-
> tion. . . .
> 2. Each campaign was pervaded by an atmosphere of controversy
> generalized beyond the specific issues and directed against the experts
> and the local leaders. . . .
> 3. During the period of community conflict there was the paradoxical
> phenomenon of heightened but often undirected power consciousness
> among persons in low positions, whose perspectives, a disposition to see

the world in a certain way, seemed to color their reactions to the issue and the direction and extent of their political action. (p. 488).

In such communities school programs become the victims of a general political situation (Beal, Hartman, Lagomarcino, 1968).

Meanwhile, teachers are doing what they can to teach civics and the ways in which local government operates, frequently taking their classes to various agencies of local government in this process. Although attitudes toward government and citizen participation may not actually be formed in school, much information on which future action will be based may be gained there.

Edgar Litt (1963) analyzed three communities with respect to the political themes found in civic education texts, the attitudes of community leaders, and the effects of courses upon student political attitudes. He assumed that one function of the school was that of indoctrinating the younger generation in the outlooks and values of the existing political order. But the indoctrination was not uniform among the three communities. Litt finds:

> . . . students in the three communities are being trained to play different political roles, and to respond to political phenomena in different ways. In the working-class community, where political involvement is low, the arena of civic education offers training in the basic democratic procedures without stressing political participation or the citizen's view of conflict and disagreement as indigenous to the political system. . . .
>
> In the lower middle-class school system of Beta—a community with moderately active political life—training in the elements of democratic government is supplemented by an emphasis on the responsibilities of citizenship, not on the dynamics of public decision-making.
>
> Only in the affluent and politically vibrant community (Alpha) are insights into political processes and functions of politics passed on to those who, judging from their socio-economic and political environment. will likely man those positions that involve them in influencing or making political decisions.

In the 1970's the programs of school desegregation which earlier faced the Southern communities are facing many Northern communities where there has been de facto segregation. The courts have consistently held that the school populations must be racially or ethnically mixed to conform to the ratios in the community at large. This has meant busing children from all-white or all-black schools to the other kind so that there will be a better racial mix (Jordan, 1974). Some communities, particularly selected neighborhoods of Boston, Massachusetts, have done all in their power to contravene the busing procedures. The rhetoric is all in favor of "the neighborhood school," and the hazards inherent in transporting young children long distances, especially into an unfriendly neighborhood. One approach being tested legally and practically is including the whole metropolitan region, not just the city limits of a statutory community, as the geographical base in terms of which busing patterns will be worked out. In this instance, suburban schools, not just the schools in the central city, would be involved in the efforts at desegregation.

Some Characteristics of the Educational Field

Supplementing and in some ways summarizing the pages just preceding, one might mention seven important characteristics of education which relate to the fate of its programs.

First, contrary to the situation in most countries, education in the United States is primarily supported by local property taxes. This makes people feel very close to the schools through their pocketbooks as well as through their children. Local taxes go up usually because of increased school expenditures, a fact duly noted by the local residents.

Second, many parents feel that the only area of their lives in which they can exercise some control is over local schools. Schools are near by; teachers, principals and superintendents are real people to whom one can talk for they are in the same community; extracurricular activities frequently involve the parents and are even dependent upon their assistance.

A third point, related to the second, is the differing expectations which various parents have about school outcomes. There seem to be class, income level, and ethnic group differences in these respects. With some parents, as we have noted, college attendance is a major goal for their children, while others wish an easy entry to a good job for their sons and daughters. In fact, one study (Collins, 1971) shows the importance of the conflict perspective in interpreting the struggle among various social strata to control the educational requirements for various kinds of jobs since in this way they can control social mobility.

The fact that a school district may cut across three or four "communities," or distinct neighborhoods, leads to a fourth consideration: namely, a mix of pupils who bring to the school the antagonisms or stereotypes built up about youngsters from neighborhoods other than their own. One school administrator told of having to deal with four overlapping neighborhoods, one of which was all-white where blacks were not allowed to linger and where a local resident was on duty at all times to protect the "integrity" of the neighborhood. When the principal drove on opening day to the school he was much impressed by the fact that this white neighborhood seemed to be much more spruced up than he had remembered it. However, when he got to the new school he understood why, for residents of that neighborhood had appropriated for their own yard many of the shrubs planted the day before in the school yard.

Five, a school system is often change-resistant. This is not just because teachers, trained in the past, feel comfortable with material and procedures that they know and thus hesitate to launch out into new areas of rapidly-expanding knowledge; it is also due in part to the unwillingness of many parents to see the school do things which are very different from that to which they were exposed in their own childhood. Herriott and Hodgkins (1969) summarize a study of the social context and the school as follows:

> . . . the reform of public schools in the less modern areas of America through local initiative is likely to be a very slow and sporadic process. . . . We expect that the greatest change . . . will come not from local, state, or federal initiative focused directly upon the schools, but rather from external forces that can modify the socio-cultural context in which these schools exist. (p. 163).

This stress upon the social context and the intrusion of external forces is in keeping the unbounded character of the social field as set forth by Kaufman and Wilkinson (1967).

The local educational system, to mention a sixth point, is often highly centralized in many phases of administration. The school superintendent and school board (or committee) speak for the system and their role will vary in keeping with the basic social traits of the community where they work (McCarty and Ramsey, 1971). This administrative unit interacts with the other decision-making units in the community, sometimes in a competitive, sometimes in a cooperative manner.

Finally, the educational field becomes ever more complex and crowded as, with more leisure, people begin to think of education as something that continues all during one's life, not ending with the completion of formal schooling. This accounts for the expansion of adult education activities, within and without the public school system. Libraries and museums seek to find their place, along with the schools, in supplying the demand.

Such a list could be continued at much greater length, but these points illustrate the divergent cross-cutting interests within and without the educational field.

20

Health and Welfare
Programs

THE HEALTH FIELD

Prominent in the organization field of any community are those programs designed to bring better health to its members. Earlier reference has been made to controversies which arise in some communities with the proposal to fluoridate the local water supplies (Chapter 16) and to four health programs that illustrate the nature of the social action field (Chapter 17). Here attention will be called to the various ways of looking at the health field in any community.

Health Subsystems

First, there is the system of private office practice, which the local medical association strongly defends. Characteristic of this is the belief in the almost sacred individuality and inviolability of the doctor-patient relationship. To some extent this inhibits the community activities of the physician.

In addition to being a member of a profession, the doctor, like the lawyer, has extraprofessional roles. Harry W. Martin (1957) studied these roles in a New England community of about 42,000 persons, where he interviewed 90 per cent of the physicians. Some of his findings are the following:

> The physicians averaged a total of eight memberships in all associations, a very high figure in comparison with other groups where data were available. Fifty per cent of these were professional affiliations.
>
> In the non-professional and non-religious groups to which they belonged the physicians held few offices unless the group had health interests, for then their specialized knowledge could be used. They are not generally expected to hold offices in associations not having health concerns. (pp. 14–15).
>
> Up until some fifteen years ago, non-Yankee physicians had been effectively excluded from the community's sole hospital, but even today the Yankee physicians—though outnumbered by the Irish, Jewish, French, Polish physicians—hold most of the key staff physicians. This pattern also prevails in the business and industrial life of the community. (p. 115).
>
> In this New England community some hypotheses might be made about the physicians' political behavior and sentiments: (1) Physicians have a high level of political interest and a low degree of active individual participation. (2) Induction into this high status profession re-inforces Republican Party sentiments and weakens Democratic Party allegiance. (3) Their perceptions of their professional role and the nature of politics limits direct participation in the frequently emotionally-laden area of partisan politics. (4) Physicians, unlike lawyers, are not expected by the community to participate in politics. (pp. 17–18).

This study also showed that the physicians' participation was affected by the beliefs that they were too busy to take part in community life, that "people can't depend on them in planning their programs," and that "it is unethical for a physician to appear to advertise, and he must not let his name or picture appear in the paper too frequently." Another aspect of the extraprofessional role is shown in this remark of a physician: "I can't go out and take part in the activities of these groups. The first thing I knew they would be calling me 'Doc' or by my first name, and when they need a doctor, they wouldn't think of me as one, and they would call in someone else." Thus, according to Martin, the physician may be compelled to behave in terms of his professional role even outside the professional context so that he will not be thought of as something less than a physician.

Group Health Care is a second type of medical subsystem. People, by virtue of employment or membership rights, have access to medical and other health services in facilities set up by factories, stores, business or governmental agencies, schools, labor unions, and the like.

Prepaid group practice (or third-party medicine), according to Dennis C. McElrath (1961), is a marked departure from traditional methods of distributing medical care to a community. It affects the classic relations between physicians and patients in that a collective element is introduced into the allocation process on the level of both physicians and patients. The practitioner in a prepaid health plan may become known as a "group doctor," which may mean that he is a deviant as far as the medical profession in his community or county is concerned. How he adjusts to this "deviance" and maintains his "professional character" is an interesting sociological phenomenon, which McElrath explores.

A current term for group health care is *health maintenance organization*, (HMO), which consists of prepaid members who receive total health care, ranging from diagnostic services, treatment in a doctor's office, to hospital and post-hospital care. The emphasis is upon prevention and early detection of health problems. The HMO is being viewed increasingly, even by those who opposed group health care in the past, as an important mode for delivery of health services, particularly prevention and outpatient care. It could bring about greater efficiency and economy of scale in providing the general population with comprehensive care. Federal legislation passed by the 93rd Congress provides aid to the HMO's.

The "world" of the hospitals, clinics, and other health agencies providing medical treatment is a third identifiable subsystem. Although medical professionals can move easily from office to hospital and back again, the shift by a patient from his home to the hospital calls for serious reorganization of roles. Many studies have been made of the hospital as a large-scale organization (Anderson and Warkov, 1961; Seeman and Evans, 1961), with some studies showing that the role of the hospital administrator has increased at the expense of the physicians who formerly ran the institution (Wilson, 1954). Other studies reveal the problems faced by those who wish to introduce innovations (Dykens, Hyde, Orzack, and York, 1964), especially when opposed by the least secure nurses. From the community standpoint, however, the financial support a hospital needs over and above its fees for service leads to public fund-raising drives or a search for private gifts.

This is why the constitution of the Hospital Board is so important to the success of the hospital in many communities.

A fourth subsystem revolves around the local health department, which will vary in size with the needs of the community and the available financial support. The structure of roles within public health differs from that in the other subsystems, since public-health officers seek to protect, administer, and perform services such as detection of health problems but not treatment of the individual patient. They may immunize to reduce incidence of disease; they try to educate the public on health matters, inspect dairies to protect the public against unsanitary conditions, visit work sites to enforce standards protecting the workers' health, and visit homes to check on communicable diseases. Their work is often unnoticed except in cases of serious health problems.

One of the problems faced by public-health workers is the incorporation of middle-class values into public-health goals, whereas the target groups are usually lower-status families. This may lead to apathetic response to public-health programs. Ozzie Simmons (1957) illustrates this by pointing out that for

> . . . middle-class people, cleanliness is not simply a matter of keeping clean but also an index to the morals and virtues of the individual. . . . Middle-class norms place great emphasis on the ability to defer gratifications in the interest of long-run goals. Readiness to sacrifice the present for some possible gain in the future may not be nearly so pervasive a pattern among lower status people, who may accord priority to immediate rewards.

Within any local department of health, there is a division of labor leading to differences in status, but it will be sufficient here to outline the six basic local public-health functions with the understanding that specialists with their own titles have charge of each function. Four of these functions, as described by Haven Emerson (1951) are as follows:

> The statistical function consists of the collection, verification, tabulation, analysis, interpretation, publication and practical use of the facts of birth, of certain notifiable diseases of communicable, occupational, nutritional, or other important categories, and of deaths.
> Control of communicable diseases is a second function. Diseases which spread from the sick to the well, directly or by intermediate means, carriers, insect and other vectors, or by contamination of foods and fluids used by man, are all, theoretically at least, preventable. . . . This was the first field of direct attack by health departments.

The third function of a local health department is to control conditions of the physical and biological environment of man. It includes the protection of the source, processing and distribution of water and foods, especially milk and milk products, against contamination or pollution; the disposal of man's personal and industrial wastes, insects, vermin, and animals capable of causing or spreading disease in the human being; the cleanliness of air; the occupancy of living and working quarters; the conditions of employment, particularly such as permit dusts, fumes, smoke and contact with irritating or poisonous materials in the course of manufacture. Concern with housing standards, with noise as an annoyance bearing upon rest and comfort, and with the abatement of public nuisances . . . accident prevention . . . fall within the scope of environmental sanitation. The public health or sanitary engineer is a professionally qualified associate of the medical officer of health. . . .

The fourth function . . . is the operation of the public health laboratory . . . [which offers] a wide variety of diagnostic and analytical tests of biological, chemical and physical character, serving the needs of physicians, the general public and the technical purposes of the various bureaus and divisions of the local department of health. . . . Most state laws require blood serological tests of applicants of marriage licenses and also of the expectant mother to make possible the easy prevention of marital and congenital syphilis. (p. 20–22).

The fifth function has to do with "maternity, infancy and child hygiene," considered broadly enough to cover "genetics, eugenics, marriage counseling, prenatal guidance and the whole range of bodily, mental and emotional growth and development of the child from birth until it has completed the years of required school attendance and enters upon self-support." The sixth function, which, like the fifth, has been more recently recognized as necessary, is that of public health education, which provides "program, plan and performance to promote by an informed and understanding public the development of healthful habits of living and a conscious desire to avoid preventable disease." (p. 22)

Dr. Emerson, long a student of public-health practice, points out that a population of not less than 50,000 is needed to give tax support to, and to justify, the employment of the 16 persons required to conduct a good local health department. These 16 include a medical health officer, educationally qualified; 10 public-health nurses (one for each 5000 people); a sanitary or public-health engineer; a nonprofessional assistant; and 3 clerks. He makes a strong plea for consolidation of local health jurisdiction so that more efficient service can be rendered, estimating that 1200 local health departments would satisfactorily cover the entire continental United States.

Allied with the official health departments in the public-health subsystem are a number of health associations that stress prevention and mass education. The local chapters of the National Tuberculosis Association seek to mobilize the community against respiratory ailments, relying on both board members and volunteers to widen the reach of the small professional staff. The same holds true for the associations directing their efforts against cancer, multiple sclerosis, musclar dystrophy, to mention but a few. Because of the extent of the problem and the availability of government funds, the establishment of local or county mental health associations has been one of the most notable accomplishments of the past few years.

Health Insurance Programs make up a fifth subsystem. The United States now has an interesting mix of governmental programs, such as Medicare and Medicaid, for those over 65, and private insurance plans promoted by salesmen representing important insurance firms. The move toward a national health insurance program, though legislated at the federal level, will have local community effects in the way it distributes funds to local health-related agencies, business and non-profit. (Colombotos, 1969)

The Business-Sponsored Health Subsystem may be seen as a sixth type. Since health is such an important concern of so many people, it is not surprising that some business firms concentrate on providing health products and covering the cost of health services. Pharmacy is semiprofessional in that the pharmacist must receive professional training and be licensed; at the same time, he serves as the business outlet for drugs dispensed according to physicians' prescriptions and for a variety of patent medicines requiring no prescriptions. Behind the druggist are the large drug firms spending millions of dollars annually on research in an effort to discover new ways to cure or alleviate different disease. These firms make an impact on the community not only through the products on the druggists' shelves but also because of the nationwide advertising that finds its way into every community.

The pharmacist, or druggist, tends to see his occupation as one of the medical-scientific occupations. However, it is a marginal occupation, since it seeks to incorporate the conflicting goals of business and profession. Although these cross-pressures of the business and professional worlds are not unique to pharmacy, they are particularly acute there. With the growth of large-scale retail enterprise, according to Thelma H. McCormack (1956) the businessman status of the pharmacist is threatened because of the growth of chain stores and other economic forces, so he turns to professionalization as a counteracting force. As a consequence, the training for a pharmacist has been lengthened to four years beyond high school and may even extend to five or six years in some states. In concluding her study, Dr. McCormack writes:

> The young pharmacist today is trained as a professional; his interests and ability for scientific research are carefully developed, preparing him for the laboratory work required by hospitals, schools and pharmaceutical companies. Yet few pharmacists see themselves in this position. Most expect to become proprietors, with the status of independent professionals, thus fusing the two systems and avoiding a final choice. In this process the entrepreneurial drive is modified by criticism of big business and by retreat from highly competitive circumstances; the professional drive is blunted by subordinating a service goal to individual achievement for its own sake. (p. 315).

Although the druggist's occupation is marginal—neither wholly a business nor yet a profession—it is an important link in the treatment of illness. He has a major responsibility as a check on the physician, who in the pressure of work occasionally makes an error in a prescription, which should be checked by the druggist.

Interaction Among the Health Agencies and Associations

Health as an *interest* field in the overall field of community action can be seen from the foregoing illustrations to be a complicated series of diverse groups ministering to health needs. (Levine and White, 1972) At times an individual in some official capacity, such as health officer, can make his influence felt. More often, however, individuals prefer to work through associations to accomplish some important objective. The county medical or dental associations, an organization of pharmacists, or a mental health association interact with official bodies such as the health board or a hospital board. Private groups often see issues differently from public bodies; those supported by contributions from the general public maintain different public relations postures from those agencies financed entirely from governmental funds disbursed from tax revenues. Furthermore, the interests of those who dispense health care in its varied forms are not necessarily identical with the concerns of those who receive this care. Nursing homes provide a notorious illustration of this gap.

As we turn to a brief look at welfare programs we see that they frequently interact with the health groups, and are often viewed by social scientists as sharing many sociological characteristics in common.

SOCIAL WELFARE PROGRAMS

Major Components of the Social-Welfare System

The chief unit of the system is the "agency," which can cover a wide variety of organizational patterns dealing with many different kinds of problems. The definition of a "welfare agency," not always the same in every community, may include the juvenile court and the YMCA, the Family Service Society and the Florence Crittenton Home for unmarried mothers, the county child-welfare department and a day camp for underprivileged children, the Travelers' Aid Society, the Salvation Army, and the Girl Scouts. All these units are staffed with professional people who think of themselves either as social workers or as closely allied to welfare work; each group has a board of directors, which determines policies for the agency; and each (unless heavily endowed) must depend on the public for funds, in the form of either taxation or contributions to some financial drive. Such organizations all seem to share the philosophy of rehabilitation and personal enrichment of those with whom they work and usually think of themselves as acting in behalf of the community as a whole in offering their services (Hasenfeld, 1972).

One type of agency does what is known as *casework*. Its staff members seek to help individuals overcome their personal, family, or employment problems through counseling and through providing physical resources when these seem an important aid in making the individual independent again. One pilot project designed to find out how dependence can best be dealt with in a community has been carried out by Community Research Associates, Inc., in Winona, Minnesota (Page, 1956). The county is populated by about 40,000 people, with about 25,000 of these living in the city of Winona, the county seat. Those in charge of the project set up a family center, to which all regular agencies reported family data they collected.

This center, with its staff of experienced professional caseworkers and other consultants, first surveyed the welfare needs of Winona County. It found that (1) out of every 1000 families in the county, 118 received services to meet health and welfare needs in the month of the initial study; (2) in the same year, $33.57 per capita were spent on these families requiring community help; (3) dependence was Winona's top-ranking community problem; (4) there was considerable overlap between dependence and indigent disability; and (5) dependence in Winona was due primarily not to industrial unemployment but to other factors such as an unusually large family with insufficient income to meet the important needs of all members.

In its effort to find out how problems of dependence can be controlled or reduced through rehabilitation and prevention, those conducting this study devised and tested seven different processes and precise tools as follows:

1. Defined goals, without which prevention planning cannot start and problems cannot be measured statistically
2. Community-wide reporting, which seeks to get comparable facts about the social problems from any agencies with diverse professional reporting systems
3. Family diagnosis, the key process in dealing with individual cases, under which data are structured in terms of the individual members of the family, key relationships between parents and between parents and children, and the identification of problems and factors affecting them
4. Treatment planning, based on the diagnosis, which specifies particular services needed and what agency should provide them, and identifies responsibility for integrating and coordinating the various services
5. Prognosis, or a prediction as to whether the family's problem status will improve, deteriorate, or not change
6. Evaluation, after a period of at least six months, as to the actual problem status to determine the correctness of the prediction
7. Redeploying staff, or having them concentrate on the cases that are the "best bets" for return to self-support or self-care

This project is especially significant in its stress on the seventh point, which leads to better utilization of skilled resources and assists in more recovery than would otherwise take place.

One feature of the casework approach is the preparation of a case record that puts in systematic form pertinent facts about a client's past and provides to the skilled interpreter an insight for current treatment. Much energy and time goes into the preparation of these case records, and this partially explains why such a social worker can only "carry" a small number of cases at any given time.

Another type of agency specializes in *group work*. The Boy Scouts and Girl Scouts and the YWCA and YMCA are illustrations of this type. These usually have national and international connections and frequently offer a program of activities that are for the most part determined outside the community. The executive directors of such agencies are considered by social workers as part of their number, although they may not be accepted into some of the professional social-work organizations if they have not had formal graduate training in social work. The essential skill of the group worker is to develop leaders, stimulate participation, maintain a circular response within the group, and constantly keep in mind what the group experience can mean to the individual member.

A third type of agency concerns itself with *community organization for social welfare*. Hertha Kraus (1948) makes seven important points about this area of social work:

> 1. Community organization in social work has developed in a democratic community as an expression of common responsibility for the sum total of all service units and their combined production on all levels of community life. It aims at an increasingly better balance between welfare needs and welfare resources. . . .
> 2. . . . The relationship of all agencies to each other within a given community, the agency's own internal relations with its goal of service, and the area of needs served and the actual output in service are an appropriate matter of concern and action within community organization.
> 3. Each community service agency requires recurring study and review of its service objectives. . . .
> 4. Social needs should be a determining factor initiating, continuing, modifying or terminating'a service program. . . .
> 5. In any classification of needs, the rank of each item will largely be dependent on the culture in which this classification has been developed, and may not necessarily fit another culture. It will also be strongly influenced by the point in time. . . .
> 6. All social needs can be met in a variety of ways. The selection of a certain pattern of response in the form of an organized service implies an important choice. . . . In selecting suitable service patterns choices must be made, among others, between providing a temporary or a more lasting solution; a preventive or a curative approach; a common provision for needs recurrent among considerable numbers of people, or an individualized response, to be produced on a case by case basis. . . .

7. Community organization as a process, and every one of its instrumentalities—the public and the voluntary service agencies—are subject to economic laws. They must recognize the principle of economy as basic to their production: the necessity to produce the greatest possible yield in return for a given investment. (pp. 54–56).

In order to carry out these ideas inherent in community organization for social welfare, different types of coordinating or planning councils are set up. They may bring together only those interested in children or may unite the so-called character-building agencies, or they may be large enough to encompass all kinds of agencies of whatever type. The Council for Social Planning or a community welfare council is the latter type, since it plans for groups involved in a community-chest or a united-community-services campaign and also seeks to draw into its committee work and deliberations representatives of the public agencies. Such councils also have executive directors who are trained social workers with a specialization in administration rather than in casework or group work.

In many communities also there is a social-service exchange where the names of individuals and families served in the past by various agencies are kept on file on a confidential basis. Thus, when a client approaches an agency for the first time, the agency can find out from this exchange what other agencies have had dealings with this client. Further coordination is worked out informally by social workers at their professional meetings, since these often provide the only opportunities they have to see each other on an unhurried basis.

The components of the social-welfare system need not be viewed only in terms of casework, group work, and community organization. A division is frequently made between public and private agencies. The public agency is tax-supported and thus restricted as to how its money can be spent; the private agencies theoretically have more flexibility in what they do with their money, but, if their funds are raised in a joint community campaign, the finance committee of the campaign organization may have much to say about how budgeted items may or may not be spent. Furthermore, the board members of a private agency may have quite fixed ideas as to how the program should operate, and may obstruct any deviation from past procedures. One characteristic feature of the public agency is the basic insecurity many social workers feel in their jobs unless a thoroughgoing system of civil service is in effect. It is a great temptation for a new state administration to try to use the child-welfare and parole-officer positions as rewards for those to whom they are indebted. The spoils system in politics, therefore, menaces the development of a highly competent and experienced personnel in public agencies, particularly when the general public assumes that anyone of good intent and a pleasing personality "can do social work," without realizing the complex nature of the task and the amount of training needed for successfully carrying it through.

In concluding this discussion of the components, it is well to remember that welfare activities even twenty years ago were becoming more and more bureaucratized. As Noel P. Gist and L. A. Halbert (1956) point out:

> A bureaucracy organized as a behavior system of statuses, roles and authority is commonly segmentalized into bureaus, departments, agencies, or divisions of one kind or another, depending on the size and functions of a particular organization. . . . If the central feature of bureaucracy is formal organization and a hierarchy of authority and status, within this framework, there is an informal organization in which relationships between personnel tend to be intimate. (p. 368).

And then these authors have this to say about welfare bureaucracies:

> Public welfare bureaucracies in the United States are rather tightly structured, with a complex hierarchy of functionaries in which the chain of administrative command stretches from the local organization to the state or national level in a gigantic social security system. Private welfare bureaucratic organizations tend to be loosely structured, at least as far as inter-organizational relationships are concerned, many of them being established on the federated principle. (p. 377).

Almost a decade ago a study (Aiken and Hage, 1966) of sixteen welfare and health organizations showed that both alienation from work and from expressive relations were found to be more pronounced in those organizations that were highly centralized and highly formalized. Such groups tended to restrict work freedom and the participation by the professional staff in helping set the goals of the organization.

SOCIAL PROCESSES AT WORK WITHIN THE WELFARE SYSTEM

Once a person has delineated the pattern of the welfare subsystem, he can observe how the social processes flow within that pattern. In other words, he can apply the type of analysis described in Chapter 2, identifying the cases of cooperation, competition, conflict, or accommodation. He does this, not by listening to the reports of the agency executives, who may not be entirely objective about their own agency, but by finding out how members of welfare groups interested in a common problem behave toward those in other groups when dealing with that problem.

Where the community has a social-planning or welfare council or a community-chest agency, or any body made up of representatives in the welfare field, a study of the accomplishments of such a body reveals much about the flow of these processes. How is action initiated? Who rallies to the cause? How is coordination achieved? What representatives (or groups) oppose or lose interest, and for what reasons? A series of questions designed to describe the playing of specific roles shows that the welfare work in any community is not merely a structural setup demanding money simply to keep itself standing still; it is a dynamic field of activity in which individuals, often as representatives of some recognized group, behave toward each other in ways that have frequently become traditional and even predictable.

No one is omniscient enough, even if predisposed to do so, to trace all of the behavior connected with welfare in any one community, since it may range all the way from a neighbor taking care of a sick person next door to a caseworker of the Family Service Society providing enough fuel to tide a family over until the sick breadwinner is able to get back on a job. But if a person uses the types of processes ordinarily treated by the sociologist, he will have a simple scheme for classifying the kinds of behavior that are observed. And, when this has been done, he can take an overall view of the community and reach some judgment as to the degree to which welfare activities are efficient or inefficient as gauged either by the professional standards of welfare workers themselves or by the expectations of the majority of people in the local community.

Cooperation

Cooperation implies that those involved in the interaction have common goals and the willingness to subordinate individual or narrow group interests for the achievement of a purpose or program greater than themselves. In classifying the instances of cooperation, one might use a twofold scheme: (1) those that are intended to avoid duplication and (2) those that combine action in a joint undertaking.

There are many ways in which duplication of effort is avoided. If, for instance, civic groups or church organizations are interested in distributing baskets to the poor at Christmas time, they usually check with the social workers about cases of genuine need and indicate the ones for which they will assume responsibility. Likewise, as already indicated, social workers cooperate in maintaining a social-service exchange where the names of all clients are confidentially filed and services reported. This avoids the possibility that two or more agencies may unknowingly be giving help to an indigent family at the same time. Duplication, however, may exist not only with respect to clients or recipients of welfare, since there may be serious duplication of services. Through cooperative discussion, a division of labor acceptable to all parties may be worked out, and the community may be provided with a wider range of welfare activities.

Sometimes community events concerned with welfare programs are scheduled on the same day or too closely together; willingness on the part of the interested groups to space the events at more appropriate times is an example of cooperation. An even more pressing need is that of timing fund campaigns so as not to overlap with those of other welfare groups, since a community can absorb just so many such drives before it is ready to react unfavorably to any and all drives.

Somewhat related to the matter of duplication is the practice of referral of a client from one social-work agency to another. This calls for cooperation between the two agencies, since the agency contacted first may not only pass on to the client the necessary information about the second agency but may also send the second agency whatever information it may have collected in its prior dealing with the client. By tone of voice or actual statement the representative of the first agency sets up in the client an expectation of favorable or unfavorable treatment that affects the success with which the second agency can treat the case.

Many instances of cooperation, however, do not relate primarily to the avoidance of duplication but rather to combined action in settling some pressing welfare problem. If juvenile delinquency is a major community concern, no one agency can claim to have all of the answers, nor can any one agency be given the blame. What is called for is an attack on the problem by all agencies having any conceivable contribution to make. Those best equipped to deal with some of the more important aspects of the problem may be given greater responsibility; yet all have some stake. Some communities rely almost automatically on joint action by groups interested in a social problem; in other communities, each organization continues to go its own way with little effort being made to join forces with other groups concerned with the problem.

Cooperation of this sort need not involve many groups, however. For a program dealing with a deeply rooted problem involving large numbers of people, the multiple approach is usually applied. Nevertheless, there are in every community innumerable examples of cooperation of two or three groups. This is not spectacular in nature or very broad in scope but does add greatly to the quality of community living. For example, the Boy Scouts may collect broken toys from the better residential districts, and the city firemen may repair these toys for later distribution by one or more social-work agencies to the poorer children of the community. The Travelers' Aid Society may find two young people at the railway station who need shelter but lack funds; the Salvation Army may agree to house them, and the Travelers' Aid Society may help them move on to their destination the following day. Such instances could be multiplied hundreds of times, indicating that there is much teamwork in the welfare field.

Competition

Not all welfare groups cooperate all of the time. They are frequently forced by the community situation to compete. This competition may center about four organizational activities: (1) financing, (2) recruiting board members, (3) obtaining clients, and (4) publicity.

1. *Financing.* Private agencies who are associated in a community-services organization must justify their budgets and their expenditures before the finance committee of such an overall group. In order to get additional funds for the following year, the Boy Scouts may have to try to convince the members of this committee that they deserve a greater increase than the YMCA, although the norms do not permit them publicly to comment adversely on another orga-

nization. A day nursery may try to show that its needs are greater than those of a community-supported milk fund for babies. Simply because of the financial mechanism that is set up for these privately supported agencies, each of them must often take a stand against the rest in order to persuade a committee to support its requests. Furthermore, the executives who are most successful in obtaining funds for their agencies often spend much time in keeping the finance committee well informed about the work of the agency so that when budget time does come the selling job is already half completed.

Public agencies, however, have their problems too. They must get appropriations from local fiscal courts or other local governmental agencies. For instance, if a reduction in the total welfare budget is to be made, should the greatest amount be taken from the local public child-welfare agency (such as the Children's Bureau), or should it be taken from the local recreation department? In which agency is money being spent most efficiently? Which is serving a greater community need? The mere asking of such questions makes the agencies involved realize that they are in a competitive position even though their programs have nothing in common and may touch entirely different groups of participants.

There are various other agencies that do not have any affiliation with local community chests and are not connected with local governmental budgets. They conduct individual drives and are in competition with all other welfare units in their search for contributions. Strategy and tactics of fund-raising campaigns are planned as carefully as those of an army going into battle, and diversionary moves by competitive agencies must be considered as possibilities with which to deal. Many rumors are set in motion in some communities about the unwise use of funds by a particular group, and competing agencies probably do not go out of their way to stop and contradict these rumors.

Thus, because welfare agencies have to get some of their funds—whether private contributions or appropriations from taxes—from the same community, they are of necessity placed in competition with each other. The greater the difficulty in raising quotas, the greater the competition is apt to be.

2. *Recruiting board members.* Agencies are also in competition for status and prestige. With private groups, in particular, the social standing of voluntary board members has something to do with the

way the agency is viewed by many of the substantial donors of the community. It often happens that some community residents who embody or symbolize many of the highest values are asked to serve on three, four, or more boards. Such people frequently have to make a choice in order to restrict their activities, thus favoring one or two groups above the others.

Even public agencies operate within the general framework of public commissions on which respected members of the community serve without pay. The individual abilities of these members, as well as their community standing, have much to do with the general approbation given by the community, since they, rather than the agency executive, make official interpretations of policy to the community. The persons most sought after are apt to be involved in other things; even so, agencies continue to compete for their services. The same holds true for leaders of fund-raising drives; the choice of one man may be a guaranty of success, while the choice of another may mean that the undertaking is handicapped from the beginning. Most of the leaders of the welfare groups are not always conscious of the existence of this type of competition, but their board members frequently are and tend to maintain a self-perpetuating board that comes to be viewed as a "clique" identified with that particular agency. This leads to competition between these "cliques," with one seeking to make a given welfare activity more fashionable in the community than that endorsed by a rival "clique."

3. *Obtaining clients.* It may at first seem strange that agencies set up to serve the needy would actually compete for clients. In order to justify budget requests, agency executives also have to show heavy case loads. This means more clients, even at the expense of competing with other groups also interested in the same clients. In the case of the character-building agencies, it may mean competition for the support of people to use their facilities or to join their youth groups.[1] Numbers and statistics, like primitive magic, still cast a charm over many uncritical people who seek to evaluate the accomplishments of any agency. More clients mean high statistics. Such competition is fortunately much less common than the other types, but it must be recognized as intrinsic within the welfare system of most communities (McKinlay, 1972).

---

[1] Strains between clergymen playing the role of counselor and social workers are cited in Elaine Cumming and Charles Harrington, "Clergyman as Counselor," *American Journal of Sociology,* 69 (November, 1963), 234–43.

4. *Publicity.* A fourth evident competition is that for space in the newspapers and time on radio and television. That agency that can tell its story throughout the year in carefully prepared news accounts or dramatic presentations over the air is apt to win the race for funds and board members with much greater ease. Some types of agencies are in a much better competitive position than others, since their activities lend themselves to a warm, human-interest appeal. Others deal with individuals who have made news by some personal misfortune or by some notorious action; agencies to which they are referred are possibly publicized and thereby indirectly thanked for assuming the burden of this problem case in behalf of the community.

Studies continue to show, however, that most social-welfare agencies do a very poor job of interpretation, and this is in part due to the fact that the system of welfare itself is in a disadvantaged position when trying to compete with other systems for the attention of mass media.

Conflict

Social agencies are human instruments as are any other organizations and reflect in their behavior the personality or other differences that develop among their functionaries. In almost every community with diversified social agencies, one can find instances of conflict among some of these agencies. It may originate in friction between the boards of two of these agencies and the refusal of one board, for what it considers good reasons, to accede to a request of the other. The conflict may grow out of personality differences between the respective directors, who may have a low opinion of the professional competence of the members of another board or who may feel that some wrong has never been righted. The reasons for conflict are numerous, and the official explanation is not necessarily the real reason. Anyone who wishes to work intelligently within the social-welfare system of the community needs to know where such strains and stresses exist, in order to avoid being drawn into a partisan fight that would seriously affect the program in which one is interested.

Accommodation

But conflict does get resolved. The passage of time often dims the dispute, or the good graces of some interceding third party may be secured. In any case, those who have been involved in conflict work out a modus vivendi without necessarily yielding in principle. As a result, the clients receive better service, and the community is not plagued by a division that carries over into nonwelfare activities as well. Just how accommodation comes about will depend on the organization of the welfare system and the hierarchy of statuses it possesses, as well as on the personalities of those who fill some of the key statuses. Too few social workers, who spend hours trying to figure out the complex interpersonal relationships of their clients, ever take time to see the network of social relationships in which they are involved and how strains can be eased through the accommodative process.

Sol Levine and Paul E. White (1961) have studied the interaction among health and welfare agencies in several cities. They use exchange as a conceptual framework, defining "exchange" as any voluntary activity between two organizations that has consequences, actual or anticipated, for the realization of their respective goals or objectives. But exchange involves the idea of scarcity, as the earlier discussion of competition among agencies has brought out. The three elements, according to these writers, that organizations need and for which they must enter into exchange are (1) clients, (2) labor services, and (3) other resources. Whether any particular agencies in the community enter into exchange is contingent on three related factors: (1) the accessibility of each organization to necessary elements from outside the health or welfare system, (2) the objectives of the organization and the particular functions to which it allocates the elements it controls, and (3) the degree to which domain consensus exists among the various organizations. We shall discuss in Chapter 19 this matter of domain consensus, or agreement as to where one agency takes up and another leaves off. Such agencies stake out claims for themselves with respect to (1) a need to be met, (2) population served, and (3) services rendered. Exchange agreements rest on prior consensus regarding domain.

THE SOCIAL CONTROL OF PHILANTHROPY

The discussion of the welfare system thus far has implied that its control is in the hands of the professional staffs and the agency boards of directors. There is also a community dimension that must not be overlooked. Aileen D. Ross (1953) in describing the city-wide campaigns of Wellsville, an eastern Canadian city, shows how the most influential people of the community exercise control over the welfare activities in much the same way as the inner core of doctors guides the fortunes of the individuals in the system of public health and medical care. Anyone interested in the mechanics of control and in the statements of those interviewed should refer to Ross's original article, which concludes as follows:

> The controls supporting philanthropy in Wellsville now form a well-established system. This means that, although powerful positive sanctions now induce people to participate in philanthropy, there are also corresponding devices for resisting them when they are resented. Some of the controls of philanthropy are almost universally accepted. Indeed, little conscious thought has been given by most interviewees as to why they actually *did* participate in philanthropic activity.
>
> In Wellsville members of the inner circle may decide the success of a campaign by sponsoring it or withholding sponsorship from it. This is equivalent to saying that they can decide which campaigns shall be held and for what objective. They can control the success of a campaign through the size of their own or company donations of money. They can control the personnel of any campaign through sponsoring individual participants or withholding sponsorship from them. They can control the amount of money raised in any campaign through granting or withholding permission to canvass employees in any corporation which they direct. And yet their total position was never clearly stated or recognized by those participating in leading positions in the different city-wide campaigns, nor were the implications of this control clear to the majority of them. (p. 460).

Yet, the importance of the individual giver, even though his contribution is relatively small, cannot be overemphasized. Voluntary contributions, for example, provide major support to 64 per cent of the nation's colleges and universities, 51 per cent of its hospitals, 18 per cent of its major museums, virtually all its symphony orchestras, and all its religious institutions. Thousands of local agencies throughout the country that are concerned with recreational programs, care of the elderly, family service, and civic betterment are maintained with private funds. Donations are made to such national organizations as the Boy Scouts and Girl Scouts, the 4-H Clubs, the Red Cross, the YMCA, the YWCA, and the YMHA, as well as organizations devoted to the conquest of disease—the American Heart Association, the American Cancer Society, and others. In 1973, voluntary giving in America totaled about $20 billion.

In 1971 the United Way of America in 2,230 local campaigns raised $865 million, up 3 per cent over 1970, and topped $915 million in 1972. Contributions to 21 national health agencies rose from $312 million in 1970 to $335 in 1971, up 7.5 per cent.[4]

Governmental expenditures in traditional fields of philanthropy —education, health, and social welfare—are growing, but so is private giving for the public good. This does not take into account the time that over 50 million citizens contribute to voluntary agencies in their communities.

THE INTERORGANIZATIONAL FIELD

The discussion so far has centered around the kinds of economic and social programs and agencies which "populate" the social field of a community. Attention has just been called to some of the interactions among health and welfare agencies. Suppose, however, that we were to go to nine cities and look at six important organizations and their interconnections. But, even more, suppose that the six we picked were *community decision organizations* "legitimated for making decisions and/or taking action on behalf of the community in specific sectors of concern." That is what Warren, Rose and Bergunder (1974) did. They selected some of the organizations which have been included in this and the preceding chapters: model cities agency, the community action agency (OEO Program), public school system administration, health and welfare planning council, urban renewal agency, and mental health planning agency. Their main purpose was to get an understanding of the model cities program, but realized that such a program did not exist in isolation but had to be understood with reference to the interorganizational field.

One of their chief findings is that there is a common institutional thought structure, including norms and goals, which those manning these community decision organizations share. Each organization has its own legitimation and is expected by others to make certain decisions affecting its interest; there is also more agreement than conflict over organizational domain, or the sphere of activity to

---

[3] Sources: Council for Financial Aid to Education; American Hospital Association; American Association of Museums; American Symphony Orchestra League.

[4] *Americana Yearbook*, 1973, p. 534.

[5] Ford Foundation, *American Philanthropic Foundations* (New York: 1964), pp. 2–3.

which a given group can lay claim. These common norms and beliefs lead to a placidity in the interorganizational field and much less contact than one might at first assume.

Of the limited interaction that did take place the pair of agencies that were in contact most frequently were the model cities agency and the school system administration; next most frequent was contact between the model cities agency and the community action agency; followed by that between the community action agency and the school administration (p. 40). The writers indicate that the stability of the interorganizational field is maintained by preventing, blunting, and repelling actual or potential threats to the structure of the field.

A brief reference to this study cannot hope to convey the richness of its insights nor the wealth of data which it has presented. It shows in a concrete way the value of viewing the community as an interorganizational field.

21

Community Development

The community as a field of interaction contains approaches to planned change which go beyond the specific programs discussed in the preceding chapters. Suppose economic, educational, health, welfare and similar programs were combined into one overall effort to improve a particular community. Two terms have been used in the past to describe these comprehensive programs: community organization and community development.

COMMUNITY ORGANIZATION

Community organization has at least three well-defined meanings whose understanding will tell us much about the nature of planned change at the local level.

Community organization as social structure. Just as each generation inherits the physical community (streets, houses, public facilities) and the values and belief systems from the prior generation, so it inherits a social organization, which at the community level we can call community organization. This includes the mechanisms (sets of social relationships) set up to deal with recurring problems or to meet basic needs (family, religion, and the like). The particular constellation of such arrangements, including all formal groups as well as informal patterns of mutual aid, is sometimes referred to as community organization; it is the way a community is *organized*

445

to carry out the usual and exceptional aspects of daily life. Such an organizational structure comes into being over a long period of time, is a part of the traditional heritage, and in its totality was unplanned. Thus, in looking at any community a sociologist might very well begin with a description of its social organization.

Community Organization as Coordination

The experience that most Americans have with community development is through club projects—women's clubs, men's service groups, and many other types of associations. Some organization with which they are connected decides singlehandedly or in conjunction with other groups to undertake some enterprise for the community. As a matter of fact, it is hard for an association in many American communities to consider itself wide-awake unless it has one or more communities involved in some activity of a constructive or philanthropic nature. One way of viewing community development would be to think of it as the totality of all of these sporadic projects, occurring over a given period of time, which fire away at problems of the aged, juvenile delinquency, relief to the poor, more support to the schools, or commemoration of some historic event. But these widely diversified activities, when uncoordinated, temporarily alleviate the problem without moving toward any long-run solution. Most of the problems are too big for any one organization to handle alone, and only through concerted, community-wide efforts can some of them be effectively dealt with.

The Community Council. It is correct to speak of community organization—as far as club projects are concerned—when some formal body such as a community council has been set up to keep each organization informed about what others are doing, to plan for unmet needs, and to combine resources when this seems to be the best approach. A community council comes into existence in any one of the following several ways.

1. Representatives of all interested organizations come together to work out means of avoiding duplication or otherwise to make the efforts of their organizations in community development more fruitful

2. Representatives of different neighborhoods, various professional and occupational interests may be called together to provide a cross-section of opinion and a bulwark of support for those that have current community programs underway; and

3. A combination of organization representatives and citizens at large, who speak for segments not ordinarily involved in the types of organizations sending spokesmen, may unite in a council.

The mistake is sometimes made of giving this community council the right to dictate, though gently, to member organizations as to what they should or should not do in the way of community activities. Community councils tend to last much longer, however, if they serve as a clearing-house of information and as a place where those groups who want to cooperate can do so without any overall authority telling them that they must do so.

To many people, especially in the social work profession, community organization refers primarily to the coordination of already existing health and welfare organizations into a more efficient "delivery system."[1] In this arrangement representatives meet regularly in a Council to discuss mutual problems and to develop ways of avoiding duplication of effort, of finding better staff, publicity, and the use of voluneers. The representatives who attend the meetings of the Planning Council often "jockey" in behalf of their organization, but they nevertheless become familiar with what other groups are doing. Coordination, however, is achieved in ways other than discussion of problems, or in program planning. Budgeting becomes very important when organizations are requested to make financial reports on the basis of which they are or are not included in the annual United Way, or annual fund-raising drive.

Some communities make use of a President's Council, which consists of the presidents of the major civic and service clubs, who meet to inform each other about projects being sponsored and to discuss which groups might develop projects to meet some new need that has arisen or become recognized. This mild form of coordination can have its uses.

A helpful discussion of citizen participation in community organization is provided by F. Stuart Chapin, Jr. (1947), who uses the following figures to show the difference between unorganized and coordinated community development activities. In Figure 21–1 every group is on its own, each trying perhaps conscientiously to do a good job but wasting much energy and resources in the process. In Figure 21–2 coordination takes place first among those in sim-

---

[1] See the section on *community organization for social welfare* in the preceding chapter.

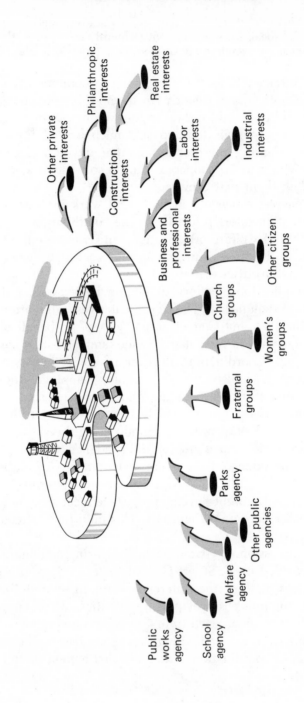

Figure 21-1. Unorganized community development activities. *Source:* F. Stuart Chapin, Jr., "A Plan for Citizen Participation in Community Development," *Social Forces* 25 (March, 1947), pp. 314–15.

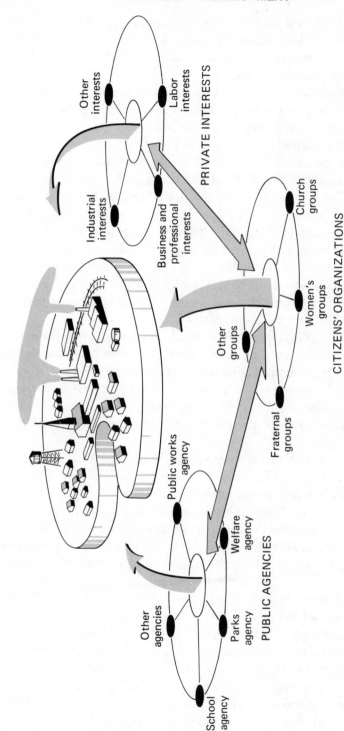

Figure 21-2. Coordinated community development activities. *Source:* same as Figure 21-1.

ilar areas of interest and then occurs again at a higher or more inclusive level. Chapin goes into a depth of detail not possible here about organizational procedures as he indicates how this coordination can be achieved and maintained.

Many people have discovered that the community approach is an effective approach in the furtherance of some campaign or organizational program. They "organize" the community. This has been done to such an extent by state and national organizations that some of the local leaders feel that they are being "used" to serve outsiders' interests and not those of the community. One man put it this way: "The representative of the State Health Department came around to ask if I would serve as a member of a Community Health Advisory Committee. I agreed. Then we began to have meetings every month or six weeks, and the representative would spend the whole time telling us about the work of the department and what we were supposed to do to help its program in this community. He never asked us what we thought ought to be done or how it ought to be done, but kept telling us instead."

This same individual also recounted how many organizations to raise money for national programs sent specialists in to assure that all segments of the community were being represented in the drive so that a good showing could be made. According to him, the community was being organized to take money out of the community, not to bring money into the community or to realize objectives of the local people.

This is an aspect of the problem of horizontal and vertical coordination that Roland L. Warren (1956) has so well described. "As the schools, churches, social agencies, business establishments and other community facilities multiply and differentiate, there is need for keeping these facilities in some sort of adequate coordination with respect to each other. This coordinating function can be performed within the community, along the *horizontal axis*, through the community welfare council or various types of local planning agencies." (p. 9) Or the coordination can be carried out at what he calls "the supercommunity level." This brings in the *vertical axis*. "Thus the national organization of the labor union, the Red Cross, the Methodist Church or a state department of education can lay down rules and procedures for the structure and function governing its particular community association or agency, thus fitting the community organization into the vertical system of local members, local units, district, regional, state and national organization, and in this way the

efforts can be coordinated along the vertical axis of common interest." (p. 9)

Warren then indicates that many of the organizations in the
supercommunity may or may not be good "citizens" of the communities where they have representative groups:

> The conflict between vertical and horizontal axes of orientation is no-
> where more readily apparent in our communities today than in the two
> competing systems of fund-raising for health and welfare. I am referring,
> of course, to the all-inclusive community chest campaign, on the one
> hand, and the special fund-raising campaigns, particularly of the various
> health groups, on the other. Here is the horizontal orientation of agen-
> cies getting together for fund-raising on a locality basis, and the vertical
> orientation of state and national organizations reaching into the local
> community through their individualized, task-oriented branches, to carry
> on fund-raising activities in little relation to what this adds up to on the
> local community level. (p. 7).

The implications of this state of affairs are clear: At the very time
when more horizontal coordination is needed because of the increasing complexity of fund-raising, it becomes more difficult to
achieve in the face of the vertical coordination which is being
forced upon local groups. The representatives of the supercommunity, such as the official of the State Health Department mentioned at the beginning of this section, may already think they "have
all the answers" before they come into the community; they may be
paternalistic, but they are also—if successful—a disruptive force in
the community. On the other hand, the local community coordinator is permissive; a nonspecialist "whose chief concern is with what
happens to the interrelated parts of the community in planning,
coordinating and changing." (p. 11) Such a person is more interested in the process, in what happens to the people than in a
particular program to be "sold."

The importance of the local community as an area for problem-
solving is heightened by such moves as revenue-sharing, which
operates on the premise that local authorities are in better position to
determine what needs to be done about local problems than the
officials in the government bureaus in Washington.

In 1972 the federal administration announced the revenue-sharing plan, under which 38,000 state, county, city, town and village
governments around the country were given money from the central
treasury. Each had to decide how it chose to spend the amount.
One account in *The Boston Globe* follows.

The tiny farm community (Taopi, Minn.), which has a population of 59, is one of about two dozen villages around the United States which draw the minimum revenue-sharing payment allowed by law. (New York City receives over $198 million, Taopi $194) . . .

Under the revenue-sharing law communities have a wide range of options to choose from when they come to decide what to do with their money.

The Treasury Department, which runs the program, has listed eight "priority expenditure areas" in which the recipients can spend revenue sharing money. They are health, recreation, library, social services, environmental protection, law enforcement, rapid transit, and financial administration . . .

Taopi, Minnesota, decided after a meeting of its four-man village council to get the cemetery mowed and the mayor added: "With all this money coming in, we may even be able to build sidewalks now."

Two limitations of the revenue-sharing plan have been pointed out since it started to operate. One is that the federal government may cut out some funding of programs already being operated in local communities on the ground that these can be funded out of the revenue-sharing resources if local people consider them important enough. This would, of course, mean that the purpose of bringing additional funds, over and above ongoing programs, would be thwarted and in the long run leave local communities short-changed. A second question about the revenue-sharing procedure is the reluctance of local officials to use the funds for any kind of program that really introduces changes in the status quo, because in the past federal agencies have often "attached strings" to the sums made available. If a local government wanted these financial resources it had to accept the necessary accommodations (for example, employment of the groups being discriminated against, etc.).

Despite these limitations, it is true that leaders of local communities have had much experience in dealing with varied social and economic problems, some recurring and some appearing only once in a while. The discussion of how they achieve certain kinds of results, often termed "progress" by those involved, can be described as community development.

Community Organization as Community Development

In the 1920's, in the wake of World War I, there was a noticeable "community organization movement" throughout much of the United

States. It was an effort at community improvement through the more rational use of available resources; it was also designed to maintain the momentum of citizen participation which wartime co-operation had generated.

By the late 1940's the ups and downs of this movement had caused sociologists to be more cautious about its potentials for problem-solving. Hayes (1949) sagely advised:

> Community organization is a means of collective action to achieve some end or purpose assumed to be worth while. Community, then, refers to people who identify themselves with a particular local area and with purposes and actions to control or develop their collective life and interest. Therefore, the community must know itself and know its values and interests if it is to bring about balanced and satisfactory living conditions. It must be this in spite of internal differentiation, stratification and mobility of persons and groups. Therefore, for the best interests of the community, it is not sufficient for conditions to be known to a few experts who "devise and sell" the citizens on a program which is good for them. The community must not only know what purpose it wishes to achieve, but it must understand how organization and what organization will serve to achieve the purpose. More important still the community must know the nature of the situation in which it finds itself in order to develop feasible and fundamentally desirable ends. If it enthusiastically embraces the rosy and fantastic proposals of misguided reformers, it may become disillusioned and cynical. If it passively submits to this and that suggestion of its paid professional servants, it will find itself in a confused and defeated state. (p. 5).

In the 1950's a number of social scientists and educators formed the American Council on the Community, a relatively short-lived organization whose purpose was to institutionalize the scattered efforts throughout the country to improve American community life. This, too, reflected the experience during World War II when millions of Americans participated in volunteer efforts and organized to deal with local problems.

This also was the time when United Nations agencies and the technical assistance programs of the developed countries sought to help the "developing nations" move along the road to "modernization." Community development became one of the vehicles for attempting this transformation. The term received such wide international usage that it came to displace "community organization" even in the United States. Programs to help the impoverished areas of Appalachia or large metropolitan centers were legislated into existence and were labeled either as Community Development or

Rural Development in the statutes. The essential feature was resource mobilization (people as well as material possessions) at the community level so as to introduce a new quality of life. It went beyond the coordination discussed above to a new kind of stock-taking by local residents, the help of outside consultants in interpreting the facts collected and in planning programs to meet the needs that were identified. This is one case where we can better understand the logic and the reality of what was happening in the United States when we relate it to community development in other countries.

COMMUNITY DEVELOPMENT

In the 1960's over sixty countries either had well-formulated national community development programs or were in the process of bringing them into existence. Although the interest in this approach to raising rural living standards has begun to wane or to be redefined, any student of community life should be familiar with this significant focus upon localities on every continent. Many sources can provide fuller documentation of these national programs, but here we will mention four points: the appeal of community development, some of its basic principles, various interpretations of community development, and some of the lessons learned.

The Appeal of Community Development

Leaders of nations in Africa, Central and South America, and Asia after World War II faced tremendous tasks of nation building. Some of this came about because former colonies gained their political independence; in other countries, long independent, decisions were made to bring about economic and social development, hopefully to reduce the differences between their own standard of living and that in Western Europe and the United States and Canada.

Faced with large-scale problems and relatively inadequate resources, national leaders embraced the idea of mobilizing local people to carry out community projects. The Community Development Programme of India, for instance, was set up to aid the inhabitants of 558,000 villages attain a higher social and material level of well-being. The program was based on the idea of self-help. Multi-purpose village level workers, especially trained for this new role, met with the villagers, helped them recognize their needs and potentialities, and then assisted in bringing the technical, financial and moral backing to meet these needs. The technical assistance was given by specialists in agriculture, roadbuilding, irrigation, education, health and sanitation, rural cooperatives, etc. who were transferred from their regular government agencies (Ministry of Agriculture, for example) to the Community Development Programme. The basic unit was the block, which consisted of 100 villages.

Other countries, of course, worked out the kind of community development programs best fitted to their needs, but a key element was that of guided self-help and the contributed labor of local people on projects that they thought important. Any compensation for the labor was often turned over by the outside funding agency to the community authorities rather than to the individuals so that other projects could thereby be financed.

These community development programs were often fitted into national five-year or ten-year plans to assure the allocation of sufficient resources to these efforts at the "grass-roots" level. To many national leaders such programs seemed a way toward democratization and decentralization of the political process; they gave local people a feeling of being involved in nation-building and showed that the central government was actually beginning to show an interest in their welfare.

Principles of Community Development

In an effort to promote the systematic study and practice of community development, many people have drawn up series of what they have termed "principles," on the valid assumption that one does not transfer an actual experience from one country to another but rather the principles which that experience reinforced or demonstrated. The United Nations, in a Report on Concepts and Principles of Community Development, set forth ten such principles. These are listed here not because they comprise a final, definitive, or necessarily the best list, but because they illustrate the type of thinking that one finds in the community development field. Remember that these are supposedly applicable to most parts of the world and were not formulated to deal with just a particular community in South Dakota or Ohio.

*Ten Principles Stated in the UN Report on Concepts and Principles as
Reported by the Secretary-General, 12 March 1957*

Principle 1: Activities undertaken must correspond to the basic needs
of the community; the first projects should be initiated in response to the
expressed needs of people.

Principle 2: Local improvements may be achieved through unrelated
efforts in each substantive field; however, full and balanced community
development requires concerted action and the establishment of multi-
purpose programmes.

Principle 3: Changed attitudes in people are as important as the
material achievements of community projects during the initial stages
of development.

Principle 4: Community development aims at increased and better
participation of the people in community affairs, revitalization of existing forms of local government and transition towards effective local administration where it is not yet functioning.

Principle 5: The identification, encouragement and training of local
leadership should be a basic objective in any programme.

Principle 6: Greater reliance on the participation of women and youth
in community development projects invigorates development programmes,
establishes them on a wide basis and secures long-range expansion.

Principle 7: To be fully effective, communities' self-help projects require both intensive and extensive assistance from the Government.

Principle 8: Implementation of a community development programme on a national scale requires: adoption of consistent policies, specific administrative arrangements, recruitment and training of personnel,
mobilization of local and national resources and organization of research,
experimentation and evaluation.

Principle 9: The resources of voluntary non-governmental organizations should be fully utilized in community development programmes
at the local, national and international levels.

Principle 10: Economic and social progress at the local level necessitates parallel development on a wider national scale.[2]

These principles, looked at one by one, reveal many of the basic
tenets of those who work professionally in community development
programs. They have learned that a program cannot be imposed arbitrarily but, if it is to take root, must be thought necessary locally. Sometimes the community development worker over
a period of time sets in motion the process whereby people learn

[2] United Nations Economic and Social Council, *Report on Concepts and Principles
of Community Development and Recommendations on Further Practical Measures
To Be Taken by International Organizations* (New York: 1957), p. 13. Mimeographed. These are summarized from an earlier UN report, entitled *Social Progress
Through Community Development* (New York: 1955).

to feel that something is necessary Many Americans may find the stress on government help, as expressed in Principle 7, too strong, but they would probably be equally surprised to learn how much help actually comes into their local community from state and Federal sources. Nevertheless, the genius of community development as defined and carried out in the United States is the emphasis it gives to the nongovernmental aspects of the program. In a country so rich in economic resources and trained leadership, the private, voluntary approach is feasible; whereas in many underdeveloped countries, much time will have to elapse before physical and human resources are sufficiently developed to the point where the government can assume a more minor role.

At the present time much of the thinking, both nationally and internationally, in community development is so *diffuse,* with so many new experiments and approaches being tried that no one has satisfactorily sifted the evidence to formulate and then demonstrate through controlled experimentation the fundamental hypotheses involved in planned community change. The Community Development approach is more and more being used in urban areas. There are many statements, many "principles," many case studies, but as yet little validated social science theory. This represents a challenge to anyone interested in pushing back the frontiers of knowledge and systematizing the accumulated facts about community development—its nature, its operational principles, its successful techniques, the part played by the factors of the setting.

Various Interpretations of Community Development

A term which describes programs in so many countries and for so many purposes is bound to mean different things to different people. Figure 21–3 characterizes four ways in which community development has been viewed. Some think of it as a process in which the main emphasis is upon what happens to the people and their development; some think of it as a method or a very useful approach to accomplish some important goal such as improved agricultural productivity; some think of it as a program which embodies a set of activities to be carried out by officials, specialists and local people in some time sequence and at budgeted costs; and some view it as a movement with strong emotional commitments—a crusade to make life better for everyone.

1. As a Process

CD as a process moves by stages from one condition or state to the next. It involves a progression of changes in terms of specified criteria. A neutral, scientific term, subject to fairly precise definition and measurement; expressed chiefly in social relations; e.g., change from condition where one or two people or a small elite within or without local community make decision for rest of the people to condition where people *themselves* make these decisions about matters of common concern; from state of minimum to one of maximum cooperation; from condition where few participate to one where many participate; from condition where all resources and specialists come from outside to one where local people make most use of their own resources, etc. Emphasis is upon what happens to *people*—socially and psychologically.

2. As a Method

(Process and Objective)

CD is a means to an end; a way of working so that some goal is attained. Other methods (such as change by decree or fiat; change by use of differential rewards; change by education) may be supplementary to the CD method which seeks to carry through the stages suggested under *process* in order that the will of those using this method (national government, private welfare agency, or local people themselves) may be carried out. The process is guided for a particular purpose which may prove "harmful" or "helpful" to the local community, depending upon the goal in view and the criteria of the one passing judgment. Emphasis is upon some *end*.

3. As a Program

(Method and Content)

The method is stated as a set of procedures and the content as a list of activities. By carrying out the procedures, the activities are supposedly accomplsihed. When the program is highly formalized, as in many five-year plans, the focus tends to be upon the program rather than upon what is happening to the people involved in the program.

It is as a *program* that CD comes into contact with subject-matter specialties such as health, welfare, agriculture, industry, recreation.

Emphasis is upon *activities*.

4. As a Movement

(Program and an Emotional Dynamic)

CD is a crusade, a cause to which people become committed. Not neutral (like process) but carries an emotional charge; one is either for it or against it.

It is dedicated to *progress*, a philosophic and not a scientific concept, since progress must be viewed with reference to values and goals which differ under different political and social systems.

CD as a movement tends to become institutionalized, building up its own organizational structure, accepted procedures, and professional practitioners.

Stresses and promotes the *idea* of community development.

Figure 21–3. Four ways of viewing community development.

Some Lessons Learned About Community Development

India, which for a decade or so placed great reliance in a national community development program, has shifted to other emphases while still trying to apply some of the program's better features in its drive toward rural improvement. The same fate has befallen several other national programs. This, however, does not negate the idea that certain kinds of activities can be carried out effectively in local communities through guided self-help and participation by the residents to be affected by these activities. Yet, crucial weaknesses can be found in some of the national programs.

The first weakness is the fact that many of the technical specialists who were assigned to work in community development programs maintained their basic loyalty to the bureaucracy best serving their career interests. If they were in agriculture or in public health, they realized that they would have to maintain strong contacts within the Ministry of Agriculture or the Ministry of Public Health even though it might mean some diversion of time and sympathy from the community development program. Many did not believe in the comprehensive approach which sought to tie into one package for a local community a program which drew upon several specialties simultaneously in a coordinated manner. They were accustomed for each professional field to have its own agency and representatives in rural areas, with each field having its own program not always geared in with what other government agencies were doing.

A second problem came with the selection and training of community development workers. They were expected to be a generalist in the more traditional technical fields, but to be a specialist in "working with people." They understood group processes, individual motivation, the local social organization, the way to analyze recurring problems, and where to obtain needed outside technical help. The problem then was not with the concept, but rather in the task of trying to find thousands of people who could quickly move into a new professional role that had not previously existed in the country before. In addition, each community development worker at the local level had to know how to get along with superiors who were primarily administering a program but who might not have a very clear insight into the nature of village life or the rationale for certain demands made by local people.

A third problem developed when national leaders tried to politicize the program. When national elections were held, there was a temptation for some leaders to expect community development workers to influence votes in favor of those then in power. Where this occurred, political opponents, upon coming to power, dismantled the community development program or gave it quite a different complexion. Local people became cynical as they realized that what was supposedly to be in their own interests turned out to be a political tool for outside politicians.

Finally, the realization grew that many problems being undertaken at the local level really had to be approached at a regional level. One village might try to improve its irrigation system but this proved ineffectual unless neighboring villages using the same water source also did what they were supposed to do. Furthermore, providing material resources (fertilizer, inoculations, textbooks, etc.) could not be done on an individual village basis, but had to be set up so as to serve many villages in the same region. It did prove useful from time to time to have one village competing with another to see which one could more quickly achieve certain targeted goals, but such competition sometimes turned to conflict, thereby causing much difficulty for district and regional officials.

When we turn to lessons learned from attempts at community development in the United States we find some of the same factors at work: a social program initiated by one of the major political parties is discarded or quickly phased out when the other political party comes into power. The Great Society of one president was succeeded by the New Federalism of another and this in turn has given way to other means of dispensing federal funds to help meet local needs. In other words, political considerations do enter into community development. Furthermore, in the community as a field of social action coordination is often difficult to achieve since each health group, hospital board, chamber of commerce, labor union, religious denomination, neighborhood association has its own goals which it does not want to see endangered or submerged in any comprehensive plan for community improvement.

As our discussion of various programs in earlier chapters has shown, we still have much to learn about the nature of planned social change. We cannot begin to anticipate all of the consequences for an action program launched with great enthusiasm, nor do we know how to sustain such programs long enough to bring about concrete, announced results. There is agreement that every community could be made a much more attractive place in which to live, physically and socially. There is also agreement that many problems cannot be solved by decision-makers in Washington or the state capital; nor can there be long-term solutions if only a few people in a community decide for the rest who are uninvolved. The development of a community comes about best when social relations are developed to the point that the participants have a broader conception of local social life and how their own activities and groups relate to others. In some ways, it means experiencing the community at a deeper level of knowledge and feeling.

VI

CONCLUSION

22

Paradigms, Profiles
and Participation

Three different paradigms, or ways of organizing concepts about the community, have served as the organizing principle of this book. To fail to list any one of them would have reflected only incompletely the contemporary state of community sociology. In this the concluding chapter we compare the three paradigms, pointing out that one paradigm can be used for a particular purpose and another paradigm for a different purpose. In order to review for the reader the main emphasis of each approach, we will cite a community study illustrating that paradigm. Then, we will turn to a recently conducted community profile and show how within a single study each paradigm illuminated certain community characteristics which others might have missed. Finally, in the last section we return to the theme of the first chapter—namely, the sense of community—to point out that theorizing about the community, or even studying it at first-hand is not the same as participating in its life as a concerned citizen. This raises the question of the connection between theory and practice, between research and involvement, between prescribing and participating.

THE THREE PARADIGMS COMPARED

Three observations should be made before we turn to the brief comparison of the paradigms.

1. As stated in Chapter 2, all three are within the interactional framework. The social system is conceived by most theoriests attracted to that perspective as a system of interacting units and much attention is paid to the ways in which these units are prepared for and guided in this interaction. Likewise, the conflict approach is basically one in which interaction is seen chiefly as antagonistic, with much of it being exploitative. But the essence of conflict is that some groups are behaving toward other groups; they are interacting. The same holds true for those who see the community as a field of social action. Though some of the adherents of this approach may claim the concept of interaction as their own, they do not have exclusive theoretical jurisdiction over it. To summarize, underlying the three paradigms and their seeming divergences is the simple fact that social interaction is a basic concept and knowing more about it sheds additional light on each of the three approaches.

2. Interdependence is a second reality that the three paradigms share in common. This is implied in social interaction, which is processual in emphasis; but out of this social behavior of groups toward each other there develop certain structures which tend to persist through time. These structures may be institutionalized in class, caste, employer-employee, or other terms, but they do exist in every community. They, in fact, give a predictability to community life. So it is by no mere chance that a possible subtitle of this book —Locality and Interdependence—would stress the continuing relationships of some segments or units of the community toward each other. Interdependence, it goes without saying, is an essential feature of social systems; it also characterizes the social order which social conflict theorists view and for whom they design programs to overcome and even upset the interdependence they and other people do not find to their liking. Even in the interorganizational field, there is a fluctuating interdependence which can be tabulated in terms of the number of contacts one agency has with another and the assistance that the agency can count upon from other groups if a particular group is to discharge its overall community responsibilities.

Without in any way suggesting that the three paradigms not only present different perspectives as well as ardent proponents, we can conclude that there are general considerations even more basic than a single approach. Describing the social interaction in a given living space and pointing out the interdependence of various groups and institutional complexes within that space is the major sociological undertaking. Emphases and labels, terms and examples may vary with the ideological or philosophical bent of the investigator, but such an ordering of social data according to a predetermined scheme more congenial to the investigator does not in itself change the nature of social reality.

3. This, of course, suggests that in the comparison to be made below we are not trying to determine which approach is best in general, which one is true and which ones are false, which one is right and which ones are wrong. Each paradigm has its inadequacies, but each also has its utility for certain kinds of research problems. A community sociologist, though more attracted to one paradigm than others because its theoretical stance more closely approximates his way of viewing a society or a community, may nevertheless use other paradigms when they serve his purpose. Before illustrating this with concrete cases we can perhaps review a few of the points brought out about the paradigms in the separate chapters (7, 12, 17) devoted specifically to them.

For one thing, the basic assumptions of each approach tend to differ. The purpose, of course, is to gain an understanding of the community, to see it as part of the real world. We have noted that looking at the community *as if* it were a social system stresses the totality of the social interaction; seeing it in conflict terms emphasizes antagonistic relationships, structural inequalities and differential allocation; defining it as a field of social interaction stresses process much more than structure, fluidity more than a stable order.

Each set of assumptions does lead toward a certain predictability. The social system approach highlights the local institutional order and the organized patterns in these inherited social mechanisms; the conflict approach predicts the maintenance of the status quo until there is a redistribution of power to the point that those who now have only residual power move into central positions of influence and control; whereas the social field theorists are busy deriving principles about interorganizational behavior as an expression of community needs and associating such behavior with variables such as size of membership, type of constituent, power patterns, and group purposes. In all three cases, the search for understanding of community behavior is a search for basic clues to help one interpret predictable outcomes as well as signs for changes in the offing.

The three approaches do differ considerably in their efforts to delimit the community as a space and as a concept. One feature of the social system analysis is "boundary maintenance," or the requirement that those in one system know where its limits are with reference to other interacting systems. Much attention, according to social system theory, should be given to the demarcation of boundaries, recognizing their tendency to shift through time, but important at any given point in time in specifying the arena of interaction. Having such boundaries makes it possible to talk about change within the system in contrast to exogenous changes forced upon it from outside.

Conflict theorists are less concerned with the problem of boundaries, although most of them frequently refer to the unit they are describing (be it a community or a society) as a system. Their focus is upon specific problem areas of the community (which illustrate the assumptions they set forth) and upon situations which they think must be changed if the normative community they have in mind is to be achieved.

A major difference between the social field theorist and the social system proponent lies in this matter of domain. To the former, the community as a social field is unbounded; to try to set limits is self-defeating because the patterns of interaction change so quickly with the coming and going of participating groups that the primary responsibility is to concentrate upon the core groups in the interaction and study the peripheral groups as they become germane to the aspect of the interaction being studied. The social system theorist argues back that he is not saying that the community, with fixed boundaries at a given point in time, *is* a system but that it can be viewed *as if* it were for heuristic purposes, thereby providing a much larger and richer analytical framework than that obtained in the field approach. Yet, confusion becomes greater when we find some of the more important advocates of the social field perspective speaking of the community as a social system, but indicating that they are looking at only one part of major interest to them—namely, certain kinds of *social actions* or *interorganizational complexes*.

The three approaches can also be contrasted in terms of the treatment of the fact of change. The tendency, though not exclusively so, in describing the community as if it were a social system is to think chiefly in terms of adaptive change, of modifications that will help the system persist through time and its various parts to operate as expected. The conflict theorists see change as in the order of things, following certain sequences through which social contradictions will be resolved; the powerful if unjust will be displaced by those better able to serve the public good, the wealthy exploiters will be subdued by the exploited. This goes beyond mere adaptation of the system to various stimuli; it requires basic modifications of the system itself.

The social field analysis treats social change as purposive, not automatic. Through carefully formulated programs carried out with a wise sense of strategy, those who wish to accomplish something in and/or for the community are able to achieve planned goals. Planned change is more congenial to this perspective, although the field theorists are ready to recognize the intervention of unplanned variables in any organizational field.

One could, of course, devote much more attention to these general statements about the three paradigms. More helpful, however, is the specific instance of where and how a given paradigm was used, as well as the reasons why it was chosen.

THREE COMMUNITY STUDIES

The Social System Model

In the spring of 1965 social scientists at the University of Illinois (Summers, Hough, Scott, Folse, 1969) learned that the Jones-Laughlin Steel Corporation planned to develop a major production complex in the Hennepin area of Putnam County, Illinois. They thought that this would provide an excellent opportunity to test various theories of urbanization and industrialization by describing the area sociologically before the plant was begun and then after its completion.

The first task was that of deciding what kind of study to do to and what kind of theoretical scheme to use. They chose the structural-functional (social systems) framework for the following reasons:

> First, the structural-functional orientation is well adapted to the need to establish relative integration of a number of studies being conducted from different social science discipline perspectives. This integrative function can be performed by structural-functional theory through the provision of a consistent, logical taxonomy which brings some semblance

of order to the diverse and specialized investigations that will be developed within the project.

Second, the Rural Industrial Development Project was developed with the idea that the location of a huge industrial plant in a relatively rural area would lead to changes throughout the social and economic life of the area. Structural-functional theory is particularly well adapted to the tracing out of possible interrelationships between different segments of society through which changes would take place . . .

Third, the taxonomy of structural-functional theory is used in selecting and categorizing the secondary data available on different aspects of the area. (p. 5).

The primary focus of the study was on social relationships and interaction, with the demographic, ecological, cultural and personality factors being part of the environment within which the social system operates. Great care was taken to provide as much data as possible on these background factors. Only in this way could one get a picture of the system adapting to and even seeking to modify its environment. The investigators make it clear that they do not mean to "reify" the system, or treat it as though it were a single comprehensive unit with a "mind" of its own. Instead, the interaction between the system and the setting factors "takes place through myriads of separate decisions and actions as individuals make decisions about proper ways to relate to environmental factors in the context of their social setting." (p. 6)

It was acknowledged at the outset that the "system" being studied here was not a single, small rural community because the influence of the new industrial installation would affect a much wider area. They then recognized that the application of the "community system" model to "an area that includes a number of small rural communities, several former mining communities, and a few urbanized industrial areas" might be considered problematical. Yet, it seemed clear that these small community systems, lying in close proximity to each other, were interdependent in the sense that they all would be changed by the new industrial establishment, and would perhaps become more interdependent with increased industrialization. The same kinds of components found in the single small community could be found in the larger "system" analyzed here. At the same time, the research team recognized the haziness of the boundaries of their system and the possible effect of changes imposed by the larger society. They saw this, however, as the kind of problem one faces in applying any paradigm to an actual, empirical situation and still felt that the structural-functional approach was best for their purposes.

As one would expect, a major concern of their study was the description of the economic system because this was the component that would be most visibly and directly affected. In their analysis, each economic subsystem was characterized and related to other economic subsystems. But then they moved from the economic sphere to the other aspects of the system, particularly the inter-relationships among the economic, educational, and governmental systems.

Here we have a "benchmark" against which to view various social changes which can be attributed to the forthcoming indus-trialization. The social system paradigm provided, as already in-dicated, a taxonomy for the kinds of interrelationships discovered and described; it helped—like any theoretical scheme—to introduce some order into the data. It dealt chiefly with the components of the system, while recognizing the operations through which the connections among the varied units of the system were maintained —though these operations were not covered in detail.

To bring the story of this study up-to-date, one should mention a series of reports that have been prepared by the research team. One is titled "Problems and Challenged Faced by Rural Com-munities with Industrial Development" (Scott and Summers, 1972) and another "Profile Change When Industry Moves into a Rural Area" (Scott, 1973).

In should be clear from the above that one advantage of the social systems approach is its comprehensiveness, since no iden-tifiable social structure is purposely excluded from the system but can be assigned a place within it. This is particularly important in preparing a "before" and "after" picture since the first account must cover as many areas as possible because one cannot predict accurately in advance just which features of the system will be found to be most critical or important in the follow-up study. To have done the earlier study from a very narrow perspective will either (1) cause the later study to conform to such a perspective even though the facts would seem to dictate a broader schema or else (2) omit altogether items which are really relevant to the problem being analyzed but which have not been perceived. The obvious disadvantage, of course, is the heavy requirement of time and money if one is to carry out an all-embracing study.

The Conflict Paradigm

Alvin H. Scaff, in studying change agencies in "Medium City" (1974), recognized at the outset the dilemma in choosing between the Durkheimian view that "conceives of the city as a community of increasingly specialized parts that are interrelated so as to support and maintain the whole" and the other tradition of Robert E. Park which emphasizes the conflict between the multiplicity of interests in the city and Max Weber's emphasis upon the "dialectical processes of change which transform the social structure of cities."

He chose the conflict or second model, though recognizing the need to keep one's mind open about the values inherent in the other model. His line of argument was the following:

> By choice and by logical necessity the study of change agencies in Medium City meant that the city be viewed in terms of its diverse and conflicting elements. The concept of change implies that there is an existing condition with its defending bodies and other bodies that want to make changes. If efforts to make changes become active they must be organized, and if organized, then change agencies must exist. On this assumption we looked for change agencies in Medium City. Along the same line of logic we assumed that efforts to make changes would produce conflict, not necessarily violent conflict but conflict that would be observable and definable.

The city he studied had a population of about 150,000, many of whom had come into this southern city from the north and east; it is diversified with respect to business and industry; it is one-third black and two-thirds white. Public schools are fully integrated; housing neighborhoods are segregated, but there are no slums in the usual sense.

The research team, including twenty-one students and the supervising professor, first identified those action groups, agencies, or organizations whose purposes were to bring about changes in Medium City. In order to qualify an agency:

> had to have a stated purpose to change some existing condition in the community
> have some recognizable organization, an identity in the community, and an active program for change
> had to aim the change at the community, not individuals separately. This meant changes in the interrelated institutions, laws, rules, ordinances, codes, regulations, and culturally patterned behavior that structures the work and common life of the people in the city.

The search for qualified agencies turned up twenty-three, of which ten were selected for more intensive study according to organization, leadership, membership, dominant interests, opposition, conflict, tactics, and results.

Two sharply different kinds of change agencies appear. One type fits the mold of established institutional agencies:

> These agencies receive wide community support; they are dominated by professionally trained personnel; their objectives are reformist—to keep the institutions of society functioning better—and their tactical style disavows open conflict and friction.

The second type emerges from disestablished poverty elements in the community:

> . . . mostly blacks, whose low class position excludes them from access to the privileges and opportunities enjoyed by others. As they formulate and state their wants for jobs and housing and their claims for fair wages and more adequate welfare payments, they clash with constituted authorities of the community. They challenge the power structure, which, acting defensively, eliminates the means of support for these agencies and brings their life to an end.

Scaff makes use of Dahrendorf's formulation (See Chapter 12) in distinguishing between the two kinds of agencies: one group has access to authority which it serves, while the other group or type lies outside the bounds of constituted authority and challenges that authority. The Durkheimian (social system) tradition helps one understand how the first type tries to keep the establishment in a healthier tradition; but the Marxian-Dahrendorf model of class conflict helps clarify the differences between the two types of agencies. This is because the effort to change the community outside the bounds of constituted authority is class-based, but from the lower class. "Any change for the better from that viewpoint means a change in the exercise of authority. Pressure to bring this about unavoidably produces conflict."

This research group uncovered less conflict than they had expected but in looking for conflict found the reason why it was so low: "Most of the change agencies studied were middle class-based and their tactics were to avoid conflict in order to persuade authorities to accept reforms."

If the team had relied only upon the social system model it would not have been in position to make such a firm statement about the small amount of conflict. By looking for it in the beginning they could identify its existence or lack. The conflict model also provided a rationale to explain the absence of extensive conflict as well as an analysis of what would have to happen if major structural change were ever to occur in Medium City.

The Social Field Paradigm

As was noted in Chapter 17, there are variations of the social field paradigm. One looks upon individuals as actors within the field; another considers groups, organizations, or agencies as the actors. Common to both, however, is the concept of the social field, the question of linkages, and the various processes of interaction.

An illustration in which individuals are seen as social actors is found in one study of community field structure, based on data collected about action programs over a five-year period in two communities of about 20,000 population each. (Wilkinson, 1974). One topic investigated dealt with behavioral indicators of connections among actions in the local society. The raw data from which interfield dynamics are inferred are acts of individuals. These acts are "amassed, sorted, classified and examined." They are then seen as "fitting into projects and episodes, and these into fields of action concerning specific interests and goals."

In order to understand an individual's performance (or role) in the action program, his acts were classified according to a five-phase model, which expresses at what stage he became involved. The five phases are awareness, organization, decision, resource mobilization, and resource allocation. In this particular study, roles were identified for 68 actors in one community and 61 in the other, with a count being made of the number of phases of a program any one individual participated in.

The purpose of the analysis reported here was to study significant interfield linkages. This was done by seeing to what extent an actor's roles linked programs and interest fields. Some actors play roles primarily within a single interest field, such as health; others link across interest lines, such as between health and industry, and thereby have a broader scope of activity in terms of their community role. The study of these two communities identified nine such interest fields.

The idea of scope also includes the type of role an actor might play in multiple programs. Does he do so as a generalist, pursuing multiple interests, or as a specialist who plays much the same role in any program in which he is involved? This paradigm gives us insights into community life, such as the following:

> . . . The behavior of generalized actors provides the basic structure of the community field. The more-generalized, highly influential of these actors play roles which appear to be essential to the existence of the kind of multi-interest field of central concern to the study of community interaction. They are the individuals who likely exert a variety of types of influence in a succession of action programs and whose persistence of appearance in major community efforts and on major public issues provides much of the continuity of local interfield structure. Less generalized actors probably provide fewer and less influential links among programs and thus make less diffuse contributions to interfield connectedness. (253–254).

The study reported here admittedly deals only with one aspect of the community field: namely, how the field becomes structured by those who play multi-interest, generalized roles. Yet it does illustrate how this approach differs in its conceptualization, the data collected, and the questions asked from either the social system or conflict paradigms. There is no effort to describe the parts of a system for the field is viewed as emergent with the interests being identified empirically from the observed actions of the participating individuals. The social field, like the social system, does have a concern for the process by which structuring occurs and linkages are maintained. Unlike the conflict approach, patterns of cooperation (linkages) are more central to the community field approach in which conflict can be viewed as disruptive to and even at times fatal to a particular field being described. The community can be seen as the sum total of the intended, conscious, identifiable acts of individuals. Since one cannot study all inhabitants in most communities, part of the strategy in a social field study is the method of determining just what actors should be embraced in the sample covered. The emphasis in the field approach may be on process, not necessarily upon change. Building a recreation center definitely constitutes an action program, it involves various actors playing certain roles, but it does not inevitably lead to the kind of structural change which is of interest to many conflict theorists.

If one were to designate social groups or agencies as the actors in the social field, then many other studies could be cited. Since each would tend to deal with a slightly different aspect of the field, it would highlight the complexity of this approach.

THE COMMUNITY SOCIAL PROFILE

Though many studies of American communities tend to follow one of the paradigms mentioned above, some are eclectic in that they combine two or more of the approaches in the investigation of a single locality. The Community Social Profile is an illustration of this reliance upon two or three conceptual frameworks.

Basically, the Profile is a description of the basic social traits of the community (Sanders, 1960). It is based on the assumption that, though all American communities have many traits in common, each community has its own individuality, its own combination of traits which distinguish it from other communities nearby. Another feature is the reliance upon a reconnaisance methodology which makes it possible for five or six researchers to spend a week or so interviewing a carefully chosen sample of local people and then, on the basis of the interviews and available documentary and census information, write up the community profile.

A recently completed study of a New England community of just under 200,000 can illustrate the importance of having more than one theoretical perspective when preparing a profile with a minimum of research expenditure. In order to arrive at a comprehensive view of the community, though no one topic is actually explored in great depth, local people are asked a number of questions, whose answers reveal their perceptions of how things get done in the community. The more involved they are in the matters on which they report, the greater the details they provide. When the combined perceptions are put together topic by topic a social portrait of the community emerges which is much richer in texture and interpretation than that held by any single informant, but which admittedly does not pretend to be the exhaustive study which would result if a research team spent a year or more looking into every conceivable social relationship that might be uncovered. Only those community traits for which there seems to be convincing evidence are included in the profile; what makes the evidence convincing is the fact that it stands the test of examination from more than one theoretical approach.

The Social System Perspective

When viewed as a social system the New England city seemed to have great social stability. Through the years it has maintained a relative isolation, pursuing its own autonomy even to the point of seeing that a major high speed thruway did not come very near "because that would bring a number of undesirable people in." The stability depended as well upon several "old" families, each generation of which felt a strong sense of community responsibility and endowed museums, institutions of higher education, music associations, youth centers, and even welfare organizations. Moreover, as a city whose economy has been centered around metal industries, no one company dominated the local scene. Most companies up until recently have been locally owned, thus sharing the same fate as the community and interested in its welfare. Large numbers of immigrants have arrived during the past hundred years, and continue to do so, but they had no problem in submitting to the paternalism which prevailed in employment, in the church, and in other local institutions. Each group tended to maintain its own ethnic enclave and there was no attempt to combine forces in a working class movement. Consequently, labor unions are relatively weak.

Moreover, religious bodies have tended to avoid major competition and conflict, preferring to stress ecumenicalism. Cooperation is the preferred and accepted way of conducting religious affairs locally. Changes which have occurred in local government have provided a city manager (Plan E) who can deal directly with the major business and industrial leaders in order to get things done, although there is implicit recognition that any changes in governmental policy must be determined by the city council chaired by a "weak" mayor more ceremonial than administrative in function.

A relatively few leaders, easily identified by any well-informed citizen, are involved in all major decisions affecting the community. In fact, it is stated authoritatively that unless these ten or eleven people agree to a proposal it is not likely to go through. Needless to say, the tendency is to maintain traditional stability except when some reform must be made to prevent any major conflict situation from arising. Stability is further guaranteed by the interlocking directorates of the industrial concerns, the banks, the insurance companies, the universities, welfare and hospital boards, and the redevelopment and housing authorities.

This picture of the community as a stable social system is one that is largely accepted by a number of those in the more affluent classes. This would probably be the picture we would portray in the profile if we only viewed the community in terms of the social system paradigm for what is most striking is the degree to which this community has maintained its own identity and perpetuated flourishing local cultural and other institutions in the face of a rapidly changing American society.

The Conflict Perspective

When we began to ask about antagonistic, problem-causing relationships within the community we added a new dimension to our analysis. We found, for instance, that a few thousand Spanish-speaking people had come into the community and were not assimilating into its daily life in the same way that other migrants had in years past. We also found that there were some questions about continuing stability for the following reasons: (1) some of the outstanding leaders are becoming increasingly less active because of advancing age and will not be replaced by others with their wealth, knowledge of the community, and spirit of public service; (2) a managerial-professional class is becoming much more numerous as outside conglomerates buy up the local industries and send in non-local people to manage them. Furthermore, the community is becoming a magnet to increased medical personnel, who bring with them life styles that may not correspond with the traditional values; (3) there is also a shift from emphasis on industry to business, with the businessmen—those in commerce—wanting to have more of a say in local affairs. Bankers remain an influential broker group between the two; (4) citizen unrest in local government is increasing, much of it at the time of the study centering around the re-evaluation of property which had the effect of raising taxes for the homeowner at a stiffer rate than for business or industry. The schools were also becoming a focus for conflict, particularly over increased school costs which are attributed to an expanded educational bureaucracy. There is even a movement, just getting off the ground, to do away with the city manager form of government in favor of a strong mayor-city council elected on the basis of wards. This would mean that a councilman or councilwoman would be accountable to a definite geographical constituency and not to the "powers-that-be," as one person put it.

Furthermore, a study of the relatively small black community showed that the blacks whom the white community leaders thought representative of this minority were almost unknown in that community. They faced a number of discriminatory practices all too common in American society but which they felt had not been recognized sufficiently by the community leadership.

The community was also facing some unanticipated results of urban redevelopment, one of these being the atrophy of the businesses along the main street. This is blamed on the building of an attractive shopping mall not far away which had attracted outside business chains who were competing far too successfully with locally-owned stores and services.

The field work and the brevity of time spent in the community do not provide a satisfactory answer to the question of whether these unsettling features will actually lead to structural change or whether the traditional stability will be maintained with a minimum of adaptation to changing demands. Suffice it to say, unless the research team had been sensitized to look for the conflict potentials some of the facts stated above might not have been as fully documented. At this stage class conflict does not seem to be very marked, although the community does reflect some of the changes occurring in American society as a whole. This was borne out in the study of attitudes toward welfare, unemployment compensation, and public assistance employment.

The Social Field

The liveliest area of interaction in the community was that among agencies. This was most noteworthy in the social welfare field. The traditional system had accommodated to the existence of and competition within bounds of the United Way, the Catholic Charities, and the Jewish Welfare Fund. Money is no longer available to support these in the style to which they have become accustomed or to meet the new kinds of demands being made upon them. What has greatly changed the picture, however, is the coming in of state and federal agencies with large sums for the asking. The War on Poverty, the Housing Act, the Urban Redevelopment Act are only a few of those which have modified both the physical and social landscape of the community. A central problem being considered at the time of the study was the possibility of setting up a Social Welfare Corporation through which public agencies would receive funds due them and then contract with the private agencies to supply some of the services needed, thus in effect putting public funds into private agencies and requiring fewer private contributions to keep these traditional agencies financially viable.

Without necessarily going into great detail, one can show that the perspective which views these private and public agencies in the same social interactional field provides the most meaningful interpretation of their behavior. This involves the study of goals, leadership, clientele, images in the community and competitive advantages over each other. Each has a recognized function, each seeks to stake out and protect a legitimate domain, and—as was shown in the discussion of the social field above—there are important linking personalities who help maintain a kind of structure of the field.

When one adds to welfare and physical planning areas the educational system and the recreational structures, one find a complex array of actors, each claiming its share of public attention.

The community also has depended upon local initiative for improving the quality of community life and for meeting certain problems which can be dealt with by limited resources. This whole approach may be in jeopardy as greater reliance is placed upon governmental programs and as disadvantaged groups demand services which the more traditional methods cannot easily provide.

This fleeting glimpse into some of the characteristics of a single New England city is an inadequate representation of what the full community social profile contains. However, sufficient traits have been indicated here to show that the more limited the methodology used the greater the need for one or more theoretical perspectives. Reliance on only one approach would stultify the effort to reveal the distinguishing characteristics of the community.

Such a profile raises of course a number of interesting questions which can be stated as hypotheses and subjected to later testing. The more precise one becomes in terms of a very few such hypotheses then the more limited one's perspective can become. The hypotheses reveal the nature of the assumptions being used and define the variables to be investigated and correlated. That is a different kind of research effort than the quick reconnaissance into which many crosschecks must be built. To understand community life we need both kinds of studies: those that delve deeply into well-defined aspects in an effort to test hypotheses and add to our theory of the community and those that try to give an overview so that local people get a better idea of the perceptions of their fellow citizens and can think more constructively about ways of dealing with problems which are recognized differentially by various social segments. Cross-community comparisons are essential in both of these kinds of community studies. And it would not be surprising if the three paradigms elaborated in this book are all used to advantage in these research undertakings.

PARTICIPATING IN THE COMMUNITY

The paradigms and the community social profile just described relate to the *understanding* of the community; they deal with the cognitive element. A sense of community, dealt with in Chapter 1, involves more than *knowing;* it also involves *feeling* or *experiencing.* In fact, there is an emotional as well as an intellectual aspect to community life. The alienation which writers from Marx on down have analyzed at great length grows from a lack of participation in or feeling a part of the local or national society. Only a few readers of this book will play the sociological role which calls for community analysis; but many readers will play the participant role of active involvement in community affairs.

Not only does an individual know something about his living space; he or she also feels positively, or negatively, or apathetically toward it. This is because one's numerous experiences, occurring day by day, reinforce the perceptions gained in applying personal assumptions, biases and values as to what a community ought to be. Far too often in our study of social phenomena we deal with the cognitive, or knowing, aspect but overlook the deep-rooted emotional overtones tied in with what we know. Such realities are brought forcibly to one's attention in the heat of community controversies: school busing to overcome racial segregation, fluoridation of the public water supply, content of school textbooks or the disputed books in a public library; treatment of those considered deviant locally; and a strike by public employees. Emotions run much more deeply than anyone anticipated; the real issue becomes clouded over with side-issues centering upon the personalities of the contestants; and what is often described as "a nasty mood" descends upon the town.

An emotional pitch can run the other way too. Community members can mobilize to deal constructively with some problem needing immediate attention and gain a rich sense of satisfaction in their accomplishment. But such emotional fervor cannot be maintained for long.

There are two ways, not always easily distinguishable, in which individuals *experience* their communities. One is as a recipient and the other is as a participant.

As a Recipient

Many community residents are recipients rather than participants in local life. First of all, they view the community as a service center and their feelings about it are closely tied in with their assessment of how well these services are provided. Some of these are, of course, institutional: religious, educational, governmental. The quality of family life is also institutional. Other services are primarily economic: the business-centered establishments which provide goods and services and the professional cadre of doctors, dentists, lawyers, and others who deal with patients or "clients" rather than "customers."

A second assessment is made of the community as a place. What it looks like; how easy it is to get from one part of town to another either with mass transportation or by private car; how the streets, trees, parks and other facilities are maintained; and the extent to which planning and zoning is controlling the spread of residential and business uses in the interest of a more aesthetic environment. One's feelings about the community also relate to the quality of the air and water, since all residents share these as recipients.

The more mobile the population, the greater the likelihood that its impressions will be formed as recipients since it takes time to develop into the participant role. Just the same, there will be a feeling of shame or pride, or a mixture of the two. Those from a community or a neighborhood with a less desirable name will often mention the name of a better place close by when asked where they are from. Or, they may use the place name of the larger metropolitan area, thereby avoiding the identification with a specific place which they consider stigmatized. We do not yet know enough about the factors which lead to this pride and shame because some of the communities with seemingly the greatest pride are often those that impress outsiders with their lack of services, their unimpressive housing, and rundown public facilities. On the contrary, in some of the communities with the most expensive houses, churches and schools one finds a feeling of distrust and bitterness toward community leaders and even one's neighbors which, though not to be characterized as shame, is certainly far removed from local pride.

As recipients, local residents do make a contribution that must be recognized. They provide purchasing power that maintains local businesses, they pay local taxes that underwrite governmental services, and they form a part of that nebulous public opinion that has to be taken into account in the formulation of any major change in community life. As recipients, they are inclined to vote on an issue only if it affects them very closely.

As a Participant

In the discussion of the community as an interactional field (Chapter 17) much attention was given to the extent of local participation. Although the majority of people belong to some local organization, such as a church, labor union, service club relatively few are involved in the decisions which are continually being made by the leaders supposedly in behalf of the community.

The affiliation with even one organization should not be minimized, however, since most of these groups carry out some function not only for their members but for the community as a whole, though the wider contribution is often quite modest. The participants are those, therefore, who run the groups that keep the community operating as a social system (if one uses that approach to the community) or those groups (if one is a conflict theorist) that exist to try to reduce local inequalities, antagonisms or to change the system drastically. It is also as participants in groups that community residents become a part of the field of social action, in which programs are carried through or stymied, as the case may be.

Of course, many of the community organizations considered most basic to social life are staffed by professionally-trained personnel, but these are dependent to a great degree upon the volunteer participants who serve on the agency boards without compensation or who perform a variety of tasks on an unpaid basis. The distinction between lay and professional workers becomes acute when the latter question the qualification of the former to carry out certain duties; it may even become quite blurred at the lower ranks of the professional staff.

Participants in community life usually go beyond their membership role in groups; they are also good communicators. As earlier discussion has shown (Chapter 10), communication of information and ideas is essential for effective and satisfying social life. The information conveyed helps recipients and participants alike make better use of the services available, particularly the new ones that have not been widely publicized; and it also gives feedback to those who are responsible for the local associations and governmental agencies.

The participants communicate more than information, however. They frequently express their ideas about what should or should not be done; they help structure public opinion to the point that some proposed change becomes acceptable; they exercise a certain degree of social control by reaffirming the dominant local values.

Participants, like recipients, develop strong feelings about certain aspects of community life. It is in this sense that they truly experience their community. In their efforts to play a participant role they feel either rewarded or rejected, appreciated or unappreciated, hopeful or pessimistic about the future. Their attempt to describe their community in rational, objective terms is tinged with the emotional overtones derived from their participation.

The social gain from participation is the sense of interdependence that it provides. The individual and the group do not stand alone. It is a part of a social network, a community, a society. Thus we close this book upon the same theme with which we began in the first chapter: the sense of community in a complex society comes only as we recognize and act upon the fact of interdependence. The neighborhood and the local community form the arena where this drama is played, a drama where the actors as participants derive more benefit than the spectators or recipients; also a drama where knowledge of the community gained through sociological insight can be added to one's emotional investment to make community living a satisfying experience not only to oneself but also to one's fellows.

Literature Cited

AGGER, ROBERT E. and GOODRICH, DANIEL. 1958. "Community Power Structures and Partisanship," *American Sociological Review* 23 (August), pp. 383–92.

AIKEN, MICHAEL and ALFORD, ROBERT R. 1970. "Community Structure and Innovation: The Case of Urban Renewal," *American Sociological Review* 35 (August), pp. 650–65.

———, and HAGE, JERALD. 1966. "Organizational Alienation: A Comparative Analysis," *American Sociological Review* 31 (August), pp. 497–507.

ALEXANDER, C. NORMAN, JR. 1972. "Status Perceptions," *American Sociological Review* 37 (December), pp. 767–73.

ALEXANDER, JOHN W. 1955. *The Economic Life of Oshkosh.* Madison: University of Wisconsin, Bureau of Community Development, Parts 1 and 2.

ALFORD, ROBERT R. and SCOBLE, HARRY M. 1968. "Community Leadership, Education and Political Behavior," *American Sociological Review* 33 (April), pp. 259–72.

ALLEN, IRVING L. 1968. "Community Size, Population Composition, and Cultural Activity in Smaller Communities," *Rural Sociology* 33 (September), pp. 328–38.

ALLEN, MICHAEL PATRICK. 1974. "The Structure of Interorganizational Elite Cooptation: Interlocking Corporate Directorates," *American Sociological Review* 39 (June), pp. 393–406.

ANDERSON, THEODORE R. and WARKOV, SEYMOUR. 1961. "Organizational Size and Functional Complexity: A Study of Administration in Hospitals," *American Sociological Review* 26 (February), pp. 23–28.

ANDREWS, WADE H. and ESHLEMAN, J. ROSS. 1963. *The New Community: I. Characteristics of Migrant and Non-Migrant Residents in the Rural Fringe of a Metropolitan Area in Ohio.* Wooster: Ohio Agricultural Experiment Station Research Bulletin 929 (April, 1963) II. *Adjustment to Living in the Changing Rural Fringe of a Metropolitan Area,* Research Bulletin 955 (November).

ANGELL, ROBERT COOLEY. 1951. "The Moral Integration of American Cities," *American Journal of Sociology* 47 (July), pp. 575–92.

The Annals of the American Academy of Political and Social Science. 1967. *Social Goals and Indicators for American Society,* Vol. II (September). Entire issue.

ARENSBERG, CONRAD. 1965. "The Community as Object and Sample," *American Anthropologist* 63 (April), 241–64.

———, and KIMBALL, SOLON T. 1968. "Community Study: Retrospect and Prospect," *American Journal of Sociology* 73, pp. 691–705.

485

AXELROD, MORRIS. 1956. "Urban Structure and Social Participation," *American Sociological Review* 21 (February), pp. 13–18.

BABCHUK, NICHOLAS and BOOTH, ALAN. 1969. "Voluntary Association Membership: A Longitudinal Analysis," *American Sociological Review* 34 (February), pp. 31–45.

BACON, LLOYD. 1971. "Poverty Among Interregional Rural-to-Urban Migrants," *Rural Sociology* 36 (June), pp. 125–40.

BANFIELD, EDWARD C. 1958. *The Moral Basis of a Backward Community.* New York: Free Press.

———. 1961. *Political Influence.* New York: Free Press.

BARTH, ERNEST A. T. and ABU-LABAN, BAHA. 1959. "Power Structure and the Negro Sub-Community," *American Sociological Review* 24 (February), pp. 69–76.

BATES, FREDERICK L. 1962. "Some Observations Concerning the Structural Aspects of Role Conflict," *Pacific Sociological Review* 5 (Fall), pp. 75–82.

BEAL, GEORGE M. 1964. "Social Action: Instigated Change in Large Social Systems" in James H. Copp (ed.), *Our Changing Rural Society: Perspectives and Trends.* Ames: Iowa State University Press, pp. 233–64.

———, HARTMAN, JOHN J., and LAGOMARCINO, VIRGIL. 1968. "An Analysis of Factors Associated with School Bond Elections," *Rural Sociology* 33 (September), pp. 313–27.

BEBOUT, JOHN E. and BREDEMEIER, HARRY C. 1963. "American Cities as Social Systems," *Journal of the American Institute of Planners* 29 (May), pp. 66–67.

BECKER, HOWARD. 1956. "Looking at Values and Value-Systems," in Irwin T. Sanders (ed.), *Societies Around the World.* Shorter ed. New York: The Dryden Press, Inc., pp. 378–98.

BECKER, HOWARD S. and STRAUSS, ANSELM L. 1956. "Careers, Personality and Adult Socialization," *The American Journal of Sociology* 62 (November), pp. 253–63.

BELL, COLIN and NEWBY, HOWARD. 1972. *Community Studies: An Introduction to the Sociology of the Local Community.* New York: Praeger.

BELL, WENDELL and FORCE, MARYANNE T. 1956. "Social Structure and Participation in Different Types of Formal Associations," *Social Forces,* 34 (May), pp. 345–50.

BENSMAN, JOSEPH and VIDICH, ARTHUR J. 1971. *The New American Society: The Revolution of the Middle Class.* Chicago: Quadrangle Books.

BERELSON, BERNARD and STEINER, GARY A. 1964. *Human Behavior: An Inventory of Scientific Findings.*

BERGER, BENNETT M. 1960. *Working-Class Suburb: A Study of Auto Workers in Suburbia.* Berkeley and Los Angeles: University of California Press.

BERNARD, JESSIE. 1950. "Where Is The Modern Sociology of Conflict?" *American Journal of Sociology* 56 (July), pp. 11–16.

———. 1962. *American Community Behavior.* New York: Holt, Rinehart and Winston. Revised edition.

———. 1973. *The Sociology of Community.* Glenview, Ill.: Scott, Foresman and Co.

BERREMAN, GERALD W. 1960. "Caste in India and the United States," *The American Journal of Sociology* 66 (September), pp. 120–27.

BERRY, BRIAN J. L. and GARRISON, WILLIAM L. 1958. "The Functional Bases of the Central Place Hierarchy," *Economic Geography* 34 (April), pp. 145–54.

BERTRAND, ALVIN L. 1962. "School Attendance and Attainment: Function and Dysfunction of School and Family Social Systems," *Social Forces* 40 (March), pp. 228–33.

———— and OSBORNE, HAROLD W. 1959. *Rural Industrialization in a Louisiana Community.* Bulletin 524. Louisiana State University and Agricultural and Mechanical College and Agricultural Experiment Station.

BIRNBAUM, NORMAN. 1969. *The Crisis of Industrial Sociology.* New York: Oxford University Press, Ch. 1.

BLACK, GORDON S. 1974. "Conflict in the Community: A Theory of the Effects of Community Size," *American Political Science Review* 68 (September), pp. 1245–61.

BLACK, RUSSELL VAN NEST and BLACK, MARY HEDGES. 1948. *Planning for the Small American City.* Chicago: Public Administration Service.

BLACK, THEREL R., FREDERICKSON, CARMEN, and MAITLAND, SHERIDAN T. 1960. *Industrialization of Box Elder County.* Bulletin 420. Agricultural Experiment Station, Utah State University.

BLACKWELL, GORDON W. 1954. "A Theoretical Framework for Sociological Research in Community Organization," *Social Forces* 33 (October), pp. 57–64.

BOGART, LEO and ORENSTEIN, FRANK E. 1965. "Mass Media and Community Identity in an Urban Setting," *Journalism Quarterly* 42 (Spring).

BOGUE, DON J. 1949. *The Structure of the Metropolitan Community: A Study of Dominance and Subdominance.* Ann Arbor: University of Michigan Press.

BONACICH, EDNA. 1972. "A theory of Ethnic Antagonism: The Split Labor Market," *American Sociological Review* 37 (October), pp. 547–59.

BONJEAN, CHARLES M. 1966. "Mass, Class, and the Industrial Community: A Comparative Analysis of Managers, Businessmen, and Workers," *American Journal of Sociology* 72 (September), pp. 149–62.

———— and OLSON, DAVID M. 1964. "Community Leadership: Directions of Research," *Administrative Science Quarterly* 9 (December), pp. 278–300.

BOOTH, ALAN. 1972. "Sex and Social Participation," *American Sociological Review* 37 (April), pp. 183–93.

BOSKOFF, ALVIN. 1962. *The Sociology of Urban Regions.* New York: Appleton-Century-Crofts, Inc.

BOTT, ELIZABETH. 1957. *Family and Social Network.* London: Tavistock.

BRAND, DONALD D. 1951. *Quiroga: A Mexican Municipio.* Washington, D. C. Smithsonian Institution, Institute of Social Anthropology, Publication No. 11.

BRESSLER, MARVIN and WESTOFF, CHARLES F. 1954. "Leadership and Social Change: The Reactions of a Special Group to Industrialization and Population Influx" *Social Forces* 32 (March), pp. 236–43.

BRITT, DAVID and GALLE, OMER R. 1972. "Industrial Conflict and Unionization," *American Sociological Review* 37 (February), pp. 46–57.

BROTZ, HOWARD M. 1959. "Social Stratification and the Political Order," *The American Journal of Sociology* 64 (May), pp. 571–78.

BROWN, JAMES S., SCHWARZWELLER, HARRY K., and MANGALAM, JOSEPH J. 1963. "Kentucky Mountain Migration and the Stem-Family: An American Variation on a Theme by Le Play," *Rural Sociology* 28 (March), pp. 48–69.

BROWNELL, BAKER. 1950. *The Human Community: Its Philosophy and Practice for a Time of Crisis.* New York: Harper and Row.

BRUNN, STANLEY DAVID. 1968. "Changes in the Service Structure of Rural Trade Centers," *Rural Sociology* 33 (June), pp. 200–6.

BUELL, BRADLEY and ROBINSON, REGINALD. 1940. "A Composite Rate of Social Breakdown," *American Journal of Sociology*, pp. 887–98.

BURCHINAL, LEE G. 1957. "Marital Satisfaction and Religious Behavior," *American Sociological Review* 22 (June), pp. 306–10.

BURGESS, ERNEST W. 1925. "The Growth of the City," in Robert E. Park, Ernest W. Burgess, and R. D. McKenzie, *The City.* Chicago: University of Chicago Press.

BUTLER, JAMES E. and FUGUITT, GLENN V. 1970. "Small Town Population Change and Distance from Larger Towns: A Replication of Hassinger's Study," *Rural Sociology* 35 (September), pp. 396–409.

BUTTEL, FREDERICK H. and FLINN, WILLIAM L. 1974. "The Structure of Support for the Environmental Movement, 1968–1970," *Rural Sociology* 39 (Spring), pp. 56–69.

CANCIAN, FRANCESCA. 1960. "Functional Analysis of Change," *American Sociological Review* 25 (December), pp. 818–27.

CAPENER, HAROLD R. et al. 1973. *Perceptions of Environmental Quality Problems in the Hudson River Region: A Preliminary Investigation of Issues, Organizations and Socio-Economic Processes.* Ithaca, N. Y.: Department of Rural Sociology, New York State College of Agriculture and Life Sciences, Cornell University. (Multilithed.)

CARDEN, MAREN LOCKWOOD. 1974. *The New Feminist Movement.* New York: Russell Sage Foundation.

CARY, LEE J. (ed.). 1970. *Community Development as a Process.* Columbia: University of Missouri Press.

CENTERS, RICHARD. 1949. *The Psychology of Social Class.* Princeton: Princeton University Press.

CHAPIN, F. STUART, JR. 1947. "A Plan for Citizen Participation in Community Development," *Social Forces* 25 (March), pp. 313–20.

CHERMAYEFF, SERGE and TZONIS, ALEXANDER. 1971. *Shape of Community: Realization of Human Potential.* Harmondsworth: Penguin Books.

CHRISTALLER, WALTER. 1960. *The Central Places of Southern Germany.* Translated by C. Baskin. Englewood Cliffs, N. J.: Prentice-Hall, Inc.

CHU, GODWIN C. 1968. "Impact of Mass Media on a Gemeinschaft-like Social Structure," *Rural Sociology* 33 (June).

CLARK, TERRY NICHOLS. 1968. "Community Structure, Decision-Making, Budget Expenditures, and the Urban Renewal in 51 American Communities," *American Sociological Review* 33 (August), pp. 576–93.

———. 1973a. *Community Power and Policy Outputs: A Review of Urban Research.* Beverly Hills, Calif.: Sage Publications.

———. 1973b. "Community Social Indicators: From Analytical Models to Policy Applications," *Urban Affairs Quarterly* 9 (September), pp. 3–36.

CLAUSEN, J. A. (ed.). 1968. *Socialization and Society.* Boston: Little, Brown, and Co.

CLELAND, CHARLES L. 1960. "Characteristics of Social Systems Within Which Selected Types of Information are Transmitted," *Rural Sociology* 25 (June), pp. 212–18.

CLELLAND, DONALD A., and FORM, WILLIAM H. 1964. "Economic Dominants and Community Power: A Comparative Analysis," *American Journal of Sociology* 69 (March), pp. 511–21.

CLEMENT, FRANK, ROJEK, DEAN, and BECK, E. M. 1974. *Trade Patterns and Community Identity: Five Years Later.* Working Paper RID 73,8. Center of Applied Sociology, University of Wisconsin (Madison). Mimeographed.

COCHRAN, THOMAS C. 1972. *Social Change in America: The Twentieth Century*. New York: Harper and Row.

COLEMAN, A. LEE, and MARSH, C. PAUL. 1955. "Differential Communication Among Farmers in a Kentucky County," *Rural Sociology* 20 (June), pp. 93–101.

COLEMAN, JAMES S. 1958. *Community Conflict*. New York: Free Press.

COLLINS, RANDALL. 1971. "Functional and Conflict Theories of Educational Stratification," *American Sociological Review* 36 (December), pp. 1002–19.

————. 1975. *Conflict Sociology: Toward an Explanatory Science*. New York: Academic Press.

COLOMBOTOS, JOHN. 1969. "Physicians and Medicare: A Before-After Study of the Effects of Legislation on Attitudes," *American Sociological Review* 34 (June), pp. 318–34.

Committee for Economic Development. 1974. *More Effective Programs for a Cleaner Environment*. A Statement on National Policy by the Research and Policy Committee. New York.

CONANT, JAMES B. 1961. "Social Dynamite in Our Large Cities," *Children* (September–October). (U. S. Department of Health, Education and Welfare).

COSER, LEWIS A. 1956. *The Functions of Social Conflict*. New York: Free Press.

COUGHENOUR, C. MILTON. 1964. "The Rate of Technological Diffusion Among Locality Groups," *American Journal of Sociology* 69 (January), pp. 325–39.

CRAIN, ROBERT L. and ROSENTHAL, DONALD B. 1967. "Community Status as a Dimension of Local Decision-Making," *American Sociological Review* 32 (December), pp. 970–84.

CRAVEN, PAUL and WELLMAN, BARRY. 1973. "The Network City," *Sociological Inquiry* 43, pp. 57–88.

CURTIS, JAMES. 1971. "Voluntary Association Joining: A Cross-National Comparative Note," *American Sociological Review* 36 (October), pp. 872–80.

DAHRENDORF, RALF. 1959. *Class and Conflict in Industrial Society*. Stanford, Calif.: Stanford University Press.

D'ANTONIO, WILLIAM V. and ERICKSON, EUGENE C. 1962. "The Reputational Techniques as a Measure of Community Power: An Evaluation Based on Comparative and Longitudinal Studies," *American Sociological Review* 27 (June), pp. 362–76.

DANZGER, M. HERBERT. 1964. "Community Power Structure: Problems and Continuities," *American Sociological Review* 29 (October), pp. 707–17.

DAVIS, ALLISON and GARDNER, BURLEIGH. 1941. *Deep South*. Chicago: University of Chicago Press.

DAVIS, KINGSLEY. 1959. "The Sociology of Demographic Behavior," in R. K. Merton, L. Broom, and L. S. Cottrell, Jr. (eds.). *Sociology Today: Problems and Prospects*. New York: Basic Books, Inc.

DEAN, JOHN P. 1949. "The Myths of Housing Reform," *American Sociological Review* 14 (April), pp. 281–88.

DeFLEUR, MELVIN L. and CROSBY, JOHN. 1956. "Analyzing Metropolitan Dominance," *Social Forces* 35 (October), pp. 68–75.

———— and DeFLEUR, LOIS B. 1967. "The Relative Contribution of Television as a Learning Source for Children's Occupational Knowledge," *American Sociological Review* 32 (October), pp. 777–89.

DENISOFF, R. SERGE, CALLAHAN, OREL, and LEVINE, MARK H. (eds.). 1974.

Theories and Paradigms in Contemporary Sociology. Itasca, Ill.: F. E. Peacock Publishers.

DEVINE, RICHARD P. and FALK, LAURENCE L. 1972. *Social Surveys: A Research Strategy for Social Scientists and Students.* Morristown, N. J.: General Learning Press.

DOBRINER, WILLIAM M. 1963. *Class in Suburbia.* Englewood Cliffs, N. J.: Prentice-Hall, Inc.

DOLLARD, JOHN. 1937. *Caste and Class in a Southern Town.* New Haven: Yale University Press.

DOTSON, FLOYD. 1951. "Patterns of Voluntary Associations among Urban Working-Class Families," *American Sociological Review* 16 (October), pp. 687–93.

DOWNS, ANTHONY. 1970. *Who Are The Urban Poor?* New York: Committee for Economic Development. Revised Edition. Supplementary Paper Number 26.

DRABICK, LAWRENCE W. and BUCK, ROY C. 1959. "Measuring Locality Group Consensus," *Rural Sociology* 24 (June), pp. 107–17.

DUNCAN, BEVERLY, SABAGH, GEORGES, and VAN ARSDOL, MAURICE D., JR. 1962. "Patterns of City Growth," *American Journal of Sociology* 67 (January), pp. 418–29.

DUNCAN, OTIS DUDLEY and SCHNORE, LEO F. 1959. "Cultural, Behavioral, and Ecological Perspectives in the Study of Social Organization" *American Journal of Sociology* 65 (September), pp. 132–46.

DYKENS, JAMES W., HYDE, ROBERT W., ORZACK, LOUIS H., and YORK, RICHARD H. 1964. *Strategies of Mental Hospital Change.* Boston: Department of Mental Health, Commonwealth of Massachusetts.

DYNES, RUSSELL R. 1955. "Church-Sect Typology and Socio-Economic Status," *American Sociological Review* 20 (October), pp. 555–60.

EDELSTEIN, ALEX S. and LARSEN, OTTO N. 1960. "The Weekly Press' Contribution to a Sense of Urban Community," *Journalism Quarterly* 37 (Autumn), pp. 489–98.

EISENSTADT, S. N. 1964. "Social Change, Differentiation and Evolution," *American Sociological Review* 29 (June), pp. 375–86.

EITZEN, STANLEY D. 1974. *Social Structure and Social Problems in America.* Boston: Allyn and Bacon, Ch. 5.

———. 1970. "A Study of Voluntary Association Memberships Among Middle-Class Women," *Rural Sociology* 35 (March), pp. 84–91.

ELKIN, STEPHEN L. 1974. "Comparative Urban Politics and Interorganizational Behavior," *Comparative Urban Research* No. 5, pp. 5–21.

ELLIS, ROBERT A., LANE, W. CLAYTON, and OLESEN, VIRGINIA. 1963. "The Index of Class Position: An Improved Intercommunity Measure of Stratification," *American Sociological Review* 28 (April), pp. 271–77.

EMERSON, HAVEN. 1951. "Essential Local Public Health Services," *The Annals* 273 (January.)

ERWIN, ROBERT. 1974. "Traffic is Heavy Tonight on Three Stooges Parkway," *Boston University Journal* 22 (Spring), pp. 23–30.

ETZIONI, AMITAI. 1968. *The Active Society.* New York: The Free Press.

———. 1957. "Solidaric Work-Groups in Collective Settlements," *Human Organization* 16 (Fall), pp. 2–6.

EVAN, WILLIAM. 1966. "The Organization Set: Toward a Theory of Interorganizational Relations," in James D. Thompson, ed., *Approaches to Organizational Design.* Pittsburgh: University of Pittsburgh Press, pp. 173–91.

EVERS, HANS-DIETER. 1966. "The Formation of a Social Class Structure: Urbanization, Bureaucratization and Social Mobility in Thailand," *American Sociological Review* 31 (August), pp. 480–88.

FALLDING, HAROLD. 1963. "Functional Analysis in Sociology" *American Sociological Review*, 28 (February), pp. 5–13.

FARLEY, REYNOLDS. 1964. "Suburban Persistence," *American Sociological Review* 29 (February), pp. 38–47.

FAUNCE, WILLIAM A. and SMUCKER, M. JOSEPH. 1966. "Industrialization and Community Status Structure," *American Sociological Review* 31 (June), pp. 390–99.

FAVA, SYLVIA F. 1956. "Suburbanization as a Way of Life," *American Sociological Review* 21 (February), pp. 34–37.

FEATHERMAN, DAVID L. 1971. "The Socioeconomic Achievement of White Religio-Ethnic Subgroups: Social and Psychological Explanations," *American Sociological Review* (April), pp. 207–22.

FELLIN, PHILLIP and LITWAK, EUGENE. 1963. "Neighborhood Cohesion under Conditions of Mobility," *American Sociological Review* 28 (June), pp. 364–76.

FELSON, MARCUS et al. 1972. "Commentary on Racially Changing Neighborhoods," *American Journal of Sociology* 78 (November), pp. 674–84.

FIREY, WALTER. 1945. "Sentiment and Symbolism as Ecological Variables," *American Sociological Review* 10 (April), pp. 140–48.

FLACKS, RICHARD. 1971. *Youth and Social Change.* Chicago: Markham Publishing Company.

FLORO, GEORGE K. 1955. "Continuity in City-Manager Careers," *American Journal of Sociology* 61 (November), pp. 240–46.

FONER, ANNE. 1974. "Age Stratification and Age Conflict in Political Life," *American Sociological Review* 39 (April), pp. 187–96.

FOOTE, NELSON N. 1951. "Identification as the Basis for a Theory of Motivation," *American Sociological Review* 16 (February), pp. 14–21.

FORM, WILLIAM H. 1973. "The Internal Stratification of the Working Class: System Involvement of Auto Workers in Four Countries," *American Sociological Review* 38, pp. 697–711.

———— and D'ANTONIO, WILLIAM V. 1959. "Integration and Cleavage and Community Influentials in Two Border Cities," *American Sociological Review* 24 (December), pp. 804–14.

———— and NOSOW, SIGMUND, with GREGORY P. STONE, and CHARLES M. WESTIE. 1958. *Community in Disaster.* New York: Harper & Row.

———— and RYTINA, JOAN. 1969. "Ideological Beliefs on the Distribution of Power in the United States," *American Sociological Review* 34 (February), pp. 19–31.

———— and SAUER, WARREN L. 1960. "Organized Labor's Image of Community Power Structure," *Social Forces* 38 (May), pp. 332–41.

FOSKETT, JOHN M. 1955. "Social Structure and Social Participation," *American Sociological Review* 20 (August), pp. 431–38.

FRANKLIN, BEN A. 1973. "Inexorably, A Copper Mine is Eating Away Butte, Montana," *New York Times* (February 15).

FREEMAN, HOWARD E., NOVAK, EDWIN, and REEDER, LEO G. 1957. "Correlates of Membership in Voluntary Associations," *American Sociological Review* 22 (October), pp. 528–33.

FREEMAN, LINTON C., FARRARO, THOMAS J., BLOOMBERG, WARNER, JR. and SUNSHINE, MORRIS H. 1963. "Locating Leaders in Local Communities: A

Comparison of Some Alternative Approaches," *American Sociological Review* 27 (October), pp. 791–98.

FREILICH, MORRIS. 1963. "Toward an Operational Definition of Community," *Rural Sociology* 28 (June), pp. 117–127.

FUGUITT, GLENN V. 1959. "Part-Time Farming and the Push-Pull Hypothesis," *American Journal of Sociology* 64 (January), pp. 375–79.

———. 1971. "The Places Left Behind: Population Trends and Policy for Rural America" *Rural Sociology* 36 (December), pp. 449–70.

FURSTENBERG, FRANK F., JR. 1971. "The Transmission of Mobility Orientation in the Family," *Social Forces* 49 (June), pp. 595–603.

GALLAHER, ART, JR. 1961. *Plainville Fifteen Years Later*. New York: Columbia University Press.

GALLION, ARTHUR B. 1950. *The Urban Pattern: City Planning and Design*. New York: Van Nostrand-Reinhold.

GAMSON, WILLIAM A. 1966. "Rancorous Conflict in Community Politics," *American Sociological Review* 31 (February), pp. 71–81.

———. 1968. *Power and Discontent*. Homewood, Ill.: The Dorsey Press.

GANS, HERBERT J. 1962. *The Urban Villagers*. New York: Free Press.

GIEBER, WALTER. 1960. "Two Communicators of the News: A Study of the Roles of Sources and Reporters," *Social Forces* 39 (October), pp. 76–83.

GIST, NOEL P. and HALBERT, L. A. 1956. *Urban Society*. New York: Thomas Y. Crowell Co. 4th edition.

GLAZER, NATHAN and MOYNIHAN, DANIEL PATRICK. 1963. *Beyond the Melting Pot: The Negroes, Puerto Ricans, Jews, Italians, and Irish of New York City*. Cambridge: M.I.T. Press and Harvard University Press.

GLENN, NORVAL D. and ALSTON, JON P. 1968. "Cultural Distances among Occupational Categories," *American Sociological Review* 33 (June), pp. 365–82.

——— and HYLAND, RUTH. 1967. "Religious Preference and Worldly Success: Some Evidence from National Surveys," *American Sociological Review* 32 (February), pp. 73–85.

GOLDSTEIN, BERNICE and EICHHORN, ROBERT L. 1961. "The Changing Protestant Ethic: Rural Patterns in Health, Work, and Leisure," *American Sociological Review* 26 (August), pp. 557–65.

GOODE, WILLIAM J. 1960. "A Theory of Role Strain," *American Sociological Review* 25 (August), pp. 483–96.

———. 1972. "The Place of Force in Human Society," *American Sociological Review* 37 (October), pp. 507–19.

GOODENOUGH, WARD HUNT. 1963. *Cooperation in Change: An Anthropological Approach to Community Development*. New York: Russell Sage Foundation.

GORDON, DANIEL N. 1970. "Immigrants and Municipal Voting Turnout: Implications for the Changing Ethnic Impact on Urban Politics," *American Sociological Review* 33 (August), pp. 665–81.

GORDON, MILTON M. 1949. "Social Class in American Sociology," *The American Journal of Sociology* 55 (November), pp. 262–68.

GREELEY, ANDREW M. 1972. *The Denominational Society: Sociological Approach to Religion in America*. Glenview, Ill.: Scott, Foresman.

GREEN, JAMES W. and MAYO, SELZ C. 1953. "A Framework for Research in the Actions of Community Groups," *Social Forces* 31 (May), pp. 320–27.

GREENBERG, MARTIN. 1974. "A Concept of Community," *Social Work* 19 (January).

GREENSTONE, J. DAVID and PETERSON, PAUL E. 1973. *Race and Authority in Urban Politics: Community Participation and the War on Poverty.* New York: Russell Sage Foundation.

GREER, SCOTT and GREER, ANN LENNARSON. (eds.). 1974. *Neighborhood and Ghetto: The Local Area in Large-Scale Society.* New York: Basic Books, Inc.

GREER, SCOTT and ORLEANS, PETER. 1962. "The Mass Society and the Parapolitical Structure," *American Sociological Review* 27 (October), pp. 634–46.

GREIFER, JULIAN L. (ed.). 1974. *Community Action for Social Change: A Casebook of Current Projects.* New York: Praeger.

GRIGG, CHARLES M. 1965. *Community Satisfaction and Community Involvement in Brevard County.* Tallahassee: Florida State University. Mimeographed.

GROSS, LLEWELLYN. 1949. "The Use of Class Concepts in Sociological Research," *The American Journal of Sociology* 54 (March), pp. 409–21.

GROSS, NEAL. 1953. "Social Class Identification in the Urban Community," *American Sociological Review* 18 (August), pp. 398–404 .

GUMPERZ, JOHN J. 1964. "Religion and Social Communication in a Village in North India," *Journal of Asian Studies* 23 (June), pp. 89–97.

HAER, JOHN L. 1955. "A Comparative Study of the Classification Techniques of Warner and Centers," *American Sociological Review* 20 (December), pp. 689–92.

HAGA, WILLIAM J. and FOLSE, CLINTON L. 1971. "Trade Patterns and Community Identity," *Rural Sociology* 36 (March), pp. 42–51.

HAGEDORN, ROBERT and LABOVITZ, SANFORD. 1968. "Participation in Community Associations by Occupation: A Test of Three Theories," *American Sociological Review* 33 (April), 272–283.

HALLER, ARCHIBALD O., HOLSINGER, DONALD B., and SARAIVA, HELCIO ULHOA. 1972. "Variations in Occupational Prestige Hierarchies: Brazilian Data," *American Journal of Sociology* 77 (March), pp. 941–56.

HAMILTON, RICHARD F. 1966. "The Marginal Middle Class: A Reconsideration," *American Sociological Review* 31 (April), pp. 192–99.

HANSON, ROBERT C. 1959. "Predicting a Community Decision: A Test of the Miller-Form Theory," *American Sociological Review* 24 (October), pp. 662–71.

HARDEE, J. GILBERT. 1961. "Social Structure and Participation in an Australian Rural Community," *Rural Sociology* 26 (September), pp. 240–51.

HARDEN, W. R. 1960. "Social and Economic Effects of Community Size," *Rural Sociology* 25 (June), pp. 332–39.

HARLAN, WILLIAM H. 1954. "Community Adaptation to the Presence of Aged Persons: St. Petersburg, Florida," *American Journal of Sociology* 59 (January), pp. 332–39.

HARP, JOHN. 1973. "Formal Voluntary Organizations: Agents of Stability and Change," *Search:* Agriculture, Rural Sociology 2. Vol. 3, No. 7. Ithaca: New York State College of Agriculture and Life Sciences, Cornell University.

――― and GAGAN, RICHARD J. 1969. "Changes in Rural Social Organizations: Comparative Data from Three Studies," *Rural Sociology* (March), pp. 80–85.

HARRISON, GORDON SCOTT. 1972. "Flow of Communication Between Government Agencies and Eskimo Villages," *Human Organization* 31 (Spring), pp. 1–9.

HASENFELD, YEHESKEL. 1972. "People Processing Organizations: An Exchange Approach," *American Sociological Review* 37 (June), pp. 256–63.

HASSINGER, EDWARD. 1961. "Social Relations Between Centralized and Local Social Systems," *Rural Sociology* 26 (December), pp. 354–64.

HATCH, DAVID and HATCH, MARY G. 1949. *Under the Elms: Yesterday and Today.* Syracuse, New York: Syracuse University Press.

HAUSER, PHILIP M. (ed.). 1955. "World Urbanism" *American Journal of Sociology* 60 (March), entire issue.

HAUSKNECHT, MURRAY. 1962. *The Joiners: A Sociological Description of Voluntary Association Memberships in the United States.* New York: Bedminster Press.

HAWLEY, A. H. 1950. *Human Ecology: A Theory of Community Structure.* New York: The Ronald Press Co.

———. 1963. "Community Power and Urban Renewal Success," *American Journal of Sociology* 68 (January), pp. 422–31.

———. 1968. "Human Ecology," *International Encyclopedia of the Social Sciences.* New York: The Macmillan Company and The Free Press, Vol. 4, pp. 328–36.

———. 1971. *Urban Society: An Ecological Approach.* New York: The Ronald Press Co.

HAYES, WAYLAND J. 1949. "Revolution—Community Style," *Social Forces* 28 (October).

HEALTH INSURANCE INSTITUTE. 1972–73. *Source Book of Health Insurance.* New York. 14th edition.

HELFGOT, JOSEPH. 1974. "Professional Reform Organizations and the Symbolic Representation of the Poor," *American Sociological Review* 39 (August), pp. 475–91.

HENRIOT, PETER J. 1972. *Political Aspects of Social Indicators: Implications for Research.* New York: Russell Sage Foundation. Occasional publication 4.

HERMALIN, ALBERT I. and FARLEY, REYNOLDS. 1973. "The Potential for Residential Integration in Cities and Suburbs: Implications for the Busing Controversy," *American Sociological Review* 38 (October), pp. 595–610.

HERRIOTT, ROBERT E. and HODGKINS, BENJAMIN J. 1969. "Social Context and the School: An Open-System Analysis of Social and Educational Change," *Rural Sociology* 34 (June), pp. 149–66.

HILL, MOZELL C. and McCALL, BEVODE C. 1950. "Social Stratification in 'Georgia Town'" *American Sociological Review* 15 (December), pp. 721–29.

HILL, RICHARD CHILD. 1974. "Unionization and Racial Income Inequality in the Metropolis," *American Sociological Review* 39 (August), pp. 507–22.

HILLER, E. T. 1941. "The Community as a Social Group," *American Sociological Review* 6 (April), pp. 189–202.

HILLERY, GEORGE A., JR. 1961. "The Folk Village: A Comparative Analysis" *Rural Sociology* 26 (December), pp. 337–53.

———. 1968. *Communal Organizations: A Study of Local Societies.* Chicago: University of Chicago Press.

———. 1972. "Selected Issues in Community Theory," *Rural Sociology* 37, pp. 534–52.

HODGE, GERALD. 1966. "Do Villages Grow? Some Perspectives and Predictions," *Rural Sociology* 31 (June).

HODGE, ROBERT W. 1962. "The Status Consistency of Occupational Groups," *American Sociological Review* 27 (June), pp. 336–43.

—— and TREIMAN, D. J. 1968. "Social Participation and Social Status," *American Sociological Review* 33 (October), pp. 722–40.

HOFFER, CHARLES R. 1958. "Social Action in Community Development," *Rural Sociology* 23 (March), pp. 43–51.

——. 1964. *Michigan Communities: Social Organization and Change in Rural Areas.* Agricultural Experiment Station Research Bulletin 1. East Lansing: Michigan State University.

HOLLINGSHEAD, AUGUST B. 1949. "Class and Kinship in a Middle Western Community," *American Sociological Review* 14 (August), pp. 469–75.

—— and REDLICH, FREDERICK C. 1953. "Social Stratification and Psychiatric Disorders," *American Sociological Review* 18 (April), pp. 163–69.

HOLMBERG, ALLEN R. and DOBYNS, HENRY F. 1962. "The Process of Accelerating Community Change," *Human Organization* 21 (Summer), pp. 107–9.

HOMANS, GEORGE. 1950. *The Human Group.* New York: Harcourt Brace Jovanovich, 1950, chap. 11.

——. 1961. *Social Behavior: Its Elementary Forms.* New York: Harcourt Brace Jovanovich, chap. 7.

HORTON, JOHN E. and THOMPSON, WAYNE E. 1962. "Powerlessness and Political Negativism: A Study of Defeated Local Referendums," *American Journal of Sociology* 27 (March).

HOSELITZ, BERT F. 1955. "The City, The Factory, and Economic Growth," *The American Economic Review* 45 (May).

HOYT, HOMER. 1939. *The Structure and Growth of Residential Neighborhoods in American Cities.* Washington, D. C.: Government Printing Office.

HUBER, JOAN (ed.). 1973. *Changing Women in a Changing Society.* Issue of *American Journal of Sociology* 78 (January). 22 articles.

HUNTER, ALBERT. 1974. *Symbolic Communities: The Persistence and Change of Chicago's Local Communities.* Chicago: The University of Chicago Press.

HUNTER, FLOYD. 1953. *Community Power Structure*, Chapel Hill: University of North Carolina Press.

HURST, CHARLES E. 1972. "Race, Class, and Consciousness," *American Sociological Review* 37 (December).

HYMAN, HERBERT H. and WRIGHT, CHARLES R. 1971. "Trends in Voluntary Association Memberships of American Adults: Replication Based on Secondary Analysis of National Sample Surveys," *American Sociological Review* 36 (April), pp. 191–206.

INKELES, ALEX. 1955. "Social Change and Social Character: The Role of Parental Mediation," *Journal of Social Issues* 11, pp. 12–23.

——. 1960. "Industrial Man: The Relation of Status to Experience, Perception, and Value," *American Journal of Sociology* 66 (July), pp. 1–31.

——. 1969. "Making Men Modern: On the Causes and Consequences of Individual Change in Six Developing Countries," *American Journal of Sociology* 75 (September), pp. 208–25.

JACKMAN, MARY R. and JACKMAN, ROBERT W. 1973. "An Interpretation of the Relation Between Objective and Subjective Social Status," *American Sociological Review* 38 (October), pp. 569–82.

JACKSON, ELTON F. and CROCKETT, HARRY J., JR. 1964. "Occupational Mobility in the United States A Point Estimate and Trend Comparison," *American Sociological Review* 29 (February), pp. 5–15.

JACKSON, ELTON F., FOX, WILLIAM S. and CROCKETT, HARRY J., JR. 1971. "Religion and Occupational Achievement," *American Sociological Review* 35 (February).

JANSYN, LEON R., JR. 1966. "Solidarity and Delinquency in a Street Corner Group," *American Sociological Review* 31 (October), pp. 600–14.

JENCKS, CHRISTOPHER and RIESMAN, DAVID. 1968. "On Class in America," *The Public Interest* 10(Winter), pp. 65–85.

JESSER, CLINTON J. 1967. "Community Satisfaction Patterns of Professionals in Rural Areas," *Rural Sociology* 32, pp. 56–69.

JOHANSON, H. E. and FUGUITT, G. V. 1973. "Changing Retail Activity in Wisconsin Villages: 1939–1954–1970," *Rural Sociology* 38 (Summer), pp. 207–18.

JOHNSON, BENTON. 1963. "On Church and Sect," *American Sociological Review* 28 (August), pp. 539–49.

———. 1967. "Theology and the Position of Pastors on Public Issues," *American Sociological Review* 32 (June), pp. 433–42.

JOHNSON, ELDON L. 1955. "Co-ordination: The Viewpoint of a Political Scientist," *The Annals* 302 (November).

JOHNSON, RONALD L. and KNOP, EDWARD. 1970. "Rural–Urban Differentials in Community Satisfaction," *Rural Sociology* 35 (December).

JORDAN, VERNON E., JR. 1974. "School Integration Still an Issue Despite Quiet Progress," *The New York Times*, January 16, p. 75.

KADUSHIN, CHARLES. 1968. "Power, Influence and Social Circles: A New Methodology for Studying Opinion Makers," *American Sociological Review* 33 (October), pp. 685–99.

KAHL, JOSEPH A. 1959. "Some Social Concomitants of Industrialization and Urbanization," *Human Organization* 18 (Summer), pp. 53–74.

KANTOR, ROSABETH MOSS. 1972. *Commitment and Community: Communes and Utopias in Sociological Perspective*. Cambridge: Harvard University Press.

KASARDA, JOHN D. and JANOWITZ, MORRIS. 1974. "Community Attachment in Mass Society," *American Sociological Review* 39 (June), pp. 328–39.

KATZ, ELIHU. 1960. "Communication Research and the Image of Society: Convergence of Two Traditions," *American Journal of Sociology* 65 (March).

——— and LAZARSFELD, PAUL F. 1955. *Personal Influence: The Part Played by People in the Flow of Mass Communications*. New York: Free Press.

——— and LEVIN, MARTIN L. 1963. "Traditions of Research on the Diffusion of Innovation," *American Sociological Review* 28 (April).

KAUFMAN, HAROLD F. 1952. "An Approach to the Study of Urban Stratification," *American Sociological Review* 17 (August), pp. 430–37.

———. 1959. "Toward an Interactional Conception of Community," *Social Forces* 38 (October), pp. 8–17.

——— and WILKINSON, KENNETH P. 1967. *Community Structure and Leadership: An Interactional Perspective in the Study of Community*. Mississippi State University. Social Science Research Center Bulletin 13.

———, et al. 1975. *Villages Upward Bound*. Calcutta: Editions Indian.

KELLER, SUZANNE. 1968. *The Urban Neighborhood: A Sociological Perspective*. New York: Random House.

KEMPER, THEODORE. 1968. "Reference Groups, Socialization and Achievement," *American Sociological Review* 33 (February), pp. 31–45.

———. 1972. "The Division of Labor: A Post-Durkheimian Analytical View," *American Sociological Review* 37 (December), pp. 739–53.

KERR, CLARK. 1954. "Industrial Conflict and Its Mediation," *American Journal of Sociology* 60 (November), pp. 230–45.

KEYES, FENTON. 1958. "Correlation of Social Phenomena with Community Size," *Social Forces* 36 (May), pp. 311–15.

KIMBALL, SOLON T. 1949. *The New Social Frontier: The Fringe.* East Lansing: Michigan State College, Special Bulletin 360 (June).

―――― and PEARSALL, MARION. 1954. *The Talladega Story: A Study in Community Process.* University: University of Alabama Press.

KIRSCHENBAUM, ALAN. 1971. "Patterns of Migration from Metropolitan to Nonmetropolitan Areas: Changing Ecological Factors Affecting Family Mobility," *Rural Sociology* 26 (September), pp. 315–25.

KISER, CLYDE V. 1962. "The Aging of Human Populations: Mechanisms of Change" in Clark Tibbitts and Wilma Donahue (eds.), *Social and Psychological Aspects of Aging.* New York and London: Columbia University Press, pp. 18–35.

KLAPP, ORRIN E. and PADGETT, L. VINCENT. 1960. "Power Structure and Decision-making in a Mexican Border City," *American Journal of Sociology* 65 (January), 400–06.

KLUCKHOHN, CLYDE. 1951. "Values and Value-Orientations in the Theory of Action: an Exploration in Definition and Classification," in Talcott Parsons and E. A. Shils (eds.), *Toward a General Theory of Action.* Cambridge: Harvard University Press.

KLUCKHOHN, FLORENCE R. and STRODTBECK, FRED L. 1961. *Variations in Value Orientations.* New York: Harper and Row.

KOHN, MELVIN L. 1969. *Class and Conformity.* Georgetown, Ontario: The Dorsey Press.

―――― and SCHOOLER, CARMI. 1969. "Class, Occupation, and Orientation," *American Sociological Review* 34 (October), pp. 659–78.

KORNBLUM, WILLIAM. 1974. *Blue Collar Community.* Chicago: University of Chicago Press.

KRAMER, RALPH M. and SPECHT, HARRY. 1975. *Readings in Community Organization Practice.* Englewood Cliffs, N. J.: Prentice-Hall. 2nd ed.

KRAUS, HERTHA. 1948. "Community Organization in Social Work: A Note on Choices and Steps," *Social Forces* 27 (October), pp. 54–57.

KREITLOW, BURTON W., and KOYEN, ROLAND. "First Progress Report: Longitudinal Study of Newly Formed Centralized Rural School Districts in the State of Wisconsin." Unpublished Ms., Department of Rural Education, University of Wisconsin.

LADINSKY, JACK. 1967. "Occupational Determinants of Geographic Mobility Among Professional Workers," *American Sociological Review* 32 (April), pp. 257–64.

LANDECKER, WERNER S. 1960a. "Class Boundaries," *American Sociological Review* 25 (December), pp. 868–77.

――――. 1960b. "Class Crystallization and its Urban Pattern," *Social Research* 27 (Autumn), pp. 308–20.

――――. 1963. "Class Crystallization and Class Consciousness," *American Sociological Review* 28 (April), pp. 219–29.

LANE, ANGELA. 1968. "Occupational Mobility in Six Cities," *American Sociological Review* 33 (October), pp. 740–49.

LANSING, JOHN and MUELLER, EVA. 1967. *The Geographic Mobility of Labor.* Ann Arbor: University of Michigan Survey Research Center. Part II.

LARSEN, OTTO N. and EDELSTEIN, ALEX S. 1960. "Communication, Consensus and the Community Involvement of Husbands and Wives," *Acta Sociologica* 5 (Fasc. 1), pp. 15–30.

LARSEN, OTTO N. and HILL, RICHARD J. 1958. "Social Structure and Interpersonal Communication," *American Journal of Sociology* 63 (March), pp. 497–505.

LASSWELL, THOMAS ELY. 1959. "Social Class and Size of Community," *American Journal of Sociology* 64 (March), pp. 505–8.

LAUER, ROBERT H. 1971. "The Scientific Legitimation of Fallacy: Neutralizing Social Change Theory," *American Sociological Review* 36 (October), pp. 881–89.

LAUMANN, EDWARD O. 1969. "The Social Structure of Religious and Ethnoreligious Groups in a Metropolitan Community," *American Sociological Review* 34 (April), pp. 182–97.

———— and PAPPI, FRANZ URBAN. 1973. "New Directions in the Study of Community Elites," *American Sociological Review* 38 (April), pp. 212–30.

————, VERBRUGGE, LOIS M., and PAPPI, FRANZ U. 1974. "A Causal Modelling Approach to the Study of a Community Elite's Influence Structure," *American Sociological Review* 39 (April), pp. 162–74.

LEGGETT, JOHN C. 1963. "Uprootedness and Working-Class Consciousness," *American Journal of Sociology* 68 (May), pp. 682–92.

LEIF, IRVING P. and CLARK, TERRY NICHOLS. 1972. "Community Power and Decision-Making," *Current Sociology* 20 (No. 2). A Trend Report and Bibliography. (Entire issue).

LERMAN, PAUL. 1968. "Individual Values, Peer Values, and Sub-Cultural Delinquency," *American Sociological Review* 33 (April), pp. 219–35.

LEVINE, SOL and WHITE, PAUL E. 1961. "Exchange as a Conceptual Framework for the Study of Interorganizational Relationships," *Administrative Science Quarterly* 5 (March), pp. 585–601.

————. 1972. "The Community of Health Organizations," in Howard E. Freeman, Sol Levine, and Leo G. Reeder (eds.) *Handbook of Medical Sociology.* Englewood Cliffs, N. J.: Prentice-Hall, Inc., Second edition, pp. 359–85.

LEVY, MARION J. 1952. *The Structure of Society.* Princeton: Princeton University Press.

LEWIN, KURT. 1951. *Field Theory in Social Science: Selected Theoretical Papers.* New York. Harper and Row.

LEWIS, GORDON. 1975. "The Sociological Study of Community: Is There a Case for Micro Analysis?" *Journal of the Community Development Society* 6 (Spring).

LEWIS, OSCAR. 1951. *Life in a Mexican Village: Tepoztlan Restudied.* Urbana: University of Illinois Press.

LIONBERGER, HERBERT F. 1960. *Adoption of New Ideas and Practices.* Ames: Iowa State University Press.

———— and COPUS, GARY D. 1972. "Structuring Influence of Social Cliques on Farm-Information-Seeking Relationships with Agricultural Elites and Nonelites in Two Missouri Communities," *Rural Sociology* 37 (March), pp. 73–85.

LIPPITT, RONALD, WATSON, JEANNE, and WESTLEY, BRUCE. 1958. *The Dynamics of Planned Change: A Comparative Study of Principles and Techniques.* New York: Harcourt Brace Jovanovich.

LITT, EDGAR. 1963. "Civic Education, Community Norms, and Political Indoctrination," *American Sociological Review* 28 (February), pp. 69–75.

LITWAK, EUGENE. 1961. "Voluntary Associations and Neighborhood Cohesion," *American Sociological Review* 26 (April), pp. 258–71.

LITWAK, EUGENE and MEYER, HENRY J. *School, Family, and Neighborhood: The Theory and Practice of School-Community Relations.* New York: Columbia University Press.

——— and SZELENYI, IVAN. 1969. "Primary Group Structures and Their Functions: Kin, Neighbors, and Friends," *American Sociological Review* 34 (August), pp. 465–81.

LONG, LARRY H. 1974. "Poverty Status and Receipt of Welfare Among Migrants and Nonmigrants in Large Cities," *American Sociological Review* 39 (February), pp. 46–56.

LONG, NORTON E. 1958. "The Local Community as an Ecology of Games," *American Journal of Sociology* 64 (November), pp. 251–61.

LOOMIS, CHARLES P. 1960. *Social Systems: Essays on Their Persistence and Change.* New York: Van Nostrand-Reinhold.

LOOMIS, WILLIAM P. and MOORE, LOUISE. 1955. "Occupational Education in the Schools," *The Annals* 302 (November).

LOPREATO, JOSEPH. 1961. "Social Classes in an Italian Farm Village," *Rural Sociology* 26 (September), pp. 266–81.

LORING, WILLIAM C., JR. 1956. "Housing Characteristics and Social Disorganization," *Social Problems* (January), pp. 160–68.

LOWI, THEODORE J. 1967. "Machine Politics—Old and New," *The Public Interest* 9 (Fall), pp. 83–92.

LOWRY, RITCHIE P. 1962. "The Functions of Alienation in Leadership," *Sociology and Social Research* 46 (July).

———. 1968. *Who's Running This Town: Community Leadership and Social Change.* New York: Harper and Row.

LYMAN, STANFORD M. and SCOTT, MARVIN B. 1970. *A Sociology of the Absurd.* New York: Appleton-Century-Crofts.

LYND, ROBERT S., and LYND, HELEN M. 1929. *Middletown.* New York: Harcourt Brace Jovanovich.

———. 1937. *Middletown in Transition.* New York: Harcourt Brace Jovanovich.

MacIVER, ROBERT M. 1970. *Robert MacIver on Community, Society, and Power.* Selected, edited and with an Introduction by Leon Bramson. Chicago: The University of Chicago Press.

MANN, PETER H. 1954. "The Concept of Neighborliness," *American Journal of Sociology* 60 (September), pp. 163–68.

MARCONDES, J. V. FREITAS. 1948. "*Mutirao* or Mutual Aid," *Rural Sociology* 13 (December), pp. 374–84.

MARK, HAROLD and SCHWIRIAN, KENT P. 1967. "Ecological Position, Urban Central Place Function, and Community Population Growth," *American Journal of Sociology* 73 (July), pp. 30–41.

MARRIS, PETER and REIN, MARTIN. 1973. *Dilemmas of Social Reform: Poverty and Community Action in the United States.* Second Edition. Chicago: Aldine Publishing Co.

MARSHALL, DOUGLAS G. 1964. *The Story of Kenosha County, Wisconsin: Population Change in an Urbanized Area.* Madison: University of Wisconsin Agricultural Experiment Station Research Bulletin 251 (July).

MARTIN, HARRY W. 1957. "Physician Role Conflict in Community Participation," *Research Previews* 5 (March), Institute for Research in Social Science, University of North Carolina, Chapel Hill.

MARTINDALE, DON and HANSON, R. GALEN. 1969. *Small Town and the Nation: The Conflict of Local and Translocal Forces.* Westport, Conn.: Greenwood Publishing Co.

MARX, GARY T. (ed.). 1971. *Racial Conflict: Tension and Change in American Society.* Boston: Little, Brown and Co.

MATZA, DAVID and SYKES, GRESHAM M. 1961. "Juvenile Delinquency and Subterranean Values," *American Sociological Review* 26 (October), pp. 712–19.

MAYER, ALBERT J. and MARX, SUE. 1957. "Social Change, Religion and Birth Rates," *American Journal of Sociology* 62 (January), pp. 383–90.

MAYER, KURT. 1956. "Recent Changes in the Class Structure of the United States, *Transactions of the Third World Congress of Sociology.*

McCARTY, DONALD J. and RAMSEY, CHARLES E. 1971. *The School Managers: Power and Conflict in American Public Education.* Westport, Conn.: Greenwood Publishing Co.

McCORMACK, THELMA HERMAN. 1956. "The Druggists' Dilemma: Problems of a Marginal Occupation," *American Journal of Sociology* 61 (January), pp. 308–15.

McELRATH, DENNIS C. 1961. "Perspective and Participation of Physicians in Prepaid Group Practice," *American Sociological Review* 26 (August), pp. 596–607.

McGUIRE, CARSON. 1950. "Social Stratification and Mobility Patterns," *American Sociological Review* 15 (April), pp. 195–204.

McKEE, JAMES B. 1953. "Status and Power in the Industrial Community," *American Journal of Sociology* 58 (January), pp. 367–71.

McKINLAY, JOHN B. 1972. "Some Approaches and Problems in the Study of the Use of Services—An Overview," *Journal of Health and Social Behavior* 13 (June), pp. 115–52.

MEAD, MARGARET (ed.). 1937. *Cooperation and Competition Among Primitive Peoples.* New York: McGraw-Hill Book Co., Inc.

MEDALIA, NAHUM Z. and LARSEN, OTTO N. 1958. "Diffusion and Belief in a Collective Delusion: The Seattle Windshield Pitting Epidemic," *American Sociological Review* 23 (April), pp. 180–86.

MELBIN, MURRAY. 1972. *Alone and With Others: A Grammar of Interpersonal Behavior.* New York: Harper and Row.

MERCER, BLAINE E. 1956. *The American Community.* New York: Random House, Inc.

MERTON, ROBERT K. 1949. "Patterns of Influence: A Study of Interpersonal Influence and of Communications Behavior in a Local Community," *Communications Research 1948–1949*, Paul F. Lazarfeld and Frank N. Stanton (eds.). New York: Harper & Row, pp. 180–219.

———. 1957. *Social Theory and Social Structure.* New York: The Free Press.

METROPOLITAN APPLIED RESEARCH CENTER, INC. 1969. *A Relevant War Against Poverty: A Study in Community Action Programs and Observable Social Change.* New York.

MIDDLETON, RUSSELL. 1973. "Do Christian Beliefs Cause Anti-Semitism"? *American Sociological Review* (February), pp. 33–52.

MILLER, DELBERT C. 1958. "Decision-Making Cliques in Community Power Structure: A Comparative Study of an American and an English City," *American Journal of Sociology* 64 (November), pp. 299–310.

————. 1963. "Town and Gown: The Power Structure of a University Town," *American Journal of Sociology* 68 (January), pp. 432–43.

MILLER, PAUL A. 1952. "The Process of Decision-Making Within the Context of Community Organization," *Rural Sociology* 17 (June), pp. 153–61.

MILLER, S. M. 1960. "Comparative Social Mobility," *Current Sociology* 9 (No. 1), whole issue.

————. 1974. "Types of Equality: Sorting, Rewarding, Performing." Paper presented at Seventh World Congress of Sociology, Montreal, Canada (August).

———— and RIESSMAN, FRANK. 1961. "The Working Class Subculture: A New View," *Social Problems* 9 (Summer).

MILLS, C. WRIGHT. 1951. *White Collar: The American Middle Classes.* New York: Oxford University Press.

MINAR, DAVID W. 1966. "The Community Basis of Conflict in School System Politics," *American Sociological Review* 31 (December), pp. 822–35.

MOLOTCH, HARVEY and LESTER, MARILYN. 1974. "News as Purposive Behavior: On the Strategic Use of Routine Events, Accidents, and Scandals," *American Sociological Review* 39 (February), pp. 101–12.

MOORE, WILBERT E. 1960. "A Reconsideration of Theories of Social Change," *American Sociological Review* 25 (December), pp. 810–18.

————. 1963. *Man, Time, and Society.* New York: John Wiley & Sons, Inc.

————. 1974. *Social Change.* Englewood Cliffs, N. J.: Prentice-Hall, Inc., 2nd ed.

MORRIS, RICHARD T. and MURPHY, RAYMOND J. 1959. "The Situs Dimension in Organizational Structure," *American Sociological Review* 24 (April), pp. 231–39.

MOSS, LEONARD W. and CAPPANNARI, STEPHEN C. 1960. "Patterns of Kinship, Comparaggio and Community in a South Italian Village," *Anthropological Quarterly* 23 (January), pp. 24–32.

MOTT, PAUL E. 1970. "Configurations of Power," in Michael Aiken and Paul E. Mott (eds.), *The Structure of Community Power: An Anthology.* New York: Random House, Inc.

MOYNIHAN, DANIEL P. 1969. *Maximum Feasible Misunderstanding: Community Action in the War on Poverty.* New York: Free Press.

MUNSON, BYRON E. 1968. "Structural Analysis of the Community," *Rural Sociology* 33, pp. 450–59.

MURDOCK, STEVE H. and SUTTON, WILLIS A., JR. 1974. "The New Ecology and Community Theory: Similarities, Differences, and Convergencies," *Rural Sociology* 39 (Fall), pp. 319–33.

MYRDAL, GUNNAR. 1944. *An American Dilemma: The Negro Problem and Modern Democracy.* New York: Harper and Row.

NATIONAL ADVISORY COMMISSION ON CIVIL DISORDERS. 1968. *Report.* New York: New York Times Company.

NELSEN, HART M., YOKLEY, RAYTHA L. and MADRON, THOMAS W. 1973. "Ministerial Roles and Social Actionist Stance: Protestant Clergy and Protest in the Sixties," *American Sociological Review* 38 (June), pp. 375–86.

NELSON, LOWRY. 1960. *The Minnesota Community: Country and Town in Transition.* Minneapolis: University of Minnesota Press.

————, RAMSEY, CHARLES E., and VERNER, COOLIE. 1960. *Community Structure and Change.* New York: The Macmillan Co.

NISBET, ROBERT A. 1962. *Community and Power* (formerly *The Quest for Community*), New York: Oxford University Press.

NIX, HAROLD L. and SEERLEY, NORMA R. 1973. "Comparative Views and Actions of Community Leaders and Non-Leaders," *Rural Sociology* 38 (Winter), pp. 427–38.

OGBURN, WILLIAM F. 1922 & 1950. *Social Change*. New York: The Viking Press, Inc.

OLSEN, MARVIN E. 1970. "Social and Political Participation of Blacks," *American Sociological Review* 35 (August), pp. 682–97.

———. 1972. "Social Participation and Voting Turnout: A Multivariate Analysis," *American Sociological Review* 37 (June), pp. 317–33.

———. 1973. "A Model of Political Participation Stratification," *Journal of Political and Military Sociology* 1 (Fall), pp. 183–200.

ORZACK, LOUIS H. and SANDERS, IRWIN T. 1961. *A Social Profile of Levittown, New York*. Boston: The Research Institute, Department of Sociology and Anthropology, Boston University. Multilithed.

PAGE, HARRY O. 1956. "Progress Toward Control and Prevention of Dependency," *Public Welfare* (October).

PAPPENFORT, DONNELL M. 1959. "The Ecological Field and the Metropolitan Community: Manufacturing and Management," *The American Journal of Sociology* 64 (January), pp. 380–85.

PARK, ROBERT E. 1952. *Human Communities*. Glencoe, Ill.: The Free Press.

PARKER, RICHARD. *The Myth of the Middle Class: Notes on Affluence and Equality*. Chicago: Aldine.

PARSONS, TALCOTT. 1951. *The Social System*. New York: Free Press.

———. 1961. "Some Considerations on the Theory of Social Change," *Rural Sociology* (September), pp. 219–39.

———. 1968. "Systems Analysis: Social Systems," *International Encyclopedia of the Social Sciences*. New York: The Macmillan Co., Vol. 15, pp. 458–73.

PELLEGRIN, ROLAND J. and COATES, CHARLES H. 1956. "Absentee-Owned Corporations and Community Power Structure," *American Journal of Sociology* 61 (March), pp. 413–19.

PERRUCCI, ROBERT and PILISUK, MARC. 1970. "Leaders and Ruling Elites: The Interorganizational Bases of Community Power," *American Sociological Review* 35 (December), pp. 1040–57.

PETERSON, WARREN A. and GIST, NOEL P. 1951. "Rumor and Public Opinion," *American Journal of Sociology* 57 (September), pp. 228–29.

PHILLIPS, HERBERT. 1963. "Personality and Social Structure in a Siamese Community," *Human Organization* 22 (Summer), pp. 105–8.

PHOTIADIS, JOHN D. 1967. "Community Size and Aspects of the Authoritarian Personality," *Rural Sociology* 33 (March), pp. 70–77.

PINARD, MAURICE. 1963. "Structural Attachments and Political Support in Urban Politics: The Case of Fluoridation Referendums," *American Journal of Sociology* 67 (March), pp. 513–26.

PLOTNICOV, LEONARD. 1973–74. "Some Thoughts on Anthropological Research in Cities of Modern Society," *Comparative Urban Research* (Winter), pp. 5–22.

POHLMANN, EDWARD W. 1952. "Semantic Aspects of the Controversy over Negro–White Caste in the United States," *Social Forces* 30 (May), pp. 416–19.

POLSBY, NELSON W. 1962. "Community Power: Some Reflections on the Recent Literature," *American Sociological Review* 27 (December), pp. 838–41.

POPLIN, DENNIS E. 1972. *Communities: A Survey of Theories and Methods of Research*. New York: The Macmillan Co.

PORTER, JOHN. 1968. "The Future of Upward Mobility," *American Sociological Review* 33 (February), pp. 5–19.

QUINN, J. E. 1950. *Human Ecology.* Englewood Cliffs, N. J.: Prentice-Hall, Inc.

RAINWATER, LEE. 1970. *Behind Ghetto Walls: Black Family Life in a Federal Slum.* Chicago: Aldine.

RANSFORD, EDWARD. 1972. "Blue Collar Anger: Reactions to Student and Black Protest," *American Sociological Review* 37 (June), pp. 333–46.

REDFIELD, ROBERT. 1930. *Tepoztlan—A Mexican Village.* Chicago: University of Chicago Press.

———. 1955. *The Little Community: Viewpoints for the Study of a Human Whole.* Chicago: University of Chicago Press.

REES, ALWYN D. 1961. *Life in a Welsh Countryside; A Social Study of Llanfihangel yng Ngwynfa.* Cardiff: University of Wales Press.

REICH, CHARLES A. 1970. *The Greening of America.* New York: Random House.

REINHOLD, ROBERT. 1973. "Trying to Get Desire on a Graph," *New York Times,* Sunday, September 2. Section E, page 8.

REISS, ALBERT J., JR. 1954. *A Review and Evaluation of Research on Community: A Working Memorandum Prepared for the Committee on Social Behavior of the Social Science Research Council.* Mimeograph. Nashville, Tenn (April).

———. 1959. "The Sociological Study of Communities," *Rural Sociology* 24 (June), pp. 118–30.

——— and RHODES, ALBERT LEWIS. 1961. "The Distribution of Juvenile Delinquency in the Social Class Structure," *American Sociological Review* 26 (October), pp. 720–32.

REISSMAN, LEONARD. 1954. "Class, Leisure and Social Participation," *American Sociological Review* 19 (February), pp. 76–84.

RIEGER, JON H. 1972. "Geographic Mobility and the Occupational Attainment of Rural Youth: A Longitudinal Evaluation," *Rural Sociology* 37 (June), pp. 189–207.

RIEGER, J. H. and BEEGLE, J. A. 1974. "The Integration of Migrants in New Settings," *Rural Sociology* 39 (Spring), pp. 42–55.

RIESMAN, DAVID, GLAZER, NATHAN, and DENNEY, REUEL. 1953. *The Lonely Crowd: A Study of the Changing American Character.* Garden City, N. Y.: Doubleday and Co., Inc.

RILEY, JOHN W., JR. and RILEY, MATILDA WHITE. 1959. "Mass Communication and the Social System," in Robert K. Merton, Leonard Broom and Leonard S. Cottrell, Jr. (eds.), *Sociology Today: Problems and Prospects.* New York: Basic Books, Inc., pp. 537–78.

RILEY, MATILDA WHITE. 1973. "Aging and Cohort Succession: Interpretations and Misinterpretations," *The Public Opinion Quarterly* 37 (Spring), pp. 35–49.

——— and FLOWERMAN, SAMUEL H. 1951. "Group Relations as a Variable in Communication Research," *American Sociological Review* 16 (April), pp. 174–80.

RITCHEY, P. N. 1974. "Urban Poverty and Rural to Urban Migration," *Rural Sociology* 39 (Spring), pp. 12–27.

ROGERS, EVERETT M. (with SVENNING, LYNNE). 1969. *Modernization Among Peasants: The Impact of Communication.* New York: Holt, Rinehart, and Winston.

ROHRER, W. C. and SCHMIDT, J. F. 1954. *Family Type and Social Participation*. College Park: Agricultural Experiment Station, University of Maryland, Misc. Publication No. 196 (June).

ROSE, ARNOLD M. 1951. "Communication and Participation in a Small City as Viewed by Its Leaders," *International Journal of Opinion and Attitude Research* 5, pp. 367–90.

————. 1955. "Voluntary Associations Under Conditions of Competition and Conflict," *Social Forces* 34 (December), pp. 159–63.

ROSENTHAL, ERICH. 1960. "Acculturation Without Assimilation: The Jewish Community of Chicago, Illinois," *The American Journal of Sociology* 66 (November), pp. 275–88.

ROSS, AILEEN D. 1953. "The Social Control of Philanthropy, *American Journal of Sociology* 58 (March), pp. 451–60.

ROSS, H. LAURENCE. 1962. "The Local Community: A Survey Approach," *American Sociological Review* 27 (February), pp. 75–84.

ROSSI, PETER H. 1957. "Community Decision Making," *Administrative Science Quarterly* 1 (March), pp. 415–43.

————. 1960. "Power and Community Structure," *Midwest Journal of Political Science* 4 (November), pp. 390–401.

ROSZAK, THEODORE. 1969. *The Making of a Counter Culture*. Garden City, N. Y.: Doubleday and Co.

RUBIN, MORTON. 1960. "Migration Patterns of Negroes from a Rural Northeastern Mississippi Community," *Social Forces* 39 (October), pp. 59–66.

————. 1971. *Organized Citizen Participation in Boston*. The Boston Urban Observatory (October).

RYAN, BRYCE. 1952. "Primary and Secondary Contacts in a Ceylonese Peasant Community," *Rural Sociology* 17 (December), pp. 311–21.

————. 1969. *Social and Cultural Change*. New York: The Ronald Press Co.

RYAN, WILLIAM. 1971. *Blaming the Victim*. New York: Vintage Books.

RYTINA, JOAN HUBER, FORM, WILLIAM H., and PEASE, JOHN. 1970. "Income and Stratification Ideology: Beliefs about the American Opportunity Structure," *American Journal of Sociology*, pp. 703–16.

SANDERS, IRWIN T. 1949. *Balkan Village*. Lexington: University of Kentucky Press.

————. 1956. "Selection of Participants in a Mutual Aid Group in Rural Greece," *Sociometry* 18, pp. 326–29.

————. 1960. "The Community Social Profile," *American Sociological Review* 25, pp. 75–77.

————. 1961. "The Stages of a Community Controversy: The Case of Fluoridation," *Journal of Social Issues* 17, pp. 55–65.

————. 1970. "The Concept of Community Development," in Lee J. Cary, ed., *Community Development as a Process*. Columbia: University of Missouri Press, pp. 9–31.

————. 1972. "Public Health in the Community" in Howard E. Freeman, Sol Levine and Leo G. Reeder (eds.), *Handbook of Medical Sociology*. Englewood Cliffs, N. J.: Prentice-Hall, Inc., pp. 407–34.

————. 1973. "The University as a Community," in James A. Perkins (ed.), *The University as an Organization*. New York: McGraw-Hill Book Co., pp. 57–78.

————, et al. 1974. *Framingham, Massachusetts: A Profile of a Rapidly*

Growing Community. Boston: Boston University, Community Sociology Series 1.

SARAPATA, ADAM. 1974. *Occupational Prestige Hierarchy Studies in Poland.* Paper presented at VIII World Congress of Sociology, Toronto, Canada.

SCAFF, ALVIN H. 1974. *Change Agencies in Medium City.* Unpublished paper presented to the Community Section, American Sociological Association meeting, Montreal, August 28.

SCHEFF, THOMAS J. 1967. "Toward a Sociological Model of Consensus," *American Sociological Review* 32 (February), pp. 32–46.

SCHERER, JACQUELINE. 1972. *Contemporary Community: Sociological Illusion or Reality?* London: Tavistock.

SCHMID, CALVIN F. 1950. "Generalizations Concerning the Ecology of the American City," *American Sociological Review* 15 (April), pp. 264–81.

SCHNORE, LEO F. 1962. "Municipal Annexations and the Growth of Metropolitan Suburbs, 1950–1960," *The American Journal of Sociology* 67 (January), pp. 406–17.

———. 1963. "The Socio-Economic Status of Cities and Suburbs," *American Sociological Review* 28 (February), pp. 76–85.

SCHULZE, ROBERT O. 1958. "Economic Dominants in Community Power Structure," *American Sociological Review* 23 (February), pp. 3–9.

——— and BLUMBERG, LEONARD U. 1957. "The Determination of Local Power Elites," *American Journal of Sociology* 63 (November), pp. 290–96.

SCHUMAN, HOWARD. 1971. "The Religious Factor in Detroit: Review, Replication and Reanalysis, *American Sociological Review* 36 (February), pp. 30–48.

SCHUR, EDWIN M. 1969. "Reactions to Deviance: A Critical Assessment," *American Journal of Sociology* 75 (November), pp. 300–22.

SCHWARZWELLER, HARRY K. and BROWN, JAMES S. 1967. "Social Class Origins, Rural-Urban Migration, and Life Chances: A Case Study," *Rural Sociology* 32 (March), pp. 5–19.

SCOFIELD, NANETTE E. 1960. "Some Changing Roles of Women in Suburbia: A Social Anthropological Case Study," *Transactions,* New York Academy of Sciences, Series II, Vol. 22 (April).

SCOTT, JOHN C. 1957. "Membership and Participation in Voluntary Associations," *American Sociological Review* 20 (June), pp. 315–26.

SCOTT, JOHN T., JR. 1973. *Profile Change When Industry Moves Into a Rural Area.* Madison: University of Wisconsin, Center of Applied Sociology, Working Paper RID 73.7. (February).

——— and SUMMERS, GENE F. 1972. *Problems and Challenges Faced by Rural Communities with Industrial Development.* Center of Applied Sociology, University of Wisconsin, (Madison). Mimeographed.

SEELEY, JOHN R., SIM, R. ALEXANDER and LOOSLEY, ELIZABETH W. 1956. *Crestwood Heights: A Study of the Culture of Suburban Life.* New York. Basic Books, Inc.

SEEMAN, MELVIN and EVANS, JOHN W. 1961. Stratification and Hospital Care, Part I," *American Sociological Review* 26 (February), pp. 67–80; "Part II," *idem* (April), pp. 193–204.

SENNETT, RICHARD and COBB, JONATHAN. 1972. *The Hidden Injuries of Class.* New York: Random House.

SEWELL, W. H. 1949. "Field Techniques in Social Psychological Study in a Rural Community," *American Sociological Review* 14 (December), pp. 718–26.

———. 1961. "Social Class and Childhood Personality," *Sociometry* 24 (December), pp. 340–56.

———. 1963. "Some Recent Developments in Socialization Theory and Research," *Annals* 349, pp. 163–81.

———. 1971. "Inequality of Opportunity for Higher Education," *American Sociological Review* 36 (October), pp. 793–809.

SHIBUTANI, TAMOTSU. 1955. "Reference Groups as Perspectives," *American Journal of Sociology* 60 (May), pp. 562–69.

SIMMONS, OZZIE G. 1957. "Implications of Social Class for Public Health," *Human Organization* 16 (Fall).

———. 1961. "The Mutual Images and Expectations of Anglo-Americans, And Mexican Americans," *Daedalus* (Spring), pp. 286–99.

SIMPSON, GEORGE. 1933. *Emile Durkheim on the Division of Labor in Society.* New York: The Macmillan Co.

SIMPSON, MILES E. 1970. "Social Mobility, Normlessness and Powerlessness in Two Cultural Contexts," *American Sociological Review* 38 (December), pp. 1002–13.

SIMPSON, RICHARD L. 1956. "A Modification of the Functional Theory of Social Stratification," *Social Forces* 35 (December), pp. 132–37.

———. 1965. "Sociology of the Community: Current Status and Prospects," *Rural Sociology* 30, pp. 127–49.

SIRJAMAKI, JOHN. 1947. "A Footnote to the Anthropological Approach to the Study of American Culture," *Social Forces* 25 (March), pp. 253–63.

SLATER, PHILIP. 1970. *The Pursuit of Loneliness: American Culture at the Breaking Point.* Boston: The Beacon Press.

SMITH, JOEL, FORM, WILLIAM H., and STONE, GREGORY P. 1954. "Local Intimacy in a Middle-Sized City," *The American Journal of Sociology* 60 (November), pp. 276–84.

SMITH, LUKE M. 1949. "Territorial Variables in American Local Government," *Social Forces* 27 (May), pp. 350–58.

SOROKIN, PITIRIM A. 1927. *Social Mobility.* New York: Harper and Row.

———. 1937–41. *Social and Cultural Dynamics.* 4 Vols. New York: American Book Co.

———. 1947. *Society, Culture and Personality.* New York: Harper and Row.

SOWER, CHRISTOPHER et al. 1957. *Community Involvement: The Web of Formal and Informal Ties That Make for Action.* New York: The Free Press.

SPAULDING, IRVING A. 1959. "Change in Rural Life and the Reintegration of a Social System," *Rural Sociology* 24 (September).

SPECTOR, P., TORRES, A., LICHTENSTEIN, S., PRESTON, H. O., CLARK, J. B. and SILVERMAN, S. B. 1971. "Communication Media and Motivation in the Adoption of New Practices: An Experiment in Rural Ecuador," *Human Organization* 30 (Spring), pp. 39–46.

SPEIGHT, J. F. 1973 "Community Development Theory and Practice: A Machiavellian Perspective," *Rural Sociology* 38 (Winter), pp. 477–90.

SPILERMAN, SEYMOUR. 1971. "The Causes of Racial Disturbances: Tests of an Explanation," *American Sociological Review* 36 (June), pp. 427–42.

SRINIVAS, M. N. et al. 1959. "Caste," *Current Sociology* 8, whole issue.

STACEY, MARGARET. 1960. *Tradition and Change: A Study of Banbury.* London: Oxford University Press.

————. 1969. "The Myth of Community Studies," *British Journal of Sociology* 20, pp. 134–47.

STARR, BERNICE C. 1971. "The Community," in Matilda White Riley, Marilyn E. Johnson, Anne Foner, and Associates: *Aging and Society. Volume 3: A Sociology of Age Stratification*. New York: Russell Sage Foundation, chap. 10.

STEEVES, ALLAN D. 1972. "Proletarianization and Class Identification," *Rural Sociology* 37 (March), pp. 5–26.

STEIN, MAURICE R. 1960. *The Eclipse of Community: An Interpretation of American Studies*. Princeton, N.J.: Princeton University Press.

STERNLIEB, GEORGE S. and BEATON, W. PATRICK. 1972. *The Zone of Emergence: A Case Study of Plainfield, New Jersey*. New Brunswick, N. J.: Transaction.

————, BURCHELL, ROBERT W., and SAGALYN, LYNNE B. 1971. *The Affluent Suburb: Princeton*. New Brunswick, N.J.: Transaction.

STOECKEL, JOHN and BEEGLE, J. ALLAN. 1969. "Urban Dominance and the Rural-Farm Status Structure," *Rural Sociology* 34 (March), pp. 56–66.

STOLL, CLARENCE. 1974. *Female and Male: Socialization, Social Roles and Social Structure*. Wm. C. Brown Co.

STONE, GREGORY P. and FORM, WILLIAM H. 1953. "Instabilities in Status: The Problem of Hierarchy in the Community Study of Status Arrangements," *American Sociological Review* 18 (April), pp. 149–62.

STOUFFER, SAMUEL A. 1955. *Communism, Conformity, and Civil Liberties*. New York: Doubleday & Co., Inc.

SUMMERS, GENE F., HOUGH, RICHARD L., SCOTT, JOHN T., JR., and FOLSE, C. L. 1969. *Before Industrialization: A Rural Social System Base Study*. Urbana-Champaign, Ill.: University of Illinois, College of Agriculture, Agricultural Experiment Station Bulletin 736.

SUTTLES, GERALD D. 1972. *The Social Construction of Communities*. Chicago: University of Chicago Press.

SUTTON, WILLIS A., JR. 1964. "Toward a Universe of Community Actions," *Sociological Inquiry* 34 (Winter), pp. 48–59.

————. 1965. *Power Structure and the Rural-Urban Variable: A Comparison of Two Kentucky Communities*. Mimeographed. Lexington, Ky.

————. 1970. "The Sociological Implications of the Community Development Process," Chapter 3 in Lee J. Cary (ed.), *Community Development as a Process*. Columbia: University of Missouri Press.

———— and KOLAJA, JIRI. 1960a. "Concept of Community," *Rural Sociology* 25, pp. 197–203.

————. 1960b. "Elements of Community Action," *Social Forces* 34 (May), pp. 325–31.

SWEETSER, FRANK L. 1961–1963. *The Social Ecology of Metropolitan Boston: 1950; The Social Ecology of Metropolitan Boston: 1960; and Patterns of Change in the Social Ecology of Metropolitan Boston: 1950–1960*. Division of Mental Health, Massachusetts Department of Mental Health.

SYKES, GRESHAM M. 1951. "The Differential Distribution of Community Knowledge," *Social Forces* 29 (May), pp. 376–82.

TAEUBER, IRENE B. 1951. "Family, Migration and Industrialization in Japan," *American Sociological Review* 16 (April), pp. 149–57.

TAEUBER, KARL E. and TAEUBER, ALMA F. 1964. "White Migration and Socio-Economic Differences between Cities and Suburbs," *American Sociological Review* 29 (October), pp. 718–29.

TAIT, JOHN L., and BEAL, GEORGE M. 1965. *An Analysis of Power Structures in Five Iowa Communities.* Ames, Iowa. Multilith.

TALMON, YONINA. 1961. "Aging in Israel, a Planned Society," *American Journal of Sociology* 67 (November), pp. 284–95.

TAMBIAH, S. J. and RYAN, BRYCE. 1957. "Secularization of Family Values in Ceylon" *American Sociological Review* 22 (June), pp. 292–99.

TANNENBAUM, ARNOLD S. 1961. "Control and Effectiveness in a Voluntary Organization," *American Journal of Sociology* 67 (July), pp. 33–46.

TARVER, JAMES D. 1972. "Patterns of Population Change Among Southern Nonmetropolitan Towns, 1950–1970," *Rural Sociology* 37 (March), pp. 53–72.

TERRIEN, FREDERIC W. and MILLS, DONALD L. 1955. "The Effect of Changing Size Upon the Internal Structure of Organizations," *American Sociological Review* 20, pp. 11–13.

THOMAS, DARWIN L. and WEIGERT, ANDREW J. 1971. "Socialization and Adolescent Conformity to Significant Others: A Cross-National Analysis," *American Sociological Review* 36 (October), pp. 835–47.

THOMAS, JOHN L. 1951. "Religious Training in the Roman Catholic Family," *American Journal of Sociology* 57 (September), pp. 178–83.

THOMPSON, J. D., and McEWEN, W. J. 1958. "Organizational Goals and Environment: Goal-Setting as an Interaction Process," *American Sociological Review* 23 (February), pp. 23–31.

THOMPSON, WARREN S. 1953. *Population Problems,* 4th Ed. New York: McGraw-Hill Book Co., Inc., chap. 14.

THORNDIKE, EDWARD L. 1939. *Your City.* New York: Harcourt Brace Jovanovich.

TIMASHEFF, N. S. 1952. "The Basic Concepts of Sociology," *American Journal of Sociology* 58 (September), pp. 176–86.

TOBY, JACKSON. 1975. "The War on Poverty: Politics of Unrealistic Expectations," *Contemporary Sociology* 4 (January), pp. 11–18. (A Review Article.)

TOFFLER, ALVIN. 1971. *Future Shock.* New York: Random House.

TUMIN, MELVIN M. and ROTBERG, ROBERT. 1957. "Leaders, and the Led, and the Law: A Case Study in Social Change," *Public Opinion Quarterly* 21 (Fall), pp. 355–70.

TURBEVILLE, GUS. 1949. "Religious Schism in the Methodist Church: A Sociological Analysis of the Pine Grove Case," *Rural Sociology* 14 (March).

TURK, HERMAN. 1970. "Interorganizational Networks in Urban Society: Initial Perspectives and Comparative Research," *American Sociological Review* 35 (February), pp. 1–19.

TURNER, RALPH H. 1969. "The Public Perception of Protest," *American Sociological Review* 34 (December), pp. 815–31.

USEEM, RUTH HILL, USEEM, JOHN, and GIBSON, DUANE L. 1960. "The Functioning of Neighboring for the Middle Class Male," *Human Organization* 19 (Summer).

VAN DEN BAN, ANNE WILLEM. 1960. "Locality Group Differences in the Adoption of New Farm Practices," *Rural Sociology* 25 (September), pp. 308–20.

VAN DEN BERGHE, PIERRE L. 1963. "Dialectic and Functionalism: Toward a Theoretical Synthesis," *American Sociological Review* 28 (October), pp. 695–705.

VANECKO, JAMES J. 1969. "Community Mobilization and Institutional Change: the Influence of the Community Action Program in Large Cities," *Social Science Quarterly* 50 (December), pp. 609–30.

VIDICH, ARTHUR J. and BENSMAN, JOSEPH. 1958. *Small Town in Mass Society: Class, Power, and Religion in a Rural Community.* Princeton, N. J.: Princeton University Press.

VOGT, EVON Z. and O'DEA, THOMAS F. 1953. "A Comparative Study of the Role of Values in Social Action in Two Southwestern Communities," *American Sociological Review* 18 (December), pp. 645–54.

VON HENTIG, HANS. 1952. "The Sex Ratio: A Brief Discussion Based on United States Census Figures," *Social Forces,* 30 (May), pp. 443–49.

WALTON, JOHN. 1966. "Discipline, Method, and Community Power: A Note on the Sociology of Knowledge," *American Sociological Review* 31 (October), pp. 684–89.

WANCE, WILLIAM and BUTLER, RICHARD. 1948. "The Effect of Industrial Changes on Occupational 'Inheritance' in Four Pennsylvania Communities," *Social Forces* 27 (December), pp. 158–62.

WARNER, W. LLOYD, et al. 1949. *Democracy in Jonesville.* New York: Harper and Row.

———, and LUNT, PAUL S. 1941. *The Social Life of a Modern Community,* New Haven: Yale University Press.

———, MEEKER, MARCHIA and EELLS, KENNETH. 1949. *Social Class in America.* Chicago: Science Research Associates.

WARREN, ROLAND L. 1955. *Studying Your Community.* New York: Russell Sage Foundation.

———. 1956. "Toward a Reformulation of Community Theory," *Human Organization* 15 (Summer), pp. 8–11.

———. 1967. "The Interorganizational Field as a Focus for Investigation," *Administrative Science Quarterly* 12 (December), pp. 396–419.

———. 1970. "Toward a Non-utopian Normative Model of the Community," *American Sociological Review* 38 (April), pp. 219–28.

———. 1971. *Truth, Love and Social Change and Other Essays on Community Change.* Chicago: Rand McNally and Co.

———. 1972. *The Community in America.* Chicago: Rand McNally & Co., 2nd Edition.

———, ROSE, STEPHEN M., and BERGUNDER, ANN F. 1974. *The Structure of Urban Reform: Community Decision Organizations in Stability and Change.* Lexington, Mass.: D. C. Heath and Co.

WASHBURNE, NORMAN F. 1954. *Interpreting Social Change in America.* Garden City, N. Y.: Doubleday & Co., Inc.

WEAVER, THOMAS and WHITE, DOUGLAS (eds). 1972. *The Anthropology of Urban Environments,* The Society for Applied Anthropology Monographs Series, Monograph No. 11.

WEINBERG, MARTIN S. and WILLIAMS, COLIN J. 1969. "Disruption, Social Location and Interpretive Practices: The Case of Wayne, New Jersey," *American Sociological Review* 34 (April), pp. 170–182.

WEISS, MELFORD S. 1974. *Valley City: A Chinese Community in America.* Cambridge, Mass.: Schenkman Publishing Co.

WELLMAN, BARRY and CRAVEN, PAUL. 1973. "Informal Interpersonal Relations and Social Networks," *Sociological Inquiry* 43.

WEST, JAMES. 1945. *Plainville, U. S. A.* New York: Columbia University Press.

WESTIE, FRANK R. and WESTIE, MARGARET L. 1957. "The Social-Distance Pyramid: Relationships Between Caste and Class," *The American Journal of Sociology* 63 (September), pp. 190–96.

WIESE, LEOPOLD VON and BECKER, HOWARD. 1932. *Systematic Sociology.* New York: John Wiley & Sons, Inc.

WILDAVSKY, AARON. 1964. *Leadership in a Small Town,* Totowa, N. J.: The Bedminster Press.

WILENSKY, HAROLD L. 1961. "Orderly Careers and Social Participation," *American Sociological Review* 26 (August), pp. 521–39.

WILEY, NORBERT. 1967. "America's Unique Class Politics: The Interplay of Labor, Credit and Commodity Markets," *American Sociological Review* 32 (August), pp. 529–41.

WILKINSON, KENNETH P. 1969. "Special Agency Program Accomplishment and Community Action Styles: The Case of Watershed Development." *Rural Sociology* 34 (March), pp. 29–42.

————. 1970a. "The Community as a Social Field," *Social Forces* 48 (March), pp. 311–22.

————. 1970b. "Phases and Roles in Community Action," *Rural Sociology* 35 (March), pp. 54–68.

————. 1972. "A Field-Theory Perspective for Community Development Research," *Rural Sociology* 37 (March), 43–52.

————. 1974. "A Behavioral Approach to Measurement and Analysis of Community Field Structure," *Rural Sociology* 39 (Summer), pp. 247–56.

WILKINSON,, THOMAS O. 1960. "Urban Structure and Industrialization," *American Sociological Review* 25 (June), pp. 356–63.

WILLEMS, EMILIO. 1953. "The Structure of the Brazilian Family" *Social Forces* 31 (May), pp. 339–45.

WILLIAMS, J. ALLEN, JR., BABCHUK, NICHOLAS, and JOHNSON, DAVID R. 1973. "Voluntary Associations and Minority Status: A Comparative Analysis of Anglo, Black, and Mexican Americans," *American Sociological Review* 38, pp. 637–46.

WILLIAMS, JAMES M. 1973. "The Ecological Approach in Measuring Community Power Concentration: An Analysis of Hawley's MPO Ratio," *American Sociological Review* 38 (April), pp. 230–42.

WILLIAMS, ROBIN M. 1969. *American Society: A Sociological Interpretation.* New York: Alfred A. Knopf, Inc., 3rd Edition.

WILSON, JAMES Q. 1968. "The Urban Unease: Community versus City," *The Public Interest.* (Summer), pp. 25–39.

WILSON, ROBERT L. 1962. "Livability of the City: Attitudes and Urban Development," in F. Stuart Chapin, Jr. and Shirley F. Weiss (eds.), *Urban Growth Dynamics in a Regional Cluster of States.* New York: John Wiley and Sons. Inc., pp. 364–65.

WILSON, ROBERT N. 1954. "Teamwork in the Operating Room," *Human Organization* 12 (Winter), pp. 9–14.

WINCH, ROBERT F., GREER, SCOTT, and BLUMBERG, RAE LESSER. 1967. "Ethnicity and Extended Familism in an Upper-Middle-Class Suburb," *American Sociological Review* 32 (April), pp. 265–72.

WINNER, IRENE. 1971. *A Slovenian Village: Zerovnica.* Providence, R.I.: Brown University Press.

WINSBOROUGH, HAL H. 1963. "An Ecological Approach to the Theory of Suburbanization," *The American Journal of Sociology* 68 (March), pp. 565–70.

WOOD, JAMES R. 1970. "Authority and Controversial Policy: The Churches and Civil Rights," *American Sociological Review* 35 (December), pp. 1057–69.

YOUNG, FRANK W. and YOUNG, RUTH C. 1960. "Two Determinants of Community Reaction to Industrialization in Rural Mexico," *Economic Development and Cultural Change* 8 (April), pp. 257–64.

―――― and ――――. 1960. "Social Integration and Change in Twenty-four Mexican Villages," *Economic Development and Cultural Change* 8 (July), pp. 366–77.

―――― and ――――. 1962. "The Sequence and Direction of Community Growth: A Cross-Cultural Generalization," *Rural Sociology* 27 (December), pp. 374–86.

―――― and ――――. 1973. *Comparative Studies of Community Growth.* Rural Sociological Society Monograph, No. 2. Morgantown: West Virginia University.

YOUNG, KIMBALL. 1949. *Sociology: A Study of Society and Culture.* 2d ed. New York: American Book Co.

YOUNG, RUTH C. and LARSON, OLAF F. 1965. "A New Approach to Community Structure," *American Sociological Review* 30 (December), pp. 926–34.

―――― and ――――. 1970. "The Social Ecology of a Rural Community," *Rural Sociology* 35 (September), pp. 337–53.

ZEHNER, ROBERT B. and CHAPIN, F. STUART, JR. 1974. *Across the City Line: A White Community in Transition.* Lexington, Mass. Lexington Books, D. C. Heath and Co.

ZIMMER, BASIL G. and HAWLEY, AMOS H. 1959. "The Significance of Membership in Associations," *The American Journal of Sociology* 65 (September), pp. 196–201.

ZIMMERMAN, CARLE C. 1938. *The Changing Community.* New York: Harper and Row.

ZUICHES, JAMES J. 1970. "In-Migration and Growth of Nonmetropolitan Urban Places," *Rural Sociology* 35 (September), pp. 410–20.

Name Index

513

Subject Index